America's Lawyer-Presidents

America's Lawyer-Presidents

From Law Office to Oval Office

Edited by Norman Gross

Foreword by
Justice Sandra Day O'Connor

Defending Liberty
Pursuing Justice

ABA MUSEUM OF LAW   NORTHWESTERN UNIVERSITY PRESS | EVANSTON, ILLINOIS

Northwestern University Press
629 Noyes Street
Evanston, Illinois 60208-4170

ABA Museum of Law
321 North Clark Street
Chicago, Illinois 60610

Book design: Herman Adler Design

Printed in China
10 9 8 7 6 5 4 3 2 1

ISBN 0-8101-1218-3

Library of Congress Cataloging-in-Publication Data
are available from the Library of Congress.

The paper used in this publication meets the minimum
requirements of the American National Standard for
Information Sciences—Permanence of Paper for Printed
Library Materials, ANSI Z39.48–1992.

CONTENTS

FOREWORD

Lawyers have played a pivotal role in the shaping of the political and civic life of this country. Their role remains a vital one today. Legal education continues to provide the training ground for significant numbers of our nation's leaders. Individuals with law degrees currently occupy roughly half the state governorships, more than half the seats in the United States Senate, and more than a third of the seats in the House of Representatives.[1]

Lawyer-presidents have made significant contributions to the third branch as well as to the political branches of government. Eight lawyer-presidents have appeared as advocates before the United States Supreme Court.[2] Beginning with then-Senator John Quincy Adams's arguments in the early days of the Marshall Court, and ending with Richard M. Nixon's sole argument before the Warren Court, these appearances provide interesting footnotes to distinguished careers.

Lawyer-presidents' arguments before the Court have provided opportunities for the statesmen to advocate their deeply held beliefs. For example, John Quincy Adams's abolitionist views led to his retention and fervent advocacy in the *Amistad* case.[3] This famous case considered the rights of a group of Africans who in 1839 had been kidnapped and sold as slaves. On board a Spanish ship bound for Cuba they mutinied, and the ship eventually landed in New York. Criminal charges were brought and dismissed, but the individuals remained in federal custody. They sought writs of habeas corpus, and their claims came before the Supreme Court when the Van Buren administration appealed the circuit justice's order that the Africans be released and returned to their homeland.

Adams visited the Africans and met with their leader, and he was deeply impressed with their cause.[4] Adams's eloquent argument to the Supreme Court included what was described as a "withering attack" on Spain's charge that the Africans were robbers and pirates.[5] One historian recounts the argument:

"Who were the merchandise and who were the robbers?" he asked. "According to the construction of the Spanish minister, the merchandise were the robbers and the robbers were the merchandise. The merchandise was rescued out of its own hands and the robbers were rescued out of the hands of the robbers."[6]

Justice Story's opinion for the Court declared that the Africans were freemen and ordered their release from federal custody. The Court did not agree that the government had a duty to transport the Africans to their homeland,[7] but after Adams failed in an effort to secure federal legislation assisting in their return, American missionaries eventually transported the group to Sierra Leone.[8]

President Nixon's personal views—his disdain for the press—similarly animated his participation in the case of *Time, Inc. v. Hill.*[9] The *Time* case involved the Hill family, which in 1952 was taken hostage in their home by three escaped convicts. *Life* magazine later published an article about a play titled *The Desperate Hours*, by Joseph Hayes, describing the play as a reenactment of the family's experience and including photographs of scenes staged in the Hills' former home. Whereas the play portrayed a violent experience and a family brutalized by the convicts, the Hills had been released unharmed. The Hills sued, alleging that the article gave a knowingly false impression that the play, with its considerable violence, was an accurate depiction of their ordeal.

Nixon took three weeks away from campaigning in the 1966 congressional elections to prepare for the oral argument in the Supreme Court, which would be his only argument before any appellate court.[10] Although he lost the case five to four, the argument helped him gain the respect of his fellow lawyers after his devastating defeat in California's 1962 governor's race.[11] Nixon was critical of his own performance but won praise from the press, the legal community, and several justices.[12] Nixon later commented that "there is only one ordeal which is more challenging than a Presidential press conference, and that is to appear before the Supreme Court of the United States."[13]

As this book aptly demonstrates, our constitutional democracy has always relied on the talents and hard work of lawyers in private practice, public service, and political office. This book reminds us of the endless twists and turns legal careers are apt to take and of the invaluable contributions the profession has made to the effective functioning of our nation. It is my hope that the chapters that follow will inspire countless others to dedicate some part of their own careers to strengthening the political and civic life of this country. Our forefathers have left us with a remarkable legacy upon which to build.

SANDRA DAY O'CONNOR
Associate Justice, United States Supreme Court

Notes

1. See *Grutter v. Bollinger*, 539 U.S. ___ (2003) (citing Brief for American Association of Law Schools as *amicus curiae* 5–6).

2. See Judge Allen Sharp, *Presidents as Supreme Court Advocates: Before and after the White House*, J. SUP. CT. HIST., Vol. 28, No. 2, at 116 (2003). The eight are John Quincy Adams, James Polk, Abraham Lincoln, James A. Garfield, Grover Cleveland, Benjamin Harrison, William Howard Taft, and Richard M. Nixon. *Ibid.*

3. *United States v. Libellants of Schooner Amistad*, 40 U.S. (15 Pet.) 518 (1841).

4. Sharp, *supra* note 2, at 120.

5. Lynn Hudson Parsons, JOHN QUINCY ADAMS 239 (Madison House, 1998).

6. *Ibid.*

7. 40 U.S. (15 Pet.) at 597–98.

8. Sharp, *supra* note 2, at 121.

9. 385 U.S. 374 (1967).

10. Sharp, *supra* note 2, at 138.

11. *Id.* at 139.

12. Sharp, *supra* note 2, at 139.

13. Sharp, *supra* note 2, at 138–39. Another lawyer-president, William Howard Taft (who as U.S. solicitor general argued more cases before the Court than any other lawyer-president), reported an altogether different experience: "[The justices] seem to think when I begin to talk that that is a good chance to read all the letters that have been waiting for some time, to eat lunch, and to devote their attention to correcting proof. . . . However, I expect to gain a good deal of practice in addressing a lot of mummies and experience in not being overcome by circumstances." 1 Henry F. Pringle, THE LIFE AND TIMES OF WILLIAM HOWARD TAFT 115 (Farrar & Rinehart, 1939).

PREFACE

The law taught Lincoln more than merely the technical knowledge of rules of practice, of demurrers, of pleas in abatement and pleas at bar," wrote Albert Woldman in his book *Lawyer Lincoln*. "It proved for him a study of human institutions and of history itself."

Woldman's observation suggests the nature, purpose, and potential of the ABA Museum of Law and its America's Lawyer-Presidents project. Though many people might initially associate the law with legal technicalities, procedures, and documents, those of us associated with the ABA Museum of Law view the law as Lincoln did—as an instructive mirror of the issues, institutions, events, and people that have shaped American history and continue to affect us on a daily basis. We believe that a nation founded on the rule of law and committed to its free and democratic principles and processes requires a citizenry that understands our laws and justice system. The museum addresses this goal through exhibits and related programming that provide engaging and informative insights into a wide variety of legal topics and the role that law and lawyers have played in American history.

The America's Lawyer-Presidents project is the Museum of Law's most recent undertaking. Project plans include this book, published through the good offices of Northwestern University Press, as well as a major exhibit, educational materials, Web site, special programming, and other complementary activities. The objective is to convey to as many people as possible (both lawyers and the general public) the fascinating—and largely untold—stories of our nation's lawyer-presidents' legal careers and their impact on their presidencies.

The exhibit, which will premiere in the ABA's new headquarters building in downtown Chicago in September 2004, is the most recent of the museum's major initiatives and follows on the heels of our current exhibit, Famous Trials in American History: Cases That Shaped and Shocked the Nation.

The Museum of Law, which first opened in 1996, offers exhibits and related programming about the role of law in America and around the world. It is open to the public six days a week, and there is no admission fee. The museum is a not-for-profit organization associated with the American Bar Association. It is governed by a distinguished thirteen-member board of directors and operates with the generous support of the ABA and many law firms, corporations, foundations, and individual contributors.

We hope you enjoy this book on our nation's lawyer-presidents, and we extend a warm invitation for you to visit the Museum of Law and its America's Lawyer-Presidents exhibit when you are in Chicago. If you have a group interested in having a guided tour or special event at the museum, please visit our Web site at www.abanet.org/museum, which provides planning details and contact information. The museum is located in downtown Chicago adjacent to the Chicago River and thus provides a convenient and picturesque setting for programs and events. We also plan to have a traveling version of the exhibit appearing in cities throughout the country. To find out about the traveling exhibit and its schedule, please check the museum Web site for such information.

We look forward to having you visit the museum and the America's Lawyer-Presidents exhibit.

James R. Silkenat
Chair, ABA Museum of Law Board of Directors

Robert A. Stein
Executive Director and Chief Operating Officer,
American Bar Association

August 2003

INTRODUCTION

The study of the law qualifies a man to be useful to himself, to his neighbors, and to the public," wrote Thomas Jefferson, America's second lawyer-president. "It is the most certain stepping stone to public preferment in the political line."

As early as colonial times, lawyers exerted significant political influence. British statesman and writer Edmund Burke offered this explanation:

> This study of law renders men acute, inquisitive, dexterous, prompt in action, ready in defense, full of resources. No other profession is more closely connected with actual life as the law. It concerns the highest of all temporal interests of man—property, reputation, the peace of all families, the arbitrations and peace of nations, liberty, life even, and the very foundations of society.

Later, Alexis de Tocqueville observed:

> The government of democracy is favorable to the political powers of lawyers. . . . [T]hey are the only men of information and sagacity, beyond the sphere of the people, who can be the object of the popular choice. . . . [Without] this admixture of lawyer-like sobriety with the democratic principle, I wonder whether democratic institutions could long be maintained.

Given this powerful nexus between law and politics, it should be no surprise that twenty-five of our nation's forty-three presidents have been lawyers. Though of common profession, each followed a distinctive legal career and path to the high office.

The first lawyer-president, John Adams, had an appreciation of "law as politics, law as philosophy, and law as jurisprudence" that was reflected in his high-profile colonial cases and his contributions to our nation's founding documents. In contrast, Andrew Jackson was "the most roaring, rollicking, game-cocking, horse-racing, card-playing, mischievous fellow" who "did not trouble with the law-books much [and] was much more in the stable than in the office." Despite this reputation, young Jackson built a thriving frontier law practice and served as one of the early judges on the new state of Tennessee's superior court, all before he gained fame on the battlefield and in the political arena.

Some lesser-known presidents were very accomplished lawyers. Franklin Pierce displayed courtroom "eloquence which stirs and rules the heart and conquers the reason," Rutherford Hayes (the only Harvard Law School graduate to serve as president) gained prominence prosecuting sensational murder cases and representing runaway slaves, while the diminutive and oft-mocked Benjamin Harrison had the most extensive law practice following his presidency—including frequent appearances before the U.S. Supreme Court. More notable presidents such as Woodrow Wilson and Franklin Delano Roosevelt had undistinguished law careers. FDR's announcement of his first law job in 1907 succinctly conveyed his view of law practice: "Unpaid bills a specialty. Briefs on the liquor question furnished free to ladies. Small dogs chloroformed without charge." Still other chief executives, including James Monroe and Bill Clinton, pursued the law primarily as an entry point to their ultimate goal—careers in politics.

This book explores the legal careers of America's lawyer-presidents and the influence of these careers upon their political lives and presidencies. It thereby also provides a mirror to American law and history over more than two hundred years. The legal careers of Adams and Jefferson, for example, reveal much about daily life in colonial Massachusetts and Virginia as well as events that shaped the Revolution. Abraham Lincoln's legal career tells the story of law and life in antebellum Illinois, while the more recent legal careers and presidencies of Richard Nixon and Bill Clinton reflect the changing nature of law and politics during the latter part of the twentieth century.

Surprisingly, there has been relatively limited research and writing on these topics. With some exceptions, scholars, presidential historians, and biographers have generally accorded but passing reference to presidents' legal careers, focusing instead on their political and personal lives.

This book begins to fill that gap, exploring the careers of lawyer-presidents through successive periods of American history. Each historical period is introduced by an overview of American law of the time, followed by articles on the lawyer-presidents of that period.

The first section, "Founding Fathers and Sons," covers colonial-era lawyers John Adams and Thomas Jefferson as well as the legal careers of James Monroe and John Quincy Adams, whose practices occurred during the early years of the new republic. Adams's and Jefferson's contributions to the legal and political framework of our constitutional form of government are explored, followed by a review of Monroe's brief years of practice and John Quincy Adams's unique experience of arguing significant cases before the U.S. Supreme Court both prior to and following his presidency.

"Antebellum Presidents" covers the frontier justice of Andrew Jackson through the presidency of James Buchanan, who, though known as a "constitutional lawyer," could not avert the constitutional crisis that ultimately drew our nation into civil war. This section also examines Martin Van Buren's long and successful legal career; the courtroom eloquence of John Tyler and Franklin Pierce; James Polk's brief law practice (which included an argument before the U.S. Supreme Court); and Millard Fillmore's partnership in a Buffalo, New York, law firm that would later claim another president, Grover Cleveland, among its members.

Abraham Lincoln's law practice spanned twenty-five years and more than fifty-one hundred cases, including four hundred before the Illinois Supreme Court. Though he proclaimed, "I am not an accomplished lawyer," Lincoln's clientele included railroads, banks, and corporations in the decade before he was elected president. A special series of articles on "Lawyer Lincoln" conveys the story of his legal career and its impact on the man and his presidency.

"Gilded Age Presidents" covers the uninterrupted series of lawyer-occupants in the White House from 1877 to 1901. Few people are familiar with the presidencies of Hayes, Garfield, Arthur, Cleveland, Harrison, and McKinley, much less their legal careers, which included a surprising number of cases before the U.S. Supreme Court and other precedent-setting cases.

"New Century Presidents" marks a significant change in the number of lawyer-presidents. While lawyer-presidents comprised 76 percent of those elected to the Oval Office through the nineteenth century, that percentage dropped by almost half, to 39 percent, in the twentieth century.

The first lawyer-president of the twentieth century, William Howard Taft, had the most diverse legal career of any lawyer-president, serving as a law reporter, prosecuting attorney, superior court and federal judge, law school professor and dean, U.S. solicitor general, and, following his presidency, chief justice of the United States. His successor, Woodrow Wilson, pursued an unproductive, year-long legal practice in Atlanta before turning his attention to academia and politics, while Franklin Delano Roosevelt's periodic ventures into law practice were always secondary to his political interests and ambitions. In contrast to Wilson and FDR, Calvin Coolidge enjoyed the practice of law and "expected to become the kind of country lawyer I saw all about me, spending my life in the profession, with perhaps a final place on the bench."

The most recent period, covering the second half of the twentieth century, was marked by two of its three lawyer-presidents—Richard Nixon and Bill Clinton—facing the challenge of impeachment, and the third lawyer-president, Gerald Ford, issuing a controversial pardon for Nixon that, in President Ford's words, would end "our long national nightmare." Of the three, Nixon had the most accomplished and varied legal career, including a high-profile case before the U.S. Supreme Court.

The concluding chapters examine lawyer-presidents' appointments to the Supreme Court and their appointments of attorneys general, solicitors general, and White House counsel. Each article explores whether a president's legal training and experience affected his appointments to the highest judicial and legal offices in the land.

This volume is the result of the talented contributions of many people. First and foremost are the book's authors, who responded magnificently to the challenging assignment of crafting concise, informative articles about each of our nation's lawyer-presidents. I thank them for lending their expertise and writing skills to the volume and for being so accommodating in addressing the various requests presented to them.

The numerous images and illustrations that appear in this volume were provided through the cooperation of staff at presidential libraries, historical societies, government agencies, and many other institutions. Often their efforts exceeded what might have been reasonably expected. While this book's illustration credits acknowledge the institutional sources of its many images, my special thanks go to the people who provided such invaluable assistance in identifying and providing those images for this book.

Northwestern University Press has been a wonderful publishing partner. When presented with the book proposal, they shared the Museum of Law's excitement about it, and then they provided expert editorial, production, and promotional support to make it a reality. I thank them for the professional and collegial manner in which they addressed the many issues that arose in assembling this book. The final product is a testament to their publishing talents.

Finally, my thanks are extended to the ABA leadership and the Museum of Law's board of directors for their critical support, without which this book and the museum's many other initiatives would not be possible. We all share the belief that a nation founded upon and committed to the rule of law requires a citizenry that understands and appreciates the law and its history, principles, issues, and procedures. Hopefully, the *America's Lawyer-Presidents* book has succeeded in contributing to this important objective.

Norman Gross
Director, ABA Museum of Law

America's
Lawyer-
Presidents

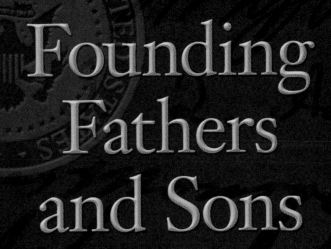

Founding
Fathers
and Sons

Law in Colonial America

The legal world in which the first American presidents lived was very different from the world of today. It was a world with relatively few lawyers and essentially a world without law schools. Young men—and only men—who wanted to become lawyers served a kind of apprenticeship. They worked for a lawyer in his office, principally as a kind of gofer. There were also almost no American law books. Colonial cases were not printed and reported. Lawyers knew the local statutes and some of the more prominent English cases. A few had manuscript collections of homegrown decisions. When Blackstone's *Commentaries*, a convenient summary of English law, appeared in the middle of the eighteenth century, American lawyers snapped it up. Yet men like John Adams and Thomas Jefferson learned their law, and learned it well, by hook or by crook.

The situation changed, of course, after independence. The Declaration of Independence came in 1776, but true independence had to wait for the end of the war, when the British reluctantly gave up their attempt to stamp out the rebellion. The newborn country was now obliged to find its way in the world. It succeeded dramatically. The men who wrote the Constitution, and who put it into effect, were brilliant innovators—and brilliant masters of compromise. They pieced together a plan that managed to gain the approval of the thirteen refractory children that made up the family of states. The Constitution, like the Revolution itself, represented in some ways a sharp break with the legal past. But in a larger sense, there was far more continuity than change in the legal system. The common law tradition, like the English language, remained firmly in place. There was no real alternative. It was part of the tradition and culture of the settlers. It soon became part of the tradition and culture of the new Republic as well.

The states were now independent, however, and they began to cultivate their own gardens. A volume of Connecticut reports appeared in 1789; by 1810, there were reports in New York, Massachusetts, and New Jersey as well. The states slowly built up a body of genuinely native common law out of their own decisions and those of neighboring states, and they pieced together a new system out of old materials and new needs. The dominance of English precedent ebbed. Great state court judges—men like Lemuel Shaw of Massachusetts and James Kent of New York—created a distinctive American system of common law.

The structure of this body of law rested on two foundations. One was the colonial experience itself, which lasted more than 150 years. For most of this time, the colonies were essentially on their own. England was very far away, and travel was slow and perilous. It took months to cross the Atlantic on boats that depended on wind, will, and luck. The English slowly blundered their way into true imperial rule. Of course, much of colonial law was solidly based on English legal traditions; this was, after all, the only law the colonists knew. They knew it, however, as a kind of dialect of common law, reflecting local customs and habits. Moreover, the colonial situation was profoundly different from the English situation; consequently, colonial law was in many ways itself profoundly different. The law of the colonies was a rich stew of English legal memories and the rules dictated by colonial experience. The colonists picked and chose what they wanted and needed from the mother country. They also innovated boldly, inventing new legal institutions like the recording of deeds to land, and discarding old institutions like primogeniture (inheritance by the oldest son). They greatly simplified court structures and procedures.

At least one major innovation is hardly a matter of pride. England had no slaves or slavery. The American law of slavery was essentially an American invention, crudely carved out of scraps of doctrine and molded to the needs of a cruel system of chattel slavery. It was also a race-based system. The owners of slaves were white, the slaves themselves blacks from Africa and their descendants. There were slaves in every colony. But only in the South did slavery become an essential prop of the economy, and only in the South did slavery outlast the revolutionary generation.

The colonies at first had few lawyers—and there was even some hostility to the very idea of lawyers. But by the time of the Revolution, the colonies had grown in size and in commercial sophistication. A vigorous trading community is a community that wants, needs, and gets its share of legal skills. And many of the leaders of the Revolution were lawyers. Lawyers, too, were prominent in drafting and lobbying for the Declaration of Independence and the Constitution. They put their stamp on the very shape and structure of the country.

LAWRENCE M. FRIEDMAN

* * *

John Adams

Second President (1797–1801)

BIRTH
October 30, 1735
Braintree (now Quincy), Mass.

EDUCATION
Local schools
Harvard College
Law study with James Putnam in Worcester, Mass.
Admission to the bar: November 6, 1758

OTHER OCCUPATIONS/PUBLIC OFFICES
Schoolteacher
Provincial legislator
Delegate, First and Second Continental Congress
First chief justice of the Commonwealth of Massachusetts
Committee to draft Declaration of Independence
Head of Board of War
Minister to France, the Netherlands, and Great Britain
Vice president with George Washington
Member, First and Second Massachusetts constitutional
    conventions

DEATH
July 4, 1826
Quincy, Mass.

LAW CAREER IN BRIEF

During Adams's extensive twenty-year law practice (1758–78) he was primarily a trial lawyer who handled commercial and real estate litigation as well as tort, family law, and criminal matters. He rode circuit throughout Massachusetts, including what is now Maine, in a few years building the largest practice in his province. As the Revolution approached, he defended high-profile political cases, such as those involving the Boston Massacre, Michael Corbet, and John Hancock. Adams was a legal scholar schooled in history, philosophy, and literature. His early writings provided the legal and political bases for independence from Great Britain. Later, his draft of the Massachusetts Constitution served as the model for other state constitutions and had a major influence on the U.S. Constitution.

John Adams: Patriot Lawyer

L. Kinvin Wroth

To the end that it might be a government of laws, and not of men." With these words framing the Declaration of Rights in the Massachusetts Constitution of 1780, John Adams stated an aspiration that has guided our constitutional republic ever since. The Massachusetts Declaration of Rights, like the first ten amendments to the U.S. Constitution, set forth limits of law upon the powers of those who govern. In the life of Adams, our first lawyer-president, we see the cataclysmic events of revolutionary America that made the need for such a principle self-evident, and the ways in which he sought to develop and implement the principle as lawyer and statesman.

Born in 1735, the brightest offspring of devout but practical Massachusetts farmers, Adams at the age of fifteen entered upon a time-honored career path—Harvard and then the Congregational ministry. Though Harvard whetted his intellectual appetites, it also directed him along secular paths in moral and political philosophy and the natural sciences. Resisting the ecclesiastical call, he became a schoolteacher in Worcester upon his graduation in 1755. After further consideration, a year later he began to read the law with James Putnam, the leading lawyer there. Adams had at first resisted a life "fumbling and raking amidst the rubbish of Writs, indightments, Pleas, ejectments, enfiefed, illatebration, and a 1000 other lignum Vitae words" as well as "the noise and bustle of Courts and the labor of inquiring into and pleading dry and difficult Cases." He was soon drawn into the literature of the law, however, reading Coke, Fortescue, and other monuments of the common law that were essential preparation for the bar.

When Adams came to Boston to begin his practice in Suffolk County two years later, a new mentor, Jeremiah Gridley, acknow-

★ ★ ★

"Then and there the child Independance was born."

John Adams, commenting on James Otis's stirring arguments in the Writs of Assistance case

"The village has become so petty quarrelsome that a popular saying is going around, 'As litigious as Braintree.'"

John Adams, commenting on the many lawsuits in his hometown

ledged dean of the Massachusetts bar, gave him timeless advice that set him on the path to legal statesmanship and public leadership. Said Gridley, "A Lawyer in this Country must study common Law and civil Law, and natural Law, and Admiralty law." Most important, "pursue the Study of the Law rather than the Gain of it. Pursue the Gain of it enough to keep out of the Briars, but give your main attention to the study of it."

Stirred, the young Adams embarked upon a ferocious course of reading in the Roman-based civil law that became a lifelong intellectual pursuit. In 1765 he joined "the Sodality," a small group of Boston lawyers organized by Gridley to study the great civil-law writers. This study of jurisprudence provided the foundation for broad policy arguments that Adams would make in courts and political forums as the Revolution approached. It also served as the basis for his later service to the new nation as constitution maker, international diplomat, and ultimately chief executive.

But first Adams had to obtain a foundation among the rubbish of writs and amidst the noise and bustle of courts in order to keep out of the briars. Daily life in the British royal province of Massachusetts was governed by a mixture of English common law adapted for simpler colonial circumstances, acts of the British Parliament, and acts of the Massachusetts legislature, then as now known as "the General Court." Civil disputes and criminal cases were tried in county courts and the superior court, which sat in each county as both the highest trial court and the provincial court of appeal.

In 1758, Adams was admitted to the Suffolk County bar. After losing his first case, involving the then-common problem of stray livestock, he wrote: "The Writ was defective. It will be said, I undertook the case but was unable to manage it." Despite this initial setback, Adams rapidly expanded his practice from the local courts of his native rural Braintree to the farthest reaches of the province, "riding circuit" with the superior court from Lincoln County (in what is now Maine) to Barnstable County on Cape Cod and Hampshire County in western Massachusetts. By 1768, he was well established as a superior court practitioner, and by 1772 he had the largest practice in the province.

"The bar" was the trial bar, and like his fellow attorneys Adams was primarily a trial lawyer, handling both petty and complex commercial and real estate litigation as well as criminal cases and family law disputes. His clients ranged from farmers and artisans to the highest levels of the provincial social and economic elite. In the latter group, he not only rubbed shoulders with leaders of His Majesty's provincial government but formed business and political relationships with individuals such as James Bowdoin and John Hancock, wealthy merchants who were becoming leaders of the rapidly growing revolutionary movement in Massachusetts.

While Adams had become politically active on the local scene, it was by applying his legal skills and knowledge for clients such as Bowdoin and Hancock that he entered upon a wider stage. Britain's efforts in the 1760s to fund its growing empire through colonial customs duties and other taxes were nowhere felt or resisted more strongly than in Boston. From the beginning, the courts, where customs laws were enforced, were a principal arena for that resistance, and its rhetoric was that of constitutional law. Adams's initial exposure to these issues came in 1761 when the young lawyer heard the brilliant James Otis argue the famous "Writs of Assistance" case. Otis contended that the act of Parliament that authorized writs allowing customs officers to search for smuggled goods without specific warrants was unconstitutional. "Then and there," Adams later wrote, "the child Independance was born."

It was a measure of Adams's professional growth that a mere four years later, Boston merchants selected him to argue before the governor and council that the courts should not be closed for want of paper bearing the revenue stamp imposed by the notorious Stamp Act. Adams brought his learning to bear in this august forum, citing the law of nature and "the antient Roman Law" and declaring that "a Parliament of Great Britain can have no more Right to tax the Colonies than a Parliament of Paris." That his political views had personal roots is revealed in his private comment that "this execrable Project [that is, the Stamp Act] was set on foot for my Ruin as well as that of America in General, and of Great Britain."

★ ★ ★

"[From his classical education] came the appreciation of law as politics, law as philosophy, and law as juris-prudence which so colored Adams's later approach to the prob-lems of his time and . . . their solutions."

L. Kinvin Wroth and
Hiller B. Zobel, in *Legal
Papers of John Adams*

Adams's best-known prerevolutionary case was his defense in 1770 of the British soldiers charged with the murder of unarmed civilians in the episode known as the Boston Massacre. Though this representation has often been characterized as the paradigm defense of the unpopular client, in fact Adams was serving the patriot cause by presenting a defense that did not implicate the revolutionary leadership. Nevertheless, his strong case resulted in the acquittal of all but two of the soldiers, who were convicted of the lesser offense of manslaughter.

The Massacre trials and many of Adams's other politically connected cases were tried in the common-law courts, whose juries were unsympathetic to actions brought by customs officers to enforce the hated British duties. To improve the chances of success in such actions, Parliament had also provided that they could be pursued in royal courts of vice admiralty, which followed the civil law and sat without juries. In that venue, customs officers in 1768 sought substantial penalties against John Hancock for smuggling a cargo of Madeira wine on which duties had not been paid. Armed with his knowledge of civil law and procedure, Adams eloquently challenged the court's jurisdiction as a violation of fundamental rights. Similarly, in *Corbet's Case*, the 1769 prosecution of an American seaman for killing a British naval officer aboard a vessel on the high seas, Adams used that same knowledge to bolster his ultimately successful defense of justifiable homicide.

In the fifteen years before the Revolution, Adams made significant contributions to the legal and political theories that ultimately justified independence from Great Britain. His "Dissertation on the Canon and Feudal Law," published in 1765 in Boston and London newspapers, took his legal arguments to a broader constitutional level in asserting the colonists' political and legal rights on the basis of both the law of nature and the common law of property.

Ten years later, his "Novanglus" letters—a series of twelve anonymous newspaper pieces published in response to the loyalist writings of "Massachusettensis," the pen name for fellow lawyer Daniel Leonard—asserted that resistance to tyranny was legally justified and that the authority of Parliament had no legal basis. It thus could and should be resisted, Adams argued, because the colonists were not represented in Parliament and owed allegiance only to the King, who had granted them their charters. Though Adams denied that he sought colonial independence, in the Novanglus letters "the child Independance" had surely reached its young adulthood.

In April 1775, events at Lexington and Concord overtook rhetoric and Adams found himself in the thick of the political action. In June 1774, he had been appointed to the First Continental Congress and typically expressed self doubts: "A more extensive Knowledge of the Realm, the Colonies, and of Commerce, as well as of Law and Policy, is necessary, than I am master of." Once among the distinguished array of lawyers and other leaders assembled in Philadelphia, however, he quickly saw that he was up to the task.

He assumed a leading role then and in the increasingly complex business of the Congress for the next three years. In the Second Congress, he was a workhorse, chairing at least twenty-five committees, including the Board of War. His prior legal experience was called upon in drafting codes of military justice for the army and navy and rules for dealing with naval "prizes"—captured enemy vessels that could be sold by an admiralty court for the benefit of the captors. He also served on a standing committee that heard appeals from state admiralty courts in prize cases. The committee, which followed judicial procedure, was a direct ancestor of the U.S. Supreme Court.

Adams's most profound contribution was in pushing for, and framing, the Declaration of Independence. With Thomas Jefferson, he served on a five-person committee charged with drafting the document, and though Jefferson was its primary draftsman, its legal theories were those developed by Adams in his prerevolutionary writings. The most forceful arguments in Congress for its adoption were his as well. As Jefferson later said, Adams spoke "with a power of thought and expression that moved us from our seats."

Despite the impact of the Declaration of Independence, Adams believed that his most important contributions were the theories underlying the constitutions of the newly independent American states, and ultimately the United States. His *Thoughts on Government*, published in 1776, countered what Adams viewed as the excessively "democratical" tenor of Thomas Paine's *Common Sense*. While Paine had called for concentration of all state

"REMEMBER THE LADIES"
As the Declaration of Independence was being drafted, Abigail Adams spoke out for women. "[N]otwithstanding all your wise Laws and Maxims," she wrote to her unmoved spouse, "we have it in our power not only to free ourselves, but to subdue our Masters, and without violence throw your natural and legal authority at our feet."

SIGNING THE DECLARATION OF INDEPENDENCE

Its drafting was assigned to a five-man committee that included Jefferson and Adams; Jefferson crafted its language while Adams convinced others of the need for its passage.

power in a single legislative assembly, Adams recognized the flaws in Britain's parliamentary system. He instead proposed a balanced separation of powers among a bicameral legislature, an independent executive, and a judiciary "distinct from both the legislative and executive and independent [from] both, so that it may be a check upon both, as both should be checks upon [it]." He felt that the true declaration of colonial independence from Britain had occurred in May 1776 when Congress passed his resolution calling upon each state to adopt its own form of government so "that the Exercise of every kind of Authority under the . . . Crown should be totally suppressed and all the Powers of Government exerted under the Authority of the People of the Colonies."

In 1779, during a brief interlude between diplomatic missions, Adams put theory into practice. He was principal drafter of the Massachusetts Constitution of 1780, which served as an elegant model for other state constitutions and the federal constitution of 1787. Under the Massachusetts Constitution, the state was a commonwealth in which government should act for the public good. The document combined Adams's separation of powers principle with a Declaration of Rights that consolidated provisions of other states' constitutions and foreshadowed the federal Bill of Rights of 1791.

Adams's legal skills were also the foundation of his career in diplomacy—a totally unknown and untried field for America's fledgling statesmen. In September 1776, Congress adopted the plan for a treaty with France that Adams had drafted. The framework of the proposed treaty, intended to "avoid all Alliance, which might embarrass Us in after times and involve Us in future European Wars," became the basis for most foreign treaties entered into by the United States in the eighteenth century. Adams's role in its preparation made him a natural choice as one of the commissioners to negotiate the treaty when U.S. diplomat Silas Deane was ordered home from Paris in 1777.

Sailing in February 1778—and effectively concluding his active legal practice—Adams spent all but four months of the next ten years working the chanceries and palaces of Europe with Benjamin Franklin, Thomas Jefferson, John Jay, and others on behalf of the new nation's diplomatic and financial interests. In 1779, when it became apparent that the British ministry was not ready to enter into a treaty recognizing American independence, he turned to the Netherlands and ultimately succeeded in obtaining Dutch recognition of American sovereignty, a treaty of amity and commerce, and a substantial loan to the United States. In 1782, he was one of five commissioners to negotiate a peace treaty with Great Britain. Provisions of the resulting 1783 Treaty of Paris—including New England fishing rights off the Grand Banks, commercial debt collection, property claims of American loyalists, and the boundary with Canada—reflected his legal, drafting, and negotiating skills. After further diplomatic missions, Adams was appointed the first American minister to Great Britain in 1785. The ultimate symbolic realization of American independence occurred when the colonial country lawyer was presented to his royal foe, George III, in a brief but moving moment of mutual recognition.

Though diplomatic assignments caused Adams to miss the frantic period of institution-building that occurred during the decade of the Revolution and its aftermath, his Massachusetts Constitution of 1780 and his massive three-volume *Defence of the*

★ ★ ★

"Adams was a colorful, articulate lawyer . . . a learned man, well read, intellectually growing, who placed great confidence in the bar and the legal system."

Jack Shepherd, in *The Adams Chronicles*

"[Adams's] tone is uncommonly bold and animated, for that period. He calls on the people, not only to defend, but to study and understand their rights and privileges."

Daniel Webster

Constitutions of Government of the United States of America (1787–88), elaborating upon his basic theme of separation of powers, served as its bookends. When he returned from London in 1788, Adams was well recognized as an intellectual and political leader of the nascent republic. At the same time, he was untainted with much of the petty scandal and enmity attached to those who had worked at close quarters in Congress and state government during the preceding years. In the presidential election of 1789, though the intrigues of Alexander Hamilton left Adams with only a plurality of the sixty-nine electoral votes cast, Adams was clearly a popular choice for the second highest office in the new republic and was duly elected George Washington's vice president.

In his constitutional role as president of the Senate, Adams's skills and experience as a lawyer in public service allowed him to have a significant impact on the framework of the new nation. Though sometimes criticized for taking too active a part, he presided over debates in the first Congress concerning the adoption of the Bill of Rights, many of the provisions of which were anticipated in his Massachusetts Declaration of Rights of 1780, and the Judiciary Act of 1789, still the cornerstone of the federal judiciary. In a closely divided Senate, Adams cast more tie-breaking votes than any of his successors. One of his most important votes defeated a measure that would have weakened the principle of separation of powers by taking away the exclusive presidential power to remove executive officers.

Adams's second term as vice president saw the coalescence of foreign and domestic issues that was to form the politics of the next thirty years. The French Revolution gave definition to the first political parties—the Federalists of Washington, Adams, and Hamilton, who were repelled by revolutionary excesses that departed from the rule of law, and the Republicans of Jefferson, who hailed the appeal to reason and basic human rights in revolutionary rhetoric. In *Discourses on Davila* (1790–91), Adams reacted to the turmoil of the French Revolution, emphasizing his earlier warnings against the excesses of Republicanism. Though his political enemies often cited these writings to show that Adams was a monarchist at heart, in fact they were consistent developments of his theory of balanced government. As the newly militant French went to war with Britain, Adams, on familiar ground, cast the deciding vote in the Senate to defeat a measure to suspend commerce with Britain. He also presided over the nomination of John Jay as special envoy to Britain and the ratification of the Jay Treaty in 1795 that averted war with that country.

These and other events provided the context for Adams's election as president in 1796 by three electoral votes over Thomas Jefferson, who became vice president. During Adams's administration, French excesses in seizing American shipping weakened the Republican position and allowed him to build a strong navy that withstood the French at sea and allowed time for diplomacy that averted war, despite pressures from Hamilton and other Federalist hawks. The domestic impact of these issues resulted in the enactment by Congress in 1798 of the Naturalization, Alien, and Sedition Acts and a direct federal property tax to support military expansion. Prosecutions under the Sedition Act raised grave constitutional issues about the scope of federal power to criminalize political utterances and even graver political issues for the Federalists. John Fries of Pennsylvania was convicted of treason for leading a rebellion against collection of the direct tax. Adams's pardon of Fries, based on his analysis of the law of treason, infuriated the Federalist hawks and won him no ground with the Republicans. In the election of 1800, these issues produced substantial Republican majorities in the House and Senate and Jefferson's ultimate election as president by a margin of eight electoral votes.

In the last days of his administration, Adams took two major steps that reflected his legal and political past. The Judiciary Act of 1801 reorganized the circuit courts established in the first Judiciary Act and eliminated the circuit-riding role of the U.S. Supreme Court justices by creating sixteen new circuit court judgeships that Adams quickly filled. This measure, intended both to bring about an essential judicial reform and to preserve a Federalist

presence in the national polity, was excoriated as the "Midnight Judges" Act by the victorious and indignant Republicans and was quickly repealed.

MIDNIGHT JUDGES EPISODE
During his last night in office, Adams signed commissions for forty-two justices of the peace, who were confirmed by the Federalist-controlled Senate the following day. President Jefferson, however, refused to have some commissions delivered, including one for William Marbury (pictured here). Marbury and others then filed suit, resulting in the landmark *Marbury v. Madison* ruling that affirmed the Court's power to review the constitutionality of executive and legislative actions.

GEORGE WASHINGTON, ESQ.?

With the "Esq." likely referring to his status as a gentleman and landholder, rather than his brief tenure as a county justice of the peace in 1770, the Father of Our Country was thus described in the 1775 report of the Continental Congress's unanimous election of Washington as commander-in-chief of the Continental army. John Adams had a leading role in choosing Washington, to the dismay of Adams's fellow Bostonian and former client John Hancock.

The second step was more lasting and of far greater significance. In January 1801, Adams appointed his secretary of state, the staunch Federalist John Marshall, as chief justice. Serving until 1835, Marshall established the federal judiciary as a truly independent branch fully implementing the concept of separation of powers at the heart of Adams's theory of American constitutionalism. In the 1803 case of *Marbury v. Madison*, Marshall echoed Adams's timeless phrase "a government of laws, and not of men" in articulating the fundamental principle of judicial review under which courts may hold acts of the executive and legislative branches unconstitutional.

A bitter Adams departed from Washington on the morning of Jefferson's inauguration and returned to his Massachusetts farm, where he thereafter engaged neither in public life nor the practice of law. His son, John Quincy Adams, as America's sixth president, and Marshall as chief justice carried forward his spirit and ideas through the first great period of the new republic. Adams, though, did not give up his pen. From his rural seat, he relived the great issues and encounters of his past in a never-completed autobiography and in extensive correspondence with old friends and former enemies, including Jefferson, with whom he was reconciled in 1812. He also published new editions of works such as *Discourses with Davila* and *Novanglus* and addressed both past and current issues in newspaper writings and pamphlets.

Adams cannot be assessed as lawyer and president without consideration of the role of his wife Abigail, a parson's daughter from nearby Weymouth whom he married in 1764. As he assumed a leadership role on the national and international stage, Abigail emerged as an independent intellectual force and confidante whose ideas and support were critical to Adams's ability to stay the course. When his necessary absences from home lengthened into months and years, she maintained their children, their properties, and his law clerks through all the stresses and deprivations of wartime and postwar Massachusetts.

Her letters not only detailed these activities but spurred him on with ideas. For example, she reminded him half-humorously of the need of the new society to "remember the ladies" and expressed deep reservations about the institution of slavery. Until her death in 1818, she provided Adams with shrewd analyses of politics, both domestic and foreign, as well as with words of warm affection.

Adams's last public service was at age eighty-five as a delegate to the Massachusetts constitutional convention of 1820. There, he argued unsuccessfully for the retention of property ownership as a qualification for voting and proposed an equally unsuccessful amendment to the Declaration of Rights that would have extended equality under the law to "all men of all religions." A couple of months later, responding with unusual modesty to Jefferson's congratulations on this effort, Adams wrote, "My appearance in the late convention was too ludicrous to be talked of . . . I boggled and blundered more than a young fellow just rising to speak at the bar. What I said I know not; I believe the Printers made better speeches than I made for myself."

On July 4, 1826, an era ended when Adams and Jefferson died within a few hours of each other on the fiftieth anniversary of the great moment of independence that they had shared as advocate and author. In his last words, Adams, unaware that his old friend was already gone, epitomized their ultimately unbreakable bond: "Thomas Jefferson still survives."

"He was unyielding in his belief that good government depends upon the impartial operation of just laws."

Adrienne Koch, in *Selected Writings of John and John Quincy Adams*

★ ★ ★

Third President (1801–09)

BIRTH
April 13, 1743
Goochland (later Albemarle) County, Va.

EDUCATION
Private tutors
College of William and Mary
Law study with Virginia attorney George Wythe
Admission to the bar: Fall 1765

OTHER OCCUPATIONS/PUBLIC OFFICES
Farmer/planter
County justice of the peace
Member, Virginia House of Burgesses
Member, First and Second Continental Congress
Virginia governor
Minister to France
Secretary of state with George Washington
Vice president with John Adams

DEATH
July 4, 1826
Charlottesville, Va.

LAW CAREER IN BRIEF

Jefferson's eight-year law practice (1767–74) focused primarily on real estate matters and totaled about nine hundred cases. Known more for his legal scholarship than for his oratorical skills, Jefferson made significant contributions to Virginia law reform, served as a law reporter, established the first American law professorship (at the College of William and Mary) and, like Adams, published treatises providing legal and political justification for the American Revolution. His draft of the Declaration of Independence has been described as "a legal document based on lawyerly study of English constitutional history."

Thomas Jefferson: Legal Wordsmith

David T. Konig

It was entirely fitting that in June 1776, the draftsman and the chief advocate for the Declaration of Independence were Thomas Jefferson and John Adams. Political factors aside, the two men were ideally suited for the task, as the statement justifying the American decision to reject British sovereignty demanded a skilled and concise legal argument, grounded in principle and eloquently expressed.

Unlike most lawyers of their generation, Adams and Jefferson were scholars of the law as well as practitioners. Whereas other budding lawyers trained amidst the drudgery of law office work, Adams and Jefferson also read widely in such areas as history and philosophy. By 1776, they were seasoned legal practitioners who had each crafted essays challenging the British Parliament's authority to tax and govern the colonies.

Jefferson drew on his legal background to conceive and express the political argument embodied in the Declaration of Independence. He found the appropriate frame of reference in the legal concept that a trustee might forfeit his position through neglect and misuse of authority. Fusing political philosophy with practical legal pleading, Jefferson assailed the king as a failed trustee of the rights of his subjects and demanded in the court of public opinion that the relationship be dissolved.

Jefferson was joining law and politics in 1776, but he had done so before and would do so many times again. Emblematic of the man, law and politics would reappear together throughout his presidency and even during his retirement, as he held government accountable to the trust placed in it democratically by the people.

Jefferson enjoyed all the educational advantages available to a person of his background. His mother's status as a Randolph

★ ★ ★

"I consider trial by jury as the only anchor ever yet imagined by man, by which a government can be held to the principles of its constitution."

Thomas Jefferson

GEORGE WYTHE, AMERICA'S FIRST LAW PROFESSOR

Jefferson studied law under noted lawyer and legal scholar George Wythe. In 1779, Jefferson appointed Wythe to the first American law professorship at the College of William and Mary.

conferred social rank, while his father's skills as a surveyor and land speculator provided the funds for his son's tutoring and education at the College of William and Mary. Despite the young Jefferson's patrician background and tastes, he never felt at ease with his classmates. He regarded them as idle scions of the Virginia landed elite who admired a man "who powders most, parfumes most, and talks most nonsense." His distrust of aristocracy never abated, and it shaped both his legal and political thinking.

After graduation, he turned to the study of law under the eminent attorney George Wythe, who quickly recognized his student's talents. In addition to providing guidance in practical matters and directing Jefferson to observe the General Court, Wythe allowed his pupil considerable freedom in reading, an opportunity that led him to devour not only legal treatises and reports but also works in history, literature, political philosophy, and natural philosophy (now known as science). Years later, a grateful Jefferson wrote of law students, "We are all too apt by shifting on them our business, to incroach on that time which should be devoted to their studies. The only help a youth wants [that is, needs] is to be directed what books to read and in what order to read them."

In the mountains at Shadwell and Monticello, Jefferson perfected his ability to identify the material points of a case and to express them concisely and effectively. He later recommended to any law student to "enter in a commonplace book every case of value, condensed into the narrowest compass possible which will admit of presenting distinctly the principles of the case . . . never using two words where one will do." It was a forensic talent that served him well.

Jefferson was admitted to the bar of the General Court, the colony's highest, in 1766. At twenty-three he was the youngest member of the superior court bar, joining an elite group of only six other practitioners. In his eight-year practice he accepted more than nine hundred cases and provided numerous opinions, but like other practitioners of that time, he found it hard to collect fees, which were fixed by statute and collectible only at the conclusion of a case. Trying a case in equity usually took eight years, but even common law cases dragged on slowly. Some that he began in 1767, his first year of actual practice, were among the unfinished cases he turned over to Edmund Randolph when he retired from the profession in 1774.

Jefferson's law practice provided the template for his later political career. Recognizing his diffident powers of oratory, he never became a great speaker in the courtroom or the political arena. Instead, he honed his skills of forensic research and became known as an "office lawyer." Comparing him to fellow lawyer Patrick Henry, Randolph remarked, "Mr. Jefferson drew copiously from the depths of the law, Mr. Henry from the recesses of the human heart."

The law of real property comprised the primary focus of Jefferson's practice. As the sole General Court attorney in the western part of the colony, he was called on repeatedly to quiet or contest land titles. Much of his practice involved assisting speculators in acquiring title to frontier lands for which other claimants had failed to make proper legal settlement. These lucrative but often questionable endeavors did his reputation little credit, but he gained distinction in other real property matters, where he represented well-known clients in contentious and complex court battles over property rights.

Jefferson's practice was also notable for his work in another area of property law—the law of slavery. Jefferson was a major slave owner; over the course of his life he owned as many as two hundred slaves, and he used legal instruments to control and transfer his human property. He did so when he settled slaves on his daughters and sons-in-law when they married, bought and sold slaves through contracts enforceable at law, or drew up documents and provided legal advice for others doing the same. He was a trustee for the disposition of slaves in estates and represented clients disputing ownership of their human chattel.

At the same time, the role of slavery in his law practice reveals the same deep ambivalence about slavery seen in his political life. In 1769, his first year as a member of the assembly, he supported an unsuccessful bill empowering owners to manumit their slaves—that is, to make the law an instrument of freedom as well as enslavement. With the failure of the bill, the only legal assault on slavery remained individual freedom suits, and in 1770 Jefferson became one of a small and unpopular group of attorneys who took slave freedom cases on a pro bono basis.

"Mr. Jefferson drew copiously from the depths of the law, Mr. Henry from the recesses of the human heart."

Edmund Randolph, commenting on each man's talents as a trial lawyer

> *"In the selection of our Law Professor, we must be vigorously attentive to his political principles."*
>
> Thomas Jefferson, writing to Madison about the new position at the University of Virginia

In one of them, he argued with vigor and ingenuity that a mixed race plaintiff, Samuel Howell, was being held in servitude contrary to several legislative acts which, if read strictly, made him a free man. His radical argument, which would have opened the doors to scores of similar suits, startled the court and his opposing counsel, George Wythe. As his old law teacher rose to respond for defendant, Jefferson reported, "the court interrupted him and gave judgment in favor of his [Wythe's] client." Just as tersely, Jefferson recorded in his Memorandum Book that he "Gave pauper client 2 [shillings]."

Jefferson's interest in politics overwhelmed his desire to practice law, and in 1774 he concentrated on the movement to protect American rights. That summer, Virginia's royal governor dissolved the assembly after it protested the Boston Port Bill. Lacking statutory authorization to charge fees, Virginia's courts could not function. Although numerous burgesses used this controversy to press for closing the courts as a political protest, Jefferson provided a learned legal case to urge the closing on the basis of strict statutory construction and legislative supremacy.

As the confrontation between the colonies and Britain worsened and Virginia delegates were chosen for the Continental Congress, Jefferson drafted a statement of instructions. Though modest in purpose and intended for local circulation, the *Summary View of the Rights of British America* was widely distributed. "Our ancestors . . . were laborers, not lawyers," he wrote in providing a powerful lawyerly critique of "fictitious" legal principles introduced by sly "Norman lawyers" to strip freeborn Englishmen of their rights and property.

Even as the Declaration of Independence was being read publicly in Philadelphia for the first time on July 8, 1776, Jefferson was preparing to return home and draft a new Virginia constitution and code of laws. For Jefferson, American independence was an unprecedented opportunity to begin dismantling the old regime of "lawcraft and priestcraft" and replace aristocracy with democracy. Though somewhat progressive, the Virginia constitution of 1776 left him dissatisfied as it still contained "many capital defects" that boded ill for the future. Most adult white men still could not vote, representation was not proportional to population, and the influence of wealth remained great. The rich, he feared, "will purchase the voices of the people" and form "an elective despotism."

Jefferson's most controversial proposals struck at vested privilege, as he sought to create a legal "system by which every fibre would be eradicated of antient or future aristocracy." This goal reflected not only his political and economic views, but also his experience as a real estate lawyer. Observing how primogeniture and entail had entrenched artificial privilege, he proposed their outright abolition. Even though his efforts were denounced as befitting "a midday drunkard," they prevailed. The legislature ended the entail of estates in 1776, although primogeniture survived until 1785.

As a lawyer Jefferson had tangled with the established church, which he regarded with scarcely concealed contempt. The "adoption in mass" of Christianity into the common law, he believed, had been achieved "by usurpation of the Judges alone, without a particle of legislative will having ever been called on," with the result that the state was interfering in matters of a strictly private nature. Conceding that the law should prevent injuries, he countered, "But it does me no injury for my neighbor to say that there are twenty gods, or no god. It neither picks my pocket nor breaks my leg." With the help of James Madison, his bill to separate church and state finally passed in 1786.

Jefferson viewed the American Revolution as "a contest which was to change the condition of mankind over the civilized globe," and he never ceased to fear for its success. Though he tried to withdraw from public service in order to be with his family—and even returned briefly to legal practice, providing several opinions in 1782—he watched the progress of events with ever-increasing concern. As secretary of state in Washington's administration and vice president to John Adams, he had grown alarmed at the concentration of power in the national government, especially in the executive and judicial branches. To Jefferson, Treasury Secretary Alexander Hamilton had created a powerful government financial engine and the federal courts had become the instrument of partisan advancement by "monocrats," a term that Jefferson coined to describe those favoring a monarchical style of government.

Federalist judges represented the threat most clearly. To Jefferson, they had shamelessly distorted the law and flagrantly used the courts to punish their enemies, most notably in prosecutions under the Alien and Sedition Acts. He suspected, too, that they

"Their trade is to question everything, yield nothing and talk by the hour. That one hundred and fifty lawyers should do business together ought not to be expected."

Thomas Jefferson

Chief Justice John Marshall

Jefferson was constantly at odds with Marshall, whom he accused of "twistifications" of the law. In the hands of Marshall, Jefferson wrote Madison in 1810, "the law is nothing more than an ambiguous text, to be explained by his sophistry into any meaning which may serve his personal malice." Marshall would head the high court for thirty-four years, handing down scores of landmark decisions and earning him the moniker "the Great Chief Justice."

sought to impose a federal common law, which he called an "audacious, barefaced and sweeping pretension to a system of law for the U S, without the adoption of their legislature, and so infinitely beyond their power to adopt." For Jefferson and the nascent Republican Party he helped create, the election of 1800 that ousted the Federalists was nothing less than a second revolution ending what Jefferson called "the reign of witches." But the struggle had only begun when he took the presidential oath of office from Chief Justice John Marshall.

Most of the crowd at the Senate Chamber knew that the superficial courtesies of the ceremony masked an intense political distrust and personal hostility between the two men. Though distant cousins with shared backgrounds, including legal study under George Wythe, their political opinions had divided them for more than a decade. While Marshall was arguing powerfully for ratification of the federal Constitution at the Richmond convention, Jefferson, then in Paris, was offering only guarded support for a plan that he distrusted as the first step toward an alarmingly powerful centralized government. When the two served in the administration of John Adams, their differences only widened.

More than political beliefs separated the two men, as their vastly differing conceptions of the role of judges became the crucible of their heated rivalry. Marshall followed the jurisprudential inclinations of England's great chief justice, Lord Mansfield, who expanded the scope of judicial intervention and introduced into English courts many principles of commercial communities. Accused of being a chancellor in common law robes, Mansfield towered over English law in this period and left a lasting imprint on it. As chief justice of the U.S. Supreme Court, Marshall would establish commerce and property rights on a secure basis, protected from incursions by legislatures, and in so doing would expand greatly the authority of the federal government over that of the states.

Jefferson, by contrast, approached law from a more theoretical perspective, studying its history with an eye to reforming it in response to popular needs. Despite his personal reverence for Wythe, who shared Marshall's judicial inclinations, Jefferson's reading of law and history revealed a legacy of excessive judicial discretion—even usurpation—against the will of the people. He deplored the "honeyed Mansfieldism" that corrupted judges and insinuated discretionary authority into common law judging. Jefferson preferred to place his trust in a reformed and representative legislature.

Moreover, Jefferson was an early and abiding apostle of states' rights. The federal bench, he believed ever more firmly as he aged, was a "corps of sappers and miners, steadily working to undermine the independent rights of the States, and to consolidate all power in the hands of that government in which they have so important a freehold estate."

Such differences would explode during Jefferson's presidency and Marshall's years as chief justice. In a new constitutional era without firm precedents, both sought to establish patterns that would secure free republican government, and both saw their rival's efforts as calamitous. Despite Jefferson's inaugural statement, "We are all republicans, we are all federalists," the new president had many reasons to distrust his opponents, and saw "federalism and Marshalism" as synonymous. Both had to be fought.

The Federalists, Jefferson believed, had been repudiated by the people but were mounting a rearguard effort to retain power through their "stronghold" in an expanded federal court system. He had good reason to believe so. The lame-duck Federalist Congress had created a new system of circuit courts staffed by Federalist judges, and Adams's appointment of "Midnight Judges" left the new president a federal judiciary controlled entirely by Federalists. While Adams and the Federalists believed that only the judiciary stood as a barrier against populist demagoguery, Jefferson was determined to reverse this "outrage on decency."

Jefferson did not wait long after assuming the presidency. His party in Congress repealed the Judiciary Act of 1801, abolishing the new system of circuit courts and its expanded original jurisdiction. The new president also discharged all those who remained in jail or indicted under the Sedition Act, which Adams had refused to do and which Jefferson defended as maintaining justice through the proper exercise of executive authority.

Jefferson was most outraged by Adams's packing the federal judiciary with Federalists, which he described to Abigail as "the one act of Mr. Adams's life, and one only, [that] ever gave me a moment's personal displeasure." The aftermath of that episode

★ ★ ★

"In the realm of the law Jefferson was even more thoroughly the scholar than in the realms of political philosophy and history."

Arthur Bestor, in *Three Presidents and Their Books*

The Trial of Aaron Burr

During Burr's trial for treason, Jefferson was subpoenaed to testify and produce documents. In refusing to appear and in providing only selective information, he helped establish the doctrine of "executive privilege," which gives the president the prerogative to withhold sensitive and confidential materials.

The trial, which involved questionable conduct on the part of both President Jefferson and Chief Justice Marshall, resulted in Burr's acquittal.

would produce yet greater displeasure for the new president, but it would be with John Marshall concerning *Marbury v. Madison*, the landmark decision asserting the judiciary's right to review the constitutionality of executive and legislative actions.

The conflict was ignited in 1801 when new Secretary of State James Madison, at President Jefferson's direction, refused to deliver many Federalist commissions left by the outgoing secretary of state, John Marshall. One of those affected, William Marbury, applied to the Supreme Court for a writ commanding Madison to do his duty and transmit the document. Jefferson believed the case reflected a simple issue that the chief justice turned into a personal and political weapon through his decision asserting the Court's power of judicial review. Though long retired, Jefferson in 1823 angrily wrote to William Johnson, his first appointee to the Supreme Court, "Besides the impropriety of this gratuitous interference, could anything exceed the perversion of the law?"

The more extreme opponents of the Federalists used the *Marbury* decision to demand an all-out attack on the judiciary. Broadening the grounds of impeachment, they impeached and removed an insane alcoholic federal district judge and, with the president's support, impeached Justice Samuel Chase of the U.S. Supreme Court. To a Baltimore grand jury, Chase had rejected the idea "that all men in a state of society are entitled to enjoy equal liberty and equal rights," and at trial he had violated numerous rules of procedure.

Jefferson was uneasy about impeaching judges for political reasons alone, however, even those like Chase who had enthusiastically supported the Sedition Act. When more radical Republicans threatened to broaden their attack among the entire federal judiciary, Jefferson withdrew his support of the prosecution, and after Chase's acquittal, he suggested instead a constitutional amendment providing for their removal by joint action of Congress.

Though temporarily abated, antagonism between the executive and judiciary erupted anew in the 1807 trial of Aaron Burr for treason. Jefferson believed that Burr was intent on separating the West from the nation, invading Mexico, and erecting a dictatorship controlling the Mississippi River and Gulf Coast, all of which would endanger an "Empire of Liberty" in the West, one of Jefferson's most dearly held goals. The president was certain, moreover, that Marshall would "shield [Burr] from punishment."

As in the election of 1800, Burr had covered his tracks very skillfully, making it difficult to prove his criminality. Adding to the problem, no Justice Department existed in 1807, the attorney general was merely a part-time legal adviser, and district attorney George Hay, who handled the prosecution, had no legal staff and had to hire Virginia lawyer William Wirt to assist in the trial.

Though he had no experience as a prosecutor, Jefferson took charge and plunged heedlessly and zealously ahead in an aggressive campaign against Burr. Publicly, he imprudently announced before trial that Burr was guilty of treason. From behind the scenes, he interviewed witnesses of questionable reliability and built the government's case on their dubious testimony. Burr and his skilled legal team were more than a match for Jefferson and exploited the "battle" between the president and Marshall, who presided at the trial before a huge crowd in Richmond.

If Jefferson's behavior diminished his status as a civil libertarian, Marshall's conduct exposed him to sharp criticism as well. He dined with Burr and his attorney, granted nearly every defense motion, and publicly accused the president of using a treason trial for political purposes. Apparently contradicting his earlier broad definition of treason, Marshall instead defined it narrowly for Burr, requiring proof of an overt act of levying war. By doing so, Marshall effectively undercut the prosecution and made Burr a free man.

The Burr trial highlighted Jefferson's tendency to overreact or bend his principles on matters that he felt endangered the future of the nation. For example, he had little trouble expanding federal authority in declaring an embargo on exports during the war between France and Britain, or in supporting internal improvements that would promote settlement of the West. Although he harbored reservations about the constitutionality of

THE LOUISIANA PURCHASE
Though Jefferson had legal and constitutional reservations about the Louisiana Purchase, he abandoned them, saying: "To lose our country by a scrupulous adherence to written law, would be to lose the law itself."

JEFFERSON'S LEGAL DISPUTES WITH EDWARD LIVINGSTON

One of the most interesting, and overlooked, examples of presidential law practice pitted Jefferson against Edward Livingston, a noted lawyer and congressman who later served as Jackson's secretary of state. The complicated controversy, which involved a batture, or beach, in New Orleans owned by Livingston, continued after Jefferson left the White House when Livingston filed an action of "trespass" against the former president and sought damages of one hundred thousand dollars. The last book written by Jefferson was a ninety-one-page pamphlet, published in 1812, which defended his actions in the batture controversy.

the Louisiana Purchase, he reached into his past as a practicing lawyer to explain his action. "It is the case of a guardian, investing the money of his ward in purchasing an important adjacent territory," he argued, "& saying to him when of age, I did this for your good." Such zealousness once prompted James Madison to remark that "allowances ought to be made for a habit in Mr. Jefferson as in others of great genius of expressing in strong and round terms, impressions of the moment."

Jefferson's retirement as president did not end his thinking or writing about law, nor did it conclude his struggles with Marshall. Indeed, actions he took as president came back to haunt him, as in 1810 when Edward Livingston sued him in the federal circuit court at Richmond, where Marshall presided. The suit was an action of trespass for the enormous sum of one hundred thousand dollars in damages over the then-president's executive order directing federal marshals to oust Livingston from river property in New Orleans.

Livingston was more interested in a quiet title than in damages, and Jefferson had more in mind than a simple matter of supposed trespass. He saw Livingston's claim as nothing less than a challenge to the public's right to a natural—and national—resource, the Mississippi River. Given that construction of a levee or dam might change its flow or impede navigation and endanger western commerce, Jefferson drafted a ninety-one-page brief citing precedent from—of all sources—Lord Mansfield. He pleaded that such a trespass action was not transitory, but rather a local action that must be tried in Louisiana, where a favorable jury would hear the case. Marshall accepted the plea and denied jurisdiction.

The nationalizing tendencies of the Supreme Court also continued to exasperate Jefferson. While the ex-president could only look on and fulminate in correspondence, Marshall wielded his powerful judicial influence, even over the three Republican justices—William Johnson, Henry Brockholst Livingston, and Thomas Todd—that Jefferson had nominated. While Jefferson continued to denounce the *Marbury* decision, he ranked Marshall's opinion in *Fletcher v. Peck* (1810) with *Marbury* and the Burr trial as equally egregious "twistifications."

As he grew increasingly embittered in old age, Jefferson's view of the law also dimmed. "I was bred to the law," he confessed, "that gave me a view of the dark side of humanity." American lawyers, once the guardians of the true principles of liberty, had become Tories, more interested in profit than liberty—"ephemeral insects of the law," he called them, seduced by the superficiality of Blackstone into neglecting the deeper wellsprings of legal knowledge. Jefferson's tendency to overstatement worsened as he aged, and his tirades reflected his political disillusionment with postrevolutionary America as well as his resentment of creditors' lawyers hounding him as he sank into debt.

Despite his outbursts against lawyers, Jefferson never ceased in his study of law, which he regarded as a template for liberty, or in his efforts at legal education. His new university included the study of law, and he set out an extensive—if unrealistic—list of source materials. "The study of law is useful in a variety of points of view," he wrote hopefully. "It qualifies a man to be useful to himself, to his neighbors, and to the public."

To discover "the real fountains of the law," Jefferson collected Virginia's ancient statutes, assembled the reported cases of others as well as those he had observed or argued, and built a vast law library that served as a resource for Virginia courts and lawyers. If the practice of law and the struggle to control its direction had disappointed both the lawyer and the president, the study of law remained a consolation and its utility an unrealized ideal.

"His legal training left a permanent impression upon him. In his most famous state papers, he is the advocate pleading a cause and buttressing it with precedents."

Biographer Dumas Malone

★ ★ ★

James Monroe

Fifth President (1817–25)

BIRTH
April 28, 1758
Westmoreland County, Va.

EDUCATION
Campbelltown Academy
College of William and Mary (did not graduate)
Law study with Thomas Jefferson
Admission to the bar: 1782

OTHER OCCUPATIONS/PUBLIC OFFICES
Farmer
Continental army officer
Virginia legislator
Delegate to Continental Congress
U.S. senator
Minister to France, Great Britain, and Spain
Virginia governor
Secretary of state and of war with James Madison

DEATH
July 4, 1831
New York, N.Y.

LAW CAREER IN BRIEF

Monroe's periodic law practice (1786–94, 1798–99, and 1808–10) was always secondary to his primary interest in public service. Contract and probate matters comprised his major areas of law practice; he also served on a prestigious commission to revise Virginia's laws. Twice he had the opportunity to pursue judicial office—once as chief justice of Virginia's supreme court—but he declined to do so. He did use his legal knowledge and lawmaking skills, however, in various aspects of his political career.

James Monroe: Occasional Lawyer

Daniel Preston

James Monroe was a reluctant attorney. He was knowledgeable about the law and his contemporaries acknowledged his skill in legal matters, but Monroe was not an avid practitioner. He was more like his mentor Thomas Jefferson, who saw the law as a tool of statecraft, than like his friend John Marshall, who made a brilliant career from the practice and interpretation of the law.

Although Monroe was an attorney and a planter, his primary career (and interest) was in public service. He spent most of his adult life in public service and held a vast array of offices. He was a member of the Virginia House of Delegates, Virginia Council of State, Continental Congress, and U.S. Senate. He held diplomatic appointments to France (twice), Great Britain, and Spain. He was governor of Virginia, U.S. secretary of state, U.S. secretary of war, and president of the United States. From 1776, when he became an officer in the Continental army, until 1825, when he left the presidency, Monroe was out of public office for a total of only eight years.

In comparison, his career as a practicing attorney was short and, as Monroe noted, occupied him only "for a moment, in the intervals of public employment." He did not commence practice until 1786—well after he began his career in public service—and pursued it for only seven years, during which time he also served in the Virginia House of Delegates and U.S. Senate. He resumed his practice in 1798 to 1799 and again in 1808 to 1810, abandoning it permanently when elected governor of Virginia in 1811. Despite the brevity of his legal career, however, Monroe found this background to be a valuable asset in his years as a legislator, diplomat, and administrator.

Monroe was born in Virginia in 1758. His father was a planter, and although the family was affluent, the Monroes were

★ ★ ★

"Since he had not yet acquired an estate on which to settle, he reluctantly turned to the law— a profession that did not interest him greatly—as offering the most immediate rewards."

Historian Harry Ammon

not as wealthy or as prominent as their neighbors, the Lees, Washington, Byrds, and Carters. Monroe inherited his father's farm when he was sixteen, and throughout the rest of his life he was a planter as well as an attorney, diplomat, and statesman. He entered the College of William and Mary in 1774 but left before completing his course of study to become an officer in the Continental army. He rose to the rank of major in the Continental army and colonel in the Virginia service. Monroe was fond of military service, but was unfortunate in his avocation, for there was then a superabundance of officers, and by 1780 he found himself a colonel without a command. Stymied in his military career, Monroe sought to continue his education in Europe. He was unsuccessful in this endeavor as well, for it was impossible to get from Virginia to Europe in 1780. Frustrated in these aspirations, Monroe turned to the study of law.

Once Monroe decided on a career in law, he turned to his uncle, the renowned Virginia jurist Joseph Jones, for advice. The young man had two choices: He could return to the College of William and Mary and study with George Wythe, one of the leading legal scholars of the day, or he could study under the guidance of Governor Thomas Jefferson. Jones, recognizing his nephew's ambition to make his mark in the new nation, gave him sound advice: Wythe represented the past and Jefferson the future. The young man, already friends with Jefferson, decided to attach himself to the governor's rising star and followed Jefferson to the new state capital at Richmond. Monroe's own star was now on the rise, for within a year he was elected to the Virginia House of Delegates.

Monroe's legal education was somewhat unorthodox, for his mentor was no longer a practicing attorney. Jefferson had abandoned his practice and was now devoting time to his farm and public service. Monroe's training, therefore, was not a clerkship or apprenticeship, but rather a course in directed readings, which he pursued both in Richmond and on his farm.

Monroe's first engagement with law was almost a sideline. During the two years he studied law, he was actively engaged in public affairs, spending time on active army duty and in the House of Delegates. The informality of his legal studies, and the interruptions to them, apparently were not an impediment, however, for he was admitted to the bar in 1782. But again, his pursuit of a legal career was secondary to other interests. He did not engage in the profession immediately, for within days of his admittance to the bar he was appointed to the Council of State. This one-year term was followed by three years as a delegate to the Continental Congress.

Monroe knew that when his term in Congress ended, he would have to embark on a career. Too ambitious and extroverted to be satisfied with life as a planter, he began to make plans for a law practice. He once again turned to his uncle for advice, and Judge Jones offered suggestions on how best to proceed. The most prestigious place in Virginia to establish a practice was Richmond, the state capital, but its corps of attorneys was more than adequate to meet the needs of the citizens. Instead, Monroe decided to make his home in Fredericksburg, which was close to his farm and where his uncle resided.

In addition to Fredericksburg, Monroe practiced before the superior court in Richmond and in circuit courts at Charlottesville, Staunton, and other towns in central Virginia. While very few records relating to Monroe's law practice survive, it seems the bulk of his practice dealt with civil matters, such as probating wills and settling estates. Like many attorneys of this period, he handled lawsuits regarding the payment of debts—including one for Thomas Jefferson regarding the payment of prewar debts owed to British merchants—as well as the fulfillment of contracts and one case of assault. He also represented clients in criminal cases; in April 1789, for example, he was defense attorney for two men charged with horse stealing.

In 1790, Monroe moved to Charlottesville and opened a law office there. He continued to have clients in Fredericksburg and, as before, attended court in Richmond and on the circuit. Although the surviving evidence suggests that Monroe worked regularly at his profession from late 1786 until he was appointed minister to France in May 1794, the scantiness of the surviving record raises questions about the extent of his practice. Indeed, Monroe may well have relied more on his farm than his law practice for his livelihood. And he remained active in public affairs, serving in the Virginia House of Delegates and U.S. Senate, where he would emerge as a leader of the Republican Party.

In such political posts, Monroe enjoyed a reputation as a fine legislator; there are indications he was equally well regarded as

★ ★ ★

"[I]f you determine to make [law] an object . . . as a man engages to a woman he marries, cleave only to her."

Judge Joseph Jones's advice to his nephew, James Monroe

an attorney with a sound knowledge of law. In 1788, for example, as a delegate to the Virginia convention for the ratification of the U.S. Constitution, Monroe took an active role in the proceedings, drawing both on his legislative experience and his legal background. Close friends James Madison and John Marshall led the fight for ratification, but Monroe joined with another friend, George Mason, in opposing ratification, arguing that the Constitution was incomplete without a bill of rights.

A second acknowledgment of Monroe's legal skills came in March 1789 when he received an appointment as assistant prosecuting attorney for the judicial circuit covering six counties in central Virginia. There is no record of how long he held this position—or of the cases he handled—but it must have been fairly brief, as he was elected to the U.S. Senate in November 1790 (and could not have continued to hold his state office).

A third incident occurred in 1791, while Monroe was in the Senate and still practicing law. He was appointed to a prestigious commission—chaired by St. George Tucker, the preeminent jurist in Virginia—to revise its laws. There had been several previous committees charged with this task; the first, chaired by Thomas Jefferson, had met in 1776. "A part of our duty," Monroe wrote, "was to consolidate (when many were drawn) all the acts on one subject. The object, to make the law more perspicuous, by drawing its scatter'd parts into one view and repealing all preceding laws on such subjects." Their work proved to be more fruitful than that of their predecessors, resulting in a complete digest of the state's laws and suggestions for revision.

A further indication of his standing in the legal community came in 1793 when Monroe was mentioned as a possible chief justice of the state supreme court. His ambitions lay in other directions, however, and he did not pursue the appointment. About ten years later, he was offered another judicial appointment—judge of the newly established chancery court of Virginia—which, he was told, would receive "almost unanimous support in the house of Delegates." Monroe was tempted but again decided to decline.

This period of Monroe's law practice came to a halt in May 1794 when he was appointed minister to France. He resumed his law practice when he returned home in early 1798 but did so for less than two years, for in late 1799 he was elected governor. He intended to resume his practice when his term as governor ended in December 1802—he even placed an announcement in the Richmond newspaper stating his intention to do so—but this was not to be, for President Jefferson appointed him special envoy to France to help with the negotiations that resulted in the Louisiana Purchase. Monroe would remain in Europe, serving as minister to Great Britain until November 1807.

Upon his return home, Monroe debated whether to "pursue the cultivation & improvement of my estate, & certain literary studies of a general nature, or return [to Richmond] & resume the duties of my profession." But the prospect did not appear promising, as he found "so little encouragement from the organization of the courts, & the absence the professional pursuit would subject me to, & the loss incident to it." Though he may have taken a few clients, he did not practice on a regular basis. Monroe's career as an attorney came to definite end in January 1811, when he was again elected governor, followed a few months later by his appointment as secretary of state in Madison's cabinet.

It was as a legislator, diplomat, and cabinet officer that Monroe was most in his element. When twenty-four-year-old James Monroe was elected to the Virginia House of Delegates and soon thereafter appointed to the Council of State, he had his first real introduction to legislative and executive matters. A year later, he was chosen as a delegate to the Continental Congress, where he thrived upon the work of drafting and shaping legislation, distinguishing himself in committee and debate.

One assignment, which was actually his first "court" appearance, proved to be anticlimactic. Monroe and Rufus King, an attorney-delegate from New York, were appointed to adjudicate a territorial dispute between Pennsylvania and Connecticut. The appointment reflected the respect that colleagues had for Monroe's legal abilities, but for some unknown reason, Monroe was unable to fulfill the duties and King had to handle the proceedings on his own.

MINISTER MONROE
Monroe's law practice was always secondary to his political career. This 1796 painting, the earliest known of Monroe, was taken during the time he served as minister to France.

★ ★ ★

After serving as minister to Great Britain, Monroe debated whether to "pursue the cultivation & improvement of my estate, & certain literary studies of a general nature, or return [to Richmond] & resume the duties of my profession."

Monroe's career moved in a new direction in 1794 when he received the first of his four diplomatic appointments. Although a legal background was not essential to the diplomatic service, his duties involved frequent interaction with the law and called upon his experience as attorney and legislator. The negotiating and writing of treaties, for example, closely resembled the writing of legislation and drew upon his knowledge of international law. His training as a lawyer was of particular value while, as minister to Great Britain, he stood at the center of the dispute resulting from British interference with American commerce. As minister—and later as secretary of state—Monroe repeatedly protested the seizure of American ships and cargoes, the impressment of American seamen, and the paper blockade of Europe as violations of the law of nations, arguing that they were "repugnant to every principle of that law." And though never directly involved in court proceedings, he carefully monitored British admiralty court proceedings regarding the seizure of American ships and cargoes.

When Monroe returned home in 1807, he was the most experienced diplomat in the United States. Political disputes kept him away from the center of power for several years, but in 1811 he returned to the national arena when President Madison asked him to serve as secretary of state. As the head of the State Department, Monroe was naturally involved with international relations and international law. But he also had domestic responsibilities that led to involvement with the judicial system. During that era, U.S. district attorneys and U.S. marshals served under the direction of the secretary of state, and Monroe worked with these officials in cases involving violations of neutrality laws and piracy.

While governor of Virginia, Monroe became involved in several matters that drew heavily on his legal experience. As chief executive, he reviewed and approved the many contracts for the construction of a penitentiary and an armory, and for the purchase of arms for the state militia. He was also charged with recommending a system of operation for the penitentiary.

The most critical event of his governorship took him from execution of the law into the realm of the administration of justice. In 1800 a conspiracy to revolt among slaves in central Virginia—"Gabriel's Rebellion"—was exposed, resulting in a large number of death sentences. Although Governor Monroe approved the execution of Gabriel and other leaders of the conspiracy, he was repulsed by the idea of mass executions. Instead, he reduced many sentences to imprisonment or transportation, and urged the assembly to enact new legislation that would provide "an alternate mode of punishment" for rebellious slaves "who under existing law might be doomed to suffer death."

This incident had a strong influence on Monroe. While he was president, some fifty or sixty men were condemned to death in federal courts, mostly for piracy. Monroe was not opposed to the death penalty; and he agreed that several offenders deserved to be executed. But he continued to be repulsed by the thought of numerous executions and gave very careful consideration to such cases, reprieving most sentences and in a few others granting pardons. Monroe tended to be fairly lenient in exercising the power of the presidential pardon. He readily granted pardons or reprieves if the judges, juries, or prosecuting attorneys in the cases recommended it.

Monroe's long engagement with the U.S. Constitution reached its culmination during his presidency. Although he had voted against ratification in 1788, he was not opposed to it, for he had become painfully aware of the inadequacies of the Articles of Confederation during his term in the Continental Congress. While in favor of "a change, and a radical one, of the confederation," he had "some strong and invincible objections to that proposed to be substituted in its stead," particularly the absence of a bill of rights.

When the first ten amendments were ratified, Monroe felt that the Constitution was complete, and he became devoutly attached to it. Throughout the rest of his life, and especially when he was president, Monroe praised the Constitution as the most perfect charter of government ever devised by man and as an embodiment of the ideals of the American Revolution, securing "equal civil, religious and political rights to all." He also saw it as an instrument for forming a "more perfect union" and repeatedly trumpeted it as a symbol of nationalism around which all Americans could unite.

JAMES MADISON, FATHER OF THE CONSTITUTION

Though thirty-three of the fifty-five delegates to the Constitutional Convention were lawyers, Monroe's Virginia colleague and the man considered the "Father of the Constitution" was not among them. A graduate of the College of New Jersey (now Princeton), Madison's classical education included intermittent law studies and a brief consideration of a law career, but he never pursued it further.

The Missouri
Compromise

The 1820 law, perhaps
the most notable domestic
legislation of Monroe's
presidency, maintained the
delicate balance between
slave and free states, admitting Missouri as a slave
state and Maine as a free
state and creating a formal
demarcation between free
and slave states. Monroe,
like many other lawyer-
presidents, considered
slavery a legal institution
and thus constitutionally
protected. A slaveholder,
he also favored a plan for
general emancipation that
included compensation to
slave owners and colonization of freed slaves outside
the United States.

During the 1790s, Monroe and other Republicans insisted upon a strict interpretation of the Constitution. For Monroe, this did not reflect opposition to a more powerful central government as much as fear of Federalist use of such power. As the nation became more secure and the national government passed firmly into the control of the Republicans, Monroe moderated his views. He had opposed chartering a national bank in the 1790s as an unconstitutional act, for example, but by 1816 he saw the necessity for a national financial institution and fully supported the Second Bank of the United States. Even so, he remained alert to unconstitutional extensions of federal power.

In the early 1800s, the presidential veto was a safeguard against unconstitutional legislation rather than the instrument of policy that it has become today. As such, it was rarely used. Monroe considered using it on one occasion and actually employed it on another. In 1819, a controversy arose over Missouri's statehood when a group of congressmen insisted on a prohibition of slavery before its admission to the union. Monroe believed that such restrictions were unconstitutional and threatened to veto any bill that required conditions beyond those specified in the Constitution. At the same time, Monroe wanted to avoid a confrontation, for he knew that the issue of slavery could destroy the Union. He thus worked quietly to support a compromise and gave his blessing to the plan once his cabinet was of the unanimous opinion that it was constitutional.

A second area of controversy involved the authority of the national government to construct and maintain public roads, canals, and other transportation facilities. While Monroe was "decidedly-friendly" to a federally funded transportation system, like many Americans, he was concerned that the authority for such an undertaking was not "vested in Congress by the constitution." Rather, he urged the passage of an amendment that would grant "an enlargement of the powers of Congress, so as to give full effect to such a system." Congress declined this suggestion, however, for a majority of congressmen believed that the right already existed.

The issue came to a head in 1823 when Congress passed a bill providing for the collection of tolls to support maintenance of the National Road. Monroe vetoed the bill and sent Congress a long essay explaining his reasons for doing so. He also circulated copies to others, asking for opinions on his position. Several responses, especially one from U.S. Supreme Court Justice William Johnson, persuaded Monroe that he was wrong, and he abandoned his opposition to government funding for these projects.

Even after his retirement from the presidency in 1825, Monroe's neighbors acknowledged his legal and legislative abilities. During that summer, he was appointed to the Loudoun County court, which served not only as a judicial body but also as the executive and legislature for the county. Monroe sat with the court only once, so it seems that the appointment was largely honorary.

A second instance occurred in 1829 when Monroe was elected as a delegate to a convention considering revisions to the Virginia Constitution. He was additionally honored when elected president of the convention. He went to the convention fully prepared to push for significant changes in the document, but ill health hampered his ability to participate and eventually forced him to resign. Thus, Monroe ended his legal and public service careers just as he began them: not as a practitioner of the law but as one nevertheless fully engaged with it.

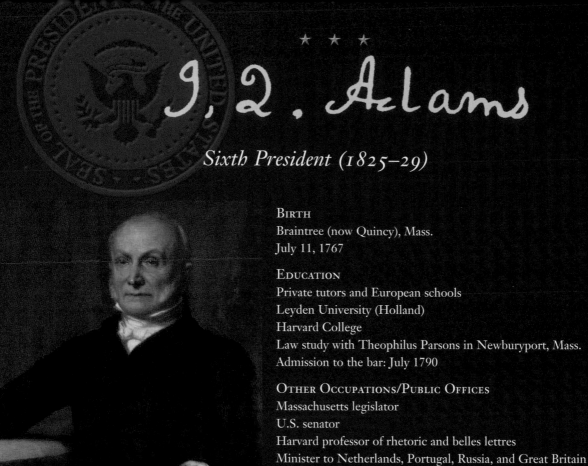

J. Q. Adams

Sixth President (1825–29)

BIRTH
Braintree (now Quincy), Mass.
July 11, 1767

EDUCATION
Private tutors and European schools
Leyden University (Holland)
Harvard College
Law study with Theophilus Parsons in Newburyport, Mass.
Admission to the bar: July 1790

OTHER OCCUPATIONS/PUBLIC OFFICES
Massachusetts legislator
U.S. senator
Harvard professor of rhetoric and belles lettres
Minister to Netherlands, Portugal, Russia, and Great Britain
Secretary of state with James Monroe
Member of the House of Representatives

DEATH
February 23, 1848
Washington, D.C.

LAW CAREER IN BRIEF

Adams had several "firsts" among the lawyer-presidents, all involving the U.S. Supreme Court. He was the first lawyer-president to argue before the high court, appearing in five such cases, two of which were landmark decisions; he was the first to decline an appointment to the Court; and he was the first to appear before the Court as a former president. Despite these notable events, John Quincy Adams's legal career was intermittent (1790–94, 1801–3, 1808–11, and 1841) and was overshadowed by his diplomatic service and his years in Congress following his presidency.

John Quincy Adams: Eloquent Advocate

Howard Jones

The seventy-three-year-old former president of the United States had not argued a case before the nation's high court in more than thirty years. But this case and its cause were of the utmost importance to John Quincy Adams, for he regarded slavery as an institution incompatible with the human rights principles emphasized in the nation's founding document of freedom. And the lives of Joseph Cinqué and his fellow African captives hung in the balance.

Every man, Adams declared in the 1841 *Amistad* case, was "endowed by his Creator with certain inalienable rights" that no one could deny to any human being. The Declaration of Independence made natural law "identical with the laws of nature's God." The conclusion was obvious, he asserted. "The moment you come to the Declaration of Independence, that every man has a right to life and liberty, an inalienable right, this case is decided."

Particularly given the high court's makeup at that time and then-president Martin Van Buren's strong opposition to the defense team's pleas, few expected Adams's arguments to prevail, but prevail they did. In many respects, this case and Adams's role in it served as a vivid reflection of the tumultuous legal and political career of America's sixth president.

Born and raised in Massachusetts, John Quincy Adams adhered to a puritanical code of morality in his private and public life that guided his efforts to build a strong nation. In politics, Adams often broke party ties in support of moral principles. Regarding slavery, he was not an abolitionist, but he opposed the institution as a violation of human rights. A lifelong student, he left behind a multivolume memoir that is a treasure for historians.

JOSEPH CINQUÉ

Leader of the *Amistad* captives, Cinqué's regal bearing generated interest in and support for the captives and lent credence to their claims of being free Africans.

SUPREME COURT
APPOINTMENT

In 1810, while Adams was minister to Russia, President Madison nominated him to the U.S. Supreme Court and the Senate confirmed his appointment. Upon learning of these actions, he declined the appointment, noting "I am also, and always will be, too much of a political partisan for a judge."

Lawyer, diplomat, writer, president, congressman, statesman, human rights advocate—all labels fit the man.

Adams had an extraordinary youth. After studying in France and Holland, the fourteen-year-old boy served as secretary to American diplomat Francis Dana in Russia and, two years later, performed similar duties for his father and later president, John Adams, during the negotiations that led to the Treaty of Paris ending the Revolutionary War in 1783. The young, well-traveled Adams already knew or spoke five languages before returning to the United States to study at Harvard, from which he graduated in 1787. He then embarked on the "dry and tedious study of law" for three years in the law office of Theophilus Parsons in Newburyport before being admitted to the bar in 1790.

In August of that year, Adams opened a legal practice in Boston that was anything but successful. His office was in a house owned by his father; he used his father's books; and his only steady income came from his father. His parents realized that their son had sunk into another bout with depression, this one caused by a broken romance and his failing practice. They invited him to the nation's capital at Philadelphia, exposing him to the city's cultural features and lifting his spirits. On his return to Boston in March 1791, however, he again became mired in boredom. "All day at court. Dull. Anxious. Heavy," he recorded in his journal. "The present a deadly calm, and the future a chilling mist."

Adams decided to pursue a public service career. President George Washington appointed him minister to the Netherlands in 1794, and three years later Adams's father, then president, appointed him to the ministerial post in Prussia, where he remained until 1801. Defeated for Congress in 1802, he was elected to the U.S. Senate the next year. In 1808, he resigned under pressure after criticizing his Federalist Party's turn from nationalism and, in an effort to avert war with England, for supporting the Republican administration's Embargo Act of 1807. This period also included a stint as professor of rhetoric at Harvard.

At the time Adams arrived in Washington to begin his term in the Senate, the U.S. Supreme Court was housed in the Senate building, as the new capital's plans had not included any facilities for the nation's highest court. Adams attended a number of its sessions, initially as a spectator and then with an eye to arguing cases and earning some much-needed income. During his first year in the Senate, he appeared as counsel in two Supreme Court cases: *Head and Amory v. Providence Insurance Co.* and *Church v. Hubbart*. Each case raised issues arising from insurance claims for the loss of vessels at sea, the latter dispute having international dimensions involving a seizure for illicit trade. Adams was impressed by his high court experiences: "I have never witnessed a collection of such powerful legal oratory as at this session of a Supreme Court."

Following his departure from the Senate, Adams appeared before the high court in another insurance case, *Hope Insurance Company at Providence v. Boardman and Pope*. However, he had not prepared well enough to handle a question about a corporate matter that the justices asked him, an experience that led him to work harder for his next Supreme Court case, *Fletcher v. Peck*, which he argued in March 1809.

The latter case involved the so-called Yazoo land controversy in Georgia and marked the first time the Supreme Court dealt with the U.S. Constitution's obligation of contracts clause. In a landmark decision, the Court upheld the sanctity of contracts, regardless of the motives behind them, and thereby extended the scope of federal judicial review to include state legislative actions. Adams had argued for the winning side, although he felt demoralized by what he called his "dull and tedious" presentation. By the time the attorneys resumed arguments in 1810, Adams had left the case to become minister to Russia. Interestingly, fellow Massachusetts lawyer and future Supreme Court Justice Joseph Story took Adams's place as counsel for the case's final arguments.

Despite this spotty record before the high court, Adams was nominated by President James Madison and confirmed by the Senate as a Supreme Court justice in 1810, all without his knowledge. From his overseas post in Russia, he declined the appointment, noting "I am also, and always shall be, too much of a political partisan for a judge."

FLETCHER V. PECK

This famous Georgia case involving the Yazoo land fraud controversies first came before the U.S. Supreme Court in 1809, with John Quincy Adams serving as counsel to John Peck, a Massachusetts investor. In its landmark 1810 decision, the Court held that the Georgia legislature was bound by the contracts clause of the U.S. Constitution and could not rescind vested property rights. The decision was the first time the Court declared a state legislative act unconstitutional, thereby extending the Court's power of judicial review to state actions.

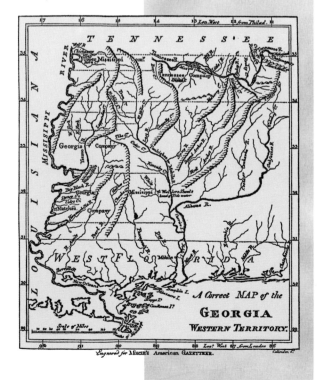

A Correct MAP of the **GEORGIA** *WESTERN TERRITORY.*

Engraved for MORSE's American GAZETTEER.

After building a lucrative
law practice through oratory
that combined "beauty and
force" and gaining fame as
a lawyer with "no equal in
Kentucky," Clay entered
the world of politics. One
of four presidential candidates in the disputed 1824
election, he was the powerful Speaker of the House
whose supporters' votes
elected Adams over Jack-
son. When Clay was then
appointed Adams's secretary
of state, charges of a "corrupt bargain" abounded.
Though Clay was unsuc-
cessful in his attempts to
gain the presidency on
several other occasions,
he still remains "one of
the most popular and
influential political leaders
in American history."

For the next thirty years, Adams devoted his time and energies
to public service. He continued to serve as minister to Russia
until 1814, headed the peace commission that negotiated the
Treaty of Ghent ending the War of 1812, and was minister to
Great Britain from 1815 to 1817, where he improved relations by
securing a commercial treaty and by defusing naval rivalries on
the Great Lakes. An illustrious tenure as secretary of state ensued
from 1817 to 1825, highlighted by the acquisition of the Floridas
and a transcontinental boundary from Spain in 1819, as well as
the formulation of the Monroe Doctrine in 1823 in a successful
effort to stave off European intervention in the Western Hemisphere. The following year, Adams became president of the
United States in a hotly disputed election.

Adams had a tumultuous four years as president and lost his
bid for reelection in 1828. His opponents falsely accused him of a
"corrupt bargain" that had sealed his victory, and they launched a
blistering attack on nearly every idea he proposed while president.
Adams's call for a national program of internal improvements
drew little interest in a period that emphasized states' rights and
rule of the people. His ventures in foreign affairs resulted in failures in Latin America and in commercial relations with England.

After leaving the executive office, however, Adams did not
retire from public life. Rather, he was elected to Congress, where
he served from 1831 to 1848. There, he became more deeply involved in stemming the growth of slavery. He opposed, for
example, the annexation of Texas in 1836 as an invitation to
its spread. When the South pressured the House of Representatives into passing a "gag rule" in 1836 aimed at
tabling all petitions against slavery, Adams denounced
the measure as a violation of free speech, finally sending
it to defeat in 1844.

His fifth and final appearance before the U.S.
Supreme Court, in the *Amistad* case of 1841, was a prominent episode in his campaign against slavery. The *Amistad*
saga began in 1839 when a Portuguese slaver took hundreds of
Africans from their homeland in violation of laws and treaties
against the African slave trade and brought them to Cuba for
auction as slaves. Fifty-three of these captives, led by Joseph
Cinqué, mutinied on board the Spanish slave ship *Amistad* in
Cuban waters that July and forced the two Spanish slave owners

aboard to navigate the vessel to Africa. The two men, however, deceived the Africans and, after nearly sixty days of zigzagging in hopes of rescue, entered the waters off Long Island, New York, where the U.S. Navy captured the *Amistad* and claimed salvage. The abolitionists, however, sought to make the incident into a cause célèbre for their antislavery crusade.

The result was a complicated mixture of politics, law, and diplomacy that developed into a long court struggle. Authorities in New Haven, Connecticut, charged the Africans with kidnapping and murder. Spain demanded their return under the reciprocity provisions of Pinckney's Treaty of 1795 and the Adams-Onís Treaty of 1819. New Haven attorney Roger S. Baldwin, grandson and namesake of Roger Sherman, who had signed the Declaration of Independence and the U.S. Constitution, led a successful defense in both the district and circuit courts, arguing that the accused were "kidnapped Africans" who had the inherent right of self-defense. But President Van Buren feared that freeing the blacks would raise the divisive issue of slavery and tear apart the northern and southern base of his Democratic Party on the eve of the 1840 election. He thus had his administration appeal the decision to the U.S. Supreme Court, hoping to establish the Africans as property of Spaniards in Cuba and thus returnable as slaves.

Abolitionists Lewis Tappan and Ellis Gray Loring convinced Adams to join in the case. Adams was familiar with the issues, having advised Baldwin in its early stages. But Adams was seventy-three years old, almost deaf, and a stranger to the courtroom for three decades. According to his memoirs, Adams demurred on the bases of his "age and inefficiency" and his "inexperience" as a trial lawyer. But the two men "earnestly entreated" him to join the team as a matter of "life and death." Adams agreed to

TRIAL OF THE AMISTAD CAPTIVES

Adams did not join in the *Amistad* captives' defense until their case came before the U.S. Supreme Court. Roger Sherman Baldwin, grandson and namesake of the signer of the Declaration of Independence and U.S. Constitution, served as the captives' lead attorney in their initial cases, one of which is depicted here in a famous mural by Hale Woodruff.

ADAMS'S "UNOFFICIAL" ARGUMENTS IN AMISTAD

Supreme Court Chief Justice Joseph Story described Adams's eight-hour argument as "extraordinary . . . for its power, for its sarcasm, and for its dealing with topics far beyond the record and points of discussion." Story was probably referring to Adams's extensive attacks during oral argument on the Van Buren administration. There is no official record of Adams's presentation, however, as he refused the reporter of decision's request for a copy that included only arguments pertinent to the case. The former president then proceeded to independently publish his arguments.

work with Baldwin and fellow counsel Theodore Sedgwick in presenting the closing argument. In his diary, Adams expressed "deep anguish of heart" regarding the "abominable conspiracy, Executive and Judicial, of this Government, against the lives of those wretched men."

The prognosis was not good. Supreme Court Chief Justice Roger B. Taney was once a slaveholder and presided with eight other justices, the majority of whom had owned or presently owned slaves. Adams intended to argue for the natural rights of life and liberty guaranteed in the Declaration of Independence. Other arguments he planned included that the U.S. Navy had no right to seize the *Amistad*, that the blacks had committed no crime and should thus go free, and that President Van Buren had interfered with the judicial process.

On February 24, 1841, Adams began his arguments before a packed courtroom by alleging that the Van Buren administration had denied justice to his clients. From the outset, he declared, it had acted on the erroneous claim that they were "slaves" and "murderers" who were extraditable to Spain. Indeed, the prosecution had purposely misinterpreted the Spanish demand for their return as property in slaves, attempting to make them subject to Pinckney's Treaty. The Supreme Court's responsibility, Adams argued, was to protect the rights of every human being. The Van Buren administration had ignored this principle by sympathizing with the white slave dealers and seeking to dispatch the African captives to Cuba for certain death.

Adams presented his arguments in two sessions—the second occasioned by the sudden death of Justice Philip Barbour—that totaled more than eight hours. He directed his most extensive and strident criticisms at the Van Buren administration, which ignored the rights of "these poor, unfortunate, helpless, tongueless, defenseless Africans."

On March 9, 1841, Justice Joseph Story rendered his decision, with all justices concurring except Henry Baldwin, who submitted no written opinion. The captives, Story wrote, were "kidnapped Africans," taken in violation of Portuguese law and Anglo-Spanish treaties against the African slave trade. Those persons held illegally had the inherent right of self-defense, even including killing their captors. His decision rested on "the eternal principles of justice and international law."

Despite the abolitionists' jubilation over the freedom accorded to the captives, the decision did not change the status of slaves as property. Story had ruled that the eternal principles of justice prevailed in instances where there was no positive law to govern circumstances—which carried the corollary meaning that when a positive law was in effect, the eternal principles of justice became of secondary importance. The *Amistad* captives went free as kidnapped Africans and not as liberated slaves.

Still, Adams's success constituted a victory in the first civil rights case to come before the U.S. Supreme Court. Story's decision had affirmed the rights of blacks to participate in the legal process. The Supreme Court had freed Africans from bondage, leaving the impression that it had approved violence in winning that freedom. The American judicial system had thus dealt a severe blow to slavery by exalting the sanctity of freedom. Adams had claimed human rights on the basis of natural rights. At one point, he asserted that the Constitution "nowhere recognizes [slaves] as property." Rather, they were persons born with the natural rights of life and liberty found in the Declaration of Independence. His argument justified a person's strike for freedom when illegally held and was as threatening to slavery as abolitionist doctrine. The Amistad decision was "a great triumph of law & justice," rejoiced Yale College student and abolitionist John P. Norton.

Adams had exposed the great chasm between manmade law and moral principles. Since the Declaration of Independence provided the spiritual basis of the Constitution, the republic had strayed far beyond its original course. During the 1850s, Abraham Lincoln declared that the nation could not exist half slave and half free—that a house divided against itself must fall. Adams had already trumpeted a similar warning, even though few Americans in 1841 grasped slavery's lethal threat to the Union. His opponents accused him of wanting to incite slave rebellions. A Virginian wrote: "Is your pride of abolition oratory not yet glutted? Are you to spend the remainder of your days endeavoring to produce a civil and servile war? Do you like Aaron Burr wish to ruin your country because you failed in your election to the Presidency? May the lightning of heaven blast you, and may the great Eternal God in his wrath curse you at the last day and direct you to depart from his presence to the lowest regions of Hell!"

"Oh, how shall I do justice to this case and to these men?"

John Quincy Adams, in preparing his *Amistad* arguments

For years afterward, Adams fought congressional efforts to indemnify the Spanish claimants of the *Amistad* captives. In 1844 President John Tyler, a Virginia slaveholder, asked the House Foreign Affairs committee to review the case. Its chair, Representative Charles J. Ingersoll of Pennsylvania, presented a report seeking seventy thousand dollars in compensation to Spain. The Supreme Court, he asserted, should not have admitted either the evidence of "ignorant, half-civilized negroes" or the testimony of British abolitionists. Adams led the fight that defeated the bill. Two years later the House returned to the matter when President James K. Polk's secretary of state, James Buchanan, recommended fifty thousand dollars in indemnities. Adams denounced the bill as "robbery" and it again failed.

Throughout his public career, Adams dealt with legal and moral issues that had threatened the American republic since its creation. At the root of his unbending position was his struggle for laws that rested on moral principles. A self-professed republic could not condone both liberty and slavery. The Constitution could not approve the enslavement of human beings when the Declaration of Independence rested on the doctrine of natural rights. The issues Adams confronted have repeatedly challenged the American nation, through a civil war, the civil rights movement, and the continuing struggle for individual freedom.

Antebellum Presidents

Effects of the Fugitive-Slave-Law.

Law in Antebellum America

The years between the adoption of the Constitution and the outbreak of the Civil War were years of change and innovation in the law. The country was growing and expanding, both geographically and economically. The Louisiana Purchase added a vast tract of new land, most of it wilderness, but all of it (in the eyes of Americans) ripe for conquest and settlement. Thousands of settlers poured into the frontier states, eager for cheap land. The federal government, a weak and tiny bundle of nerves inside a gigantic, sprawling national body, had very little in the way of assets except for the land, which it used both to raise money and to satisfy the hunger of settlers for the empty tracts in the West. Of course, these lands were not truly empty, but the settlers ruthlessly swept away the native peoples in their rush to expand the pale of settlement.

America was becoming what we would now call a middle class society—a society in which hundreds of thousands of families had a farm, a small house in town, or some other piece of property. This meant that they were in the market for basic legal services. Wills, mortgages, issues of land titles and recordings, debt collection: these were the food on which a growing number of lawyers fed. And who were these lawyers? De Tocqueville called lawyers the American aristocracy. Perhaps, but they were hardly aristocrats by birth. They were young men on the make, eager and ambitious sons of farmers, ministers, schoolteachers, and storekeepers.

The law was one way to climb up the greasy pole. There were still no law schools in the modern sense; the few institutions that called themselves law schools simply lectured to students, who took notes. There were no entrance exams, and the training was dry and didactic. Most lawyers still learned what they knew through apprenticeships as clerks, errand boys, and copyists in the offices of established lawyers. The lucky ones were clerks to lawyers who took the time and trouble to instruct them and help them in their struggle to master the law.

There were also no bar exams in the modern sense, and the testing of new lawyers was hardly rigorous. Young John Caton, later chief justice of Illinois, described how he was admitted to the bar. He went for a walk in the moonlight with one of the local judges. Suddenly, the judge began asking him questions, and Caton stuttered and answered as best he could. The judge listened, and asked more questions. It was a harrowing experience, but mercifully brief. At the end of it, the judge gave his OK; Caton had become an Illinois lawyer. Abraham Lincoln was apparently admitted to the bar without any examination at all.

Lawyers, like Americans in general, were more closely linked to their states, towns, and home communities than to the distant, feeble federal government. They were concerned with the affairs of farmers and small businesses, and above all with matters of debt, title, and land. Many of them were immersed in local politics. Their lives revolved around the county courthouse. Lawyers formed a unique kind of community; in some states, they traveled in groups, "riding circuit" from county seat to county seat, following a court that was equally peripatetic. They stayed in local inns, sometimes sharing a room and even a bed with their fellow travelers after an evening of food and drink. In the commercial centers, the practice of law became more sophisticated. There were great lawyers in this period—giants of the law like Daniel Webster—and the literature of the law grew in size and quality.

National politics, however distant, remained turbulent. And one issue came to dominate the national scene. This issue was slavery: the law of slavery, the morality of slavery, the spread or containment of slavery. More and more, the divide between North and South, between slave states and free states, grew into a yawning abyss. Legislation and litigation were unable to solve a problem so deep seated—no Missouri compromise, no fugitive slave law, no *Dred Scott* case could avoid a growing sense of alienation and sectional hatred, which erupted finally into the bloodiest of American wars.

Lawrence M. Friedman

★ ★ ★

Andrew Jackson

Seventh President (1829–37)

BIRTH
March 15, 1767
The Waxhaws, S.C.

EDUCATION
Frontier schools
Law study under Spruce Macay and John Stokes in N.C.
Admission to the bar: September 26, 1787

OTHER OCCUPATIONS/PUBLIC OFFICES
Planter
Delegate to state constitutional convention
Attorney general for territorial district
U.S. congressman
U.S. senator
Superior court judge
Militia and U.S. Army general
Military governor of Florida

DEATH
June 8, 1845
The Hermitage, outside Nashville, Tenn.

LAW CAREER IN BRIEF
Following a slow start with his law career, Jackson moved to Nashville, where his success as public prosecutor brought much new business his way. Indeed, from 1788 to 1796, he had more clients than any other attorney in his county, his caseload primarily dealing with land titles, debts, and assault and battery. A land speculator, he was also a "prodigious litigant" who hired other counsel to represent him. In 1798, the Tennessee legislature elected Jackson a superior court judge, a position he held until 1804. Though "Jackson's restless nature was not well-suited for the inevitable constraints upon a judge," his decisions were generally regarded as sound, even if they were not exemplars of legal scholarship.

Andrew Jackson: Frontier Justice

DAVID S. HEIDLER AND JEANNE T. HEIDLER

O n the early American frontier, becoming a lawyer was a road to prosperity and social standing, especially for the poor but ambitious and the young. Andrew Jackson was both of these things. He was born on March 15, 1767, in a wilderness region of South Carolina called the Waxhaws, where tragedy and want stalked his youth. His father died before he was born, and his two brothers as well as his mother died during the American Revolution. Andrew himself became a boy soldier in the conflict, suffering a saber wound from an angry British officer and nearly dying of smallpox when imprisoned under wretched conditions. Following the Revolution, the young man was virtually alone in the world, and his fits of temper soon estranged him from a maternal uncle, almost the only family he had left.

A binge in Charleston seems to have sobered him, however, and at age seventeen, Jackson began to feel the spurs of ambition. He had glimpsed, even if through boozy revels in Charleston, a life beyond the vague and unsatisfying prospects of his childhood home, a place of dead family, disapproving relatives, and unrewarding labor. Possibly the prominence and wealth of Charleston lawyers so impressed him that he resolved to become one himself. For whatever reason, he discerned that practicing law was a quick ticket for advancement, and with that aim, he headed for North Carolina in the fall of 1784.

Jackson was correct about advancement, for lawyers on the American frontier had become an indispensable part of public and private life by the 1780s. Increasing settlement gave rise to increasingly complex communities, and methods of settling disputes by casual agreement would no longer suffice. Arguments over land ownership and the affairs of growing commerce made

★ ★ ★

"He did not trouble with the law-books much; he was more in the stable than in the office."

A Salisbury, N.C., contemporary

"Apart from his law activities, [Jackson] earned money from the plantation, the cotton gin, horse breeding and racing, and . . . an occasional fling at the highly lucrative business of slave trading."

Biographer Robert Remini

an orderly system of rules imperative and the service of lawyers essential. Accordingly, lawyers always had work, and they often became influential in political and economic matters as well as legal ones.

Added to these attractions was the fact that the process of becoming a "backwoods" lawyer, while not necessarily easy, was remarkably straightforward and informal. Even someone of modest educational background could manage the regimen, and Jackson had the advantage that his schooling had been more elaborate than was usual for frontier boys. His mother's fleeting wish that he enter the clergy—the boy's violent disposition had dashed the expectation—had prompted her to enroll him in frontier schools.

Jackson absorbed some refinements, but he was never much of a student, then or later. He learned to read and write, but he remained ignorant of standard spelling for the whole of his life. One biographer has suggested that the only book he ever finished was *The Vicar of Wakefield* and that he never achieved anything other than a basic working acquaintance with the law. Yet, Jackson was intuitive and mentally nimble by nature, and though he lacked eloquent erudition, he could convey ideas with passionate power. Such ability was frequently enough for the frontier lawyer of his time.

Therefore, he was at least fit to become an apprentice to an established attorney under whom he would "read" law, the first step to pursuing a legal career. The course of study consisted of carrying out the duties of a clerk who copied briefs, researched citations, and ran errands. Jackson first approached Waightstill Avery, an eminent attorney in Morgantown, North Carolina, for such a position, but Avery declined to take him on. We can only speculate about the reason for the refusal, but Avery might have thought Jackson unworthy. In any case, the boy was undeterred. He pressed on to Salisbury, North Carolina, where he took a room in a tavern and came under the tutelage of local attorney Spruce Macay.

His mentor, who pronounced his name "McCoy," was an example of how the law could smooth the path to public life. In addition to his 1782 appointment as the judge for the Court of Oyer and Terminer in Washington and Sullivan counties, Macay had served for three years on the North Carolina Council of

State and in 1784 had just won election to the state's lower house as the representative from Salisbury.

Doubtless encouraged by proof that such public acclaim could be part of an attorney's reward, Andrew Jackson spent three years studying with Macay while growing into physical maturity. By age twenty, his appearance had set into the form of his adulthood. Always gangly, he grew to a prodigious six one when the average male was about five seven. An unsettling leanness accentuated his height as did his narrow shoulders. Smallpox had not disfigured him, but his face was strange—long and angular, with close set crystal blue eyes and topped by a shaggy mane of reddish hair that further emphasized his height.

During his three years in Salisbury, Jackson clerked, watched, learned the rudiments of how to make pleadings and prepare briefs, and gained a reputation as "the most roaring, rollicking, game-cocking, horse-racing, card-playing, mischievous fellow that ever lived in Salisbury." Such freewheeling habits doubtless contributed to the debt that continued to dog him and possibly prompted him to leave Salisbury and Macay's office before applying for admission to the bar.

In March 1787, he began completing his legal apprenticeship under Colonel John Stokes, whose courtroom presence was highlighted by a silver knob in the place of the hand he had lost in the Revolution. Here was more encouragement for the pupil. Stokes was only thirty-one years old, but he was prominent and respected for his military service, legal acumen, and compelling style. His knob would ring like a bell when he rapped it during arguments in court, and like Macay, he had vaulted into public life with service in the North Carolina legislature. Jackson was with Stokes for only six months, but he must have relished watching this colorful man, only eleven years his senior, a fellow veteran of the fight with Britain who, like Jackson, bore a physical disfigurement to prove it.

By that fall, Jackson was ready to begin his career. In September 1787, he submitted to the examination for admission to the North Carolina bar, a procedure as informal as the preparation for it. A panel of practicing attorneys or sitting judges—in Jackson's case it was Samuel Ashe and John F.

RESPECT FOR LAW OR FOR ANDREW JACKSON?

One of Jackson's primary tasks as prosecuting attorney in Nashville was ensuring that debtors paid their obligations, and in short order, he enforced seventy such cases. When one disgruntled debtor showed his displeasure by stepping on Jackson's foot, "Without batting an eye, Jackson turned around, picked up a piece of wood, and calmly knocked the man out cold." While it has been suggested that respect for the law, Jackson-style, thus arrived in Nashville, others say it was more a case of Jackson ensuring respect for Andrew Jackson. Years later, during his presidency, this editorial cartoon reinforced the latter point of view.

BORN TO COMMAND.

OF VETO MEMORY.

HAD I BEEN CONSULTED.

KING ANDREW THE FIRST.

★ ★ ★

"[S]hort, untechnical, unlearned, sometimes ungrammatical, and generally right."

A colleague's description of Judge Jackson's decisions

Williams, two judges from the state superior court of law and equity—ascertained an applicant's worthiness on the basis of his good character as much as any wide knowledge of the law.

Such loose and formless subjectivity in admitting members to the legal fraternity produced an eccentric collection of variously trained amateurs of diverse talents. In Jackson's case, it produced an unintended irony. Admitted to the bar because of his "un-blemished moral character," a month later, he was arrested for criminal trespass. The case was settled, but newly minted lawyer Jackson was not off to a good start. In fact, he drifted around the state, unable to establish a legal practice of any note, let alone a prosperous one. He accumulated debt, disregarded his bills, and possibly began to think his whole plan had been a bad idea.

A peculiar facet of Jackson's life was the way that opportunity would follow on the heels of failure, or good fortune would inter-vene to save him from disaster. Sometimes salvation was a product of his pluck and audacity, of course, but just as frequently a lucky turn rescued him at the crucial moment. When he was broke and desperate after his spree in Charleston, he had risked everything in a dice game and won enough on one toss to cover his debts and get himself home. Years later during the War of 1812, he arrived almost too late at New Orleans to defend the city from a British assault, but the British dallied long enough to give him time to construct indomitable defenses before they launched what be-came a suicidal attack. In 1787, at this pivotal moment in his early career as a struggling lawyer, fate intervened when the North Carolina legislature appointed John McNairy judge of the state's Western District, an untamed region beyond the mountains where growing settlements required a legal presence.

McNairy, a friend of Jackson's since their days as students of Spruce Macay, offered Jackson a political post as prosecutor for the district, doing so on his own authority because the legis-lature had apparently overlooked the creation of the post and the appointment of a man to fill it. Therefore, Jackson in the spring of 1788 traveled with McNairy and several other com-panions westward toward what eventually became the state of Tennessee. They paused at Jonesboro to wait until fall before pushing on toward Nashville on the Cumberland River, some two hundred miles to the west. By then, Jackson had begun the process of reinventing himself as a gentleman with a profession and property. He amused himself at the local racetrack, bought a slave girl, and fought his first duel.

The purchase of the slave marks a troubling aspect for modern observers who will certainly strain to reconcile Jackson's purported devotion to liberty and fairness with his embrace of an unpardonable system of chattel labor. Yet, reconcile it we must if we are to understand the complex social and economic organization of the plantation South and a man like Jackson's place in it.

In Jackson's world, accumulating property established the credentials of a prominent gentleman, so in his view it was as natural to own slaves as it was to accumulate and trade in land. Consequently, he would traffic in slaves, supplying them to planters, and increase the numbers he owned as he increased his land holdings. Between 1790 and 1794, he purchased no fewer than sixteen slaves, and he eventually would own almost two hundred at the Hermitage, his home outside Nashville, and another plantation in northern Alabama.

As a lawyer, Jackson occasionally argued cases involving slavery, but they were routine matters involving property disputes or status. They did not touch upon any moral questions, large or small. In 1790, for instance, he defended John Boyd and James Foster, who were accused of assaulting another man's slave, but the question centered on the owner's financial loss after the slave died. A year later, Jackson successfully defended John Williams, who was charged with being a slave and trying to gain freedom by pretending to be white—a serious charge, indeed—but there is no evidence that Jackson ever entertained any profound misgivings about the institution.

"As far as lenity can be extended to these poor creatures," he instructed one overseer, "I wish you to do so." He also believed, however, that the arrangement required dominance: "Subordination must be obtained first and then good treatment." He would tolerate no disobedience, and he turned a hard hand to those who sought freedom by running away. In 1804, he placed a disturbing advertisement for a fugitive by promising those who apprehended the slave a fifty-dollar reward plus "ten dollars, for every hundred lashes any person will give him, to the amount of three hundred."

In spite of such a disconcerting attitude, Jackson has been described by one biographer as an "ideal slave owner." But he never

LEGAL QUESTIONS ABOUT JACKSON'S MARRIAGE TO RACHEL DONELSON ROBARDS

Shortly after arriving in Nashville in 1788, Jackson impetuously courted Robards and "married" her before she had secured a divorce from her husband, Lewis Robards. Though they remarried after Lewis obtained a formal divorce decree, questions about their courtship and legal status at the outset of their marriage would trouble them for the rest of their lives. It also gave rise to occasions in which Jackson rejected the law as a remedy for serious slanders. In 1806, for example, he killed Charles Dickinson in a duel that ostensibly resulted from a dispute over a horse race but probably had more to do with Dickinson's impugning Rachel Jackson's virtue.

"A good judiciary lends much to the dignity of a state and the happiness of a people When on the Contrary a bad Judiciary involved in party business is the greatest Curse that can befall a Country."

Andrew Jackson

questioned the morality of the institution. Late in his life, during the great sectional crisis that would eventually lead to civil war, Jackson somberly contemplated how arguments over slavery were threatening to destroy the Union, but he blamed agitators rather than slavery for the turmoil. He believed abolitionists were undemocratic and elitist, at best pawns of disunionists and enemies of property and equality—at least, equality for white men.

The duel also merits explanation. It was the result of an altercation with Waightstill Avery, who was then prosecutor for North Carolina. The immediate reasons for the confrontation are unclear. Some accounts have Avery lecturing Jackson on the particulars of legal authorities during a court proceeding, and Jackson chafing under the slight and issuing a challenge. Perhaps Jackson had never forgiven Avery's refusing to accept him as a student. The prosecutor at first tried to ignore the upstart, but Jackson was insistent and the two men, accompanied by their seconds, faced off in August 1788. As in most such affairs, what happened in this one suggests that it was more a show than a real dispute. By apparent prearrangement, both men fired their weapons into the air, and thus the matter was settled.

The episode illuminates an important facet of Jackson's character and reveals much about the time and place in which he lived. Duels were not exclusively relegated to settling backwoods quarrels nor were they always a sham, as the notorious encounter between Aaron Burr and Alexander Hamilton would prove sixteen years later. However, it is doubtful that Jackson wanted to kill Avery. More than likely, he wanted to use the duel as a way of establishing himself as equal in stature to the state's respected prosecutor—only gentlemen fought duels, and Jackson's reputation, whether wounded or not by Avery's purported condescension, would have been enhanced by an encounter that put him on the same social and professional level as Avery. Jackson and Avery thus presented the peculiar scene of two armed men ostensibly prepared to shoot one another in spite of their professional dedication to the law as the supreme arbiter in personal disputes.

In addition, the code of conduct reputedly imparted to Jackson by his mother advised him against seeking legal redress for assault or slander because in her view "the law affords no remedy to such outrages that can justify the feelings of a true man." Those words stated a common belief on the frontier, where the habit of personally settling scores continued, sometimes following court decisions that left one or both of the parties unsatisfied.

Citizens of the frontier did not shy away from litigation, but they did not always see it as a way of conclusively resolving disputes. Once, when Jackson rode circuit as a public prose-cutor, a disgruntled debtor vented his anger over Jackson's diligent work for creditors by stomping on Jackson's foot. The prosecutor retorted by smash-ing a piece of wood onto the man's head. This was a world most strange to modern sensibilities, for it comfortably resorted both to the law and to the fracas.

In October 1788, Jackson and his companions arrived at Nashville. By then the North Carolina legislature had created the Mero District in the far western expanse, and Nashville was the only settlement of note in the region, a remote outpost on the Cumberland River. It consisted of a collection of blockhouses and modest merchant establishments clustered together against a hostile Indian presence. The Davidson County courthouse was a five-year-old structure just eighteen feet square with an adjoining jail only a bit smaller.

Jackson received his law license in the district in November 1788, and Judge McNairy duly appointed him the prosecuting attorney for Davidson County. At first, he received no salary for what was essentially a part-time position, but he eventually peti-tioned the legislature for compensation and a year later was awarded forty pounds per year, a sum equaling about one thou-sand dollars today. Jackson then became the attorney general for the Mero District when the North Carolina legislature appointed him to that post, probably acting on McNairy's influence, but whatever pay he received was still inadequate. Jackson later peti-tioned both the U.S. Congress and the state of Tennessee for compensation. In 1799, he finally received four hundred dollars (about six thousand dollars in today's dollars) for his entire service as attorney general.

RUSSELL BEAN
SURRENDERING TO
JUDGE JACKSON

The frontier had its own special sense of law and justice, and Jackson figured into some of its unique leg-ends. One involved Russell Bean, an armed criminal who repeatedly defied a sheriff's efforts to enforce a judgment against him. Angered over these futile attempts, Judge Jackson decided to take matters into his own hands. Ac-cording to folklore, a few choice words and a glare that left no doubt about Jackson's intentions led to Bean's immediate surrender.

FIRST CAPITOL INAUGURATION · 1829

Presidential Oath of Office

In accordance with Article II, Section I of the U.S. Constitution, each president solemnly swears to "faithfully execute the office of President of the United States, and . . . to the best of my ability, preserve, protect and defend the Constitution of the United States." Above, Chief Justice Marshall administers the oath of office to President Jackson in 1829. Jackson and the Marshall court subsequently had differing views as to whether the president's actions exceeded his constitutional powers.

In Nashville and outlying settlements, Andrew Jackson would practice law for the next nine years, riding the circuit as a prosecutor in cases involving theft, assault, and on two occasions, murder. He also carried on a private practice while he was a prosecuting attorney, mainly representing plaintiffs in debt collection cases. With both his public and private practice, he was always busy, especially because he never joined a firm or took a partner, and his success attracted additional clients. He served as cocounsel in a number of cases, a common practice in spite of legal prohibitions against the custom, and when Nashville's Josiah Love died in 1794, Jackson took over the bulk of Love's practice, purportedly the largest in Davidson County.

But all lawyers were busy on this bustling, raw frontier. They practiced in a court system haphazardly guided by a jumble of ruling authorities that included the English common law, parliamentary legislation from North Carolina's colonial era, acts of the North Carolina and later the Tennessee legislatures, and a mixture of English and American judicial rulings. Critics complained that the system was confused by imprecise jurisdictions and plagued by too heavy a caseload, created impossible backlogs, and rendered decisions most noted for their lack of uniformity. Not all was chaos, however, and after Congress imposed the strictures of the Judiciary Act of 1789, reliance on English precedents gradually brought greater stability and consistency to the frontier justice system. Nevertheless, proceedings were usually informal and relied on the character and common sense of the presiding judge to maintain decorum and process. That in itself was a difficult task because court sessions were as much social as legal events for the communities in which they occurred. Starved for amusements and diversions, citizens staged raucous festivals where hawking vendors, feasts, strong drink, and even an occasional brawl complemented the business of the court.

Jackson rode circuit with a judge and other attorneys, forming an itinerant legal caravan that gave its members the benefit of mingling with powerful and plain folk in a variety of towns and villages. Such interactions could help launch careers in business and politics, so in addition to his legal activities, Jackson became a land speculator and commercial entrepreneur—activities that nearly ruined him financially—and a political operative in the powerful faction led by William Blount.

Jackson saw the law as a way for public advancement, and politics claimed an increasing amount of his attention. He sat in the Tennessee constitutional convention and was elected as the state's first congressional representative after its admission into the Union in 1796. The following year, the legislature elected him to the U.S. Senate. At the age of thirty, one year younger than Lewis Stokes when Jackson had finished his legal apprenticeship under him, the young lawyer seemed well on his way to attaining social prominence as well as political influence.

Jackson does not seem to have enjoyed the law very much. He was a reasonably successful attorney general, prosecuting eighty-nine criminal cases during his tenure, mostly for assault and battery and various types of theft, especially horse stealing. His conviction rate of about 60 percent was normal for frontier regions. Meanwhile his private practice burgeoned. From 1788 to 1798, he tried about four hundred lawsuits, representing ordinary folk as well as prominent planters and men destined for important local political office. He sued more frequently than he defended and when representing plaintiffs, won about twice as often as he lost.

The sheer volume of his caseload, however, attests to the financial limitations of a legal career. The Tennessee legislature technically set lawyer fees, and though there were ways to avoid such statutory limitations, Jackson never received a large payment from any client and thus had to rely on modest returns from wide and sometimes harried legal labors. He averaged about eight to fifteen cases per session of the court, but that number could range as high as thirty cases. One April day in 1793, he argued an incredible eight jury trials, winning five.

Yet his salary as prosecuting attorney was not particularly lucrative, and he found private practice monotonous and unrewarding. In 1796, he resigned as attorney general for the Mero

"I have as much right to determine constitutionality as the Supreme Court and so does Congress."

Andrew Jackson

District, and two years later, he tried his last civil case as a private attorney. Had things worked out financially and politically, Jackson may have ended his legal career in 1798. Yet, bad business decisions nearly bankrupted him, and his volatile temper proved him so unsuited to service in the Senate that he resigned his seat within a year and returned to Tennessee. Financial necessity compelled him to accept Governor John Sevier's interim appointment to the Tennessee Superior Court of Law and Equity in the fall of 1798. That December, the legislature formally elected him over Bennett Searcy for the position.

It was as a judge that Jackson concluded his legal career, and he seems to have continued in the position mainly for the modest but steady salary of six hundred dollars per year. Years later, Thomas Hart Benton recalled Judge Jackson's "cordial and graceful manners, hospitable temper, elevation of mind, undaunted spirit, generosity, and perfect integrity." In keeping with such an impression, an early biographer lauded Jackson for "maintaining the dignity and authority of the bench" while issuing decisions that "were short, untechnical, unlearned, sometimes ungrammatical, and generally right."

Jackson was never happy or at ease with his duties, however, and his attendance during court sessions was occasionally spotty. In 1802, he successfully sought election as major general of the Tennessee militia while remaining a judge, a move that some thought in violation of the state constitution; he also carried on an unseemly quarrel with political rival Governor John Sevier. In addition, he continued his private business activities despite the potential for serious conflicts of interest, and he neglected to recuse himself from cases in which he had a potential personal or economic interest. His mounting outside activities and chronic ill health finally moved him to act on his frequently expressed wish to quit the bench, which he did in July 1804.

He left no written opinions—the practice of issuing such would not be initiated until his friend and successor John Overton's tenure on the bench—but we have some idea of his legal philosophy from his service on the superior court. In Philadelphia in 1797, he had purchased an extensive and far ranging collection of law books that totaled nearly forty volumes, but it is doubtful he relied much on these in his rulings. Instead, Jackson interpreted the law as merely an elaborate form of common sense that measured right and wrong to mete out fairness. He could be a hard judge, but he was not averse to tempering stern justice with compassion. In late 1801, when a young defendant was found guilty of horse stealing, Jackson joined the rest of the court, including the jury, in successfully petitioning the governor for the boy's pardon.

"Do what is right between the parties," he would instruct juries. "That is what the law always means." This seemingly decent and reasonable attitude, however, points to the overriding theme of Jackson's life as a lawyer, as a private citizen, as a military chieftain, and finally as president of the United States. For the whole of his life, Andrew Jackson sustained the view that the law was essentially an extension of his fundamental personality and basic beliefs.

As a Tennessee militia general and later as a major general in the U.S. Army, Jackson exhibited truculence toward civilian authority that more than once crossed the line into insubordination and constitutional impropriety. As president, he presumed sweeping presidential prerogatives that friends found novel and adversaries found disturbing. Insisting he was answerable only to the people, Jackson led an assault on the republicanism of the Founders and made possible its replacement with an overarching democracy.

Historians have been arguing ever since whether Jackson's leadership in the public arena was aimed at liberalizing American politics or if it was merely the accidental result of his belief that he was a law unto himself. Lawyer Jackson would doubtless be disconcerted that before the court of historical opinion, we may never have a final verdict on that matter.

★ ★ ★

M Van Buren

Eighth President (1837–41)

BIRTH
December 5, 1782
Kinderhook, N.Y.

EDUCATION
Local schools
No college
Law study with Francis Silvester in Kinderhook and
    William P. Van Ness in New York City
Admission to the bar: 1803

OTHER OCCUPATIONS/PUBLIC OFFICES
County surrogate
State senator
New York attorney general
U.S. senator
New York governor
Secretary of state with Andrew Jackson
Vice president with Andrew Jackson

DEATH
July 24, 1862
Kinderhook, N.Y.

LAW CAREER IN BRIEF

After seven years of training that earned him the moniker "boy lawyer," Van Buren had a long and successful legal career that spanned twenty-five years (1803–27). Van Buren (and his partners) quickly developed a thriving practice that included a large appellate caseload. He won almost 90 percent of his appellate cases as a private practitioner; during his four plus years as state attorney general, he won 254 cases. Though lacking formal education, Van Buren earned a reputation as a "consummate lawyer" who "exhibited a keen knowledge of the law" on all sides of the issue.

Martin Van Buren: Boy Lawyer

James A. Henretta

As Martin Van Buren rose toward the presidency, he was both disparaged and praised for his skills as a lawyer-politician. To Davie Crockett, Kentucky frontiersman, land speculator, and congressman, Van Buren was "an artful, cunning, intriguing, selfish lawyer," concerned only with "office and money." The caustic John Randolph of Virginia was equally contemptuous of the young New Yorker's machinations, calling him "too great an intriguer . . . an adroit, dapper, little managing man." But even Randolph recognized Van Buren's persuasive abilities as a legal advocate and politician. "Give him time to collect the requisite information," he admitted to Andrew Jackson in 1832, "and no man can produce an abler argument."

Van Buren began his legal career in 1796 as a fourteen-year-old apprentice to Francis Silvester, a Federalist attorney in his hometown of Kinderhook, New York, where the young lad's courtroom oratory earned him the moniker "Boy Lawyer." Breaking with Silvester over political matters, Van Buren completed his initial training in the intricacies of the common law system in the New York City offices of Republican William Peter Van Ness. Admitted to the bar in 1803, he set up practice in Kinderhook in partnership with his older half-brother, James Van Alen. The firm prospered, attracting 118 clients in the first two years, with most of the cases involving disputes over real estate and commercial debts. Because most clients were small-scale farmers with little property, they paid slowly if at all; of thirty-two hundred dollars billed in 1803, more than fifteen hundred was still due a year later. Still, by 1807 Van Buren felt sufficiently established to marry Hannah Hoes, like him a fifth-generation Dutch American and a distant relative. Seeking a broader practice, he moved to the growing river city of Hudson, entering a partnership with Cornelius Miller,

DEBTORS' PRISON

"Van Buren regarded debtors' prison as the most abominable institution existing in the Republic," wrote one biographer. The son of a tavern keeper and truck farmer, Van Buren spoke out against the institution as "fundamentally wrong," based not on crimes but "the misfortune of being poor."

the son of a prominent banker. In 1811 and 1812, the new partners won forty-nine cases, including several shipping and commercial cases involving substantial sums of money and several for the Bank of Hudson dealing with debt collection and defaulted mortgages. Already Van Buren's legal knowledge and brief-writing skills were in demand; between 1807 and 1812, he appeared before the New York Supreme Court at least five times, a record matched by fewer than fifty of the state's one thousand practicing lawyers.

Van Buren quickly built upon his early successes at the bar and in the caucus room. Thanks to his political support of Governor Daniel Tomkins, the "farmer's son" who rose to become vice president of the United States under James Monroe, Van Buren won appointment as the surrogate of Columbia County in 1808. Three years later he secured election as a state senator—and consequent service on the Court of Errors, the mixed body of judges and politicians that sat as the highest court in the state. In 1815 Governor DeWitt Clinton named him attorney general. During his four years in that post, the rising lawyer-politician chalked up an impressive record, winning 254 cases—many involving the collection of debts from public land sales—and securing about $3.8 million (in 2002 dollars) in fines, penalties, or repayments for the state.

While Van Buren served as attorney general of New York and as U.S. senator from 1821 to 1828, he maintained a private law practice in Albany in partnership with Benjamin F. Butler. By the 1820s, Butler supervised a staff of four clerks and handled at least half of the lucrative business in chancery. Gradually taking charge of the firm's ordinary business and some of the appellate work before the supreme court, Butler became a leader of the New York bar and, eventually, U.S. attorney general under Andrew Jackson. But it was Van Buren who handled the high-profile cases, many of which involved patent and inheritance claims to tens of thousands of acres of land or valuable property in New York City. These cases brought hefty fees, though Van Buren—like other lawyers of the period—had difficulty in collecting some of them. Nonetheless, twenty-five years of legal practice, in combination with his governmental salaries, thrifty habits, and careful investments in real estate made Van Buren a wealthy man. By the time he became a full-time politician in 1828, Van Buren had accumulated an estate worth (in today's money) nearly four million dollars.

"Legal training," suggests historian Major Wilson, "provided the principal discipline for his mind" because Van Buren, one of nine children of a hardscrabble farmer and tavern keeper, had only a meager education. "His knowledge of books outside his profession," his friend James A. Hamilton remarked, "was more limited than that of any other public man I ever knew." As Van Buren himself admitted, he keenly felt his lack of a broader intellectual training when engaged in "conflicts with able and better-educated men."

Despite Wilson's comment, there are a number of reasons to question the centrality of the law to Van Buren's persona—and to his presidency. Consider the contents of Van Buren's *Autobiography*, a substantial tome of some 1,250 folio pages composed in the 1850s, only one-quarter of which pertains to his twenty-five years of legal practice. It mentions only a few cases—his representation of tenants on the Livingston Manor and of claimants of Dutch ancestry for patent rights—that loomed large in his mind because they formed part of his assault against the political power of "the great landed aristocracies of the country." As for his hundreds of other cases and legal activities, Van Buren deemed them not "of sufficient interest" and therefore best "left to the judicial reports and the traditions of the times." Yet Van Buren filled page after page of these memoirs with the minutiae of minor party battles. In fact, these political struggles were the "stuff" of Van Buren's life, not his forays into court. Van Buren admitted as much in 1828, rhetorically asking Benjamin Butler whether it was possible "to be anything in this country without being a politician."

Equally telling, the appointments to the Supreme Court during Van Buren's years as vice president, when he was Andrew Jackson's closest adviser, and as president, show little concern for the legal skills of the nominees. Of the justices who served with John Marshall, only two—the eminent Joseph Story of Massachusetts and the talented Smith Thompson of New York—remained at the end of Van Buren's term. Apart from Roger B.

COURT-MARTIAL OF GENERAL WILLIAM HULL
During the War of 1812, Hull commanded military operations in the Detroit area. Despite having a larger force than the enemy and without even engaging in battle, Hull surrendered his soldiers and arms. After a series of delays, in 1814 the Senate appointed Van Buren as special prosecutor in Hull's court-martial, where Hull was charged with neglect of duty, cowardice, and treason. Van Buren secured guilty verdicts on the first two counts (he considered the treason charge "as unsupported and insupportable"). Though Hull was sentenced to be shot, President Madison spared his life on the court's recommendation.

VAN BUREN AND THE SUPREME COURT

While in the Senate, Van Buren voiced his concerns about the U.S. Supreme Court on a number of occasions. He spoke forcefully, for example, against legislation to relieve its justices from their circuit responsibilities. Noting the "idolatry for the Supreme Court" and its "almost entire exemption from human fallibilities" and accountability, Van Buren argued that the circuit court duties brought them in closer contact with the populace and the issues of the day. When the high court ruled against New York in *Gibbons v. Ogden*, he introduced a bill providing that no state law could be declared unconstitutional except by a vote of five of the then-seven members of the Court. Later, he declared that the Court had become the nation's "highest legislative body" and suggested that most of its authority be given to the state courts.

Taney, who succeeded Marshall as chief justice in 1835 and was nearly his equal in ability, the new justices were a sorry lot.

Southern and border state appointees selected for their safe political views, they wrote few influential opinions during their tenure on the highest bench. James Wayne of Georgia, who sat as an associate justice from 1835 to 1867, owed his nomination primarily to his support for Jackson during the Nullification Crisis and left almost no mark on the Court. Philip Barbour of Virginia, a states' rights Democrat, received his post as political compensation and was merely competent in his five-year stint. Peter V. Daniel of Virginia, who replaced Barbour and served for twenty years, has been termed a "knee-jerk antifederalist" who "seemed to care little for legal reasoning." John Catron of Tennessee, who had served as one of Van Buren's campaign managers, left a meager record on the Court despite his twenty-eight years as a justice. Equally ineffective during his fifteen years as a justice was John McKinley of Alabama, whose main qualification was his strong stand as a states' rights Democrat in the U.S. Senate.

As early as 1838 James Kent, the aging Federalist chancellor of New York, concluded that these appointments had gutted the intellectual quality of the Court. "Now we feel with a pang the loss of Marshall," Kent wrote to Joseph Story. "Now we sadly realize that we are to be under the reign of little men—a pigmy race." A longtime participant in party warfare, Kent understood that the Jacksonians would appoint justices who shared their ideology, but he had hoped the nominees would have strong intellectual and legal talents. That Van Buren preferred mediocre men who were politically safe choices rather than distinguished jurists again suggests the primacy of politics in his values. A quarter century of practice at the New York bar—some of it before the eminent Kent, whom he greatly admired—had apparently not convinced Van Buren of the desirability of an outstanding bench. Law was Van Buren's occupation but its intellectual challenges and doctrinal integrity did not stand at the center of his consciousness.

Nonetheless, there was a certain congruence between Van Buren's legal training and his political outlook and values. Instinctively a cautious man, inclined to compromises that produced orderly change, Van Buren's thinking embodied the evolutionary, precedent-oriented logic of the common law. Early in his career, for example, he warned his tenant clients against pressing their claims against the Livingston family. Although Van Buren was convinced that the Livingstons held their lands under a fraudulent seventeenth-century patent, he also understood that the long "possession of the claimants under it and the statutes of limitation" posed questions of great difficulty. Consequently, he refused to encourage the tenants "with a prospect of a favorable result" at law, suggesting instead that they petition for legislative redress.

As leader of the majority "Bucktail" Democrats at the New York constitutional convention of 1821, Van Buren similarly charted a cautious course on the contested question of suffrage. While he repudiated the existing Federalist doctrine of a high property qualification for voting, he opposed "mad-cap" Democrats who advocated universal white male suffrage. Rather, Van Buren proposed linking political and legal rights to the acceptance of social responsibilities and therefore restricting the vote to men who paid taxes. Most of his fellow Bucktails took a more radical stance, prompting the convention to extend suffrage not only to taxpayers but also to men who served in the militia or worked on the public roads.

Van Buren was not averse to radical change—indeed, he was the architect of a system of party government that revolutionized American politics—but he habitually sought it through orderly means. The best example comes from the 1840s, when the former president combined his superb political skills and his legal training to craft a proposal that was at once socially revolutionary in its results and deliberate and lawful in its means.

After decades of legal struggle and periodic violence, the conflict between New York's manorial landlords and their tenants had

★ ★ ★

"The factors that made Van Buren a great lawyer made him a great politician."

Historians Jerome Mushkat and Joseph Rayback

"Law was Van Buren's occupation but its intellectual challenges and doctrinal integrity did not stand at the center of his consciousness."

come to a head. Responding to a rent strike in 1839, Whig governor William H. Seward had condemned the manorial system as "oppressive, antirepublican and degrading" and searched for a way to end it. To assist the tenants, who were trapped in quasi-feudal landholding contracts, some of his state legislative colleagues sought to deprive landlords of various legal remedies. However, other Whigs opposed such legislation as unconstitutional and, in an unrelated Illinois case, the Democrat-dominated U.S. Supreme Court agreed with them, ruling that such laws violated the contract clause. An alternative Whig proposal to use the state's power of eminent domain to "take" manorial land, paying compensation to the landlords and then selling it to tenants, likewise ran afoul of constitutional objections.

When this political and legal conundrum fell into the hands of Democratic Governor Silas Wright in 1844, Van Buren proposed a solution that was legally elegant, politically feasible, and constitutionally valid. Accepting that the property rights of landlords were vested, but echoing Blackstone's declaration that "rights of inheritance and succession [are] . . . creatures of civil or municipal laws," Van Buren proposed a statute allowing tenants, upon the death of their landlord, to convert the value of all their rents and services into a five- or ten-year mortgage. As with earlier legislation abolishing entails, such a statute would neither impair existing contracts nor interfere with vested rights. Moreover, it would provide for a gradual, compensated emancipation of the tenantry, a legalistic outcome very much in accord with Van Buren's political philosophy. Only Wright's political miscalculation and the party-driven opposition of Whigs and Conservative "Hunker" Democrats prevented the implementation of this ingenious legal scheme.

During his presidency Van Buren likewise used legal and diplomatic procedures to defuse dangerous disputes with foreign nations. For example, just before leaving office in March 1837, Jackson had disregarded Van Buren's wishes and extended diplomatic recognition to the rebellious Mexican province of Texas. By suggesting the prospect of quick annexation, Jackson's action outraged New England abolitionists and raised the danger of war with Mexico. Boldly reversing Jackson's expansionist policy, Van Buren rebuffed Texas's formal request to join the United States and proposed arbitration to resolve existing financial disputes with Mexico. A longtime advocate of "mutual forbearance and reciprocal concession" on controversial national issues, Van Buren gave a higher priority to sectional harmony than to territorial expansion.

The *Amistad* incident, however, severely tested Van Buren's legalistic approach because it threatened his prosouthern political strategy. In August 1839 enslaved Africans took over the *Amistad*, a schooner that was illegally transporting slaves in the Spanish colony of Cuba. When the schooner was seized by an American ship and ended up in New London, Connecticut, its fate—and that of its human cargo—came to rest in the hands of a federal district court judge. Speaking through government lawyers, Van Buren urged the judge—and on appeal, the justices of the U.S. Supreme Court—to follow the letter of the Spanish-American (Pinckney) Treaty of 1795 and return the ship and captives to Cuba. When the courts refused and freed the enslaved Africans, on the grounds that the *Amistad*'s clearance papers were fraudulent and that the captives were free Africans, Van Buren accepted the rule of law. As his secretary of state, John Forsyth, informed the Spanish minister, the Constitution "secured the judicial power against all interference on the part of the executive authority." Although Van Buren did not appoint distinguished judges to the Supreme Court, unlike Andrew Jackson he would not ignore or repudiate its decisions.

Van Buren's views toward slavery were fairly clear, even before the politically charged *Amistad* saga. Like many New Yorkers of Dutch descent, Van Buren grew up in a slave-owning household and briefly owned a slave himself. By the late 1820s, he had come to believe that slavery was morally wrong, but he found strong political allies among antiblack Democratic workers in New York City and proslavery Democrats throughout the South. Indeed, as the architect of the Jacksonian Democratic Party, Van Buren consciously recreated the Jeffersonian alliance between the "plain republicans of the North" and the slave-owning planters of the South.

Moreover, as a lawyer committed to the Jeffersonian constitutional principle of a limited national government, Van Buren believed that slavery was a local matter to be decided by the citizens of each state. In his inaugural address in 1837, he declared himself "the inflexible and uncompromising opponent" of any attempt on the part of Congress to interfere with slavery "in the states where it exists." However, Van Buren strongly opposed the expansion of slavery as a threat to democracy and to national unity. He resisted proposals to annex the slaveholding republic of Texas, both as president in 1837 and later as a presidential candidate in 1844, a decision that cost him the Democratic nomination.

Seeking the presidency again as the candidate of the Free-Soil Party in 1848, Van Buren composed a constitutional history that established Congress's exclusive power, under Article 4, Section 2 of the Constitution, to exclude slavery from the territories. In the end, Van Buren's position closely resembled that of Lincoln in 1860: Both men saw slavery as a morally flawed institution that could not be allowed to expand but had, nonetheless, to be protected where it existed.

Beyond the issue of slavery, there are few direct links between the New Yorker's life as a lawyer and his policies as president. In a recent monograph, *Martin Van Buren: Law, Politics, and the Shaping of Republican Ideology*, historian Jerome Mushkat claims that "the practical way Van Buren implemented classical republicanism and liberal republicanism through the law forged the basis for party principles and programs . . . [and eventually] Jacksonianism."

But Mushkat fails to substantiate this provocative thesis. On occasion, Van Buren composed briefs that used "liberal republican" doctrines such as the "will" theory of contract, which differed from the "equitable" legal tenets espoused by James Kent and other Federalists. But Van Buren's primary motivation was not ideological but practical; his goal—like that of any good lawyer in an adversarial system—was to win the case for his client. When a client's interest required an argument based on nonrepublican principles, he supplied it. Thus, in an 1819 ejectment action alleging violation of a lease made in 1694, Van Buren protected the lessee by invoking the doctrine of "ancient rights," a prescriptive argument that was often used by lords to deny the claims of tenants.

Nonetheless, Van Buren undoubtedly preferred to devise legal arguments that accorded with his ideological values. With respect to banking, there is a direct line from his early political views to subsequent legal briefs and, finally, to his stunning creation of an independent treasury during his presidency. Although

New York lawmakers enacted a Restraining Act in 1804 that reserved the issue of bank notes to state-chartered corporations, by 1810 they had chartered ten commercial banks and in 1818, over Van Buren's objection, added five more. "I was always opposed to the multiplication of banks," Van Buren declared in his *Autobiography*, arguing that they were a "danger to the public weal." Not only did their directors corrupt the political process by offering free shares of bank stock to key legislators, but once in business they made unsecured loans to "insiders" and issued bank notes far in excess of their paid up capital. Such practices led to inflation and banking failures, with innocent investors bearing the loss.

As attorney general, Van Buren took decisive—and legally important—steps to curb the proliferation of banking activities. Upon receiving a state charter in 1816, the Utica Insurance Company lent funds to businesses in the form of paper money that subsequently circulated among the general public. Believing that this quasi-banking activity violated the Restraining Acts of 1804 and 1813, Van Buren initiated a quo warranto proceeding, a legal writ requiring the company to demonstrate its right to issue money. When the New York Supreme Court considered the writ, Van Buren rejected the company's argument that banking was not a franchise but a right that existed "at large" in every citizen. Rather, he demanded a strict reading of the company's charter: If the privilege of banking "was intended, why not say so in express terms?" A majority of the supreme court agreed, enjoining Utica Insurance from future banking activities.

Van Buren's quo warranto proceeding against a corporation was an innovative legal stroke, and his argument for the strict construction of a charter anticipated Chief Justice Taney's reasoning some twenty years later in the important U.S. Supreme Court case of *Charles River Bridge Company v. Warren Bridge Company*. Equally important, the Utica case foreshadowed Van Buren's future policies. In the state constitutional convention of 1821, he inserted a clause requiring a two-thirds legislative majority to approve a bank charter. As governor in 1829, he won enactment of the Safety Fund as part of a new system that kept New York banks as privately owned, profit-seeking entities but subjected them

WHIG CHALLENGER DANIEL WEBSTER

At a relatively early age, New Hampshire native Daniel Webster established himself as "the nation's leading lawyer and outstanding orator," winning such landmark Supreme Court cases as *Dartmouth College v. Woodward*, *Gibbons v. Ogden*, and *McCullough v. Maryland* among the 168 cases he represented before that tribunal. As Massachusetts congressman and senator, and as secretary of state with Presidents Harrison and Tyler, Webster was also an influential political leader. As a presidential candidate, however, he was singularly unsuccessful, carrying only Massachusetts in his campaign against Van Buren in 1836 and never thereafter gaining serious consideration for the Oval Office.

"It shall be my constant and zealous endeavor to protect the remaining rights reserved to the states by the federal constitution; to restore those of which they have been divested by [judicial] construction."

Martin Van Buren

to regulation by a state-appointed board of commissioners and required them to set aside 3 percent of their capital to reimburse note holders of failed banks.

As president during the Panic of 1837, Van Buren presented an even more dramatic financial proposal at a special session of Congress. Believing that "redundancy of credit and . . . reckless speculation" had sparked the panic, he proposed that the national government withdraw its funds from state-chartered banks (just as Andrew Jackson had pulled them out of the Second Bank of the United States). Public funds would remain in the United States Treasury, thus making the government completely "independent" of the banking industry and preventing state banks from using federal specie as backing for excessive issues of notes and loans. Despite intricate wheeling and dealing, Van Buren could not win congressional approval for an independent treasury. Whigs demanded a nationally chartered institution to replace the Second Bank, while "soft money" Democrats wanted to expand the money supply by keeping government specie in state banks. However, when a second financial deluge struck the country in 1839, Van Buren blamed the Bank of England and demanded an independent treasury to counter the "control of a foreign moneyed interest." Celebrating the resulting legislation as a "Second Declaration of Independence" from Britain, Van Buren signed it into law on July 4, 1840.

Just as the Utica injunction and the Safety Fund protected New Yorkers against banking excess, so the independent treasury would safeguard the national republic. At least with respect to banking, the policy of President Van Buren was at one with the political ideology and legal arguments of Martin Van Buren, Esquire, the rising New York lawyer-politician of the 1810s and 1820s.

★ ★ ★

John Tyler

Tenth President (1841–45)

BIRTH
March 29, 1790
Charles City County, Va.

EDUCATION
Local schools
College of William and Mary
Studied law at home with his father and cousin; later studied
    with former U.S. attorney general Edmund Randolph
Admission to the bar: circa 1811

OTHER OCCUPATIONS/PUBLIC OFFICES
Virginia legislator
U.S. congressman (Speaker of the House)
Virginia governor
U.S. senator
Delegate to Virginia constitutional conventions
Vice president with William Henry Harrison
Chancellor of College of William and Mary
Member of Confederate Congress

DEATH
January 18, 1862
Richmond, Va.

LAW CAREER IN BRIEF

Though well schooled in the law and known for his oratorical skills, Tyler pursued the "plain business" of a country lawyer, usually handling routine matters involving debts and estates during periods when he was not in public office. As few court records of the day survived, anecdotes about Tyler's rise to prominence based upon his early criminal defense work cannot be confirmed. In the political arena, he was respected for his understanding of legal decisions and technical procedures, but he never sought admission to practice before the appellate courts and thus did not establish a judicial record of such legal skills.

John Tyler: Virginia Counsel

E. Lee Shepard

In *Letters and Times of the Tylers*, the story is told of young John Tyler's "desperate case at the bar," where both the law and prominent counsel stood solidly against him. Opposing counsel Andrew Stevenson had been persuasive, citing extensively from legal authorities. Stevenson had been so eloquent that Tyler's client seemed dispirited as he awaited his counsel's argument.

In his usual manner, Tyler first complimented Stevenson and noted his own shortcomings. He then decried "the transparency of the cause," proclaiming "with a singular intermixture of tones, expressive of surprise, confidence, and contempt":

> *The gentleman has referred to authority—English authority! . . . And pray, what has a Charles City jury to do with English authority? Charles City—the birth-place of Bacon's Rebellion, the home of revolution, and the land of republican principle! When we cast off in blood the colonial dependency, we cast off the authority of England. . . . The [jury] will have none of your English authority! Away with it!*

And in five minutes, the jury returned a verdict for Tyler's client.

The tenth president of the United States was born at "Greenway," the Charles City County, Virginia, plantation of his father and mother, Judge John Tyler and Mary Armistead Tyler. Comparatively little is known of his youth and young adulthood that is not conjecture or the myth-making of political writers in the mid–nineteenth century. His mother died when Tyler was seven, so John and his six siblings were raised by their father, an attorney-turned-dedicated revolutionary statesman and jurist.

By all accounts, the senior Tyler was a loving but demanding father, pressing his sons to excel at their chosen

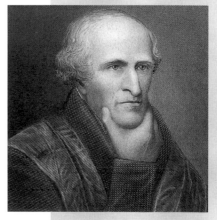

professions. The younger man idolized his father and absorbed his parent's social outlook and political philosophy virtually intact. He once described him as "amongst the most steadfast and most firm of the Whigs during the whole period of the Revolutionary War." A strong proponent of state-sponsored education, a perennial advocate of legal and judicial reform, and the strictest of constitutional constructionists, Judge Tyler inculcated his son with complete faith in states' rights, extreme Anglophobia, and a belief in the validity of a slave-based economy.

Young Tyler received his formal education at the nearby College of William and Mary in Williamsburg, from which he graduated in 1807. His father had already mapped out a career in law for him, or at least strongly encouraged his tendency toward that profession. While still a student at William and Mary, Tyler fielded frequent admonitions from his father to improve himself so that he would "be fit for law business of every description."

Upon graduation, the future president began reading law in his father's library, one of the better collections in the commonwealth, since his father was then a judge on the Virginia General Court. Reportedly, his cousin Samuel Tyler, chancellor of the Williamsburg District, also aided in Tyler's studies. When his father was elected governor of Virginia, the younger man traveled with his family to Richmond, where he continued his studies under the venerable former U.S. attorney general Edmund Randolph. In later years, he always spoke publicly of Randolph in the most respectful and admiring terms. In reality, he chafed as much under the Federalist political views espoused by his mentor as he did under the apprenticeship experience that consisted of much routine office work and little courtroom exposure. During his time in Richmond, Tyler also joined a debating society formed by his contemporaries for the purpose of gaining forensic experience before their first appearances at the bar.

Very little evidence survives about Tyler's early professional life. Tradition holds that he received his license to practice during his twentieth year, some time before gaining his majority and contrary to the laws of Virginia. On the one hand, this seems entirely possible given his intellect and advanced studies, as well as the notoriously lax approach most Virginia judges of the day took toward granting licenses. At the same time, the law was the law, and his father was, after all, as governor, the commonwealth's chief law enforcement officer. The law then in force required that, prior to appearing before a judge, a student had to secure a certificate testifying to his residence, age, and "honest demeanor" from the court of the county or corporation in which he had been living for the preceding twelve months. Complicating matters, the records of the county and municipal courts in which Tyler would have naturally acquired such a certificate and commenced his practice—Charles City County, New Kent County, and Williamsburg—all suffered extensive loss during the Civil War. So it is impossible to trace when he actually qualified to practice before the justices of each of those respective tribunals. In fact, the few pertinent records that do survive from this period point exclusively to 1811 as the year of Tyler's first legal activity—his twenty-first year.

At the time, young attorneys began their practice before the commonwealth's lower courts, starting in the county courts composed of lay justices of the peace, then gradually moving up to the local superior courts of chancery and the district courts. Those aspiring to greater legal fame and fortune marked time by gaining essential experience at the bar of these courts while setting their sights on graduating to practice before the state's highest courts in Richmond. Those courts in the capital city then included the Virginia General Court and the Supreme Court of Appeals, along with the federal district and circuit courts.

By Tyler's own testimony, at age twenty-one he took at least one case on appeal from the Charles City County Court to a higher court in Richmond where he represented his client alongside the eminent litigator John Wickham. Presumably, Tyler would not have moved into such a circle without at least some experience on the local level, no matter who his father was. But Tyler never would have a regular practice among those Richmond courts. In fact, he never even qualified to practice before the state's highest court.

Throughout his career, the bulk of John Tyler's substantial law practice came from representing clients in

THE NEWLY ADMITTED TYLER IS INTRODUCED TO HIS CRAFT

Tyler, just recently arriving in Richmond as a new member of the bar, consented "after much urgency" by a client, to assist in pleading his cause. The client's lead attorney, John Wickham, and opposing counsel William Wirt were lions of the profession, having been opposing counsel in the treason trial of Aaron Burr. Wickham (pictured here) encouraged the young attorney. Wrote Tyler, "So much (said he) for high sounding names at the bar. You must open the case. I did so,—in fear and trembling, however,—and soon after lost myself in the ingenious sallies made during the rest of the day by two eminent counsel."

"At his best, Tyler was the rhetorical equivalent of Webster, Clay, Benton, and Calhoun in his ability to move and manipulate an audience."

Biographer Robert Seager II

his own locality or in adjacent counties and towns. The routine matters of law practice—drawing deeds and wills, pursuing litigation over indebtedness and the settlement of estates, and providing opinions—proved to be his most certain means of income. Tyler called this "the plain business, which is in truth the really valuable business." Until he was much older, he routinely reverted back to his practice whenever he put politics temporarily aside.

Contemporary political writers and later biographers claim that Tyler made his real name at the bar as a neophyte practitioner who took on cases of accused felons. He certainly gained an early and sustained reputation as an orator, something that any attorney would put to good use before both judges and juries, particularly in criminal cases. Surviving evidence reveals that Tyler unsuccessfully represented an accused slave on at least one occasion, while several popular anecdotes support the view of the future president's rise to professional recognition and favor as a criminal advocate.

Tyler understood, as did all young attorneys of his day, that the law was the truest and most direct path to fortune in antebellum Virginia, and to political preferment as well—"the high road to fame," he called it. Lawyers declaiming at the bar got the community's attention, especially when they were successful. Their oratorical feats proved to be one of the most accessible forms of entertainment in the Virginia countryside. By all accounts, Tyler excelled as a litigator, knowledgeable in the law and gifted in the oral presentation of his clients' cases. This surely explains his election, just after his twenty-first birthday, to a seat in the lower house of the Virginia General Assembly for Charles City County. He consciously carried into his political career the principles that shaped his life in the legal profession. As he once told a brother-in-law, he was guided by "my moral code and my legal code, and I am yet to learn that there is a distinction between them."

Similarly, the skills Tyler developed at the bar—particularly his acknowledged abilities as an orator—played well in political settings. Sought after for his legal opinions and possessing the special ability to lucidly explain legal doctrines and procedural niceties, Tyler was also well equipped to make law and administer it.

In the legislative session beginning in early December 1811, Tyler made an immediate impression. His early prominence no doubt derived, at least in part, from his father's position and his strong advice to take an active role in the deliberations. Young Tyler served consecutive terms in the House of Delegates until 1816. While still a member of that body, he was elected to a seat on the Virginia Executive Council, the advisory body to the commonwealth's governor.

A year later, Tyler headed to the Fifteenth Congress of the United States in Washington to replace the late representative of his district, John Clopton. There, he strongly advocated strict construction of the Constitution, championed states' rights, and doggedly opposed internal improvements and the national bank. Never a robust man, he found the experience physically draining. After serving one term, he confided to his wife that "my friends in the district have a right to expect me to continue for another Congress, [after which] I should certainly cease to be a public man." True to his word, he declined renomination in 1821, citing ill health. The young congressman then returned to Virginia and to his law practice, which had been sadly neglected during his four years of extended absences in Washington. "You must know," he confided to his brother-in-law Doctor Henry Curtis, "that a station here [in Washington] and the practice of the law are almost incompatible with each other."

Although it is hard to gauge Tyler's success at the bar, by his own testimony he had a thriving practice as of the early 1820s. He told Curtis, for example, that his practice could be valued at two thousand dollars annually, a handsome sum for someone who was basically a country lawyer. The renowned Daniel Webster annually brought in only six hundred to seven hundred dollars at the same age.

The lure of political life was too great, however, and in 1823 Tyler returned to the Virginia House of Delegates. Two sessions later, in late 1825, his legislative colleagues elected him governor of the state. Following his term as Virginia's chief executive, he was elected to the U.S. Senate. In that body he continued his strict constructionist and antitariff stances, while seeking to protect the rights of the slaveholding states and of those who would extend slavery into new territories. He supported Andrew Jackson during most of his Senate career, but broke with the administration over nullification—that is, a state's right not to obey a congressional act that conflicted with its own laws and interests.

"[I am guided by] my moral code and my legal code, and I am yet to learn that there is a distinction between them."

John Tyler

For a time in 1829 and 1830, Tyler served in the Virginia constitutional convention, where he naturally sided with the Tidewater conservatives against western interests and the expansion of voting rights. Interestingly, given his father's support of judicial reform, Tyler did not follow suit, opposing any changes to the structure of the commonwealth's court system. Back in Washington, Tyler began to associate with the emerging Whig Party, but he resigned from the Senate over his refusal to reverse a resolution censuring President Jackson for removing deposits from the Bank of the United States, an action seen by many as beyond the scope of the president's constitutional authority. Elements of the Whig Party sought to capitalize on the issue and unsuccessfully promoted Tyler as a vice presidential candidate in 1836. Tyler himself again turned to the law and had perhaps the busiest time of his career as a practitioner, as he needed the work to recover his personal finances and provide for his large family.

The former senator sold his farm in Gloucester County, bought a house in Williamsburg, and found himself perfectly located to serve his local constituents, who now abundantly favored him with legal business. He concentrated his practice in the circuit superior courts, focusing largely on civil litigation, but kept a weather eye on the developing political scene. After returning briefly to the Virginia House of Delegates, he accepted the Whig Party vice presidential nomination in 1840 on the ticket with William Henry Harrison, a Virginia native from his own home county. Tyler's appeal as a vice presidential candidate stemmed from his connection with southern conservatives and the chance that he might successfully pull Virginia into the Whig column.

Harrison's untimely death a month after taking office precipitated the first true constitutional crisis for the American executive branch. While Tyler had consistently feared and challenged a powerful executive during the whole of his political life, he exhibited no hesitation in now taking the reins of government. Despite ambiguity in the language of the Constitution, hardly clarified by subsequent congressional legislation regarding elections and presidential succession, Tyler believed that he acceded to the full office and powers of the presidency upon Harrison's death. In fact, breaking sharply with his strict constructionist past, he could not visualize himself as simply a caretaker until the next national election. Harrison's cabinet, led by Secretary of State Daniel Webster, supported this view, however reluctantly. Shortly thereafter, following some heated debate, both houses of Congress similarly acquiesced in the succession, thereby assuring an orderly transfer of power.

The legal and political issues about the succession, however, haunted Tyler's entire term of office. His political opponents ridiculed him as "His Accidency," and he was not helped by his own erratic political behavior. He irritated Whigs by vetoing key economic measures, pushing the congressional delegation so far as to consider impeachment proceedings. His inept handling of the nomination of a replacement to the U.S. Supreme Court upon the death of Justice Smith Thompson of New York in 1843 further isolated him from both Whigs and conservative Democrats. The blatant politicization of the potential appointment further tarnished Tyler's already shaky public image, as a series of candidates—including his main political rival, Martin

Tyler Impeachment Vote

The controversies surrounding Tyler's ascendancy to the presidency were perhaps most vividly reflected by an attempt to impeach him. In January 1843, fellow Virginian John Minor Botts sought to charge "John Tyler, Vice President acting as President" with corruption, official misconduct, high crimes, and misdemeanors. The House resolution failed to carry the day, garnering but 83 of 210 votes.

★ ★ ★

"His immediate hope was that [in 1836] his sons Robert and John would join him in a family law practice from which all three might prosper."

Biographer Richard Seager II

Van Buren—turned him down or failed to secure confirmation. Only when he settled on a prominent attorney from New York, Samuel Nelson (who went on to serve for twenty-seven years), did the Senate at last ratify his choice. When a second Court vacancy occurred upon the death of Justice Henry Baldwin, Tyler again fared poorly. His nomination of Judge Edward King of Philadelphia languished, and when he replaced King with another Pennsylvanian, John Meredith Read, the Whig-dominated Senate rudely adjourned without acting on the nomination, leaving the appointment to the next president, James K. Polk.

Only foreign policy, which featured the Webster-Ashburton Treaty and Tyler's wooing of Texas to join the American union, offered bright spots in his administration's history. Abandoned by the mainstream Whigs and unable to wrest the Democratic Party nomination from Polk, Tyler returned to Virginia after his term of office and turned his attention to the plantation affairs that had languished during his absence in Washington. He may have again taken up his law practice briefly, but he had definitely retired from the profession by the early 1850s.

Although he did not again hold political office, he remained an interested observer of Virginia politics and offered periodic pronouncements on the issues of the day. Having opposed the African slave trade, Tyler felt that colonization would be the key to settling the slavery issue. Yet, he continued to defend the expansion of slavery into the territories and hailed the Kansas-Nebraska Act for maintaining a balance between northern and southern states in the Union. Throughout his life, whether living on his own farm in Gloucester County, or at his final home in Charles City—"Sherwood Forest," to which he retired in 1845—Tyler maintained a large enslaved work force and never appears to have seriously contemplated freeing them.

If anything, as he entered the last years of his life, Tyler moved even further toward extreme states' rights. Although he chaired the Washington Peace Convention in 1861, he harbored little hope of saving the Union. He became an early advocate of secession, only joined by a majority of his Virginia Convention colleagues following the firing on Fort Sumter and Lincoln's call for volunteers. In turn, they elected him to the Provisional Confederate Congress, but he died in January 1862 before taking office.

John Tyler the lawyer proved to be a workmanlike advocate, making a handsome living—when politics allowed—from the routine business of a country practice. Although a stellar performer at the local bar, with an apparent mastery of Virginia law, he was never an appellate attorney, and never found himself tested as a deep thinker in matters of judicial review. Whether this limited his performance in the nation's highest office is difficult to say. Certainly, politics overshadowed his administration, and the mark he may have wanted to make for himself in crafting law, influencing the interpretation of the Constitution, or controlling the burgeoning executive department fell victim to his own miscalculations and to the machinations of politicians who had little patience with his independent ways.

***

Eleventh President (1845–49)

BIRTH
November 2, 1795
Mecklenburg County, N.C.

EDUCATION
Private school
University of North Carolina
Studied law with Felix Grundy in Nashville
Admission to the bar: June 1820

OTHER OCCUPATIONS/PUBLIC OFFICES
Chief clerk of Tennessee Senate
State legislator
U.S. congressman (Speaker of the House)
Tennessee governor

DEATH
June 15, 1849
Nashville, Tenn.

LAW CAREER IN BRIEF

Polk had a "brief and sometime practice of law." Possessing a classical education, he spent but a year studying law with noted criminal lawyer and former Kentucky chief justice Felix Grundy before passing the bar. His practice benefited immensely from family connections, with most of it focusing on real estate issues, including a case before the U.S. Supreme Court. His association with Felix Grundy and Andrew Jackson, however, also drew him into the political arena, and except for a few months of law practice between his gubernatorial term and his nomination to the presidency, politics occupied most of his time and attention.

James K. Polk: Sometime Lawyer

ROBERT W. JOHANNSEN

In 1818, when twenty-two-year-old James K. Polk graduated first in his class from the University of North Carolina, he faced a decision, like all college graduates, that would determine the direction of the rest of his life. He was a young man in a hurry, forced by a frail constitution to begin his formal education later than most of his peers. He had become aware that he could catch up only through a single-minded dedication to his goals and an iron discipline in pursuing his studies.

The eldest of ten children, Polk was born in Mecklenburg County, North Carolina, in 1795. His family, prominent in the region, was of sturdy Scotch-Irish stock, staunchly Presbyterian, and strongly supportive of American independence. Like many North Carolinians following the Revolution, Polk's father had invested in land in the state's Western District, or what would become the state of Tennessee. When Polk was eleven, the family moved to a farm near the town of Columbia in south central Tennessee, and it was there that he was raised in an atmosphere of rigid Presbyterianism mixed with steadfast loyalty to Jeffersonian principles. As a student in church-related academies, he also demonstrated an intellectual capacity for Latin and Greek grammar, Caesar's commentaries, and the Greek Bible.

Polk's diligence as a student and mastery of subjects enabled him to move directly into the sophomore class of the University of North Carolina. With a curriculum modeled on that of Princeton and a faculty of clerics trained under the celebrated John Witherspoon, the university had become a bastion of Presbyterian orthodoxy. As a student at Chapel Hill, Polk developed the work habits that characterized his later life and career. He concentrated on the classics and mathematics, two subjects he felt would best discipline his mind. During his senior year a

★ ★ ★

"[In the frontier] the study of law offered a number of advantages. The lawyer, representing stability and frequently viewed as an agent of reason and restraint, often enjoyed respect and social prominence."

FELIX GRUNDY: POLK'S LEGAL (AND POLITICAL) MENTOR

As a young lawyer, Grundy was elected to the Kentucky legislature, where he successfully introduced a bill to establish the circuit court system. He was then appointed a supreme court judge and became chief justice. Unable to live on a judge's salary, he moved to Nashville, where he developed a prominent criminal practice, defending 105 capital cases and losing only one man to the gallows. His later career included several terms in the U.S. Senate and service as U.S. attorney general in Martin Van Buren's administration.

course in moral philosophy was added, reinforcing his faith in human reason and his belief in civic virtue, public order, and love of country.

Polk pursued his studies amidst the heady atmosphere of American nationalism that followed the War of 1812, America's second War of Independence. As an active debating society member, he argued the question, "Would an extension of territory be an advantage to the United States?"—a matter that would engage his attention in later years. In another address, Polk urged his fellow students to develop that "fluency of language, that connexion of ideas and boldness of delivery" that would prepare them for service with equal proficiency in the councils of the nation, in the pulpit, or at the bar—politics, religion, and the law, the young republic's trinity of service.

The work habits Polk acquired, the friendships he formed, the simple eloquence and prudent conduct he derived from his mentors, and the systematic exactness demanded by his studies prepared him for a life of professional development and competition. It is not known precisely when Polk decided to follow a career in the law. After graduation and a short visit with his family, he left for Nashville, some forty-five miles north of Columbia, to study law in the office of the noted Felix Grundy. For a young man intent on pursuing a professional career in a region that still bore the characteristics of a frontier, the study of law offered a number of advantages. The lawyer, representing stability and frequently viewed as an agent of reason and restraint, often enjoyed respect and social prominence.

It was an exciting transition period in the young history of the republic, as the classical republicanism associated with Thomas Jefferson was giving way to the new mass democracy of Andrew Jackson. Alexis de Tocqueville, the French traveler whose observations of American democracy in the 1830s became a classic, found that lawyers often constituted a privileged body in American society, for as they offered the security of the law against the excesses of democracy, they also wielded a great degree of political power. Land titles were often obscure and required legal clarification, wills had to be drawn and estates probated, and individual altercations and disagreements had to be adjudicated. The maturity of a community was often measured by the number of its lawyers, for the presence of lawyers suggested a law-abiding atmosphere. Political questions, observed de Tocqueville, became judicial questions. The practice of law brought the fledgling lawyer into close contact with the people, not only in his own community but also in nearby towns and villages, and the fact that many of these people also voted was not overlooked. For those who aspired to a career in politics, there was no better preparation than the practice of law.

Legal training on the western frontier, in contrast with the structured programs in older states, was highly informal, usually limited to a brief period of study in the office of an experienced lawyer, followed by a perfunctory examination administered by a local judge or another member of the bar. The study of the classics was thought to be essential background for legal study, and some states prescribed a formal classical education as a prerequisite to admission to the bar. Polk's studies at Chapel Hill gave him an immediate advantage, for few peers could boast the high quality education he had received there. His proficiency in Latin and Greek gave him the mental discipline he needed for a career in the law. That he chose Felix Grundy for his mentor revealed his seriousness. That Grundy accepted him was a tribute to his promise and ability, although the prominence of Polk's family in Middle Tennessee may have been a factor.

Grundy's fame as a criminal lawyer extended beyond the bounds of Tennessee. Years before, he had lived and practiced in Kentucky, where in 1807 he was appointed chief justice of the state supreme court. He resigned that post shortly afterward and moved to Nashville, where he resumed his law practice. His reputation did not rest so much on knowledge of the law as it did on being a "profound judge of Mankind." Indeed, he studied people more than he did books. Employing common sense and intuition, he developed a manner that proved irresistible to juries. Reports of his success spread throughout the West and drew him to cases far afield.

★ ★ ★

"The maturity of a community was often measured by the number of its lawyers, for the presence of lawyers suggested a law-abiding atmosphere."

Grundy, however, was much more than a successful lawyer. His political experience was equally impressive and especially important to the young Polk. Twice elected to Congress following his move to Tennessee, Grundy preached a new, aggressive, and nationalistic brand of western republicanism. He took his seat in the Twelfth Congress, where he quickly became identified with a dynamic group of like-minded men, including Henry Clay and John Calhoun. As a War-Hawk, Grundy promoted war with Great Britain as the only alternative to national dishonor. He resigned his House seat in 1814 and returned to Nashville, carrying with him a reputation as a party leader and patriotic supporter of American expansion, both of which became key elements in shaping Polk's career in politics and the law.

A frequent visitor to Grundy's law office was the man whose influence on the aspiring lawyer would surpass even that of Grundy, Andrew Jackson. The ties between Grundy and Jackson were exceptionally close; it was Grundy who later initiated Tennessee's nomination of Jackson for the presidency. The Polks themselves were no strangers to Old Hickory. Born only a few miles from the seat of the Polk family in North Carolina's Mecklenburg County, Jackson later recalled that he knew "all the old stock of Polks" and that he had known James when the latter was but a boy. The Old Hero of New Orleans also took a keen interest in Polk's legal education.

Polk had studied with Grundy for barely a year when he passed his examination before the state supreme court and qualified as an attorney. He returned to Columbia early in 1820, and in June of that year he was admitted to the bar. Family and friends immediately aided him in setting up his practice. Polk's father paid for the small one-room building that would house his office and provided him with $140 toward the purchase of a law library. Polk entered a subscription to the prestigious but soon to be defunct *Journal of Jurisprudence* and later completed his library with the purchase of over $600 worth of law books.

Polk's law practice prospered from the beginning, thanks in large part to his family connections. His entry into the profession coincided with the opening of Tennessee's Western District, the land west of the Tennessee River, which had been freed of its Indian title by a treaty with the Chickasaws in 1818. The Indian cession was not only good news to Tennesseans, but was also

received enthusiastically in North Carolina, where many individuals held land warrants dating as far back as the
1780s. Surveyors flocked to western Tennessee to
locate land claims for their clients, and lawyers
such as Polk were busy validating the warrants
according to North Carolina and Tennessee
law, which often were in conflict. In 1827,
Polk was cocounsel with Missouri Senator
Thomas Hart Benton in a successful defense
before the U.S. Supreme Court in a related
case. The high court's technical ruling, however, played but a minor part in the larger
legal and political drama surrounding such
claims at the time.

Among the members of the Polk family involved in land speculation was his cousin William,
one of the largest holders of North Carolina warrants with thousands of acres. And Polk did not overlook
his own opportunities, acquiring land in Tennessee, Arkansas,
and Mississippi. With his father, he engaged in speculative activity
involving North Carolina grants. A slave owner by inheritance
and purchase, he established two plantations in Tennessee and
Mississippi, which became important sources of income. Slavery,
Polk believed, was a common evil, "entailed upon us by our ancestors"; as a practical man, he was aware of the difficulties, if not
dangers, of trying to get rid of the institution. He regarded those
who tried (like the abolitionists) as mischief makers who placed
the Union in jeopardy.

Polk's law practice, however, encountered a formidable rival
almost from the very beginning. Felix Grundy's mentoring not
only laid the groundwork for a legal career, but also launched
Polk on a political course. In August 1819, while Polk studied in
his office, Grundy was elected to a seat in the state legislature. At
the time, Grundy encouraged a young lawyer who shared his
office, Francis Fogg, to seek the post of clerk of the state senate,
assuring Fogg that he could easily be elected, thus providing an
advantageous position for a person with political ambitions.
Fogg, however, was intent on a law career and declined. Polk,
who had overheard Grundy's offer, suggested that if Fogg was
not interested, he was. Grundy promptly put forward Polk's

WILLIAMS V. NORRIS

Polk was counsel in this
1827 U.S. Supreme Court
case. While it did not gen-
erate a significant legal
decision, it was politically
significant as one example
of the contentious disputes
over land titles in western
Tennessee that "would split
into fragments" the state's
Jackson party. It also involved prominent counsel
arguing opposing sides of
the case. Joining Polk as
counsel for Williams was
Missouri Senator Thomas
Hart Benton (pictured
here), while Tennessee's
Senators Hugh Lawson
White and John Eaton
represented Norris.

candidacy and Polk won the office. At that moment, Polk made his commitment to a career in politics.

It was an exciting moment, filled with opportunity for a young man with political aspirations. Politics was in a state of transition that soon would result in new political alignments. The economic distress in Tennessee and elsewhere, left by the Panic of 1819, aroused demands that the government be more responsive to the needs of the people. A "new politics" was called for, and Andrew Jackson became its symbol and leader.

Polk's political ambition was aroused. After serving as senate clerk for four years, he was elected to the lower house of the state legislature, and in 1825 campaigned successfully for a seat in Congress. The aftermath of the contested presidential election of 1824, when Jackson led the field of four candidates only to be defeated by John Quincy Adams in the House of Representatives, gave Polk's campaign significant new meaning. He shared the outrage of the Jacksonians, convinced that the will of the people had been thwarted by the forces of "bargain and corruption." Polk was easily elected to the House of Representatives, where he would remain for seven terms.

As congressman, Polk served his constituents much as he would have his clients in his law practice, securing pensions and bounty lands for veterans of the Revolutionary War and the War of 1812 and bringing order to the state's complex land and banking problems. He found it increasingly difficult, however, to manage both careers, and it was not surprising that his law practice suffered as a result. During his early years, he had formed partnerships to help handle his caseload, including a brief relationship with Aaron Brown, later governor of Tennessee, but he found the arrangements unsatisfactory. He relied more and more on fellow attorneys to represent his clients at circuit court sessions, and it was not long before his political career won out over his law practice.

Polk carried his success in the courtroom and on the stump into debates on the floor of the House. Following Jackson's election in 1828, he became the spokesman for the president and leader of the Jackson forces in the House. In debate, his words carried conviction without the florid elaboration so common to many of his peers; his statements were simple and direct, demonstrating a command of facts and principles and revealing a practical common sense.

Polk gained a reputation as a loyal and trustworthy Jacksonian, sharing Old Hickory's belief that the president, as chief executive of all the people, reflected the popular will more than any other federal officer. As member and later chairman of the powerful Ways and Means Committee, Polk supported Jackson's assault on the "money power" in the nation and warned against the "despotism of money" that, if not checked, would soon "control your election of President, of your Senators, and of your Representatives." He was a staunch defender of states' rights in a confederation of sovereign states, and of strict interpretation of the Constitution. He proved to be a relentless foe of Henry Clay and the Whigs, whose program he warned would lead to a "consolidated empire."

Polk was elected Speaker of the House in December 1835, a post he held for two terms during one of the most critical periods for himself and his party. With Martin Van Buren in the White House, divisions appeared in the Democratic ranks over the new president, the economic distress following the Panic of 1837, and Polk's enforcement of the gag rule against antislavery petitions. Polk struggled to hold the Democratic coalition together by wielding a tight and absolute control over deliberations of the House, for which he was often criticized.

Polk left the House in 1839 when he was persuaded to run for governor of Tennessee. He was elected to a two-year term, but it proved to be thankless and unsuccessful. Polk's subsequent effort to return to national politics as Van Buren's vice presidential candidate in 1840 came to naught. He ran for reelection as governor in 1841 and 1843, but lost both times. His political career appeared at an end.

It was then that he contemplated a return to the practice of law. "I have gone to my profession in earnest," he announced in September 1843, "& think I will *now* make some money." His friends were both approving and supportive. "I see by the papers," wrote one, "that you are engaged in professional pursuits, I hope profitably, and that you find pleasure in it." Others warned that his "absence from the bar & devotion to other subjects will demand great exertion on your part to sustain your high reputation."

"I am if possible more than ever resolved to 'fight on' for my principles, though I be in the ranks I will not be the less zealous or active."

James K. Polk, in returning to law practice following unsuccessful campaigns for Tennessee governor

*"[The slavery issue]
is a mere political
question on which
demagogues &
ambitious politicians
hope to promote their
own prospects for
political promotion."*

James K. Polk

Polk followed their advice to take a partner "to perform the drudgery" of the office, freeing him to appear only in the "great cases." At the same time, Polk wanted his friends to know that his "accustomed interest in politics" had not ceased. On the contrary, he continued to nurture a return to political life. "I am if possible more than ever resolved to 'fight on' for my principles," he declared. "Though I be in the ranks I will not be the less zealous or active."

Polk's return to the "ranks" was much briefer than even he could have predicted. Nine months after his second defeat for re-election as governor of Tennessee, the Democrats chose him as their candidate for the presidency. Polk's nomination was as unexpected as it was sudden. The Whigs reacted with ridicule and delight. "Who is James K. Polk?" they asked, implying that he was little known and poorly qualified to be president, especially when compared to the Whig candidate, Henry Clay, who enjoyed great experience, power, and popularity. Contrary to all expectations, however, Polk won a narrow victory over Clay to become, at age forty-nine, the youngest president in American history to that time. Seldom has a politician's career turned around so suddenly and dramatically.

Once again Polk put aside his practice of law, this time to concentrate on the duties of the president. He exchanged the courtroom for the challenging arena of national government and brought to the presidency a high level of discipline, diligence, and intellectual acumen—qualities he had nurtured since he sat at the feet of Felix Grundy. He pledged to serve only a single term as president, and he remained steadfast behind this promise. He set his goals early in his administration and pursued them "with undeviating resolution." Like Jackson, he made full use of the power of the presidency, including the exercise of the veto power, to accomplish his goals. He was determined to be at the center of his administration, to be his own man. "I intend to be myself President of the United States," he announced. No previous president had ever applied himself so intensely to the government's business. "I am the hardest working man in the country," he remarked.

Like Old Hickory, Polk regarded his party as the principal instrument for carrying out the popular will. Although his practice of law had been suspended, as president he could at least influence the law. He made two appointments to the Supreme Court, Levi Woodbury, whose party credentials were impeccable, and Robert Grier, who represented the party's control over Pennsylvania's factional politics. He nominated eight district judges, five of them in newly admitted states, and named judges for two territorial governments. Democratic Party ideology—strict construction, states' rights, and limited government—was the yardstick by which the judiciary was to be measured.

Polk's legislative objectives were those of the Democratic platform on which he stood, a blending of Jacksonian principles and policies and the new spirit of continental expansion: reduction of the tariff to revenue levels, establishment of the independent treasury system, annexation of Texas, and acquisition of the Oregon country. Probably the most remembered and studied event of the Polk presidency was the war with Mexico. He administered the war as he did all other objectives, with a single-minded dedication to what he perceived as his responsibilities of leadership. He was the first president to define and implement the full powers of his office as commander-in-chief in wartime. "He proved that a President could run a war," said one historian. As a result of the war, the United States acquired half a million square miles of what would become the American Southwest, including New Mexico and California, fulfilling the nation's manifest destiny. Under Polk's guidance, the United States indeed became "an ocean-bound republic."

Few presidents have achieved such an ambitious and far-reaching program in the brief space of four years, an accomplishment that has earned Polk a place among the top ten or twelve presidents of the United States. He left the presidency in March 1849 and barely three months later, he died, leaving behind a legacy of energy and dogged determination that few others have matched. Among the least known but nonetheless important aspects of that legacy is his brief and sometime practice of law.

★ ★ ★

Millard Fillmore

Thirteenth President (1850–53)

BIRTH
January 7, 1800
Cayuga County, N.Y.

EDUCATION
Limited schooling
Studied law with Cayuga County Judge Walter Wood and
     Buffalo law firm of Rice and Clary
Admission to the bar: 1823

OTHER OCCUPATIONS/PUBLIC OFFICES
Schoolteacher
State legislator
U.S. congressman
Honorary chancellor of University of Buffalo
State comptroller
Vice president with Zachary Taylor

DEATH
March 8, 1874
Buffalo, N.Y.

LAW CAREER IN BRIEF

Fillmore's law career spanned twenty-five years (1823–47), beginning with a solo practice in East Aurora, New York, that centered on real estate and debt matters. Soon admitted to practice before the state supreme court, his business and reputation prospered, leading him to move to Buffalo and a succession of partnerships involving increasingly notable and lucrative cases, including those involving business failures occasioned by the depression. Known for his professionalism and his mentoring of young lawyers, Fillmore was admitted to practice before the U.S. Supreme Court but did not argue any cases there.

Millard Fillmore: Lawyer Mentor

ELBERT B. SMITH

Millard Fillmore's illustrious political career began with the admiration he inspired as a highly successful self-taught lawyer. Fillmore combined an extensive knowledge of law with a deep understanding of people. As lawyer, legislator, state comptroller, vice president, and president, he was noted for his ability to persuade others, mainly due to his thorough knowledge of facts. He was not a flamboyant orator but one who spoke in a deep voice that slowly and clearly drew people into the substance of his arguments.

Fillmore was born at the turn of the nineteenth century in Cayuga County, New York, in a wilderness cabin four miles from the nearest neighbor. His father was a hard-working but impoverished tenant farmer who had lost his own farm through a defective title. Heavy farm labor gave Millard a powerful physique, but left little time for schooling. At fourteen, he was apprenticed to a tyrannical miller, a relationship that ended when Fillmore, with ax in hand, resisted his mentor's threatened physical punishment. Apprenticed to another employer, he spent most of his teen years operating milling machines. When he was seventeen, however, neighbors organized a library. This encouraged Fillmore, who bought a dictionary and began reading books with his every spare moment. And when the village of New Hope established an academy, he enrolled during off-season at the mill. There, he met Abigail Powers, a clergyman's daughter, who encouraged his ambitions.

FILLMORE AS A YOUNG LAWYER

Ever mindful of his poverty-stricken youth, Fillmore stressed dignity and professionalism in appearance and practice. He also believed that people seeking counsel preferred lawyers who conveyed a sense of success and propriety.

FILLMORE'S FIRST LAW OFFICE

Initially declining an offer to work with a large Buffalo firm, Fillmore maintained a solo practice in this small East Aurora building for about ten years.

In 1819, Fillmore's father became the tenant of a wealthy county judge, who suggested that Millard become a part-time clerk in his law office. He eagerly accepted, but after two months of studying Blackstone, he prepared to return to the mill. The judge, who had rarely commented on Fillmore's efforts, surprised him by suggesting he continue clerking. "If thee has an ambition for distinction, and can sacrifice everything else to success, the law is the road that leads to honors," the judge noted, "and if thee can get rid of thy engagement to serve as an apprentice, I would advise thee to come back again and study law." The judge also offered to help Fillmore pay his way by tending to some of the judge's farm business. However, Fillmore soon became disillusioned with his new employer's harsh treatment of tenants. He also made the judge angry by pleading a case for which he received three dollars, and he quit rather than promise not to repeat the offense. He left owing the judge sixty-five dollars, which he eventually paid.

Soon afterward, the family moved to Aurora, eighteen miles from Buffalo, where Fillmore taught school and took a few minor law cases that won him a clerkship with a prominent law firm. He combined teaching with his clerkship, while studying every law treatise available. Within a year, several lawyers persuaded the court of common pleas to admit him to full-time practice. The usual period of training was seven years, but he had accomplished it in twenty-seven months. Although a prominent Buffalo firm offered him a partnership, he did not yet feel qualified. Instead, he opted for East Aurora, where he opened a small office—and married Abigail. He bought and read dozens of books while winning case after case, and he was soon made commissioner of deeds for the area. Within a year he was admitted to practice before the New York Supreme Court, and soon he joined an old friend as a law partner in Buffalo.

In Buffalo, he quickly became a leader. He helped found the Buffalo High School Association. He became vice president of the Lyceum, which sponsored lectures, conducted experiments in chemistry and physics, collected rocks and plants, maintained a library, and agitated for better schools. He gave the YMCA time, money, and numerous books. He and Abigail were charter members of Buffalo's first Unitarian Society, and he helped found the University of Buffalo (where, from 1842 until his death, he was honorary chancellor).

All of this added to his professional reputation and reflected the high public regard his legal career inspired. In 1830 he formed a prestigious law firm with Nathan Hall and Solomon G. Haven. It was a fascinating mixture of personalities. Haven "was the prince of trial lawyers," said a fellow attorney, "the most rarely endowed we have ever had among us." Hall was the quintessential office lawyer and counselor, who "had a delicate sense of justice and loved the principles of equity." Fillmore was the steadying influence of the three, the consummate professional whose common sense was as strong as his knowledge of the law.

The partners were involved in most of the area's important cases—and all were later elected to high office. Buffalo was then a boomtown because of its location on Lake Erie at the end of the Erie Canal, which connected the city to the Hudson River and the great port of New York. Men competed for land, harbor facilities, friendly tax assessments, business franchises, licenses, and other advantages, usually with borrowed money. Litigation was the order of the day, and the Fillmore firm prospered. One villain of the area was the Holland Land Company, from whom most of the settlers had bought their lands. In legal cases and in public meetings citizens charged that the company was restricting

"I learned more law than I had acquired during all the time I had been reading."

One of Fillmore's legal apprentices, describing Fillmore's weekly sessions with them

★ ★ ★

"If thee has an ambition for distinction, and can sacrifice everything else to success, the law is the road that leads to honors."

Judge Walter Wood

development while enjoying unfair tax privileges. An "Agrarian Convention of the Holland Purchase," in which Fillmore was a leader, demanded lower land prices, lower mortgage interest, and the revision of state tax laws.

Fillmore's law clerks, most of whom became distinguished lawyers, remembered their experiences with affection and gratitude. In many respects, Fillmore was continuing the teaching of his earlier years, this time instructing aspiring attorneys. One evening a week, the young clerks would sit in a half circle in front of Fillmore, who would launch into discussions on various subjects, often relating to books he had assigned them. Not all was serious, as Fillmore amused the students with anecdotes about individuals and legal matters, and he would introduce them to national leaders who might be visiting him.

Fillmore also taught by example. On one occasion, when two students argued over who should go to the post office and later sweep the stairs, the senior partner himself ostentatiously performed both duties and then called a conference, after which no such disputes recurred. Remembering his poverty-stricken youth, Fillmore stressed dignity and professionalism in appearance as well as in practice. He was always clean-shaven, well dressed, and neat in appearance. He believed that most people seeking legal assistance preferred lawyers who conveyed an impression of success and propriety, and he insisted that his law clerks follow his example. On at least one occasion he scolded two clerks for personal conduct that seemed undignified and unprofessional. One student later wrote that he learned more from this than in all his time reading law, adding that Fillmore was "tenderly alive to everything that would advance the interests of his students or improve them in their profession, morals or manly bearing."

All did not remain well in Buffalo, however. Nationally, speculation had led to panic, and banks refused to honor their currency. Even though this fed Fillmore's law practice—as out-of-town creditors retained him to handle claims against Buffalo clients, and he was involved in many of Buffalo's business failures—he was dismayed by these events. "Lawyers may perhaps make money in such times," he said, "but to them they are unpleasant when they see the ruin of business men from whom they derive their patronage."

In many ways, Fillmore's political career was a projection of his legal work. The same command of facts, independence of thought, and persuasive abilities that made him a successful attorney made him a highly effective leader at every political level. He studied every issue, reached his own conclusions, and wrote his own speeches. He was always a powerful advocate for the interests of his constituents and for his own principles. Pre–Civil War political campaigns were relatively inexpensive, and Fillmore's reputation for probity and independence was impeccable. Representing a country town that was rapidly becoming a large commercial city, he believed that the state and federal governments should promote a sound money and banking system; build roads, canals, bridges, harbor facilities, and other infrastructure; and provide at least minimal protective tariffs.

He was therefore first a National Republican and then a Whig. Elected to the state assembly in 1828, he helped his constituents get charters for turnpike companies, ferries, and banks. He sponsored branch canals that would connect with the Erie. He fought the state banking monopoly held by banks in New York City. He introduced a bill to abolish imprisonment for debt and persuaded the Democratic majority to support it by allowing them to take the credit. The bill also gave new businessmen a state bankruptcy law that enabled them to take greater investment risks and protected creditors by making fraudulent bankruptcy a crime. A Unitarian who believed firmly in the separation of church and state, Fillmore introduced an unsuccessful bill to eliminate the law that required trial witnesses to first swear to a belief in God and the hereafter. He also helped write the charter incorporating Buffalo and sponsored a bill that enabled Buffalo to spend extra money for wells, reservoirs, and fire engines.

Elected to Congress in 1832 despite the overwhelming Democratic reelection of Andrew Jackson, Fillmore immediately became a friend of Daniel Webster, who arranged his admission to practice law before the U.S. Supreme Court (though he never did so). By 1834 he was building the new Whig Party in western New York but did not run for reelection. He spent the next two years promoting laws that forced landlords to treat their tenants more fairly and in 1836 began the first of three more terms in Congress.

In 1840, he was runner-up in the voting for House Speaker and became chairman of the powerful Ways and Means Committee.

OXFORD OFFERS FILLMORE HONORARY DEGREE

Fillmore declined Oxford's offer of an honorary degree of Doctor of Civil Law. "I had not the advantage of a classical education and no man should, in my judgment, accept a degree he cannot read," said Fillmore.

*"Lawyers may per-
haps make money
in [hard economic]
times, but to them
they are unpleasant
when they see the
ruin of business
men from whom
they derive their
patronage."*

Millard Fillmore

The depression beginning in 1837 had left the government in desperate financial condition, and Fillmore pushed through a bill authorizing the president to borrow twelve million dollars. He then wrote a new tariff bill, which he defined as a revenue bill, and persuaded reluctant southerners to vote for it and the equally reluctant President Tyler to sign it. Looking for safeguards against improper expenditures, he prepared a lengthy digest of the laws authorizing each appropriation and persuaded Congress to pass a resolution requiring all departments to justify each request for money with a reference to the law or laws authorizing it, a practice that is still followed. By 1842 he had won a national reputation, but he and Abigail were tired of Washington, and to the chagrin of party leaders he declined to run for certain reelection.

In 1844, Whig leaders believed that a Fillmore candidacy for governor of New York would help their presidential candidate, Henry Clay, and despite Fillmore's objections, the state convention nominated him by acclamation. The entire Whig ticket was defeated, however, in part because Archbishop John Hughes quite unfairly branded Whigs as anti-Catholic. In 1847, Fillmore was elected state comptroller and wrote a banking code based on principles later incorporated in the national banking act and federal reserve system.

In 1848, the Whigs needed a presidential ticket acceptable to both North and South. General Zachary Taylor, the hero of the Mexican War, owned some 140 slaves, but he had opposed the annexation of Texas and did not advocate the expansion of slavery. Many northern "conscience" Whigs, led by New York's Thurlow Weed, were leaning toward the new Free-Soil Party, and to keep them voting Whig, the popular Fillmore, often on record against slavery, was nominated for vice president. Despite some initial intraparty opposition, the ticket succeeded in appealing to both North and South, due in part to Fillmore's efforts in getting Taylor to publicly disavow any intent to expand slavery.

In July 1850, Taylor suddenly died and Fillmore became president. He quickly appointed a distinguished cabinet headed by Daniel Webster as secretary of state. He also sought to heal divisions within his party, particularly concerning the expansion of slavery. As a Buffalo attorney, Fillmore had sympathized with fugitive slaves and had represented at least one without payment. He agonized for days before signing the Fugitive Slave Act, which was the only concession made to the South, while the North got a free state of California, a free territory of New Mexico, and removal of the slave trade from the District of Columbia. Throughout the South, angry election campaigns were raging between radical secessionists and unionists, and Fillmore feared correctly that a veto of the act would throw the elections to the secessionists. Webster had supported the act for the same reason. Signing the bill made Fillmore unpopular with the abolitionists and a number of later historians, but the moderates won the southern elections and the end of the crisis was welcomed by most Americans, both North and South, with parades and public celebrations.

In foreign policy, Fillmore understood and upheld the laws. When his secretaries of war and state promised naval protection to American ships ready to defy the claim of Peru to the guano-rich Lobos Islands, Fillmore cancelled their orders and announced that Americans who removed guano without the consent of Peru would do so at their own risk. When four hundred young Americans joined an expedition to take Cuba, Fillmore warned that they would be violating American laws and would get no protection. He ordered the navy to stop the expedition, but the invaders escaped and landed in Cuba only to be badly defeated. Fifty of them were executed, while one hundred sixty others were taken to Spain for penal servitude. Many

The Fugitive Slave Law of 1850

The original Fugitive Slave Act, passed in 1793, was largely ineffective because the responsibility for capturing slaves rested with the owners, and northern judges and legislation sometimes made such cases difficult to pursue. As part of the Compromise of 1850, Fillmore reluctantly signed the Fugitive Slave Act that placed enforcement responsibilities in the executive branch. Though these actions were widely criticized, at least one historian viewed Fillmore's decision positively, writing that "The compromise measures of 1850 . . . placed the preservation of the Union above any specific settlement of the slavery question."

Effects of the Fugitive-Slave-Law.

"God knows that I detest slavery, but it is an existing evil . . . and [we must] give it such protection as guaranteed by the constitution, till we can get rid of it."

Millard Fillmore

American newspapers and politicians demanded war, and a mob sacked a Spanish newspaper and wrecked the Spanish consulate in New Orleans. Ignoring the pressures and criticisms, Fillmore and Webster apologized to Spain and quietly negotiated the release of the prisoners in return for twenty-five thousand dollars in damages voted by the U.S. Congress.

A sitting president can usually guarantee his renomination by using his influence in the selection of delegates, but Fillmore did not wish a second term and made no effort to this end. However, when General Winfield Scott emerged as a front runner over Fillmore's choice, Daniel Webster, Fillmore entered the contest at the last minute because he knew that Scott's nomination would destroy the Whig Party in the South. He led the convention voting for forty-six ballots, but on the fifty-third ballot the exhausted delegates nominated Scott. The prosouthern Democrat Franklin Pierce won the election by a landslide, and the Whig Party disappeared as a national institution.

During his final weeks in office, Fillmore and Abigail made happy retirement plans, but at the Pierce inauguration, Abigail stood for hours in melting snow and died three weeks later from pneumonia. The devastated Fillmore grieved for more than a year and then suffered a second blow when his beloved twenty-two-year-old daughter also died. Desperately needing a diversion, he reentered politics.

The Kansas-Nebraska Act of 1854 had repealed the Missouri Compromise barrier against western slavery and had thereby created a new cause for northern Whigs, many of whom joined with Free-Soil Democrats to form a new Republican party against the expansion of slavery. Other Whigs, like Fillmore, believed that the expansion of slavery was already forbidden by geography and climate and feared that the election of an entirely northern Republican president would start a civil war. Hoping to rebuild a national party strong in both sections, they turned to the American, or Know-Nothing, Party. The Know-Nothings were aided greatly by the aggressive public statements of Archbishop John Hughes, who urged Catholics everywhere to help fulfill God's plan for a Catholic America.

The Know-Nothings nominated Fillmore for president while he was touring Europe. During the 1856 campaign he delivered twenty-seven speeches in which he ignored the sentiments of the

party and dwelt upon the terrible sectional war that would follow the election of the Republican candidate, John Fremont. "I have no hostility to foreigners," he told one audience. "Having witnessed their deplorable condition in the old country, God forbid that I should add to their sufferings by refusing them an asylum in this." Fillmore's nearly 30 percent of the vote prevented a Fremont presidency, which James Buchanan won with 39 percent.

It was his last campaign although he was only fifty-six years old. He married a wealthy fifty-two-year-old widow, and the couple generously gave of their time and money to many charities and causes. After the Battle of Fort Sumter, Fillmore organized a giant Union demonstration and then founded and led the "Union Continentals"—a group of men too old to enlist but ready to act in any local emergency—and later raised twenty-five thousand dollars for the Union cause. After the war he continued in his role of leading citizen until his death in March 1874.

Fillmore's career embodied American ideals more often preached than realized. Born in abject poverty, he became a successful attorney, public servant, and political leader entirely through his own abilities, hard work, and unselfish devotion to his clients, his constituents, and the American public. The fact that the war he avoided in 1850 occurred eleven years later does not diminish the value of his achievements.

Compromise of 1850

Legislative efforts to preserve the Union are depicted in this symbolic, though somewhat inaccurate, group portrait. Senators John Calhoun, Henry Clay, and Daniel Webster are among those featured in the depiction. Millard Fillmore is at the right, holding a shield.

★ ★ ★

Franklin Pierce

Fourteenth President (1853–57)

BIRTH
November 23, 1804
Hillsborough, N.H.

EDUCATION
Public school
Bowdoin College
Studied law with John Burnham, Levi Woodbury, Samuel Howe,
    and Edmund Parker in N.H. and Mass.
Admission to the bar: September 1827

OTHER OCCUPATIONS/PUBLIC OFFICES
State legislator
U.S. representative and senator
Brigadier general
President of state constitutional convention

DEATH
October 8, 1869
Concord, N.H.

LAW CAREER IN BRIEF

Though Pierce began practicing in Hillsborough in 1827, politics dominated the young lawyer's interests for many years. From 1841 to 1852, Pierce practiced law in earnest, gaining a reputation as the state's preeminent trial lawyer, an advocate whose eloquence "stirs and rules the heart and conquers the reason." Pierce was part of several successful partnerships—representing banks, railroads, and towns, as well as individuals in criminal and civil matters—and was involved in more than seventy-five appellate cases.

Franklin Pierce: Courtroom Orator

Christopher M. Johnson

Most historians rank Franklin Pierce among the least successful of American presidents. Serving at a time of increasing tension between the North and the South, he sought to calm the waters and preserve the Union by signing into law the Kansas-Nebraska Act of 1854. That law repealed the Missouri Compromise of 1820, which for decades had kept a semblance of sectional peace by specifying territories in which slavery might exist and those in which it could not, while the new law empowered settlers in any territory to decide the matter for themselves. Committed abolitionists and dedicated slavers responded by competing for power in the territories, and the resulting violence in Bleeding Kansas made John Brown famous while the guerilla warfare pitting Americans against Americans brought the nation closer to civil war.

Pierce fared no better in his efforts to unite the Democratic Party. Through his policies and appointments to federal office, Pierce sought to please the many factions of his splintering party. Instead, he succeeded in pleasing no one, and his party did not renominate Pierce for a second term. In 1852, at the young age of forty-eight, Pierce had won the presidency in a landslide—only Massachusetts, Vermont, Kentucky, and Tennessee

FRANKLIN PIERCE, U.S. ATTORNEY FOR THE DISTRICT OF NEW HAMPSHIRE

Three lawyer-presidents were involved in this 1845 appointment, under which Pierce was named a U.S. attorney by President James Polk and Secretary of State James Buchanan, each of whom affixed their signatures to the authorizing document.

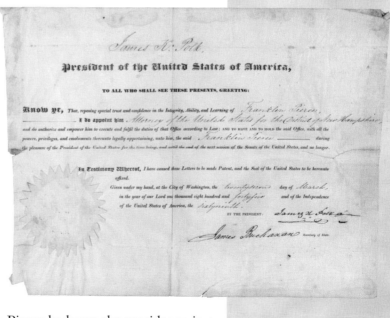

had opted for his opponent. Upon his retirement from the presidency in 1857, however, even his home state of New Hampshire regarded him as a failure.

Despite that sorry presidential record, Pierce was among the greatest trial lawyers to serve as president. Pierce was renowned in New Hampshire for his skills before a jury, and the New Hampshire of his day knew some extraordinary courtroom orators—Daniel Webster most famously. But Pierce (and others) discovered that the skills commanded by a great trial lawyer alone were insufficient to meet the demands of the nation's highest office.

Born in Hillsborough, New Hampshire, in 1804, Pierce was the son of a Revolutionary War brigadier general and New Hampshire governor. He studied at Bowdoin College, where he formed a lifelong friendship with fellow student and future novelist Nathaniel Hawthorne, who wrote a biography of Pierce for the presidential campaign of 1852. After graduating from Bowdoin, Pierce studied law with several lawyers in New Hampshire and Massachusetts before being called to the New Hampshire bar in 1827. Among those with whom Pierce studied was Levi Woodbury, who later served in the U.S. Senate and on the U.S. Supreme Court.

Pierce began to practice law in Hillsborough and, with his father's financial support, established his first office in a converted corner of an old horse shed. His attentions were quickly diverted by politics, however, as he soon added to the routine of a small-town lawyer the activities of a precociously successful politician. In 1828, the citizens of Hillsborough elected Pierce moderator of the town meeting. He held this post for six years, presiding over contentious disputes between "the friends of Mr. Jackson and those of Mr. Adams."

The spring term of the court of common pleas soon followed, but the young lawyer's first case "was a failure, and perhaps a somewhat marked one." When an older practitioner sought to console Pierce, the young advocate confidently replied, "I do not need that. I will try nine hundred and ninety-nine cases, if clients will continue to trust me, and if I fail, just as I have today, will try the thousandth." But Pierce's immediate future lay

New Hampshire Attorney Levi Woodbury

Woodbury was one of several lawyers with whom Pierce studied the law, and the most notable. Woodbury served his state in the U.S. House of Representatives and U.S. Senate before joining Andrew Jackson as secretary of the treasury during Jackson's crusade against the Bank of the United States. In 1845, James Polk appointed Woodbury to the U.S. Supreme Court, and while still on the Court, Woodbury unsuccessfully sought the 1848 presidential nomination. A second campaign for that high office was cut short by his death in 1851.

outside the courtroom. As Hawthorne noted, "The enticements of political life—so especially fascinating to a young lawyer, but so irregular in its tendencies, and so inimical to steady professional labor—had begun to operate upon him."

The citizens of Hillsborough sent Pierce to the state legislature in 1829, and in 1831 he was elected speaker of the New Hampshire House of Representatives. In 1832, Pierce moved to Washington, D.C., to serve in the U.S. Congress as one of his state's five representatives. There he remained until 1837, when he returned to New Hampshire to resume the practice of law. In November of that year, however, the state legislature made him U.S. senator, and he again suspended his law career to be the youngest member of a Senate that included such extraordinary political and oratorical talents as Daniel Webster, John C. Calhoun, and Henry Clay.

In 1841, at the behest of his wife, who hated Washington, Pierce resigned from the Senate and returned to New Hampshire and the practice of law, this time settling in the capital city of Concord. Although Pierce remained active in party politics during the next decade, the law became his principal activity until his election to the presidency in 1852. This period of practice was interrupted only in 1847 when Pierce volunteered to serve in the war with Mexico. After volunteering as a private, Pierce was commissioned a brigadier general and saw action. Otherwise, Pierce declined responsibilities outside New Hampshire, as when President Polk offered him the post of U.S. attorney general and when the New Hampshire legislature invited him to return to the U.S. Senate.

His practice of law between 1841 and 1852 was extensive and multifaceted. After moving to Concord, Pierce entered into partnerships with Asa Fowler, Josiah Minot, and others. The *New Hampshire Reports* contain more than seventy-five appellate cases in which Pierce's firms appeared and demonstrate the breadth of his legal practice. He represented banks, railroads, towns, criminal defendants, civil litigants, and others in cases raising almost every kind of dispute known to the mid-nineteenth-century law, including bankruptcies, wills, torts, contracts, property claims, and criminal cases, to name but a few. He even served as U.S. attorney for the district of New Hampshire, having been appointed to the post by President Polk in 1845.

"I will try nine hundred and ninety-nine cases, if clients will continue to trust me, and if I fail, just as I have today, will try the thousandth."

Franklin Pierce

"General Pierce was the quickest to get hold and understand a case . . . [and] was thoroughly posted in the law of evidence and procedure . . . I have never seen his equal as an advocate in New Hampshire."

Attorney Edward S. Cutter

Pierce never distinguished himself as a legal scholar. In his partnerships, it was Fowler or Minot who worked out the fine points of legal theory. But Pierce was a master of the rules of evidence, had an uncanny ability to read a witness, and, most important, possessed a personal grace and a winning eloquence that moved juries to adopt his view of the case. Said one observer, "Defending a man charged with murder, Pierce would weep out of pure sympathy, the jurors would weep with him, and after all this sentimentality there would probably be an acquittal." A New Hampshire lawyer, recalling Pierce's closing arguments in a libel case, said, "His argument in this case for ability, clear and beautiful illustration, apt quotations and pathos, has never been equaled in New Hampshire. It was the eloquence which stirs and rules the heart and conquers the reason."

Pierce also had the unique ability to influence a jury through facial expressions or telling glares of his opaque gray eyes. Trial lawyers know that such moments, though never noted in a transcript, can determine the outcome of a case. Pierce possessed the rare ability not merely to recognize such moments but to make them. Said one biographer, "People from all over New Hampshire fought for a place in his courtrooms, and he seldom disappointed them. Pierce had little interest in the drab bookwork of law, but he was a master at assessing a jury at a glance, then appealing to its most emotional—and least reasoning—aspects. He took high-profile cases regardless of whether the client was innocent, won frequently, and his fame spread."

Two largely forgotten cases illustrate the skill with which he practiced the art of persuasion. The first involves the Shakers, while the second was a murder case.

In 1848, agitation against the Shakers in New Hampshire led to proposed legislation by Asa Fowler, Pierce's former law partner, that would have prohibited "the binding of minor children to the Shakers, providing for the support of the wife and children of husbands joining that society and for the remuneration of persons leaving the same," among other provisions. The Shakers retained Pierce and two other distinguished lawyers to represent them in the legislative hearings. Pierce did not prevail in the House, but his evidentiary presentation and arguments produced a powerfully worded minority report, and the New Hampshire Senate unanimously voted to table the bill indefinitely.

"This victory, won by the courage and sagacity of Franklin Pierce and his clients, ended all attempts in this state to embarrass the Shakers by hostile legislation."

The second case began on March 26, 1845, in Manchester, New Hampshire, when a tax collector named Jonas Parker was brutally stabbed to death in a snowy patch of woods. Parker was a powerfully built man who carried large sums of money with him. Witnesses reported that a man, evidently known to Parker, had called for him at a tavern that night, after which Parker left with the man. A passerby had followed the two at a distance before turning off home, and heard Parker's screams as he was killed.

Five years passed before the investigating authorities brought three brothers—Horace, Asa, and Henry Wentworth—and William Clark to court. Asa and Henry Wentworth were sometime tavern keepers of questionable reputation, Clark was an itinerant oil cloth peddler, and Horace was a retail clerk. The evidence against them consisted principally of the testimony of persons as to statements made by the defendants admitting their guilt. Pierce and another lawyer were hired to represent Clark and Asa and Henry Wentworth. Benjamin Butler, later a Union general during the Civil War and a founder of the American Bar Association, represented Horace. On May 30, 1850, a preliminary hearing began to determine whether sufficient evidence existed to charge the men.

The newspaper transcript of the hearing indicates Pierce's skills as a lawyer (and reflects the more leisurely pace of nineteenth-century litigation). The newspaper reported, for example, that "Gen. Pierce objected to having the prosecuting counsel pointing out to the witness the points on which he should speak, with . . . notes in his hand as a prompter. It was against all usage in the Courts of this State. The speech of Gen. P. was a strong effort—equal to his best." Today, a lawyer who spoke at any length in support of such an objection would be quickly quieted.

However, a lawyer of any era would admire Pierce's cross-examination of Eliza Smith, a young woman who claimed, while working in the home of Asa Wentworth, to have seen the three Wentworth brothers the morning after the murder. According to Smith, Horace then appeared with a wounded hand while Henry wore bloody clothes and threatened her with Parker's fate, should she ever tell of the things she saw.

Pierce began gently enough by asking about her family situation, which revealed that Smith had borne two children under circumstances having a tenuous connection with her marriage, and that she soon abandoned the children with relatives. When Smith tried to mitigate her responses, Pierce compelled her to admit that her ambiguities were either lies or reflected a poor memory of the events. Having thus at a stroke proven the witness's dishonorable conduct as wife and mother, her falsehoods under oath, and her poor memory, Pierce proceeded to lead her into other inconsistencies and to admit she could not remember any other conversation she ever had with Asa.

Pierce's closing argument was predictably powerful. The judge dismissed the charges against Horace Wentworth and Clark, but bound over Asa and Henry Wentworth to the grand jury, which refused to indict the two men. Nobody was ever prosecuted for the Parker murder.

To further understand legal practice of that period and its influence upon Pierce, it is useful to know something of the courts in which he labored. At the time Pierce flourished, New Hampshire courts were just emerging from a period of extraordinary development. In 1767, only eight lawyers practiced in New Hampshire, and until 1800, most judges possessed no legal training. Appeals from decisions of trial courts were taken to the state legislature, formally known then and now as the "General Court." As a consequence, any litigant dissatisfied after trial could reverse the result by persuading a majority of legislators to vote that the litigant be "restored to his law." Because of that demoralizing circumstance, and because judges' pay was very low, few able lawyers of that period would serve as judges.

Progress toward making the judiciary independent of the legislature and staffing it with capable lawyers slowly advanced during the first decades of the 1800s. By 1830, the city of Concord, in which Pierce would soon practice, alone had eight lawyers. Still, the day was not long past when one New Hampshire judge instructed a jury as follows: "They [the lawyers] talk of law. Why, gentlemen, it is not law we want, but justice. They would govern us by the common law of England. Trust me, gentlemen, Common sense is a much safer guide for us—the common sense of Raymond, Epping, Exeter and the other towns which have sent us here to try this case

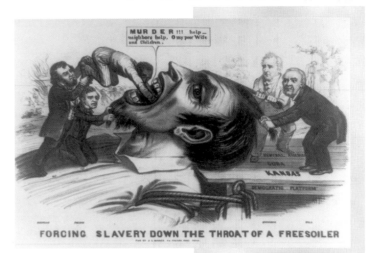

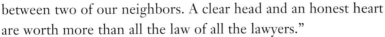

FORCING SLAVERY DOWN THE THROAT OF A FREESOILER

between two of our neighbors. A clear head and an honest heart are worth more than all the law of all the lawyers."

Such statements suggest how a lawyer like Pierce might tend toward conservatism and a rigid adherence to legal precedent, given that precedent had recently meant so little to nonlawyer judges and that litigants with legislative influence could evade the clearest commands of settled law. One can discern in Pierce's presidency an almost pathological commitment to unpopular and unsuccessful policies pursued because of their precedential standing. Pierce's support for the Kansas-Nebraska Act does not contradict this diagnosis, because he regarded the Missouri Compromise as unfaithful to an older principle of federal noninterference in a state's choice as to slavery.

Family factors and personal tragedies also influenced Pierce's thinking. His father served in the Continental army with General Washington for close to nine years, participating in such battles as Bunker Hill and in the hardships of Valley Forge. Knowing how dear a price was paid for independence, Benjamin Pierce valued as sacred the union of states it created. Indeed, young Franklin was raised to view preservation of the Union as the chief aim of the federal government.

That view of the role of government is as notable for what it does not include as for what it does. In Pierce's view, a government that exists chiefly to preserve the Union need not, and generally should not, concern itself with improving the Union. Accordingly, Pierce opposed proposals ranging from establishing the military academy at West Point to improving roads in western states.

THE KANSAS-NEBRASKA ACT CONTROVERSY

Pierce questioned the constitutionality of the Missouri Compromise. "Involuntary servitude," he said in his inaugural, "is recognized by the Constitution [and] stands like any other admitted right." The Kansas-Nebraska Act repealed the 1820 ban on slavery's expansion in the territories and replaced it with local choice. The result was "bleeding Kansas," questions about Pierce's intentions, and a tarnished presidential legacy.

"Involuntary servitude . . . is recognized by the Constitution [and] stands like any other admitted right."

Franklin Pierce

Pierce's view extended to the most important issue of his time—slavery. In his inaugural address, Pierce stated that "involuntary servitude . . . is recognized by the Constitution [and] stands like any other admitted right." Pierce despised the abolitionist movement, for he saw it as endangering the Union by promoting federal interference in the purely domestic affairs of the southern states. This view distinguished Pierce from Abraham Lincoln, another lawyer-president whom in some respects Pierce resembled. One historian offered this comparison of the two men: "Pierce was oversentimental and emotional while Lincoln, the equal of Pierce in tolerance and loving kindness, had within him a certain balancing coolness and logic that Pierce lacked. . . . [Lincoln] had also courage where Pierce was fearful, strength where Pierce had weakness. Above all, it is to be said that Pierce never saw the moral blackness of slavery, while Lincoln could never forget it."

Personal struggles and tragedies also laced Pierce's adult life and undoubtedly affected his presidency. First, there was his life-long struggle with alcoholism. Probably of greater debilitating importance, though, were a series of family tragedies. In 1834, Pierce married Jane Means Appleton, an exceptionally devout Christian with a tendency to poor health. Their first child, Franklin Jr., died three days after his birth in 1836. A second child, Frank Robert, died at age four. Their third and last child, Benjamin, was eleven years old when his father was elected president. Both Pierces doted on their only surviving child.

Early in 1853, after Pierce's election but before he took office, Benjamin accompanied his parents on a journey to Boston, where they visited with relatives and Pierce consulted with leaders as he prepared for his presidency. During the return journey to Concord, their train derailed, causing young Benjamin to be crushed before his parents' eyes. He died in their arms.

Mrs. Pierce never recovered from the tragedy. During the rest of her life, she wrote letters addressed to her deceased son. And Franklin Pierce was never afterwards the man he had been. Pierce took on the responsibilities of the presidency burdened not only with this terrible loss but by his devout wife's belief that God "had taken their boy so that Pierce might have no distraction, caused by his preoccupation in the child's welfare, to interfere with his attention to the great responsibilities which were to be his."

Pierce did not resume the practice of law after his presidency, and he and his politics grew ever more unpopular during the Civil War, as he became a harsh critic of President Lincoln's conduct. In his last years, Pierce's "propensity for alcohol overcame him," and he died in 1869.

Several circumstances make remembrance of Franklin Pierce particularly timely in 2004. The two-hundredth anniversary of his birth coincided with a presidential campaign that included the important New Hampshire primary and featured would-be lawyer-presidents seeking the nomination of Pierce's Democratic Party. In addition, President George W. Bush has a connection with Pierce, as Bush's mother Barbara is a distant relation. It is unlikely, however, that these leaders will seek lessons from the life and presidency of Pierce, a great trial lawyer but failed president who could not effectively confront the great issue of his day.

ONE-TERM PRESIDENT

Though Pierce aspired to another term, his own party repudiated him in favor of James Buchanan. Pierce never returned to the practice of law, passing his remaining years in relative obscurity.

★ ★ ★

James Buchanan

Fifteenth President (1857–61)

BIRTH
April 23, 1791
Cove Gap, Pa.

EDUCATION
Old Stone Academy
Dickinson College
Studied law in Lancaster with James Hopkins
Admission to the bar: November 17, 1812

OTHER OCCUPATIONS/PUBLIC OFFICES
State legislator
U.S. representative and senator
Minister to Russia and Great Britain
Secretary of state with James Polk

DEATH
June 1, 1868
Lancaster, Pa.

LAW CAREER IN BRIEF

Buchanan once described his years of law practice (1813–29) as "extensive, laborious and lucrative." Indeed, Buchanan handled all areas of general law and became counsel to several corporations as well, earning himself the considerable sum of $11,300 in 1821 before he left for the U.S. Congress. Buchanan gained prominence as a skilled constitutional lawyer, defending several judges against impeachment charges and, in Congress, defending the U.S. Supreme Court's power to review state court rulings. He handled more than one hundred cases before Pennsylvania's state supreme court and, though admitted to the U.S. Supreme Court bar, never practiced before that tribunal. He also had several opportunities to pursue a seat on the U.S. Supreme Court but declined to do so.

James Buchanan: Strict Constructionist

JEAN H. BAKER

I will follow the Constitution and the Laws," promised President-elect James Buchanan when he took office on March 4, 1857. But four years later, when he retired from the presidency, the Union he had intended to preserve was in shreds. Seven southern states had seceded and formed the Confederate States of America. War, a possibility when Buchanan took office, was a probability by March 1861. Yet from his own lawyerly perspective on national affairs, Buchanan believed he had kept the promise that grew out of his deep respect for the law and its application in the U.S. Constitution.

Of all America's lawyer-presidents, James Buchanan was perhaps the one most affected by his profession. Born in 1791, two years after George Washington was inaugurated as the nation's first president, Buchanan was to become America's eleventh lawyer-president and fifteenth president. Influenced by an ambitious and increasingly prosperous father of Scotch-Irish heritage, Buchanan was educated in a local academy in the small town of Mercersburg, in southern Pennsylvania. His father encouraged him to go to Dickinson College in nearby Carlisle, and after graduation in 1809 he secured an apprenticeship in a busy office with an established lawyer, James Hopkins. With only three law schools in the country, most lawyers in this period read the law while serving as unpaid versions of twentieth-century paralegals.

Hopkins was the preeminent lawyer in Lancaster, a small town in southern Pennsylvania that until 1814 was the state capital and hence the ideal place for a young lawyer to find clients. Here, Buchanan also met the state's political leaders. As Hopkins's clerk and student, Buchanan read and discussed the basic texts of Chitty and Blackstone, the constitutions of the United States and Pennsylvania, and the ever-growing statute law that

★ ★ ★

"The change from law to politics and from politics to law makes both pursuits very laborious. A man cannot do himself justice at either."

James Buchanan, writing to Andrew Jackson

★ ★ ★

"If you persist in the study of law you serve under my absolute control and if you become inattentive you shall seek another preceptor."

James Buchanan to an apprentice applicant

interpreted and applied the abstract principles of these charters of government. Buchanan also attended trials with Hopkins, and the citizens of Lancaster grew accustomed to the younger man walking about town, talking out loud as he transposed the principles he read into oral arguments—in his words, "fixing them into my memory." Later, Buchanan acknowledged that this process gave him confidence to give spontaneous political speeches.

After he registered with a notary public and passed the informal exam directed by a committee of the Pennsylvania court, twenty-year-old Buchanan was accepted into the state's bar in November 1812. Soon he had a successful practice and even some of his own apprentices, whom he told to give up "dissipations" and "serve under my absolute control." If they disobeyed, wrote Buchanan, "you shall seek another preceptor."

Some of Lancaster's twenty-six lawyers scavenged for clients, but not Buchanan. The second year of his practice he earned less than $1,000, but by 1818 his income was $7,915. In 1821, the year he left Lancaster for Washington as a congressman, he earned a substantial $11,297. It was hard work, but he was a conscientious lawyer. Buchanan once described a practice that took him into several counties adjacent to Lancaster as "extensive, laborious and lucrative and always increasing."

His cases covered all areas of general law—from writing contracts and wills, to arguing *ad litem* cases for orphans, to litigating property claims and land disputes that were at the center of much early American law. In 1821, he also handled several prominent local murder cases. That January, he successfully defended a group of men against manslaughter charges and in May "scored one of his greatest courtroom triumphs" in defending William Hamilton in the murder trial of Ann Piersol.

In time he also became counsel for several corporations. His practice focused almost exclusively on the state courts; he was reported as counsel in 108 cases that reached the state supreme court. To all, he applied a style that one lawyer described as "marching directly to the point he aimed at, ever keeping it in view and never leaving his hearers to suppose he has lost sight of it."

Even as a neophyte, Buchanan took ambitious cases that brought prominence, more clients, and larger fees that made him, before he was thirty-five, one of the best-known lawyers in southern Pennsylvania. At age twenty-four, with only three years' experience as a lawyer, Buchanan had defended Judge Walter Franklin in the latter's impeachment before the Pennsylvania state senate. In a classic case of national authority versus states' rights, Franklin had ruled that once a militia was nationalized, Pennsylvania's authority to fine a refusant ended. At a time in American history when the distinction between judicial error and impeachable offense sometimes disappeared into party prejudice, Franklin had been impeached. Buchanan successfully argued in the ensuing trial that Judge Franklin had committed no crime; he had only made an unpopular ruling.

Lancaster remained Buchanan's home throughout his life, though he never married. In 1848 he bought Wheatland, a large brick home with twenty-two acres just outside the city. Here his niece Harriet Lane, who served as his first lady, lived, as did one of his nephews who was orphaned at an early age. Lonely and yet at the same time often aloof, Buchanan divided his time before his presidency between Washington where he boarded and Lancaster, his permanent home.

Interestingly, his bachelorhood and Wheatland home had links to one of his better-known cases, which involved complex title issues surrounding the Columbia Bridge Company. During this time, Buchanan had gotten engaged to the lovely Ann Coleman, daughter of one of the richest men in the country. The Columbia Bridge case and some pressing political issues commanded Buchanan's time and attention for several months, however, leaving Ann to question his devotion to her. When Buchanan called upon one of his Columbia Bridge clients, William Jenkins, he also encountered Jenkins's charming young sister-in-law, who was visiting at the time. When gossip about this encounter got back to Ann, she broke off the engagement (and suddenly died soon afterward, prompting Buchanan to vow never to marry). Buchanan went on to secure a settlement of the legal case and several years later, William Jenkins built Wheatland, which was to become Buchanan's home.

Judge James Peck's Impeachment Prosecution

While chairman of the House Judiciary Committee in 1830, Buchanan prosecuted Missouri Judge James Peck, who had sentenced lawyer Luke Lawless to prison and suspended his law license after Lawless criticized one of Peck's decisions in a newspaper article. In the impeachment proceedings, Buchanan successfully argued that "there was criminal intention" by Peck as well as "judicial usurpation and tyranny." The Senate subsequently acquitted Peck for violations of the U.S. Constitution and abuse of judicial authority, but Congress then passed a statute that limited judicial contempt of court powers.

HIGH COURT REVIEW OF STATE COURT RULINGS

When Congress sought to repeal Section 25 of the Judiciary Act, which gave the U.S. Supreme Court powers to review and reverse certain decisions of the highest state courts, Buchanan drafted the committee minority report opposing the bill. His arguments ultimately carried the day, as the bill was defeated in the full House by a 135 to 51 vote. The report earned Buchanan many admirers and enhanced his reputation as a "well-instructed constitutional jurist."

Though his father had advised him that eminence at the bar was "preferable to being partly a politician and partly a lawyer," like other lawyer-presidents Buchanan used his legal background as a launching pad for his political career. After two years in the Pennsylvania Assembly, James Buchanan ran as a Federalist for Congress. So began his long ascent to the presidency. In 1821 he began the first of five terms in the U.S. Congress, and by the time he declined to run again in 1831, he had become a member of Andrew Jackson's new Democratic Party. After his appointment as minister to St. Petersburg, Buchanan returned to the United States and was elected three times by the Pennsylvania legislature to the U.S. Senate, where he served from 1834 to 1845.

As a senator and congressman, Buchanan's legal training served him well. He was accustomed to detailed, precise arguments based on evidence. Some of his colleagues described his lengthy speeches on topics such as the United States Bank (which he opposed) as classically legal in that they laid out the controversy, examined the evidence, took a position, and then rebutted the opposition. He was seldom witty or ironic. But mirroring his closing arguments in the local courtrooms of southern Pennsylvania, Buchanan usually finished his speeches with some boilerplate rhetoric to convince the jury, in this instance his fellow congressmen, of his case.

Given his attachment to the Democratic Party— the party that stood for a light and simple government— Buchanan was what this generation called "a strict constitutionalist." For example, he found nothing in the U.S. Constitution about the authority of the government to create a national bank and so opposed one, as did most Jacksonian

Democrats. Nor did he accept high tariffs, although this was often a difficult issue for a Pennsylvania representative, given the state's iron industry.

In time, Buchanan's dedication to the law was rewarded with a seat on, and eventually chairmanship of, the House Judiciary Committee. In this capacity Buchanan argued against the repeal of the Twenty-fifth Section of the 1789 Judiciary Act, which established appellate jurisdiction of the U.S. Supreme Court over various cases originating in state courts. Buchanan opposed restricting the federal judicial power to the limited number of cases that originated in federal court. He successfully argued, contrary to the views of most members of his committee, that the beneficial uniformity established by a national court would be lost and that there must be an authority higher than that of the sovereign states. This not only reinforced a critical role for the high court but enhanced Buchanan's reputation as a "well-instructed constitutional jurist."

In 1845, President Polk chose James Buchanan to be his secretary of state. Buchanan would have preferred to be president, for his ambitions had by this time reached the highest level. Later, he vacillated between Polk's offer of a seat on the U.S. Supreme Court or a position in the cabinet, eventually choosing the latter. Perhaps he was following a friend's advice that he would "find the field open for the Presidency unless you place yourself on the shelf by accepting the judgeship."

Now he continued his education in international law, begun twelve years earlier when he had been minister to Russia. Then he had negotiated a complex commercial treaty; in 1845 he found his legal training appropriate as he presided over a tremendous expansion in the size of the United States. As secretary of state he negotiated treaties, especially those with the British relating to Oregon. He enthusiastically supported the Mexican-American War but argued over the size of the American indemnity from Mexico. Then in 1853, after another failed effort to become president, Franklin Pierce appointed him minister to Great Britain, where he served from 1853 to 1856.

When James Buchanan returned to the United States in 1856, many Democrats considered him their strongest candidate, a man who had experience in government and who might be able to quiet the stormy waters of sectionalism. In the political

★ ★ ★

"There was a combination of physical and intellectual qualities that made him a powerful advocate."

A Lancaster judge's description of Buchanan

DRED SCOTT DECISION

Dred Scott had filed a series of suits seeking freedom for him and his slave family, alleging that such emancipation resulted from the time they had spent in free territory. In 1857, the U.S. Supreme Court finally decided the case. In a decision that hastened civil war, Chief Justice Roger Taney wrote that slaves had no rights as citizens under the U.S. Constitution, that residence in a free state did not automatically make them free, and that the Missouri Compromise's ban on slavery in the territories was unconstitutional. Buchanan was said to have "improperly intervened" in the case, encouraging a northern justice to support the Court's decision.

style of the times, he did not campaign. But he did make clear through his letters that his highest priority was to stop all agitation over the slavery question and to enforce the despised fugitive slave laws that permitted southerners to track and legally return slaves to their owners. Buchanan believed such disturbances the fault of the North and most particularly of abolitionist "fanatics" who meddled in a domestic institution protected by the U.S. Constitution.

There were three contenders in this time of partisan change—Buchanan, the Know-Nothing Millard Fillmore, and the Republican

John Fremont. Buchanan easily carried the electoral college, but he received only 45 percent of the popular vote, mostly from the South. After the election, when he sent his cabinet choices to the Senate for confirmation, some northerners were shocked that a majority were southerners, appointments that testified to his sectional bias. Of seven Buchanan cabinet officers, four were from slaveholding states and one was a Doughface like Buchanan—that is, a northern man with southern principles.

As the fifteenth president of the United States, the sixty-five-year-old Buchanan was hardly inaugurated before he was embroiled in a dispute over slavery in Kansas. He had always opposed slavery—indeed, he quietly bought slaves in Washington, D.C., and then set them free in Pennsylvania—but he believed the Constitution had established it as legally untouchable except by southern states. In his inaugural address, he condemned agitation over slavery while supporting "popular sovereignty" in the territories, a system by which before statehood the male residents in political subdivisions decided for themselves whether their community would have slavery.

Buchanan already knew that the U.S. Supreme Court had decided the case of Dred Scott. This controversial decision declared slaves property and repealed a traditional congressional barrier to the advancement of slavery. As property, slaves could be taken everywhere, and the Missouri Compromise line that prohibited slavery north of the 36/30 parallel was now null and void.

One result of his legal training was that Buchanan was a stanch believer in the legitimacy of the courts. Hence in his view the decision announced by fellow Dickinson College graduate and Supreme Court Chief Justice Roger Taney to all intents and purposes should have ended the American slave controversy. This was "a judicial question that belongs to the Supreme Court," Buchanan argued, though his position put Buchanan at odds with the growing number of Republicans who stood for no expansion of slavery into the territories.

Throughout his administration, Buchanan was ineffective in accomplishing what he most wanted to do—preserve the Union. By the spring of 1858, Kansas had erupted, with two governments in place—one in Lecompton run by the proslavery contingent and the other that of the free-state majority in Topeka. Accustomed to fraud and the incursions of illegal voters from

★ ★ ★

"To all [cases], he applied a style that one lawyer described as 'marching directly to the point he aimed at, ever keeping it in view and never leaving his hearers to suppose he has lost sight of it.'"

★ ★ ★

"You will find the field open for the Presidency unless you place yourself on the shelf by accepting the judgeship."

William R. King, discouraging Buchanan from pursuing President Polk's offer of a Supreme Court seat

Missouri, the free-state voters boycotted the elections and established their own territorial government. When the proslavery faction refused to present their charter in a statewide referendum they knew they would lose, the free-state majority boycotted the vote and wrote their own state constitution. But a stubborn Buchanan stuck by the so-called Lecompton constitution, holding against the majority in Kansas because in his legalistic view, it was the officially authorized document.

In a great presidential blunder, Buchanan tried unsuccessfully to bully the Lecompton constitution through Congress. In the process, he was condemned by many northern Democrats and split the Democratic Party, a faction of which led by Stephen Douglas supported the Topeka convention. And when the process of turning Kansas into a state was slowed and it became obvious that Kansas would not become a slave state, southerners were angry as well.

There were other controversies during his four-year term, among them his decision to send troops to the Utah territory where Brigham Young's government was defying U.S. officials. In an age in which the government did not intervene in financial panics and depressions, Buchanan did nothing when the New York Stock Exchange collapsed and the Panic of 1857 swept across the nation, bringing unemployment and economic distress especially in the more industrial and urbanized North. The president also had to contend with the treacherous behavior of his cabinet officers and others whom a congressional committee found had diverted government funds to Democratic candidates and provided kickbacks and bribes on public contracts. While there was little suspicion that Buchanan himself was involved, his administration was widely considered corrupt.

But such matters seemed unimportant compared to the great crisis developing between the North and the South. Buchanan had already announced that he would seek only one term, and having lost some leverage with that pronouncement, he lost more when in 1860, mostly as a result of his Kansas policy, the party he had served so loyally for thirty years could not agree on a platform or a candidate. Two Democrats—Stephen Douglas of Illinois and John Breckinridge of Kentucky, who had been Buchanan's vice president—ran in November 1860 against John Bell of the newly formed Constitutionalist Union Party and

Abraham Lincoln of the Republicans. As Buchanan had four years before, Lincoln swept the electoral college, carrying all the northern states. But Lincoln did not receive a majority of the popular vote. Ominously, southerners announced that they would secede from the Union if Lincoln were elected. And so they did, beginning with South Carolina and continuing with states from the lower South, such that by the time Buchanan left office, the Confederacy included seven states.

Buchanan now faced the greatest American crisis since the founding of the Republic. In his annual message to Congress in December 1860, he vowed to follow the law, according to his interpretation of it. Secession, he held, was illegal; that was obvious in reasoning he based on the preamble of the U.S. Constitution and on the legal principle that no government establishes the means of its own destruction in its fundamental law.

But, said the president, he could do nothing about secession because "the power to make war against a state is at variance with the whole spirit and intent of the Constitution." Without congressional authorization, he could not call up the militia, despite precedents in the administrations of George Washington and Andrew Jackson. And as for the coastal forts being taken over by southerners, he could not reinforce them. Meanwhile his cabinet, some of whom were in touch with what were now enemy governments, encouraged him to follow prosouthern policies.

Then, in a significant reversal of his position due in part to a change of cabinet officers (when southerners left Washington to prepare for war against the federal government and were replaced by northerners), Buchanan ordered the resupplying of Fort Sumter in January 1861. The attempt was unsuccessful, and Buchanan did little more in the six weeks remaining in his administration than to wait for his successor Abraham Lincoln to take office.

On inauguration day Buchanan told Lincoln that he hoped the incoming president was as happy in becoming president as he was to be leaving that office. Now an old man who had aged during an administration of continual turmoil, Buchanan lived for seven more years. In Lancaster, his time was spent writing a justification of his administration, which changed few minds.

In the end, James Buchanan was too bound by the letter of the law, and too little able to accept broader interpretations of constitutional principles. Indeed, many thought "Buchanan used the Constitution as a device to shield his ineptness."

To Buchanan, however, what was necessary and proper never displaced the importance of specific and enumerated powers, without which he did nothing. Ever attached to his reading of the U.S. Constitution, the legalistic Buchanan had failed in his stated presidential goal "to arrest, if possible, the agitation of the slavery question at the North, and to destroy sectional parties."

Lawyer Lincoln

Abraham Lincoln

Sixteenth President (1861–65)

BIRTH
February 12, 1809
Hardin County, Ky.

EDUCATION
Limited schooling; primarily self-educated
Admission to the bar: September 9, 1836

OTHER OCCUPATIONS/PUBLIC OFFICES
Boat operator
Store owner
Postmaster
Captain in Black Hawk War
State legislator
U.S. congressman

DEATH
April 15, 1865
Washington, D.C.

LAW CAREER IN BRIEF

Lincoln's law career spanned almost twenty-five years (1837–60), three law partnerships, and more than five thousand cases. His practice began inauspiciously, as he handled mostly simple debt and property cases. Despite Lincoln's declaration that "I am not an accomplished lawyer," by the time he ran for president, he was also representing railroads and other business interests, had argued frequently before the Illinois Supreme Court, and had appeared once before the U.S. Supreme Court (where he was involved in at least five other cases). More than any other lawyer-president, Lincoln's prepresidential years were spent in active law practice, and these experiences were reflected time and again in his presidency.

Abraham Lincoln: Prairie Lawyer

PAUL FINKELMAN

Abraham Lincoln is, by any popular measure, our greatest president. Whenever presidents are ranked, Lincoln comes out on top. Indeed, his job was the hardest of any president, leading the nation through four years of civil war. And he accomplished it so stunningly well: winning the war, preserving the Union, and ending slavery. Lincoln's place in history rests in large part on this latter role as the Great Emancipator. With a stroke of his pen he brought liberty to some four million slaves and, despite some modern critics, he was the greatest friend of civil rights to sit in the White House, at least before Lyndon Johnson. The sudden end to his life only enhanced his reputation, making him more tragic and heroic.

While many remember him as a great politician and leader, few are familiar with Lincoln's years as a "prairie lawyer." Lincoln is unique among our lawyer-presidents in the extent and prominence of his legal practice prior to his years in the White House. During his first few years of law practice, Lincoln served in the Illinois legislature. Otherwise, except for a brief stint in the U.S. Congress, the practice of law was Lincoln's only form of employment from his admission to the bar in 1836 until he became president in 1861.

He was perhaps the only president to practice immediately before running for the office and to handle cases after receiving his party's nomination. Barely a month after the Republicans nominated him, Lincoln appeared in a federal court case, filed notices and pleadings

in another case, and appeared in one of his last cases, a patent infringement suit. While presidential campaigning did not then involve speeches or trips, Lincoln's continued attention to his law practice reflects his commitment to the law as a profession and a source of income.

Lincoln's legal career is also deeply embedded in our popular culture. "Honest Abe" is viewed as the honest lawyer and conscientious advocate. Until the *Amistad* film portrayed John Quincy Adams's role in that famous case, Lincoln was probably the only president to have a movie made about his legal career. In *Young Mr. Lincoln*, Henry Fonda portrayed Lincoln as a brilliant lawyer who defended the poor, the downtrodden, and the falsely accused. Loosely based on the famous "Almanac Trial," which actually occurred late in Lincoln's career, the film was largely fictitious. In cinema at least, Lincoln was the lawyer-hero who became the heroic president.

Lincoln was born in 1809 and grew up in near-poverty, traveling with his family from Kentucky to Indiana before settling in Illinois. His father Thomas had early problems with the law, losing part of a Kentucky farm due to flaws in its title and becoming enmeshed in litigation regarding several other farm properties.

Young Abe was about eighteen when he too encountered a legal challenge regarding his operation of a ferryboat. His successful defense in the case prompted encouragement from the justice of the peace, who suggested that Lincoln "read up a bit on the law." Lincoln did so, eagerly digesting the dry contents of the *Revised Laws of Indiana*. "The more I read," said Lincoln, "the more intensely interested I became. Never in my whole life was my mind so thoroughly absorbed."

Lincoln was twenty-two when he began helping friends and neighbors in New Salem, Illinois, prepare legal documents. In the next five years, he would serve briefly in the Black Hawk War, lose a race for the Illinois House of Representatives, be sued in connection with the failure of his general store, and be elected twice to the Illinois House. Throughout this period he studied law, finally gaining admission to the bar in September of 1836. Though he lost his first case a month later, he would continue practicing law until June 1860, becoming one of the premier lawyers in the state. While never achieving great wealth,

STOVEPIPE HAT

While Lincoln's briefs were well organized—in fact he excelled at legal draftsmanship—that was not always the case with his office habits. One example was the use of his signature stovepipe hat to file away papers and notes. In apologizing to a fellow lawyer for not responding to a letter, he explained that "when I received the letter, I put it in my old hat and buying a new one the next day, the old one was set aside, and so the letter was lost sight of for a time."

Lincoln's practice brought him solidly into the upper middle class, very far from his log cabin days in Hardin County, Kentucky, and his hardscrabble, impoverished youth in Indiana. As it has for many others, it also provided Lincoln an effective complement to his political ambitions.

During his legal career, Lincoln was involved in three partnerships. In 1837 he was junior partner to John Todd Stuart. When Stuart left Springfield to serve in the U.S. Congress in late 1839, the firm essentially became a solo practice, and in April of 1841, the partnership was formally dissolved.

Within several weeks, the firm of Logan and Lincoln announced its presence in Springfield. Like Lincoln a Kentucky native, Stephen T. Logan had moved to Illinois after practicing law in his home state. A skilled attorney with far more experience than Lincoln, Logan proved to be an important mentor, as Lincoln learned to prepare his cases more carefully. Lincoln's income rose to about fifteen hundred dollars a year during this period and his reputation rose as well as he took about sixty cases to the Illinois Supreme Court. This relationship lasted until December of 1844 when Logan entered into a partnership with his adult son. The breakup was apparently amicable, and by this time, Lincoln was ready to assume the role of a senior partner in any event.

Soon, Lincoln took on William H. Herndon as his new partner. Although in theory it was an equal partnership, Herndon was clearly the junior member of the team. In the next sixteen years, Lincoln and Herndon would become one of the most important firms in Illinois, the partnership ending only when Lincoln left Springfield for the presidency.

The Lincoln Legal Papers project has identified more than fifty-one hundred cases in which a Lincoln partnership was involved. It is impossible to know how many of these he personally handled, though he seems to have played a part in most of them. Also, we will never know the full extent of Lincoln's practice because of the loss of records caused by the great Chicago fire of 1871, other catastrophes, and the vagaries of time.

We do know that Lincoln's practice was typical of the era. He began by representing clients in a seemingly endless stream of minor cases (legally and financially), mainly involving contract, debt, and property disputes. Most of his criminal cases were also run-of-the-mill, though he represented accused murderers in

"The framework of his mental and moral being was honesty, and a wrong case was poorly defended by him."

Judge David Davis

LINCOLN THE TRIAL LAWYER

Lincoln was an effective trial advocate who had the ability to get to the heart of issues and to convey his arguments in home-spun language that jurors could appreciate and understand. Lincoln also was a skilled appellate lawyer who had one of the largest caseloads before the Illinois Supreme Court.

some twenty-seven cases. In addition to his practice in Sangamon County, he "rode circuit," traveling with judges and other lawyers to courts in the state's eighth judicial district. His major caseload—comprising about two-thirds of his total practice—involved debt-related issues, with family law actions constituting the next most frequent type of case.

By the time Lincoln moved to Washington, D.C., to serve in Congress, he was representing major business interests and earning substantial fees. This later included such regular clients as the Illinois Central Railroad, which he represented in fifty-seven cases over an eight-year period starting in 1853. Ironically, Lincoln was forced to sue the railroad to obtain his fee—a hefty five thousand dollars—but this apparently did not cause a serious breach with the railroad, which continued to retain him. He also represented six other railroads in a total of twenty-four cases. Not simply "railroad lawyers," he and his partners also opposed railroads in sixty-two cases.

Such statistics suggest but the outlines of the legal career that saw Lincoln evolve into a capable office lawyer as well as a skilled trial and appellate lawyer who had one of the largest caseloads before the Illinois Supreme Court. While serving in Congress, Lincoln even appeared once before the U.S. Supreme Court and was associated with at least five other high court cases.

Stories and reminiscences suggest that Lincoln was an effective courtroom lawyer, with a fine sense of humor and an intuitive sense of how to persuade a jury. Some stories are clearly apocryphal, while others may well have been created out of whole cloth. But given time to prepare his case, most agree that Lincoln was a skillful advocate whose sense of timing, legal knowledge, down-home explanations, and engaging personality often won the day.

This is not to say he was either the quintessential advocate or one who shunned the use of legal procedure to serve the needs of his clientele. Lincoln could, in the words of historian Robert Bruce, "split hairs as well as rails." In addition, Lincoln's awkward features and style often disarmed and fooled opponents, who would discover too late that their arguments had been undone.

Yet others have questioned Lincoln's legal ability, especially in pursuing cases with equal fervor and effectiveness. Wrote one fellow attorney, "He was strong if convinced he was in the right, but if he suspected he might be wrong he was the weakest lawyer I ever saw." Judge David Davis, with whom Lincoln rode circuit and whom he appointed to the U.S. Supreme Court, agreed: "The framework of his mental and moral being was honesty, and a wrong case was poorly defended by him." Perhaps his partner, William Herndon, best summed up Lincoln's legal career when he described him as "at the same time a very great and very insignificant lawyer."

Whatever one's view of his legal talents, they no doubt had a major effect on his political life and presidency. Whether representing the downtrodden, handling a minor dispute, or advocating the cause of railroads, land speculators, and businessmen, Lincoln learned much during those years about the law, issues of the day, human nature, problem-solving, advocacy, and negotiations. His knowledge and skills, and particularly his lawyerly way of addressing issues, were repeatedly reflected in his presidency and helped him succeed during America's greatest crisis.

Few issues are more prominently associated with Lincoln than his views and actions regarding emancipation of the slaves. While such cases comprised but three-tenths of 1 percent of his total caseload, they provide a glimpse of Lincoln the lawyer and president, and the complexities inherent in each of these roles. Moreover, the evolution of his attitudes toward slavery may well reflect the influence and evolution of his legal career.

Given that Lincoln was born in a slave state and raised in states that prohibited blacks from testifying in court against whites, gave them no political rights, and rarely offered them access to the public schools, it should not be a surprise that his early racial attitudes were reflective of his surroundings.

The first clear indication of Lincoln's attitude toward slavery occurred in 1837, when at age twenty-eight, he was among the few members of the Illinois legislature to vote against a resolution declaring the right to own slaves "sacred to the slaveholding States." Not only did Lincoln vote against this resolution, he joined another legislator

THE EMANCIPATION PROCLAMATION: A LEGALLY DUBIOUS ACT?

In *Lincoln as a Lawyer*, John Frank describes the proclamation, along with Jefferson's Louisiana Purchase and FDR's exchange of destroyers with Great Britain, as "legally dubious acts." There is no doubt that Lincoln recognized the arguable legality of his actions, reflected in the proclamation's legalistic tone despite Lincoln's exceptional skill with words. This is perhaps why "Lincoln regarded the [Thirteenth] Amendment as the most important political act to be performed by Congress during his administration," as it ended slavery while putting to rest any lingering doubts about the proclamation's legality.

"The great living issues which divided the Nation were secession and slavery—questions of law, of constitutionality, and of right and wrong."

Albert Woldman,
in *Lawyer Lincoln*

in asserting slavery to be "founded on both injustice and bad policy." Significantly, Lincoln framed this protest in constitutional and legal terms. While this did not put Lincoln on the cutting edge of antislavery efforts—he also asserted that "the promulgation of abolitionist doctrines tends to increase rather than abate its [slavery's] evils"—for a young Illinois politician, this was a radical stance.

In the next decade, lawyer Lincoln was involved with slavery in at least seventeen cases, mostly representing whites. It is hard to characterize his practice as being either proslavery or antislavery; the best characterization may be that he was an attorney accepting clients. Thus, between 1838 and 1847, when he left for Washington to serve his single term in Congress, Lincoln represented slave owners, opponents of slavery, and free blacks.

In the 1841 case of *Bailey v. Cromwell*, for example, Lincoln successfully appealed a circuit court ruling involving the sale of a slave girl, arguing that the sale of a human being contravened the Illinois Constitution provision forbidding slavery. Then thirty-two years old, Lincoln's study and investigation of the slavery issue in the case may well have influenced his later political views on the issue. On the other hand, five years later Lincoln represented slave owner Robert Matson of Kentucky in a habeas corpus action involving his alleged fugitive slaves—a mother and her four children. Lincoln was unsuccessful in his pleas, which one biographer described as "spiritless, half-hearted, and devoid of his usual wit, logic, and invective."

Shortly after the Matson case, when Lincoln moved to Washington, D.C., his positions reflected what might be considered an inconsistent view toward slavery. For example, he proposed one bill allowing Washington, D.C., officials to return fugitive slaves to southern masters, while drafting another bill calling for gradual emancipation in the District of Columbia. On closer inspection, these and other actions were consistent with Lincoln's constitutionalism, respecting the existing law while seeking to curb the expansion of slavery.

After returning from Washington, Lincoln's practice changed in many respects, including his slavery caseload. He no longer defended the interests of masters in fugitive slave cases; rather, the firm of Lincoln and Herndon took a more active role in defending fugitive slaves and free blacks. Between 1849 and 1860 the firm represented free blacks at least nine times and fugitive slaves at least twice; at no point did either man represent slave owners.

During this period Lincoln also had one steady black client, William Florville, a barber who acquired much real estate and was well known as "Billy the Barber." Lincoln represented him at least four times before being elected president. This relationship was significant because Lincoln here represented a hardworking, upwardly mobile midwesterner, not unlike himself except in being black.

The lessons about equality that Lincoln learned from his black clients came slowly, and Lincoln learned them incompletely. Nevertheless, by the time he ran for the Senate in 1858, his attitudes on race were clearly evolving. Lincoln's opposition to the spread of slavery, and his wholesale rejection of Chief Justice Roger Taney's Dred Scott opinion—which made him a leader of the Republican Party and helped gain him the nomination in 1860—also framed his first presidential campaign. Indeed, Lincoln may well have been the first presidential candidate in our history to run "against" the U.S. Supreme Court.

While many presidents have found the law a useful stepping stone to politics and the White House, none have used legal argumentation so successfully in gaining the nomination and campaigning for the presidency. Lincoln the candidate was really Lincoln the advocate, arguing against Taney's position in the only forum that mattered—the court of public opinion.

Lincoln's election set the stage for secession and then civil war. In 1860 and 1861, Lincoln persistently took his case to the American people, North and South, much as he might have taken it to a jury. He argued the facts over and over again—the North had done nothing to threaten slavery, and he had never threatened slavery where it existed. While he opposed the spread of slavery into the territories, this policy would not lead to the emancipation of a single slave. Moreover, he promised to obey the existing law with regard to fugitive slaves. Abolitionists like Wendell Phillips might have called him "the Slave Hound of Illinois," but Lincoln the lawyer understood the obligations of his new office.

When not arguing the facts, he argued the law. He reminded southerners that he had no legal or constitutional power to interfere with slavery in existing slave states. Thus, masters had nothing to fear from his administration. He also argued that the

"I have always hated slavery. I consider it a great moral evil to hold one-sixth of the population in bondage."

Abraham Lincoln

★ ★ ★

"Just as his Emancipation Proclamation was precise and legalistic, reflecting the lawyer-advocate and litigator, Lincoln's second inaugural was passionate and open-ended, reflecting the lawyer-mediator seeking a settlement of the dispute."

nation's highest law—the U.S. Constitution—did not permit secession. Simply put, it was illegal.

Lincoln thus controlled the "spin" of secession, wrapping the law and Constitution around his own policies, and—at least in the free states—successfully portraying the Confederacy as a lawless and illegal entity. He also appealed to the Constitution as almost a religious document deserving great veneration and respect. Lincoln was using his legal expertise, responding to secession with constitutional and legal arguments about the nature of the Union and the need to preserve it.

A year after the war began, President Lincoln began to reshape his wartime goals and attack slavery. Fortunately, his years of legal practice gave Lincoln the tools to draft an emancipation document that would serve his purpose and, he hoped, withstand judicial scrutiny. The final Emancipation Proclamation, issued on January 1, 1863, was Lincoln's finest hour as a lawyer.

The proclamation must be understood in the context of Lincoln's experience as a lawyer and politician. He fully expected his actions to be challenged in court and hoped that by the time the issue reached the U.S. Supreme Court, proslavery Chief Justice Taney would be gone, replaced by someone of his own choosing. But Lincoln could not be sure of this. Thus, he attacked slavery on carefully chosen legal grounds.

Lincoln understood that he could not constitutionally attack slavery in the states early in his presidency. When eleven states seceded, however, he had the vehicle to do so through his war powers. In the first year of the war, he solidified support for the war effort and the Union, making preservation of the Union his first goal, biding his time to attack slavery at the right moment. Most of all, the lawyer did not want a court overturning his actions because the president had overstepped his constitutional authority.

Many scholars have attacked the notion of Lincoln as the Great Emancipator, in part because of the nature of the proclamation. For example, historian Richard Hofstadter described Lincoln as a cynical politician, "among the world's great political propagandists," whose Emancipation Proclamation had "all the moral grandeur of a bill of lading."

For Lincoln, however, this was the point of the proclamation, as he surely knew how to write a great speech and make a powerful statement. He did it in two inaugural addresses and the Gettysburg Address. But for emancipation, Lincoln understood that he needed the skill of the prairie lawyer, not the great speechwriter. His Emancipation Proclamation may have had "all the moral grandeur of a bill of lading," but it did the trick. Indeed, Karl Marx, reporting for a London newspaper during the war, had a clear fix on what Lincoln had done, and why he did it the way he did. Marx observed that the "most formidable decrees which he hurls at the enemy and which will never lose their historic significance, resemble—as the author intends them to—ordinary summons, sent by one lawyer to another."

While popular culture often portrays lawyers as men and women identified with conflict and chaos, they are also counselors and peacemakers who bring parties together, seeking to resolve conflicts and settle disputes. At the end of his life, Lincoln functioned as such a negotiator and peacemaker. Just as his Emancipation Proclamation was precise and legalistic, reflecting the lawyer-advocate and litigator, Lincoln's second inaugural was passionate and open-ended, reflecting the lawyer-mediator seeking a settlement of the dispute.

Summing up his case, Lincoln noted how "all knew" that slavery "was somehow the cause of the war," which had come to an end with the conflict. He noted its huge cost, as emancipation might mean that "all the wealth piled by the bondsman's two hundred and fifty years of unrequited toil shall be sunk" and that "every drop of blood drawn with the lash shall be paid by another drawn by the sword."

With emancipation accomplished, along with subsequent ratification of the Thirteenth Amendment outlawing slavery, Lincoln ended his inaugural, and as it turned out his life, with the promise of conciliation and, most important of all, justice. "Charity for all," he said, committing "to care for him who shall have borne the battle and for his widow and his orphan," and looking to the ultimate goal of a "just and lasting peace." Such a peace had to include justice for those whose bondage Lincoln had helped end.

Thus, the lifelong lawyer from Illinois, who like a comet briefly flashed across the sky of American politics, ended his presidency with a vision of "justice." This is a concept often lost in the practice of law and surely often forgotten in the day-to-day scramble of politics. Fittingly, it was the goal of the lawyer who became a president and the Great Emancipator.

Selected Cases of A. Lincoln, Esq., Attorney and Counsellor-at-Law

JOHN A. LUPTON

Upon moving to Springfield to practice law with John Stuart, his first partner, Lincoln proudly wrote on the flyleaf of his dictionary, "A. Lincoln, Esq., Attorney and Counsellor-at-law." With Stuart and two other law partners, he would go on to handle more than five thousand one hundred cases over a twenty-five-year legal career.

When people think of Lincoln the lawyer and the cases he handled, they generally think of his most famous ones, including *Almanac*, *Effie Afton*, *McLean County Tax*, and *Reaper*. In the *Almanac* trial, Lincoln used a farmer's almanac to discredit the eyesight of the star prosecution witness in a murder case. In *Effie Afton*, Lincoln argued for the interests of railroads over river transportation, while in *McLean County Tax*, Lincoln prevented local governmental bodies from taxing his client railroad, saving it millions of dollars (he later had to sue the railroad to recover his five-thousand-dollar legal fee, the largest of his career). And in the *Reaper* case, Lincoln was shunned by his future secretary of war, Edwin Stanton, and other cocounsel who refused to work on the patent case with the gangly, unkempt, and seemingly uneducated Lincoln.

These cases—like all of Lincoln's caseload—concerned important issues in antebellum Illinois, which placed land, money, property, reputations, careers, freedom, and lives at stake. His cases illuminate such issues while providing insight into Lincoln's legal career and Lincoln the lawyer.

Debt-related cases made up the majority of cases on the era's court docket, and Lincoln's caseload was no different. The lack of specie and dependable currency forced many people to rely on promissory notes as a form of currency. When people failed to pay their notes, creditors sued to collect their debts. The

★ ★ ★

"The law provided for [Lincoln] a study of human institutions and of history itself."

Albert Woldman,
in *Lawyer Lincoln*

"Lincoln was an aggressive and tenacious litigator whose mastery of civil and criminal procedure surfaced frequently. . . . He could, as historian Robert Bruce aptly put it, 'split hairs as well as rails.'"

Lincoln historian
Cullom Davis

creditor/debtor relationship factored heavily in federal legislation of 1841, when Congress passed a national bankruptcy act that allowed debtors to free themselves of overwhelming financial obligations.

One of the reasons Stephen Logan wanted Lincoln as his junior partner in 1841 was to help him with these bankruptcy cases. Logan and Lincoln handled more than seventy such cases during the year the law was in effect. In one case, *In re West*, Amos West owed numerous people the sizable total of $18,393. He retained Logan and Lincoln in petitioning the federal court for bankruptcy relief, indicating his assets included more than $1,700 in notes and accounts and 436 acres of land. The court declared West bankrupt and appointed an overseer to distribute his assets to his creditors. After setting aside $200 worth of household items and livestock for West, his wife, and their ten children, the remaining property brought only $39 at auction. With bankruptcy costs totaling $37, West's creditors received no money (though Lincoln was paid for his services, as legal fees were generally paid up front in bankruptcy cases).

In addition to promissory notes, land and timber were valuable commodities in central Illinois. Builders used the lumber that came from large groves of trees to construct houses, businesses, and whole communities. In 1850, five members of the Whitecraft family cut down more than three hundred trees on Horatio Vandeveer's property. Vandeveer retained the firm of Lincoln and Herndon, sued the Whitecrafts, and successfully recovered the value of the lost trees. The Whitecrafts appealed the judgment to the Illinois Supreme Court, where Lincoln continued to represent Vandeveer. Due to shortcomings in Lincoln's declaration, the court ruled for the Whitecrafts. Justice Lyman Trumbull admonished Lincoln that "the want of permission from the owner is a necessary ingredient to constitute the offense, and he who would make a party liable must allege all the facts." While there is no record of Lincoln's response to his error, it reflects the fact that Lincoln was hardly a perfect attorney; indeed, he lost cases he probably should have won. Despite the admonition and outcome in this case, however, Lincoln experienced a good measure of success in his many appeals before the state's high court.

William Herndon, Lincoln's third law partner, claimed that Lincoln was at his best as an attorney before the Illinois Supreme

Court because he had time to think about and prepare for a case. One of Lincoln's most precedent-setting cases before that court was *Barret v. Alton and Sangamon Railroad*, in which Lincoln successfully argued for the railroad that a stock subscriber had to pay his subscriptions despite the fact that the railroad's board of directors changed the promised course of the road. He argued—and the state supreme court agreed— that the public good in this 1851 case was more important than individual rights. Interestingly, in two subsequent cases later in the 1850s, Lincoln represented stockholders seeking to overturn that very precedent. Lawyer Lincoln was thus not afraid to argue different sides of issues in different cases.

In the first such case, *Sprague v. Illinois River Railroad*, Charles Sprague refused to pay his stock subscriptions because the Illinois River Railroad decided to expand its routes and build a bridge to link up with other railroads. After unsuccessfully representing Sprague at the circuit court level, Lincoln appealed to the Illinois Supreme Court, arguing that the change was a "material departure" from the original charter. In affirming the lower court judgment, Justice John Caton cited the *Barret* case, noted that these changes were for the common good of the public and the shareholders, and indicated that changes in charters would be impossible if "one stupid or obstinate holder of one share [could] tie up the hands of all the rest."

One year later, Lincoln again attempted to overturn the *Barret* precedent. Daniel Earp and sixteen fellow shareholders of the Terre Haute and Alton Railroad refused to pay their stock subscriptions because the railroad, in acquiring another railroad to Illinoistown (now East St. Louis), had changed its terminus from Alton to Illinoistown. In the circuit court, Lincoln argued that the change was material because it would economically benefit St. Louis, Missouri, more than the Illinois community of Alton. Though the court agreed and ruled for the stockholders, the railroad appealed to the Illinois Supreme Court, citing the *Barret* decision. There, Justice Caton reversed the judgment of the circuit court, noting that "the principles by which this case must be determined, have already been settled by repeated decisions of this court, and we do not feel called upon to discuss them again at length." No doubt, Judge Caton was well aware of Lincoln's role in establishing those principles.

LAW PARTNER WILLIAM HERNDON

Herndon, Lincoln's third law partner, claimed that Lincoln was at his best as an attorney before the Illinois Supreme Court because he had time to think about and prepare for a case.

★ ★ ★

"In McLean County Tax [case], Lincoln prevented local governmental bodies from taxing his client railroad, saving it millions of dollars (he later had to sue the railroad to recover his five-thousand-dollar legal fee, the largest of his career)."

In addition to his many appellate cases, Lincoln was an accomplished advocate at the trial level before juries. Isaac Arnold, a Chicago attorney who worked with Lincoln on some cases, claimed that Lincoln was the best jury lawyer in the state. In one illustrative 1846 case, Lincoln represented a Revolutionary War widow who had been overcharged by a pension agent in obtaining her pension. Lincoln asked Herndon to research the history of the Revolutionary War and used it in his remarks to the jury. According to Herndon, in one of Lincoln's most impassioned pleas to a jury, he recounted the struggles at Valley Forge and the valiant military career of his client's spouse, and then "skinned" the defendant. By the end of his argument, Lincoln had most of the jury in tears. The jury proceeded to find for the widow and awarded her thirty-five dollars in damages.

Lincoln also handled cases in the court's chancery division, which comprised those cases that did not have a remedy under the strict common law system, such as divorce, land partitions, and partnership dissolutions. Lincoln handled a large number of divorce cases during his career, as Illinois had relatively liberal divorce laws that allowed disgruntled spouses to leave difficult marriages and begin a new life.

In 1849, Robert Plunkett retained Lincoln and Herndon in suing his wife Ann for divorce, alleging that she had deserted him. Ann retained Lincoln's former partner, Stephen Logan, in the case, and answered that Robert actually had left her because she had been ill for some time and he had to assume some of her prior debts. She further charged him with having an adulterous affair with Matilda Gately. Ann repeated these charges in a cross bill for divorce against her husband, indicating she did "not object to being divorced from [Robert] but she objects to a divorce being granted for any alleged misconduct on her part."

Robert answered the cross bill by denying all her charges and claiming he was not committing adultery, but that Gately was a live-in nanny for his children from a former wife. At the trial, however, Robert withdrew his answer and confessed to the allegations. Lincoln then helped forge an agreement between the two parties under which Robert would not make any claims for her property if Ann would not seek alimony. Robert also agreed to pay one hundred dollars for the court costs and Ann's legal fees.

Lincoln's criminal caseload was quite small compared to his common law and chancery practice, but criminal cases more often garnered the attention of the local and surrounding population as well as the local press. Though most criminal cases concerned less publicized and more mundane matters—such as larceny, liquor violations, or assault and battery—murder cases in particular aroused the populace, who often knew either the accused perpetrators or the victims. Because of this familiarity, juries in murder cases generally preferred to find defendants guilty of the lesser charge of manslaughter. Not only were the lives of the defendants at stake—with convicted murderers automatically sentenced to capital punishment—but if the defendant had a family, then friends, relatives, or the local community might have to care for them.

John Bantzhouse, a German immigrant, was a tavern owner in rural Sangamon County, who became incensed when a group of people at his tavern became rowdy. Stepping outside with a rifle, he fired into the building and killed Walter Clark. The new state's attorney indicted Bantzhouse for murder, and Lincoln defended him, securing a continuance one term and a change of venue the next. When the judge finally called the case, he immediately dismissed it—thus setting Bantzhouse free—because the state's attorney had violated a statutory provision that called for an accused murderer to have a trial within two court terms. Clark's brother urged the state's attorney to indict Bantzhouse again, but "before another indictment could be framed, [Bantzhouse] had made use of leg bail and taken to the woods. It is probable that he will not be heard of very speedily in this part of the country." Lincoln thus demonstrated his willingness to use legal technicalities in serving his clients' interests.

In addition to divorce and criminal proceedings, slander was a legal action that aroused passions in the community. Social stature was an important aspect of antebellum life, and slander suits provided a means for insulted or embarrassed persons to regain their reputation. America Toney was one of those who sought such redress in the courts.

According to Toney's complaint, Emily Sconce had made some defamatory remarks about Toney's chastity. Sconce and Toney were both single women who had been living together when James Whitcomb came for a visit. Later in the evening,

Lincoln's legal and political careers were frequently intertwined. In 1856, for example, fellow circuit rider Anthony Thornton requested Lincoln's help in Shelbyville, Thornton's hometown, to argue seventeen cases for stockholders trying to cancel their payments to the Terre Haute and Alton Railroad. While there, Thornton asked Lincoln to return to debate the slavery issue. Lincoln agreed, speaking for three hours in the largely Democratic county. Noting its dearth of Republicans, he quipped, ". . . however poorly I may defend my cause, I can hardly harm it, if I do it no good."

Toney retired to her room, and not long after Whitcomb followed her. Sconce then retired to her room, which adjoined Toney's room. Sconce heard "scuffling" and "wriggling" on the bed and "was satisfied from the noise and their actions that they were doing what they ought not to be doing." Sconce reported the incident to various people. Toney denied it, retained Lincoln, and sued Sconce in an action of slander for five thousand dollars in damages. Sconce consented to a judgment against herself for the full amount, but Toney remitted all damages except for fifty dollars, which was presumably spent on Lincoln's fees. Toney—like many others who filed such suits during this period—was less interested in the money than in recovering her good name.

The courtroom was generally a serious place where reputations and finances were at stake. However, Lincoln never lost his sense of humor in the courtroom, and many of his legal colleagues noted how Lincoln would entertain the court with his humor.

Lincoln probably had a smile on his face while working on an 1852 case involving Moses Thorpe's agreement to castrate James Ford's bull. As insurance, Thorpe agreed to pay Ford twenty-five dollars if the bull did not recover from the castration. The bull died following the procedure, and when Thorpe refused to pay the insurance, Ford sued him to recover the twenty-five dollars. Lincoln represented Thorpe and sought a continuance to obtain the testimony of one Russell Thompson. In Lincoln's affidavit, he noted that Thompson claimed Ford did not own the bull "at any time during the life of said bull, or at any time after his change of condition by which he ceased to be a bull." The court granted the continuance, but at the next term of court, a jury found for Ford and awarded him twenty dollars.

Lincoln sought to resolve cases outside of court when possible. A law clerk working in the Lincoln-Herndon law office often heard Lincoln encourage clients and potential clients to settle their disputes. During his twenty-five years of practice, nearly one-third of the 5,100 cases he and his partners handled were dismissed, with many of them resolved out of court. While many of these settlements can be attributed to Lincoln's desire to forge a resolution that benefited both sides, his remaining caseload clearly indicates that Lincoln was not afraid to take a case to trial or to appeal adverse decisions to a higher court. In one federal case, Lincoln assured his clients that he would do all in his power to help them retain their land, "even if we have to go to the Supreme Court of the U.S. for it." Lincoln did not have to appeal that case, however, which he won at the circuit court level.

Though Lincoln was mainly a courtroom attorney, he also had an office practice that involved preparing deeds, wills, and other legal documents and offering opinions on legal topics. In 1857, for example, a village wanted to organize its community into a town and requested Lincoln's legal opinion as to how large or small the town's physical limits could be for its governing body. A five-dollar fee was included with the request, with a note expressing hope that it would be sufficient. Lincoln responded that he examined the Illinois statutes and concluded that the new town trustees could not exceed the original mile square town plat but could reduce the size if necessary. He also indicated that five dollars was a sufficient fee for his service.

Other than his salaries from terms in the Illinois General Assembly and the U.S. Congress, Lincoln earned practically all his income from the law. Unlike fellow lawyers such as Judge David Davis, who made a fortune from land speculation, Lincoln was content to earn a livelihood from handling cases in Illinois. While he made a comfortable living with his income, owning a nice home in an upper middle class Springfield neighborhood, Lincoln had a reputation for charging his clients relatively low fees. After he did some legal work for George Floyd, for example, Lincoln received twenty-five dollars from him. Lincoln replied, "You must think I am a high-priced man. You are too liberal with your money. Fifteen dollars is enough for the job. I send you a receipt for fifteen dollars, and return to you a ten-dollar bill."

In Lincoln's long legal career, he handled cases that demonstrate the important economic, social, legal, and political issues of antebellum Illinois. When he departed for Washington in February 1861 to become the sixteenth president of the United States, he left behind a thriving law practice that had exposed him to countless personalities and issues. These experiences were to serve him well in the executive mansion in Washington, D.C., where he would deal with the greatest constitutional crisis in American history.

★ ★ ★

"But the best training [Lincoln] had for the Presidency, after all, was his twenty-three years' arduous experience as a lawyer traveling the circuits of the courts of his district and state."

President William McKinley, in 1896 speech to Marquette Club of Chicago

Lincoln's Notes for a Law Lecture

Lincoln's White House secretaries, John Nicolay and John Hay, based their monumental biography of the president on papers owned by Lincoln's son Robert. Included in these papers were Lincoln's notes for a law lecture. While Nicolay and Hay dated the document July 1, 1850, Lincoln probably wrote it at another time as there are no sources to verify its genesis and date. One possibility is that Lincoln drafted it after receiving a November 1858 letter inviting him to speak at the Ohio State and Union Law College in Cleveland. However, Lincoln did not thereafter travel to Cleveland, and there is no known Lincoln response to this invitation. Whatever the origin and purpose, the notes offer unique insight into Lincoln's philosophy of the practice of law.

I am not an accomplished lawyer. I find quite as much material for a lecture, in those points wherein I have failed as in those wherein I have been moderately successful.

The leading rule for the lawyer, as for the man of every other calling, is <u>diligence</u>. Leave nothing for to-morrow, which can be done to-day. Never let your correspondence fall behind. Whatever piece of business you have in hand, before stopping, do all the labor pertaining to it, which can <u>then</u> be done. When you bring a common-law suit, if you have the facts for doing so, write the declaration at once. If a law point be involved, examine the books, and note the authority you rely on, upon the declaration itself, where you are sure to find it when wanted. The same of defences and pleas. In business not likely to be litigated—ordinary collection cases, foreclosures, partitions, and the like,—make all examinations of titles and note them, and even draft orders and decrees in advance. This course has a tripple advantage; it avoids omissions and neglect, <u>saves</u> your labor, when once done; performs the labor out of court when you <u>have</u> leisure, rather than in court, when you have not. Extemporaneous speaking should be practiced and cultivated. It is the lawyer's avenue to the public. However able and faithful he may be in other respects, people are slow to bring him business, if he can not make a speech. And yet there is not a more fatal error to young lawyers, than relying too much on speech-making. If any one, upon his rare powers of speaking, shall claim an exemption from the drudgery of the law, his case is a failure in advance.

Discourage litigation. Persuade your neighbors to compromise whenever you can. Point out to them how the <u>nominal</u> winner is often a <u>real</u> loser, in fees, expenses, and waste *of time. As a peace-maker, the lawyer has a superior opertunity of being a good man. There will still be business enough.*

Never stir up litigation. A worse man can scarcely be found than one who does this. Who can be more nearly a fiend than he who habitually overhauls the Register of deeds, in search of defects in titles, whereon to stir up strife, and put money in his pocket? A moral tone ought to be infused into the profession, which should drive such men out of it.

The matter of fees is important far beyond the mere question of bread and butter involved. Properly atended to fuller justice is done to both lawyer and client. An exorbitant fee should never be claimed. As a general rule, never take your whole fee in advance, nor any more than a small retainer. When fully paid before hand, you are more than a common mortal if you can feel the same interest in the case, as if something was still in prospect for you, as well as for your client. And when you lack interest in the case, the job will very likely lack skill and diligence in the performance. Settle the <u>amount</u> of fee, and take a note in advance. Then you will feel that you are working for something, and you are sure to do your work faithfully, and well. Never sell a fee-note—at least, not before the consideration service is performed. It leads to negligence and dishonesty—negligence, by losing interest in the case, and dishonesty in refusing to refund, when you have allowed the consideration to fail.

There is a vague popular belief that lawyers are necessarily dishonest. I say <u>vague</u>, because when we consider to what extent <u>confidence</u>, and <u>honors</u> are reposed in, and conferred upon lawyers by the people, it appears improbable that their <u>impression</u> of dishonesty, is very distinct and vivid. Yet the expression, is common—almost universal. Let no young man, choosing the law for a calling, for a moment yield to this popular belief. Resolve to be honest at all events; and if, in your own judgment, you can not be an honest-lawyer, resolve to be honest without being a lawyer. Choose some other occupation, rather than one in the choosing of which you do, in advance, consent to be a knave.

Gilded Age Presidents

Law in the Gilded Age

In 1870, new Harvard Law School dean Christopher Columbus Langdell, like his namesake, went off on his own voyage of discovery, and legal education has never been the same. Langdell believed that law was a "science"; the duty of law schools was to teach the principles of this science, which would be revealed through the study of appellate cases. Langdell got rid of the lecture method and introduced casebooks and Socratic dialogue. He also, in a way, invented the law professor. Before Langdell, law schools hired judges (sometimes retired) or prominent lawyers to do their teaching. Langdell, on the other hand, hired bright young men, fresh out of law school, who (he thought) would be especially good at handling the tricky new method. Langdell's method seemed slow, inefficient, and strange. It struggled at first even in its home base of Harvard. Yet it gradually took hold and began to spread beyond the confines of Cambridge, Massachusetts.

Meanwhile, apprenticeship was dying. The new law offices had typewriters, telephones, and young women with clerical skills. There was no longer a felt need for young gophers. The path to the bar ran more and more through schools of law. Some, like Harvard and Columbia, were attached to universities. Others, especially those geared to the children of new immigrants who were streaming into the country, were more modest night-time and part-time schools. These were the schools that turned out solo and small-firm practitioners, local mayors, aldermen, and municipal judges. The business lawyers and those in larger law firms came predominantly from the more elite and expensive schools. They became the "Wall Street" lawyers who worked in the financial centers of New York and other big cities. More and more, too, these lawyers banded together in partnerships—groups of attorneys that swelled in size to meet the various needs of their gigantic clients.

The South was still dominated by agriculture; its farmworkers were predominantly black—and desperately poor. They had been slaves until the Civil War freed them. There had been a kind of false dawn during the Reconstruction period. When Reconstruction ended in 1876, white supremacy replaced it. The black tenants and sharecroppers became little more than serfs on the white man's land. There were no black judges, no black jurors, and virtually no black lawyers to be seen in the courts. The courts were the white man's courts.

The North was no longer the domain of yeomen farmers. More and more it was filled with urban workers: men and women who toiled in factories, mines, and railroad yards. Industrial accidents took a terrible toll of lives and bodies, producing a rich harvest of lawsuits. Personal injury lawyers, mostly from the local and ethnic bars, made their living out of the wreckage of the industrial revolution. The elite bar sneered at these men, and called them ambulance chasers. But the companies themselves desperately sought to foreclose lawsuits; the claims adjusters of streetcar lines, for example, were in a race with the ambulance chasers, seeking to induce accident victims to sign away their rights in exchange for a modest settlement.

Nowhere was the legal struggle more intense than with regard to the rights of labor, especially organized labor. Working men and women had no capital, no assets except their hands, bodies, and sweat. They could be hired and fired at will. There was essentially no social safety net. To many workers, the only hope was in organization in labor unions. But management often resisted the unions with passion. Labor and management were often locked in combat—on the shop floor, in the streets, in the legislatures, and more and more, in the courts. This was the period that invented substantive due process and made judicial review much more of a reality— a reality that was sometimes fatal to labor and social legislation. This was the period in which the courts forged the powerful weapon of the labor injunction. Presidents like Grover Cleveland sent in federal troops to break strikes, but injunctions and convictions for contempt, granted by federal courts, were perhaps more powerful than the army itself.

By the end of the century, the country had expanded to the Pacific, the great herds of buffalo were a small remnant, and the frontier was pronounced officially dead. With it, perhaps, died the dream of unlimited horizons and unlimited resources. The fundamental job of the legal system changed from promoting an unending process of growth to monitoring a zero-sum world—controlling conflict and distributing goods within a finite, more limited domain.

The big-city machines took this task, perhaps, rather too literally. The period after the Civil War was a period of extraordinary corruption, both North and South, and especially in the cities. Scandals in New York's legal establishment inspired the creation, in 1870, of the Association of the Bar of the City of New York. A group of elite lawyers, the founders, were determined to rescue the profession from the sinkhole of corruption. An Iowa state bar association was founded in 1874, and the American Bar Association was founded in 1878. The legal profession seemed to be in crisis. It stood at a crossroads between probity and professionalism on the one hand, and corruption and greediness (as the bar association founders saw it) on the other. The new organizations took their stand for what they defined as a purified and dignified profession.

LAWRENCE M. FRIEDMAN

★ ★ ★

Nineteenth President (1877–81)

BIRTH
October 4, 1822
Delaware, Ohio

EDUCATION
Kenyon College
Read law under Thomas Sparrow in Columbus, Ohio
Harvard Law School
Admission to the bar: March 10, 1845

OTHER OCCUPATIONS/PUBLIC OFFICES
Cincinnati city solicitor
Civil War major general
U.S. congressman
Ohio governor

DEATH
January 17, 1893
Fremont, Ohio

LAW CAREER IN BRIEF

Hayes's sixteen-year law career (1845–61) involved a series of law partnerships and high-profile cases. The only lawyer-president to graduate from Harvard Law School, Hayes initially handled mundane debt collection and land disputes in Lower Sandusky before moving his practice to Cincinnati and gaining fame for his defense of Nancy Farrer, a live-in housekeeper accused of poisoning members of two families. He proceeded to handle more high-profile cases, including those involving runaway slaves, before being elected city solicitor. In 1861, Hayes left law practice entirely to serve in the Civil War.

Rutherford B. Hayes: Volunteer Counsel

Ari Hoogenboom

A junior at Ohio's Kenyon College, eighteen-year-old Rud Hayes wrote his mother he "would love to be a farmer," if he had good land. Failing that, he would spend every cent he had on "a good and complete education, and . . . practice law in some dirty little hole out West." Rud loved to tease his mother, made dour by the loss of two children and the death of her husband before Rud's birth. Sophia Hayes did not mind her son's kidding, especially since he was coming around to her way of thinking. He was also yielding to the views of sister Fanny and uncle Sardis Birchard, both of whom wished to live vicariously through him. Although he earlier argued that "all the plow joggers are happier than students," young Rud settled on law as a career.

After Hayes graduated from Kenyon College as class valedictorian, he read law in the Columbus office of Thomas Sparrow. He started with Blackstone's *Commentaries on the Laws of England*, but he was distracted by a nearby bookstore and coffeehouse as well as by newspapers and politics. A lover of literature, he also studied German for two hours daily so that he would not have to read the German poet and playwright Schiller in translation.

For ten "vexatious and tedious" months, Hayes read law under Sparrow's direction. Dissatisfied with the progress of his semi-independent study, he sought more structure and decided to attend Harvard Law School. On the strength of his training with Sparrow, Hayes was admitted to Harvard's middle class in August 1843.

At Harvard, Hayes was taught by the "eminent jurists and teachers" Justice Joseph Story of the U.S. Supreme Court and Simon Greenleaf, author of the authoritative *Treatise on the Law of Evidence*. Both Story and Greenleaf combined illustrations and explanations with the recitations of students but otherwise

★ ★ ★

"The life of a truly great lawyer must be one of severe and intense application . . . it is not by sudden, vigorous efforts that he is to succeed . . . but by patient, enduring energy."

Rutherford B. Hayes

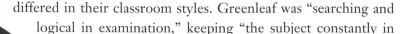

HAYES THE YOUNG ATTORNEY

Commenting on the meager nature of his early law practice, Hayes noted, "I assisted in pettifogging a case last week and have hopes of becoming quite a pettifogger in time." After he moved to Cincinnati, however, pettifogging gave way to important cases, and his reputation as a capable and clever attorney grew.

differed in their classroom styles. Greenleaf was "searching and logical in examination," keeping "the subject constantly in view" and making it "impossible for one who has not faithfully studied the text to escape exposing his ignorance." On the other hand, Story was "very fond of digressions to introduce amusing anecdotes, high-wrought eulogies of the sages of the law, and fragments of his own experience."

Story's digressions were a font of good sense, high ideals, and intense patriotism. Since "law is the perfection of human reason, the wisdom of all ages . . . precedents must not be slavishly followed," he insisted, "but in every case reason and justice should prevail." His lecture on the duty of citizens to adhere to the Constitution was "the most eloquent" Hayes had ever heard. If people "in the name of conscience, liberty, or the rights of man" disregarded the constitutional provision enabling slaveholders to reclaim a fugitive slave in a free state, Story argued, then southerners would ignore constitutional provisions that were counter to their interests and the Union would become a "rope of sand," leading to "discord and civil war." Story even had career advice for his charges, suggesting they "keep out of politics" until they were forty.

Moot court was as important for Hayes as reading and lectures. Often, Story would hear moot court arguments on knotty cases appealed to the U.S. Circuit Court, over which he presided. It was, Story declared, "the high-court of appeals for the whole world."

As during his days in Columbus, Hayes enjoyed diversions from his legal studies. He read Cicero and Aristotle but was more influenced by James Beatty and John Locke. Hayes also continued to study German and took up French, attended the theater, visited such sites as Bunker Hill and Mount Auburn Cemetery, and enjoyed the preaching of Dr. James Walker. Among politicians, Hayes heard a "poor" speech by his childhood idol Daniel Webster and an "unreasonable and very unfair" speech containing "much abolitionism" by the "venerable but deluded old man" John Quincy Adams. Nevertheless, Hayes acknowledged that the old man was "quick, sharp, fearless, and full of the wit and learning of the ages." Hayes also played ball. "I consider one game of ball worth about ten plays," he told Uncle Sardis, who was concerned that he was studying too hard. "I am now quite lame, from scuffling, and all my fingers stiffened by playing."

After a year and a half at Harvard, Hayes left for Ohio, having completed enough work to be awarded a bachelor of laws degree. Following Greenleaf's advice to settle first in an obscure place, Hayes decided on Lower Sandusky in northern Ohio. It was the hometown of Uncle Sardis, who as its most prominent citizen could steer business his way. It also would put a hundred miles between him and his strong willed mother and sister in Columbus. But first he spent a month with them while studying for the Ohio bar exam.

To take it, he journeyed by stagecoach and steamboat to Marietta, where the Ohio Supreme Court was in session. In March 1845 Hayes fielded questions from a friendly committee for an hour or two and was declared fit to practice law. The examination was neither perfunctory nor trying. A year later, Hayes served on a similar committee to examine his college chum Stanley Matthews (who later, thanks to Hayes, became a U.S. Supreme Court justice) and, with a mix of modesty and honesty, declared Matthews "beyond dispute a better lawyer than any of the examining committee. The good lawyers were all too busy in court to be sent off on such sham service."

Greenleaf's advice on where to practice proved unsound for Hayes. His clients' problems were minor, usually involving debt collection or land titles. He was less lonely and busier after he formed a partnership with Ralph Buckland in 1846, but for the junior partner of Buckland & Hayes, "Land and Collection Agents," the work was too routine. He became overwhelmed by ennui, his failure to secure a wife, and fears for his health, as his roommate had tuberculosis and he began coughing up blood. By 1847 he resolved to leave Lower Sandusky. Winding up his affairs, Hayes was instrumental in changing its name to Fremont just before he moved to Cincinnati on Christmas Eve of 1849 for "Health and stimulus."

In his last moments in Fremont, Hayes became involved in a significant suit in which some of Sardis's land titles were challenged, the case being appealed all the way to the U.S. Supreme Court. Hayes spent most of December researching disputed land

UNCLE SARDIS'S "INTERMINABLE LAWSUIT"

Just before moving to Cincinnati, Hayes was involved in a case challenging the validity of some of Uncle Sardis Birchard's land titles. Though his uncle (pictured here) had triumphed in the Ohio Supreme Court, the decision was appealed to the U.S. Supreme Court; for the case, Hayes and Judge Ebenezer Lane prepared a "short but good" brief that Henry Stanberry—a future U.S. attorney general— used in arguing the 1849 case. After an adverse decision in *Boswell v. Dickinson, Birchard, et al.*, Sardis pursued his claims again in the Ohio courts before Hayes negotiated a settlement to the dispute.

THE NANCY FARRER CASES

In 1852, Hayes received "*the* criminal case of the term" and probably the most important case of his law career. Nancy Farrer (pictured here) was a live-in housekeeper accused of poisoning four members of two families. "The poor girl is homely—very," wrote Hayes, who planned to use "the effect of original constitution, early training, and associations in forming character" to frame an insanity plea in her defense. Though Farrer was initially found guilty and sentenced to hang, Hayes pursued appeals and secured an "inquest of sanity" during which Farrer was found to be of unsound mind. "I succeeded in getting an acquittal of my first life case which has been a pet case so long," Hayes wrote, "and to which I owe so much."

titles and, with Judge Ebenezer Lane, prepared a "short but good" argument for future U.S. Attorney General Henry Stanberry's use before the high court. When Justice John McLean delivered an adverse Court ruling, Hayes encouraged pursuing the case and prepared arguments citing errors by the Court. Another hearing and postponement, however, led Hayes to propose a settlement that concluded "Uncle's interminable lawsuit."

After a month in Cincinnati, Hayes lamented, "Oh, the waste of those five precious years at Sandusky!" Despite an atmosphere reeking with coal smoke, he claimed his health was better in the professionally, intellectually, and socially stimulating new locale. Hayes shared an office with John W. Herron—who would become William Howard Taft's father-in-law—and boarded at the house of a respectable Presbyterian widow. Since business—primarily debt collecting—was slow, his brother-in-law helped him meet his thirty-dollar monthly expenses.

Interesting cases abounded in Cincinnati, and Hayes spent profitable time observing trials there. He also joined the newly formed Cincinnati Literary Society, which met weekly for "debates, conversations, . . . essays, and oysters washed down with liberal amounts of the local Catawba wine." Hayes attended to sophisticated "city belles," but found himself falling in love with Lucy Webb, who was from his home town of Delaware. Although he feared his income was inadequate for marriage, his uncle offered help as needed, and Rud and Lucy wed in December 1852.

Although Hayes's income was meager, his reputation as a clever attorney was growing. Almost a year before his marriage, he made his "maiden effort in the Criminal Court" with his sensible, energetic, but futile defense of a client found guilty of grand larceny. Impressed, the court appointed Hayes to defend Nancy Farrer, "the poisoner of two families," in "the criminal case of the term." Farrer was homely to the point of deformity, and Hayes argued that from her misfortune stemmed mental incompetence and her malignity. Catering to the prejudices and sympathies of the all-male jury, Hayes observed, "No white woman has ever yet, I believe, been executed in Ohio, and if this idiotic girl is to be the first," the rules of law guarding every man and woman's life and rights would be violated.

His insanity defense of Farrer was especially fervent, since he was personally aware of mental illness. His sister Fanny, apparently afflicted with postpartum psychosis, had become deranged and violent and spent several months in an asylum before recovering. Despite Hayes's emotional appeals, the jury found Farrer guilty, and she was sentenced to be hanged. Not giving up, Hayes secured a new trial that was partially successful, since it delayed execution of the sentence.

The Farrer case led to Hayes's defense of James Summons, convicted in 1852 of poisoning his family and scheduled to be hanged for the crime. While not doubting his guilt, Hayes prepared a bill of exceptions and successfully argued to reserve decision for the Ohio Supreme Court. Delighted "to blow off in two murder cases instead of one," Hayes chortled, "I've evidently hit upon a good lead."

Hayes was next appointed to help defend Henry Lecount, who had smashed the head of his wife's lover with a dray pin. Unable to save Lecount, Hayes felt compelled to accompany him to the gallows. For Hayes, the experience was "shattering," leaving him determined to save Farrer and Summons.

While on his honeymoon in Columbus, Hayes argued the Summons case before the state supreme court. Hayes was proud that his first effort before that court—and an audience of distinguished lawyers—went well and would be in the *Ohio Reports*. His argument that "occasional fits of delirium tremens and repeated attacks of epilepsy" reduced Summons "almost to imbecility," coupled with the questionable testimony of a witness, persuaded half the court to reverse the conviction. But Allen G. Thurman, the presiding judge who had admitted the questionable testimony and also sat on the supreme court, convinced his other colleagues to uphold the conviction, thus deadlocking the court. After the case was argued several more times, the court upheld the death sentence against Summons, though the governor proceeded to commute it to life imprisonment.

Hayes was more successful in defending Farrer, since the state's high court reversed the guilty verdict and ordered a new trial. Hayes then secured an inquest of lunacy, arguing that Farrer was not responsible for her actions. Among the experts testifying on both sides of the question, virtually all initially thought her an imbecile or an idiot, but some came to believe that she knew right from wrong. After eighteen hours, the jury declared Farrer to be of unsound mind, and she was sent to an asylum

★ ★ ★

"In September 1852, there were three prisoners in the Hamilton County jail under the sentence of death . . . and the defense attorney for all three was young Rutherford B. Hayes."

Historian Watt Marchman

"My services were always freely given to the slave and his friends, in all cases arising under the Fugitive Slave Law from the time of its passage."

Rutherford B. Hayes

rather than to the gallows. "It has been a pet case with me," Hayes remarked, "has caused me much anxiety, given me some prominence in my profession, and indeed was the first case which brought me practice in the city."

The day after Christmas 1853, Hayes had formed the partnership of Corwine, Hayes & Rogers, which assured Hayes of success since Richard M. Corwine, who brought a lucrative practice to the partnership, excelled "in beating the bush for game." Hayes would be pleasantly busy in court, Corwine tended to be diverted by politics, while William K. Rogers, who brought little to the firm beyond devotion to his college chum Hayes, would search records and do ordinary office work.

Following his marriage, Hayes began handling fugitive slave cases. While not sympathetic to slavery, Hayes had been hostile to abolitionists and had agreed with Justice Story that fugitive slaves had to be returned to their owners. Obviously influenced by Lucy, Hayes began to defend the freedom of African Americans threatened by the 1850 Fugitive Slave Law. When in 1853 John Jolliffe, Cincinnati's most conspicuous defender of runaway slaves, was assaulted, Hayes volunteered to Jolliffe his services in defense of the runaways. A few weeks later, Hayes defended a fugitive slave, whom careless—or sympathetic—court attendants allowed to slip away while attorneys were engrossed in a passionate argument.

Hayes's emerging antislavery credentials were enhanced when, with Senator Salmon P. Chase and Judge Timothy Walker, he defended Rosetta Armstead, a young slave girl. Her owner, Henry M. Dennison, placed her in the charge of a man traveling from Louisville to Richmond, and en route they crossed Ohio by rail. Alert antislavery activists detained them at Columbus, where the probate court freed the girl on a writ of habeas corpus and appointed a guardian for her. In the presence of witnesses, Dennison asked her to choose between going with him or freedom. Though she chose freedom, he later changed his mind about the offer, procuring an arrest warrant from the U.S. Commissioner in Cincinnati, where she was brought. On a writ of habeas corpus, the issue then came before the court of common pleas.

The case attracted enormous attention. Not only was the young girl's freedom at stake, the case raised intriguing legal questions. Did a slave who was not a runaway become free upon touching the free soil of Ohio? Did Dennison in effect free her

by giving her a choice and apparently accepting her decision? Did her status as a minor affect her competence to decide her fate? Who would prevail if a state court's writ of habeas corpus conflicted with the decision of a U.S. Commissioner?

The court accepted the case, declaring that Ohio's Constitution did not grant the right of transit across it with slave property. The U.S. Commissioner responded by having Rosetta rearrested and conducting his own hearing. Before a packed courtroom, Hayes made the major argument for the young girl, after which the courtroom burst into applause. A week later, the Commissioner declared Rosetta free under U.S. and Ohio law, an outcome her guardian and others credited to Hayes's "eloquent and masterly closing speech."

Although "speaking beautifully for the innocent" was more rewarding than lucrative, Hayes gradually began to prosper financially. He also helped found the Republican Party and became prominent in its counsels. In 1858, the city solicitor of Cincinnati was killed by a locomotive and the city council had to fill the office. Hayes was chosen on the thirteenth ballot, as his reputation for fairness and integrity made him acceptable to those with whom he disagreed.

The thirty-five-hundred-dollar annual salary delighted Hayes, but the solicitorship of a growing metropolis was no sinecure. Not only did he represent the city in court, but city

PRESIDENT OF PRISON REFORM ASSOCIATION

Accompanying a guilty client to the scaffold gave Hayes a lifelong unease with the death penalty, and as Ohio governor and U.S. president, he was criticized for "liberal use of the pardoning power." In retirement, Hayes became head of the Prison Reform Association "and worked hard at it." With an optimistic faith in the goodness of people and in education, Hayes believed that much crime was rooted in poverty and that criminals could be rehabilitated.

ATTORNEY BELVA ANN
LOCKWOOD

During Hayes's presidency,
he signed the bill enabling
women lawyers to practice
before the U.S. Supreme
Court. Attorney Belva
Lockwood, who lobbied
for the bill, was the first
woman to argue such
a case.

officials, agencies, and private citizens relied on him for interpretations of its charter and ordinances. And while many of the decisions facilitated the development of Cincinnati, most were routine. In 1859, the public confirmed the city council's judgment and elected Hayes city solicitor for another two years.

The Republican triumph in 1860 and the election of Lincoln overjoyed Hayes, but the secession of the lower South and the threat of war soured Cincinnati—with its close ties to the South—on the Republican Party. In 1861, Republicans—including Hayes—were swept out of office "as a means," he quipped, "of saving the Union."

He vacated the solicitor's office and tried a case on April 9, but three days later the South fired on Fort Sumter and plunged the nation into the Civil War. After briefly joining a "volunteer home company," Hayes declared that he would rather die than not participate in the war. He was commissioned a major in the Twenty-third Ohio Volunteers (which also included Private William McKinley) and never tried another case in a court of law.

Hayes's legal training, however, was an entrenched part of him. It proved of use in the military when he served briefly as judge advocate of the Army of Western Virginia. Although there were advantages in being a staff officer, including hobnobbing with generals at headquarters, he found presiding over courts-martial "a laborious and painful business," and he was happy to return full time to the Twenty-third. As an officer, Hayes proved to be able, courageous, and lucky, surviving five wounds in four years of service.

A war hero, Hayes was elected to Congress, serving from 1865 to 1867, when he resigned to successfully run for governor of Ohio, where he served two terms from 1868 to 1872. While in Congress, Hayes supported radical Republican Reconstruction measures, and in his campaigns for governor he advocated suffrage for African Americans. Hayes was more responsible than anyone else for Ohio's crucial ratification of the Fifteenth Amendment, outlawing race as a qualification for voting.

As governor, Hayes embraced enlightened and humane reform issues. He helped establish Ohio State University and sought to improve the state's "benevolent and reformatory institutions" in their care of veterans' orphans, the mentally ill, and prisoners. Believing that the spoils system had no place in asylums or prisons, Hayes called for bipartisan boards for these state institutions.

Hayes's interest in the mentally ill and prison reform resulted in large part from his experience as a defense attorney, and the connection between his legal career and his use of the pardoning power was even more direct. Although he was not bothered by the execution of a bounty-jumping deserter during the war, he disliked the death penalty ever since accompanying Lecount to the gallows. Governor Hayes did not save hardened criminals, but when he believed a murder was not premeditated, he commuted the sentence of condemned persons and was criticized for his leniency. By the end of his second term, Hayes decided to quit politics since his main goals had been achieved with the passage of the Fourteenth and Fifteenth Amendments.

Hayes's retirement from politics proved short-lived. He did not return to the practice of law but did return to Fremont to manage Uncle Sardis's banking and real estate ventures. Hard times following the Panic of 1873, coupled with corruption in the Ulysses S. Grant administration, enabled Democrats to win the Ohio governorship and control of the U.S. Congress. In 1875, Ohio Republicans once again turned to Hayes—their best vote getter—as their gubernatorial candidate.

Hayes's narrow victory in that race led to his nomination in 1876 for president. War hero, advocate of radical Reconstruction measures, loyal party man, civil-service reformer, and favorite son of a large, toss-up state, Hayes was the classic "available man" who proved least offensive to the factions at a badly divided national convention. Hayes triumphed in the ensuing election, the outcome of which was in dispute until March 1877, by only one electoral vote. In the protracted struggle, Republicans disqualified votes—at times fraudulently—to counteract the violence Democrats had employed to keep African Americans from voting in the states of Florida, Louisiana, and South Carolina. It is impossible to say who would have won in an election devoid of violence, intimidation, and fraud. Ever self-confident, Hayes was certain that he deserved to win.

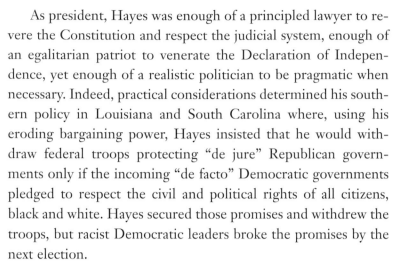

As president, Hayes was enough of a principled lawyer to re-
vere the Constitution and respect the judicial system, enough of
an egalitarian patriot to venerate the Declaration of Independence, yet enough of a realistic politician to be pragmatic when
necessary. Indeed, practical considerations determined his southern policy in Louisiana and South Carolina where, using his
eroding bargaining power, Hayes insisted that he would withdraw federal troops protecting "de jure" Republican governments only if the incoming "de facto" Democratic governments
pledged to respect the civil and political rights of all citizens,
black and white. Hayes secured those promises and withdrew the
troops, but racist Democratic leaders broke the promises by the
next election.

Hayes revered the Reconstruction Amendments, for which
he had fought so hard. He was a patient reformer certain that
in the long run equality for all would be achieved by universal
education combined with the political and legal processes, including the enforcement acts and election laws. The shortcomings of radical Reconstruction emphasized for Hayes that in the
American democracy "the people are the government. Their
character does not change with the results of elections," but
only with "generations" of education. In his inaugural address
and in retirement, Hayes advocated federal aid to supplement
education in poorer states, thus chiefly benefiting
black children. Although passed by the Senate,
the Blair bill, embodying Hayes's ideas, was defeated in the House by a combination of racist
southern Democrats and parsimonious northern
Republicans.

In the "Battle of the Riders," Hayes staunchly defended the Constitution and equal rights
against a Democratic attack on presidential
power and the election laws. In the second half of
Hayes's term, the Democrats controlled both
houses of Congress but failed to muster the two-
thirds majority needed to override a presidential
veto. To overcome that deficiency and make the
president more responsible to Congress, the Democrats attached appropriations riders that
would repeal laws enforcing the Fourteenth and

Fifteenth Amendments, especially those providing federal protection for voters. Defying the threat to shut down the government, Hayes vetoed the bills with stirring messages that reiterated his constitutional right to veto legislation and exposed the Democrats' objective to disfranchise African American southerners and corrupt northern elections. Hayes rallied public opinion to his side, united all Republican factions, and soundly defeated the Democrats.

As during his gubernatorial terms, Hayes's experience as a lawyer was most directly involved in what the hostile press called "unprecedented use of the pardoning power." In the first fourteen months of his presidency, he issued 284 pardons. Nevertheless, Hayes thought that the "pardoning power must not be used to nullify or repeal Statutes, nor to overrule the judgments of the Courts." Rather, it should be saved for "palpable mistakes, hasty decisions, newly discovered facts."

Before and after his presidency, Hayes fought for equality. With the exception of Jimmy Carter, no retired president has been more involved in social causes than Hayes. Recognizing that the American government and its laws could be no better than its people, Hayes labored constantly to broaden educational opportunities for ordinary as well as gifted students of all races, from grade school through graduate training.

Closely related to his faith in the schoolhouse and his experience as a lawyer was his interest in prison reform. In retirement, he opposed the death penalty and was president of the National Prison Reform Association. Hayes was convinced that criminals could be rehabilitated and that crime was the result of poverty and desperation and could be reduced by a more equitable distribution of wealth.

Indeed, in the last decade of his life, Hayes believed that the disparity of wealth between industrial "kings" and laboring men was the greatest problem facing the nation. Consequently, he favored confiscatory inheritance taxes, federal regulation of industry, and universal industrial education. He wanted everyone—financial moguls and political leaders as well as humble citizens—to experience and appreciate what manual labor entailed, believing that such knowledge would reduce class tensions. Sensitive, judicious, and pragmatic to the end, Hayes was a precursor of the Progressive movement.

★ ★ ★

James A. Garfield.

Twentieth President (1881)

BIRTH
November 19, 1831
Orange, Ohio

EDUCATION
Public schools
Western Reserve Eclectic Institute (now Hiram College)
Williams College
Self-study of law
Admission to the bar: January 26, 1861

OTHER OCCUPATIONS/PUBLIC OFFICES
Teacher
College president and professor
State legislator
Civil War major general
U.S. congressman and senator-elect
Minister of the Disciples of Christ

DEATH
September 19, 1881
Elberon, N.J.

LAW CAREER IN BRIEF

It is rare indeed when a lawyer's first case is before the U.S. Supreme Court and rarer still when the decision represents a landmark in the law. But that was the situation for James Garfield, whose practice was largely before our nation's high court. The 1866 landmark case was *Ex parte Milligan*, which held that Milligan and other civilians could not be tried by a military court so long as civil courts were operating. Garfield went on to argue eleven more high court cases from 1869 to 1879, none as legally or historically important as *Milligan*, though they enhanced Garfield's reputation as a skilled constitutional lawyer.

James A. Garfield: Supreme Court Counsel

ALLAN PESKIN

Although it may be accurate to describe James A. Garfield as a "lawyer-president," it is also misleading. Many nineteenth-century Americans, particularly those who grew up near the frontier, were simply too versatile to be confined in any one occupational category. The social ideal was the self-made man and the jack of all trades.

Garfield certainly qualified as a self-made man. Born into rural poverty in 1831 on a farm outside of Cleveland, Ohio, he lost his father while still an infant. As he grew up he was saved from a life of manual drudgery by his affable personality, quick mind, and phenomenal memory, all of which enabled him to shine in the district schools and later the colleges he attended. Building upon his scholastic prowess, he became a teacher and, after his conversion, a preacher as well.

Neither of these callings could completely satisfy his ambitious nature and so, like many others of his time and place, he sampled a number of trades. In his fifty years of life he managed to be a farmer, carpenter, professor of classical languages, college president, ordained minister (of the Disciples of Christ), major general, and highly successful politician. That he added lawyer to that list was something of an afterthought.

Initially he resisted the prospect of a legal career, fearing that it might conflict with his role as a minister of the Gospel. "Though I do not regard the Legal Profession [as] incompatible with Christianity," he had mused in 1854 at the age of twenty-three, "still I think it would be much more difficult to cultivate and preserve that purity of heart and devotedness to the cause of Christ while partak[ing] of those ambitious aspirations that accompany the Gentlemen of the Bar."

★ ★ ★

"I made my study of the law as complete as anyone I know of, but I did it in my own room at Hiram."

James A. Garfield

Five years later, with Garfield already a state senator as well as the president of what is now Hiram College, "ambitious aspirations" no longer seemed quite so threatening, and he began to explore the possibility of becoming a lawyer.

It was, he discovered, easy enough to do. In an age not yet committed to formalized credentials or standardized exams, legal training was often casual and haphazard. Although there were a handful of law colleges, few would-be lawyers bothered to attend them. Most were either self-taught, like Lincoln, or else served some sort of apprenticeship under the tutelage of an established attorney. Garfield was self-taught. "I made my study of the law as complete as any one I know of," he boasted, "but I did it in my own room at Hiram." His only formal assistance came from the up-and-coming young northern Ohio lawyer and novelist Albert Gallatin Riddle, with whom he registered in order to comply with Ohio regulations.

If Riddle's description of a similar interview in his semiautobiographical novel *Bart Ridgley* is any indication, then the help he gave Garfield was minimal. In that account, an aspiring lawyer was advised to read Blackstone; any further study was dismissed as superfluous. As for admission to the bar, the student was informed that "the laws of Ohio required two years study, before admission, which would be upon examination before the Supreme Court, or by a committee of lawyers appointed for that purpose; lawyers who received students usually charged fifty or sixty dollars per year for use of books and instruction, the last of which often did not amount to much."

Garfield borrowed the recommended books, mastered them and, when the two-year waiting period was up, presented himself for examination. Since the members of the examining boards were usually themselves self-taught, their exams were not, as a rule, unduly rigorous. Garfield could have avoided even that formality. By this time in early 1861, he was a member of the Ohio legislature and was assured by his friend, Jacob D. Cox, that a man in his position could forego the bar exam and be admitted "by courtesy" regardless of legal expertise (or lack of it). "So be at rest on that point, and don't overtax yourself," Cox advised.

Garfield, however, insisted on a proper examination. The board was stacked with his political antagonists who were not inclined to let him off lightly, but after a "thorough and searching examination," they declared his mastery of the law to be "unusual and phenomenal."

Garfield was now officially a lawyer but not a practicing one. Shortly after his admission to the bar the Civil War turned his career to unexpected paths. Entering the army as a lieutenant colonel, he rapidly rose to become the youngest major general in the service. In mid-war he resigned his commission upon election to the U.S. Congress. For the next few years he was too busy learning how to be an effective legislator and a leader of the Radical faction of his Republican Party to spare time for another career. Other than drawing up incorporation papers for some mining ventures in which he was involved, he allowed his legal training to rust.

Garfield was inordinately proud of having avoided the drudgery customarily endured by fledgling attorneys. "The regular channel to the law," he explained, "is to study in a lawyer's office, sweep out the office for a year or two more, then to pettifog in a justice's court, and slowly and gradually, after being subordinate to everybody, and the older heads have died off, to feel his way as a practicing lawyer. If after fifteen or twenty years' practice the man gets a case in the United States Supreme Court, and is admitted there, he considers it a red-letter day in his history."

He had not even appeared in any courtroom until a dramatic development enabled him to make the most spectacular debut in the annals of the American bar. He started at the top, with his very first legal argument made before the U.S. Supreme Court, in the 1866 landmark case of *Ex parte Milligan*.

Lambdin P. Milligan and his friends were prominent Indiana "Copperheads," as the slang of the day labeled those northerners who sympathized with the Confederate cause. There was some reason to suspect that Milligan's support went beyond sympathy and that he might, in fact, be plotting to release Confederate prisoners of war, assist rebel raids behind Union lines, and commit other acts of terror and espionage. He was arrested in October 1864 and tried before a military court rather than a civil one partly because of the fear that no civilian jury in southern Indiana would convict him and partly, it must be admitted, because the evidence against him was probably too flimsy to warrant a conviction.

★ ★ ★

"[T]hat a Republic can wield the vast enginery of war without breaking down the safeguards of liberty; can suppress insurrection, and put down rebellion, however formidable, without destroying the bulwarks of law."

James A. Garfield,
in *Ex parte Milligan*

EX PARTE MILLIGAN

Garfield's first case was his most notable, as the U.S. Supreme Court agreed with his argument that Lambdin Milligan and his fellow civilian defendants (pictured here) could not be tried by a military court when civilian courts were in operation. Politically, however, the decision unleashed a storm, and the high court was assailed as it had not been since the *Dred Scott* case.

As expected, the military tribunal did its duty. Without being hobbled by constitutional restraints or fastidious notions of due process, it summarily ordered the alleged conspirators to be hanged the following May. By that time, however, the Civil War was over and the new president, Andrew Johnson, postponed execution of the sentence while an appeal was pending before the U.S. Supreme Court.

The outcome of that appeal could have political ramifications that went beyond the fate of Milligan and his associates. In their program of reconstructing the South, the Radical Republicans who controlled Congress planned to utilize military commissions similar to the one used to try the Indiana Copperheads. An adverse ruling in the Milligan case could jeopardize these plans.

Milligan's legal team was a brilliant one. David Dudley Field was a legal scholar and codifier, hailed as "the American Justinian." He was also, not incidentally, the brother of Supreme Court Justice Stephen J. Field. Jeremiah Sullivan Black had served as secretary of state and attorney general in the Buchanan administration and was one of the most sought-after trial lawyers of his day.

What this distinguished team lacked was political balance. Black was a partisan Democrat and Field, though a Republican, was not a Radical. Not surprisingly, they sought to redress this political imbalance by recruiting a certified Radical Republican for their team. As a leading spokesman of that faction in the House of Representatives, Garfield seemed to fill the bill, with the added advantage that he was a close personal friend and political protégé of Chief Justice Salmon P. Chase. He was also on good terms with Black, despite their political differences. They prayed at the same church and shared similar literary tastes.

Black had even taken the young congressman into his law firm, though he had not yet assigned him any duties.

In later years, explaining his involvement in the Milligan case, Garfield downplayed political considerations and gave the impression that he was tapped as counsel solely because of his merits. He must have realized, however, that he was running in fast company, particularly for his first outing, for he boned up on the case with an intensity he had not displayed since his student days.

His argument before the Court was lengthy and learned but it boiled down to a question of jurisdiction—that is, that military tribunals had no right to try civilians so long as the civil courts were functioning. A majority of the Court adopted this proposition, thus freeing Milligan and his confederates. The ruling also brought down upon Garfield and the Supreme Court a flurry of angry denunciations, but over the years it became recognized as a landmark in the evolution of American freedom, justifying Garfield's claim that it would demonstrate "that a republic can wield the vast enginery of war without breaking down the safeguards of liberty; can suppress insurrection, and put down rebellion, however formidable, without destroying the bulwarks of law."

HERO OF THE COLORED RACE?

Though Garfield was not particularly known for his advocacy of black civil rights, he was a strong opponent of slavery before the Civil War, and during the war he was a vigorous advocate for enlisting blacks in the Union army. Almost twenty years later, in his presidential inaugural address, he insisted there could be no middle ground between slavery and full equality and he promised to protect the newly won rights of the freedmen. Ironically, at the inaugural ball that followed, blacks were discouraged from participating in the dancing.

HEROES OF THE COLORED RACE.

ALEXANDER CAMPBELL'S WILL CASE

Campbell founded the Disciples of Christ, into which Garfield, at the age of eighteen, was baptized. This "turning point in his life" had a transforming influence on the "hitherto lackadaisical lad." Garfield took special pleasure in successfully defending Campbell's will against some disgruntled family members who alleged that Campbell had been mentally incompetent, as the outcome vindicated the reputation of his boyhood religious hero.

Garfield's very first case was also the high point of his legal career. Never again would he be associated with such a high-profile case, though over the next two decades he would take part in about two dozen cases, the majority of which were argued before the U.S. Supreme Court. This legal work was squeezed into whatever time Garfield could spare from his increasingly demanding congressional obligations. Although a part-time attorney, Garfield was no dilettante. According to Associate Justice Stanley Matthews, he was regarded "as one of the very best lawyers at the bar in the whole country."

His practice was confined to civil cases. Some of these arose from the tangled legal issues stemming from the disruption of the Civil War. In *Bennett v. Hunter*, a Virginia tenant had tendered the real estate tax in the absence of the owner, who was off fighting in the Confederate army. State authorities refused the proffer and confiscated the property. The Supreme Court supported Garfield's appeal and overturned the confiscation.

Two more-far-reaching cases dealt with the impact of the Civil War on life insurance policies whose premiums had been uncollectible during the conflict. Were they still in force if the insured made good on the back payments? If so, Garfield argued, then only the dying and the heirs of the dead would likely take advantage of this opportunity, bankrupting the companies. In the 1874 case of *Tate v. New York Life Insurance Company*, the Court was evenly divided but two years later, in *New York Life Insurance Co. v. Statham*, a majority of the justices were persuaded by his argument.

Garfield also litigated contract disputes as well as patent infringements on inventions as varied as feather dusters, inkwells, and harvesters, including a successful challenge to the Goodyear corporation (*Providence Rubber Co. v. Goodyear* in 1869). Although he frequently represented large insurance companies, he did not always take the side of big business. He defended a Washington church against damages caused by construction of the nearby Baltimore & Potomac Railroad and unsuccessfully supported the claims of certain government workers for additional pay.

The case that gave him the greatest personal satisfaction was the Alexander Campbell will case, heard in the Virginia courts

FULL DRESS REHEARSAL OF THE GRAND PRESIDENTIAL CORPS DE BALLET.

in 1868. After the death of Campbell, the founder of the Disciples of Christ, some disgruntled family members challenged the aged preacher's will, claiming he had been mentally incompetent. Garfield represented the estate and was exceedingly pleased at being able to vindicate the reputation of his boyhood religious hero.

The case that brought Garfield the most grief was one that never went to court and to which he devoted almost no effort. Early in the 1870s, he was retained for five thousand dollars to represent the DeGolyer Pavement Company in its quest for a contract to pave Washington's muddy streets. Although he did make an appearance before the District's Board of Public Works, the records of his otherwise voluminous legal papers contain little evidence that his efforts were more than perfunctory. Cynics charged that he had not been engaged for his legal expertise but because of his position as chairman of the House Appropriations Committee, which controlled the purse strings of the District. These accusations followed him into his subsequent reelection campaigns and were never fully laid to rest, despite all of Garfield's attempts to justify his conduct.

Garfield managed to weather that storm, but it contributed to his growing discontent with public life. No longer young, and

DeGolyer Pavement Company Controversy

DeGolyer's payment of five thousand dollars to Garfield for his legal services dogged him politically, despite his repeated efforts at justifying it. In the company's quest to secure a contract to pave Washington's muddy streets, they had retained Garfield, who made an appearance before the District's Board of Public Works but did little else. Garfield was then chair of the House Appropriations Committee, and accusations of misconduct followed him throughout his subsequent campaigns.

UNEXPECTED (AND THEN
TRAGIC) DEVELOPMENTS
Garfield was on the verge
of becoming partner in a
Cleveland law firm when
the Republican convention
turned to him to lead its
1880 presidential ticket,
with Chester Arthur as
his running mate. Three
months into his presidency,
however, Garfield was assas-
sinated by Charles Guiteau.

burdened with a growing family, he found it increasingly difficult
to juggle two careers. Congressmen in Garfield's day were expected to do all their own work without the assistance of the large
staffs now taken for granted. Except for committee chairmen,
they were not supplied with offices or even desks, other than the
one they occupied on the floor of Congress. Garfield had to draft
bills, mollify constituents, prepare campaign speeches, and handle
correspondence with no help other than a part-time private secretary. Little wonder that complaints of exhaustion and mental
stagnation appeared more and more frequently in his diaries.

Something would have to give. Either he would devote himself completely to an onerous, but promising, political career or
else embark upon the untried waters of a full-time legal practice.
Yet, despite the praise lavished on his skills by Stanley Matthews
and others, Garfield harbored deep misgivings about his legal
ability. "Every case I have," he confessed, "convinces me anew

that I need a more thorough knowledge of the technical parts of the law." Had he applied himself more diligently to the profession, he now realized, it "would have placed me in a high position at the bar. . . . It may not be too late even yet and I think I must break away from public life and take care of myself."

He sounded out various Cleveland law firms and was on the verge of accepting a partnership when a startling and unexpected development intervened. In 1880, he was attending the Republican national convention as floor manager for Ohio's senator John Sherman when the delegates, frustrated by a deadlock that had lasted for thirty-six ballots, turned impulsively to Garfield and selected him to be their presidential nominee.

Garfield won election to the presidency the following November in one of the closest contests in American political history. His administration, however, was cut tragically short after only three months when this lawyer-president fell victim to America's only lawyer-assassin, Charles Julius Guiteau.

Like Garfield, Guiteau was a self-trained midwestern lawyer, but while Garfield had found success, Guiteau knew only failure. He seems to have tried only one case and made such a botch of it that the jury ruled against his client without even bothering to leave the jury box. After that setback, he, like Garfield, sampled many trades, including religion, journalism, and politics, failing in each. Determined to make his mark on the world in one way or another, he decided to assassinate the president after the voice of God told him one morning that Garfield had to be "removed" for the good of the nation and the Republican Party.

He caught up with his victim on July 2, 1881, in the waiting room of that same Baltimore & Potomac Railroad that Garfield had successfully sued a few years earlier. Guiteau pumped two bullets into the back of the unguarded president. Garfield lingered for another eighty days, dying of complications from his wounds on September 19. After his death it was discovered that this lawyer-president had neglected to make out his own will.

★ ★ ★

"Like Garfield, Guiteau was a self-trained midwestern lawyer, but while Garfield had found success, Guiteau knew only failure."

Twenty-first President (1881–85)

BIRTH
October 5, 1829
Fairfield, Vt.

EDUCATION
Union College
Studied law with E. D. Culver in New York City
Admission to the bar: May 1854

OTHER OCCUPATIONS/PUBLIC OFFICES
Teacher and school principal
Civil War brigadier general
Collector, Port of New York
Vice president with James Garfield

DEATH
November 18, 1886
New York, N.Y.

LAW CAREER IN BRIEF

Upon being admitted to the bar in 1854, Arthur was made partner in the firm of Culver, Parker and Arthur. Early on, he was counsel in several notable civil rights cases that integrated New York City's railroad cars and secured the freedom of eight slaves. After leaving the military in 1863, Arthur and partner Henry Gardiner prospered as war-claims attorneys and as lobbyists in Albany and Washington, D.C. As Arthur became more politically active in the mid-1860s, however, law became a sideline for him, even though he had such notable clients as R. G. Dun and Charles Tiffany.

Chester A. Arthur: War Claims Lawyer

Thomas C. Reeves

When President James A. Garfield was shot on July 2, 1881, the national clamor was accelerated by the thought that in the event of the chief executive's death his successor would be Chester A. Arthur. When the shots were fired in a railway station in Washington, the vice president was busily at work in Albany, New York, defending administration opponents. Moreover, when the gunman was captured, he implied that he was an agent of Arthur's. Journalists began scurrying through their files to find out just who this distinguished looking lawyer, Civil War general, and controversial politician and government administrator really was.

Chester Alan Arthur was born in Fairfield, Vermont, on October 5, 1829, the fifth child of a Baptist minister and his wife. William Arthur, a native of Ireland, was a bright, irascible, well-educated man of thirty-four who had studied law and taught school before being swept away by a religious experience in Burlington, Vermont, and deciding to become a preacher. Malvina Stone Arthur was of English descent and had been born and raised in Vermont. She could boast of a grandfather who had fought for the Continental army during the American Revolution and a father who had graduated from Dartmouth College.

While young Chester was growing up, the family moved often and was far from prosperous. Their difficulties stemmed in large part from William's often fiery temperament and his fervent belief in abolitionism. By the mid-1840s, however, William was able to devote some time and energy to scholarly and literary pursuits and was awarded an honorary Master of Arts degree by Union College in Schenectady, New York.

Chester, or "Chet" as he was known to classmates, entered Union College as a sophomore in 1845, following several years

★ ★ ★

"Arthur was also part of a landmark civil rights case in New York City . . . [that] soon led all New York City railroad companies to integrate their cars."

THE TIFFANY CONNECTION

Arthur served as attorney for Charles Tiffany (pictured here), scion of Tiffany and Company. The meager existing records of Arthur's services indicate that he provided Tiffany advice regarding relationships and dealings with early business partners. Later, President Arthur retained Louis Comfort Tiffany to help renovate the White House and handle its china business. "History only remembers a few things about [Arthur]," wrote White House historian William Seale, but "one is that he had taste."

of preparatory education. Chester took the traditional classical curriculum and was an above average student. Six foot two, handsome, amiable, and well dressed, he was president of a debating society and a popular member of a social fraternity. He taught school during two winter vacations to help pay his college expenses.

After graduating in 1848, Chester taught school briefly and traveled to Ballston Spa to begin a legal education, probably at the newly opened State and National Law School. He returned home a short time later and resumed teaching, while studying law at home. In 1853, Arthur went to New York City to become a law clerk for a family friend, E. D. Culver. In May of 1854 he was admitted to the bar and made a partner in what was now called Culver, Parker and Arthur.

When Culver became a judge in 1855, many of his duties fell to Arthur. One such assignment involved the landmark Lemmon Slave case, which was argued before the supreme court of New York in 1857 and in the court of appeals, New York State's highest court, in early 1860.

Jonathan Lemmon and his wife had brought eight slaves into New York City in 1852, traveling from Virginia on their way to Texas. A free black named Louis Napoleon appealed to the superior court of New York for a writ of habeas corpus, contending that state law prohibited slavery and that the slaves should thus be freed. Abolitionists, now gaining considerable strength in the North, joined the case and E. D. Culver, an abolitionist, was one of two attorneys hired to represent the petitioner. Many southerners were irate when the writ was granted, and the Virginia legislature ordered a suit to be filed.

The writ was upheld by both courts in which it was argued, in large part a triumph for the gifted lawyer-orator William M. Evarts, who had been added to the legal team. Arthur's role in the struggle is uncertain, but he was clearly active. When the case came before the court of appeals, he was listed as "attorney for the People" and was later awarded a one-third share of the firm's legal fees. The Lemmon case would thereafter be cited as an example of Arthur's legal acumen, industriousness, and commitment to high principle.

Arthur was also part of a landmark civil rights case in New York City. In 1854, Elizabeth Jennings, a black public school teacher, was roughed up on a New York City streetcar for failing to leave a car reserved for whites. Angry black leaders consulted Culver, Parker and Arthur, and a lawsuit was filed against the railroad company. Arthur won the suit by calling attention to a statute stating that "colored persons, if sober, well-behaved, and free from disease" could not be expelled from a common carrier. The case soon led all New York City railroad companies to integrate their cars.

Arthur was keenly interested in politics, considering himself a Whig as early as 1844. A decade later, he was active in the creation of the Republican Party in New York and began to serve as a political functionary in New York City. He learned much from political boss Thurlow Weed and allied himself with the wealthy merchant Edwin D. Morgan, who became New York's governor in 1858. Three years later, after his reelection, Morgan named Arthur engineer-in-chief of the state militia. At thirty, Chester Arthur's future looked promising indeed.

In 1859, Arthur married Ellen Lewis Herndon, Virginia-born daughter of Captain William Lewis Herndon, who had won national attention the year before by bravely going down with his ship off Cape Hatteras. Nineteen-year-old "Nell" came from a long line of southern aristocrats and was active in Washington high society.

When the Civil War broke out, Arthur became engineer-in-chief with the rank of brigadier general. He was responsible for helping to arm, equip, clothe, and feed troops for the defense of the state. His effectiveness was such that he was soon able to add "Acting Assistant Quartermaster General" to his title.

By December of 1861, more than one hundred ten thousand men were enrolled by New York, and other troops were pouring into the state on their way to battlefields. Arthur's duties were such that for several months he was able to sleep only three hours a night. He was, by all accounts, congenial, efficient, and honest. His legal talents were employed at one point when he helped draft a new state militia law and advocated it before state legislative committees. His position required him to have a sophisticated knowledge of military law. Governor Morgan, himself a general and a severe taskmaster, was highly pleased with the accomplishments of his protégé. In July 1862, Morgan commissioned Arthur quartermaster general of New York. By late that year, New York had sent a total of 219,000 men to the front.

★ ★ ★

"Returning to his legal practice [after the war], Arthur grew prosperous by handling war claims and by writing and lobbying for legislation in Albany and Washington."

Arthur left active duty in the war on the first day of 1863, when a new Democratic governor assumed office and relieved Morgan and his staff of their duties. A major reason for his decision not to reenlist involved the Confederate sympathies of his wife and her relatives. He had also lost much of his enthusiasm for President Lincoln. Moreover, wealth and power were to be had during wartime, and Arthur and his wife were ambitious on both counts.

Returning to his legal practice, Arthur grew prosperous by handling war claims and by writing and lobbying for legislation in Albany and Washington. He soon became involved with a wealthy and unscrupulous New York hatter named Thomas Murphy, and the two began pursuing real estate speculations and political opportunities. Both were members of the Republican Party's Conservative wing, led by Morgan (now a U.S. senator), boss Thurlow Weed, and William Henry Seward. Their opponents were called Radicals, headed by Horace Greeley. In the campaign of 1864, Arthur and Murphy played a small role in selecting Andrew Johnson of Tennessee for the ticket and were employed in collecting political assessments from government employees and contractors.

In 1867 Arthur became a member of the exclusive Century Club, a tribute to his good manners, charm, wealth, and political ascendancy. That same year he began serving on the city executive committee as an assembly district representative. Moving rapidly up the ranks, he soon became chairman of the executive committee of the state central committee, the top Republican body in the state. Shortly, he became an ally of Congressman Roscoe Conkling, an able, imperious, highly ambitious, and narcissistic congressman from Utica. In 1869, Conkling was elected to the Senate, largely due to his commanding oratorical abilities. Conkling and James G. Blaine of Maine, bitter personal enemies, were soon to represent the two major factions of the GOP.

With the enthusiastic support of New York Conservatives, including Conkling and Arthur, Ulysses S. Grant was elected to the presidency in the fall of 1868. At first, Arthur failed to win a desirable post from the administration and continued to concentrate his efforts on his legal practice. He handled business affairs for Tiffany and Company, among others, and took some criminal cases. But those who knew him best were convinced that Arthur was primarily interested in politics.

From 1869 to 1870, Arthur served as counsel to the New York City tax commission, one of several New York City Republicans appointed with the cooperation of Tammany Hall and Boss William Marcy Tweed. Conkling took control of the state GOP in 1870 by winning the friendship and trust of President Grant and by successfully defending his appointment of Tom Murphy as collector of the New York Customhouse, the richest source of political patronage in the country. When Murphy was forced out of the Customhouse in November 1871 amid charges of corruption, inefficiency, and undue attention to politics, the president permitted him to choose his successor. The choice was Chester A. Arthur, a selection endorsed by the entire Conkling faction. Civil service reformers, eager to take government positions out of politics and base them on merit and ability, feared the worst.

The "spoils system" had been part of American politics from the nation's beginning. Political victors drove out opponents holding government jobs and appointed their own, usually without regard to qualifications of any kind. Once in office, the new officeholders were assessed portions of their salaries for campaign purposes. Political machines of both parties were dependent upon the patronage dispersal and the funds it produced.

The New York Customhouse was a prime political plum because it was the largest single federal office. In 1877 it collected about 75 percent of the nation's custom receipts, which amounted to approximately $108 million, and employed hundreds. In fact, the collector's principal occupation was the direction of removals and appointments and the collection of assessments. When Arthur took office, Republicans could count on $36,000 a year coming from Customhouse employees. For his services, Arthur grossed more than $50,000 a year, an income superior to the president's, and a far cry from the $4,019 he made as an attorney in 1871.

Business leaders at first welcomed Arthur; he was an amiable, genteel, educated gentleman whose legal background would undoubtedly prove useful in his new office. And he, like the president, spoke earnestly of his desire for civil service reform. It soon became apparent, however, that the spoils system

LAWYER FOR R. G. DUN

In 1870, R. G. Dun—owner of the Mercantile Exchange, the forerunner of Dun and Bradstreet—hired Chester Arthur as his attorney. Few records, however, provide insight as to the nature and scope of legal work that Arthur may have performed for his friend and frequent fishing partner (pictured together here). Interestingly, Dun and Bradstreet claims that three lawyer-presidents—Abraham Lincoln, Grover Cleveland, and William McKinley—worked as "business correspondents" for the company.

PRESIDENT ARTHUR

Morrison J. Waite, chief justice of the United States, administers the presidential oath to Arthur following the assassination of President Garfield.

was in operation as never before in the Customhouse. Arthur was highly popular in Republican circles, especially within the ranks of the Conkling machine. While often giving sound business and legal advice to merchants and brokers, he devoted most of his time and energy to politics, manipulating appointments and salary kickbacks (illegal in the Customhouse after October 19, 1872) throughout the city and state and transmitting funds to campaigns across the nation.

The spoilsmen reigned during both Grant administrations, generating corruption, inefficiency, public scandal, and widespread cynicism. Conkling's Customhouse lieutenants, led by Arthur, were an integral part of the sordid picture, although the collector himself attempted with much success to conceal his role in the scandals. After a celebrated attempt to extort funds from a prominent businessman, Congress passed reform legislation that lowered Arthur's annual income to a fixed salary of twelve thousand dollars.

During the depression era of the 1870s, the Arthurs lived luxuriously in a lavishly decorated New York brownstone, complete with five servants. The couple, now with two children, participated regularly in events led by the city's wealthiest and most powerful citizens. The collector, dapper and dignified, weighed up to 225 pounds and dressed in the latest English fashions, sporting carefully trimmed side whiskers.

In 1876, Conkling made an unsuccessful effort to win the GOP presidential nomination. The convention choice, Governor Rutherford B. Hayes of Ohio, enjoyed the full support of Arthur and his Customhouse colleagues during the successful campaign. But instead of rewarding the spoilsmen for their unusually vigorous fund-raising, the new president actively embraced civil service reform. He was also eager to punish Roscoe Conkling for personal slights, the failure to carry New York in the election, and a flirtation with the Democratic presidential candidate. Historian T. Harry Williams has observed of Hayes that he was "a curious mixture of idealism and practicality." On April 9, 1877, the administration announced a full-scale investigation of the much criticized New York Customhouse.

In a series of reports, the probe revealed inefficiency, incompetence, political activity, and widespread corruption. When the

Customhouse leadership proved less than eager to carry out recommended reforms, the president, after a lengthy struggle, replaced Arthur and two of his lieutenants with reformers. Conkling thus lost his control over a major campaign tool, and intraparty warfare accelerated throughout the nation. Throughout the Customhouse crisis, Arthur portrayed himself as the champion of integrity and civil service reform, a claim that persuaded few. In early 1879, he returned to his law practice. But it was a sideline: the pursuit of power for the Conkling faction, known as the Stalwarts, won his major attention.

The Stalwarts worked feverishly for a third term for Ulysses S. Grant, but it was not to be. With Hayes voluntarily dropping out of the picture, the GOP convention in 1880 turned to Ohio senator James A. Garfield, who had a distinguished Civil War record and much political experience. He was pragmatic and moderate and was widely thought to be somewhere between the dominant factions, Conkling's Stalwarts and James G. Blaine's Half-Breeds. At the convention, in part due to a mistake by a key politico, the second place on the ticket went to Chester A. Arthur, who had sought the honor in part to elevate his battered reputation. Delegates approved, hoping that Arthur would bring Conklingites enthusiastically into the campaign and help assure victory in November.

Conkling, Arthur, and Grant labored intensely for the election of the ticket. New York made the difference in the extremely close election, and Stalwarts expected Garfield to reward them handsomely. Instead, the new president allied himself with Blaine, Conkling's archenemy, naming the Maine senator his secretary of state. Garfield rejected almost all Stalwart demands and chose an opponent to be collector of the New York Customhouse.

Conkling's power in New York began to slip badly during the Garfield administration, and he and a state colleague resigned from the Senate in protest. Arthur, despite his position, participated actively in efforts to restore Stalwart authority. He was in Albany working against the wishes of his own chief executive when word reached him, and the world, on July 2 that Garfield had been shot. The assassin, demented attorney and frustrated office-seeker Charles Guiteau, declared to the arresting officer, "I did it and will go to jail for it. I am a Stalwart, and Arthur will be President." The vice president's popularity hit rock bottom.

STAR ROUTE CASES

Though an active participant in the spoils system, Arthur surprised many friends and foes with his moderate, and sometimes progressive, agenda after assuming the presidency. In the Star Route cases, for example, he supported continued prosecution of former political allies and personal friends accused of swindling government funds.

THE PATH OF DUTY.
STAR-ROUTERS—"Be ral'd, you shall not go!"
HAMLET-ARTHUR—I say, away! Go on, I'll follow thee!"

Garfield died on September 19. During the months he suffered, Arthur rose in public esteem, being applauded for his dignified behavior. His political experience and legal background provided special hope for many, and even his sternest critics wished him well.

Once in the White House, Arthur showed few sympathies toward his fellow Stalwarts. He knew full well that fighting civil service reform and awarding Conkling with high office would earn him widespread condemnation. Instead, he pursued a moderate course, selecting a politically balanced cabinet and being willing to work with reformers. He also backed the continued prosecution of Stalwarts, former political associates and personal friends involved in a swindle of government funds called the Star Route frauds.

Arthur's first annual message, delivered to Congress on December 6, 1881, brimmed over with requests. He favored, among other things, the enlargement of the armed forces, federal aid to education, a building for the Library of Congress, assistance and protection for Native Americans, lower taxes, tariff revision, and a measure of civil service reform. The message was received with widespread approval.

During his almost full term in office, Arthur renovated the White House and entertained with elegance and good taste (his wife having died in 1879, Arthur called on his youngest sister, Mary Arthur McElroy, to serve as first lady). To the public, he was a sophisticated, handsomely dressed, and generally affable president. Privately, Arthur intensely disliked the burdens and political restraints of his office.

In 1882 the president began to suffer from Bright's disease, a fatal kidney illness in adults that sapped his strength and often left him irritable. Presidential trips to Florida and Yellowstone National Park in 1883 did little to alleviate Arthur's suffering, about which he said nothing.

Almost evenly divided politically, Congress could boast of only modest achievements during the Arthur administration. The Pendleton Act of 1882 was the nation's first civil service reform legislation, covering about 10 percent of all federal jobs, which Arthur not only signed but administered admirably. The president also supported and signed legislation initiating creation of the New Navy, a flotilla of steel ships.

Like his father, Arthur was an abolitionist before the Civil War. As president, his veto of the Chinese immigration bill also showed sensitivity toward their rights in this country. He later signed the highly popular bill, however, when the prohibition of the importation of Chinese laborers extended ten, rather than twenty, years. The legislation also denied American citizenship to all Chinese, a principle Arthur had earlier opposed.

The president's support of Indian rights was extraordinary. He sought to extend state and territorial laws to Indian reservations, made attempts to protect Indian land from encroachment, believed in individual land ownership for Indians, and supported Indian education. Arthur thus was somewhat ahead of his time on the issue of civil rights.

At the same time, the country went into an economic slump during the last two years of the Arthur administration. A pork barrel rivers and harbor bill passed over the president's veto. And efforts by the president to invigorate the nation's foreign policy got nowhere.

By early 1884, Arthur had perhaps more enemies than friends among GOP leaders, and his nomination for a second term seemed highly doubtful. A prominent New Jersey Republican exclaimed, "People look upon this Administration as a sort of summer holiday—a kind of lapse between one man who was elected and another who is going to be elected." Almost wholly secretive about his fatal illness, Arthur quietly told friends to cease efforts on his behalf. The nomination went to James G. Blaine, who narrowly lost to Grover Cleveland in November.

At the time, Arthur was given credit for restoring calm and confidence in the wake of a traumatic presidential transition and for supporting integrity and efficiency in public office. Business leaders were especially grateful. The *New York World* declared in 1886, the year of Arthur's death, "No duty was neglected in his administration, and no adventurous project alarmed the nation. There was no scandal to make us ashamed while he was in office and none to be ripped up when he went out of it. He earned and deserved the honest fame he possesses."

Chester Alan Arthur was a good president at a time when very few sought greatness in their chief executives. His record was clearly better than anyone who had known him only as a spoilsman and shifty political operative might have expected.

★ ★ ★

"After leaving the White House, Arthur announced he would resume the practice of law in New York City. His efforts were severely limited, however, by his fatal illness."

Twenty-second and Twenty-fourth President (1885–89 and 1893–97)

BIRTH
March 18, 1837
Caldwell, N.J.

EDUCATION
Public schools
Studied law in the Buffalo, N.Y., firm of Rogers, Bowen & Rogers
Admission to the bar: 1859

OTHER OCCUPATIONS/PUBLIC OFFICES
Assistant district attorney
Erie County sheriff
Buffalo mayor
New York governor

DEATH
June 24, 1908
Princeton, N.J.

LAW CAREER IN BRIEF

Cleveland initially practiced with the law firm of Rogers, Bowen & Rogers from 1859 to 1863 before serving as Buffalo's assistant district attorney, where he handled the bulk of the work due to the district attorney's health problems. Cleveland then formed a series of law partnerships, the most successful with Lyman Bass and Wilson Bissell in 1873, which included Standard Oil and other prominent businesses among its clientele. Cleveland preferred practice outside the courtroom, though one trial garnered his client a verdict of $274,000, then the largest award in western New York State. Cleveland also practiced law between his presidential terms, including a case before the U.S. Supreme Court.

Grover Cleveland: An Honest Lawyer

EUGENE C. GERHART

When young Grover Cleveland arrived as an apprentice at the Buffalo, New York, law firm of Rogers, Bowen, and Rogers—at whose predecessor Millard Fillmore had worked—few expected the firm would soon be claiming another American chief executive. Henry W. Rogers, elder partner of the firm, grabbed a copy of Blackstone and firmly planted it on the table where Grover was to work. "There's where they all begin," intoned Rogers. The seeds of Cleveland's legal career were sown.

Cleveland was born in Caldwell, New Jersey, on March 18, 1837. His father was a Presbyterian minister, a graduate of Yale and Princeton; his mother was of Anglo-Irish extraction and the daughter of a law book publisher. He was a descendant of Moses Cleaveland, an English Puritan, who came to America and settled in Massachusetts in 1635. Another descendant, also named Moses Cleaveland, was a Connecticut lawyer who distinguished himself in the Revolutionary War and who, with others, established a settlement on Lake Erie that bears his name (the Cleaveland clan and the Ohio city both later dropped the first "a" from their names). From his ancestors, Cleveland inherited traits that were held in higher esteem than money; namely, piety, self-respect, education, and courage, values that Grover respected all his life.

He was christened Stephen Grover Cleveland, the fifth of nine children. While still a boy, he dropped the name Stephen and was known thereafter only as Grover Cleveland. Young Grover entered the Academy in Fayetteville and later attended the Clinton Liberal Institute for a year. He was governed by strict rules laid down by his clergyman father who died in 1853 at the age of forty-nine. When that happened, sixteen-year-old Grover had to go to work and leave his formal education behind.

★ ★ ★

"If the boy has any brains, he'll find out for himself without anybody telling him."

Henry Rogers, on Cleveland's legal apprenticeship

"Lawyers liked him as a referee because they knew his decisions would be based on the law."

Senator Frank Loomis

Such responsibilities would soon thereafter effectively end his hope of a college education at Hamilton College.

But formal education was not then a prerequisite for a legal career, and young Grover was soon on his way to pursue the study of law in Cleveland, stopping first near Buffalo to visit his uncle, Lewis Allen, a wealthy and well-connected farmer. At Allen's initiative, Cleveland soon began an apprenticeship at the Rogers law firm, where he averaged five dollars weekly. He enjoyed his work but complained, "they won't tell me anything." Said Rogers, "If the boy has any brains, he'll find out for himself without anybody telling him," echoing an instructional principle that continued to hold sway in legal circles well into the twentieth century.

Grover decided to stay in Buffalo. The fishing was excellent in upstate New York and he enjoyed this respite from his duties at the firm, a diversion he would continue to enjoy throughout his life.

At the age of twenty-two he was admitted to the New York bar. He also worked hard for the Democratic Party. His record as a young man in Buffalo was outstanding. He was not a brilliant lawyer, but his clients trusted him and he soon became one of the leading lawyers in western New York. Given the conscientious manner in which he pursued his legal and political work, one biographer describes him as a "plodder." But there was also something about Cleveland that mirrored traits of Lincoln, who wrote: "Stand with anybody that stands right . . . and part with him when he goes wrong." As Buffalo lawyer Philip Wickser wrote, "In this philosophy he was supported by a native courage, fully equal to that of any of our greatest Presidents, and by a truly Lincolnian faith that the people, once shown all the facts, will approve the fair and equitable course."

He became managing clerk for Rogers, Bowen & Rogers at an annual salary of one thousand dollars. Partner Dennis Bowen, then but thirty-five, had the greatest influence on Cleveland, both in his approach to legal practice and in introducing him to Buffalo's Democratic conclaves. Bowen emphasized the justness of each case, not simply its legal advantage, and encouraged settlement of disputes before trial.

All was not work for young Cleveland, however, as he expanded his horizons in other ways as well. Said to include a "bar on every corner," Buffalo saloons were his early social and political haunts, as he would enjoy a drink, the manly company, and getting atop beer barrels to speak on issues of the day. He was not a boozer but thereby made many local friends and admirers.

He worked hard at the law office, often until two or three in the morning. His goal was to become master of all the facts; indeed, his exhaustive research would produce legal briefs that were "a model of detail and lucidity." He developed an extraordinary memory—he would impress judges and juries alike with his perfect pleading, without notes, of the most complicated cases. He also demonstrated a tendency to be rigidly stubborn, a quality he later carried into the presidency.

He practiced with the Rogers firm until 1863, when he accepted appointment as assistant district attorney of Erie County. The district attorney recognized Cleveland's hard-working habits and, due to health and other concerns, was delighted to let him handle the lion's share of the work. Three years on the job earned Cleveland a reputation for "legal talent and probity." According to one biographer, Cleveland "attended all thirty-six grand juries that met during his term of office, drawing up most of the indictments and trying over half the cases personally. On one occasion, he argued four major cases concurrently, winning favorable verdicts in all four."

During this time, Cleveland also made a decision that would haunt him in his first run for the presidency. Drafted early in his term as assistant district attorney, Cleveland, then still the primary provider for his mother and two youngest sisters, instead opted to secure a substitute—Polish seaman George Benninsky—to take his place. While the draft law permitted this option, opponents would highlight Cleveland's decision and his avoidance of military service in future campaigns.

Given his notable on-the-job performance, however, this did not prevent the Democrats from nominating Cleveland to run for district attorney, but he lost a close election to Lyman Bass, who would later join Cleveland in a law partnership. Instead, Cleveland formed a three-year law partnership with Isaac Vanderpoel, and when Vanderpoel left to become police magistrate, the law firm of Laning, Cleveland, and Folsom was formed.

YOUNG LAWYER

Though he often appeared in court while Buffalo's assistant district attorney, Cleveland was primarily an "office lawyer" who discouraged clients from even pursuing litigation. Said Cleveland, "A lawsuit, like a gun, is a dangerous thing 'without lock, stock, and barrel.'"

BATTLE OF LIMESTONE RIDGE

In 1866, about fifteen hundred Irish nationalists conducted an ill-fated invasion of Canada. When they were brought back to Buffalo and tried for organizing the expedition, Cleveland volunteered his services and successfully defended them against the charges. Though they subsequently raised money to pay for their defense, Cleveland refused to accept a fee for his services.

Like Cleveland, Oscar Folsom and Albert Laning were young lawyers on the rise. Cleveland was more the legal workhorse than the politician or rainmaker of the firm, roles effectively carried out by Folsom and Laning, respectively. The firm handled many corporate clients and grew in stature. Several cases in particular enhanced Cleveland's reputation. In one, he organized a successful pro bono defense of fifteen hundred Irish nationalists who were captured during an ill-fated "invasion" of Canada and then tried for organizing the expedition. In another, he successfully defended a local newspaper against libel charges brought by a prominent and well-connected businessman.

Then in 1870, despite the firm's success and his growing reputation as an accomplished lawyer, Cleveland opted to run for public office again, this time being elected sheriff of Erie County. Though the post was known as one occupied by political hacks, he may have been attracted to the considerable fees and other perks it offered. Whatever the reason, Cleveland aggressively eliminated graft during his three-year term and earned a reputation for incorruptibility that would follow him throughout his career. He also earned the considerable sum of forty thousand dollars during that time.

The story of one crime and its aftermath reflects another unique quality that Cleveland brought to his post—one that had a great impression on the populace. A drunkard named Patrick Morrissey lived in a slum section of the Buffalo waterfront where he treated his mother with cruelty. One day he knocked her to the floor and she said he had better kill her and have done with it. At these words Morrissey grabbed the knife with which he had been cutting bread and drove it into her breast. The crime was too horrible to admit of any mercy, and he was sentenced to death. Sheriff Cleveland investigated the execution evidence with proper solemnity. He excluded sensation-seekers and at the hanging, he sprang the trap. Although Cleveland was never opposed to capital punishment, he described the execution as "grievously distasteful." But he did not want to hire a hangman or ask his assistant in the sheriff's department to do something he would not do himself.

At the end of his term, he returned to private law practice, this time forming a partnership with Wilson Shannon Bissell, his dear friend whom he would later appoint postmaster general during his second presidency, and with Lyman Bass who, due to poor health, was soon replaced by George Sicard. The firm of Cleveland, Bissell & Sicard would prosper, as would Cleveland's reputation as an attorney and political leader.

He tried cases in both state and federal courts and was one of several counsel to secure a jury award of $240,000, then the largest amount ever rendered in western New York. By all accounts, he was doing extremely well. Bissell later noted that Cleveland would devote himself to a case "absolutely and completely, whether it was large or small, whether with fee or without, and for a rich client or for a poor one." Journalist George Parker told of how Cleveland was a mentor for young lawyers, and how judges, recognizing Cleveland's fairness and integrity, often called upon him to serve as an impartial third party in complicated or contentious cases. "He was now a man of some property," wrote biographer Rexford Tugwell, "head of a respected firm having custody of many estates, and attorney for banks and industrial concerns of the highest standing. He could imagine himself going to only one further post—that of a judgeship, preferably a federal one."

But in a surprising turn of events, Buffalo Democrats, having been turned down by a string of possible candidates, convinced Cleveland to run for mayor in 1881. Cleveland had recently rejected an offer to become regional counsel for the New York Central Railroad, and his successful mayoral campaign effectively placed his law practice on hold until the period between his presidencies. "This office-seeking is a disease. It is even catching," Cleveland would later quip.

In a period when patronage was the norm and graft was fairly common, the new mayor set a much different tone for Buffalo upon assuming office in 1882. Voters demanded municipal reform, and they found a like-minded, effective public servant in Cleveland. "Good and pure government lies at the foundation of the wealth and progress of every community," said the new

★ ★ ★

"It was his invariable rule to master every detail of any legal matter entrusted to him."

Buffalo lawyer Philip Wickser

★ ★ ★

"[Cleveland] attended all thirty-six grand juries that met during his term of office [as assistant district attorney], drawing up most of the indictments and trying over half the cases personally."

Historian Charles Armitage

mayor, who didn't hesitate to challenge political patronage and set former sweetheart contracts out to bid.

Though he was mayor for but a brief time, the Democrats drafted the relative political neophyte to run for governor, a race Cleveland handily won. During the next two years he sponsored modest reforms, including the protection of workers during a period of widespread economic growth, and he vetoed legislation he considered wasteful. "Cleveland was only moving slowly past the mainstream of public thinking," writes historian Henry Graff. "He was a legalist committed to a legal system not yet able to rein in the cutthroat forces of the marketplace."

As governor, Cleveland strengthened his reputation of being a plain man who acted consistently and in accordance with what he believed to be right. Many respected him for his stands against Boss Kelly of Tammany Hall and other Democratic Party leaders in New York. "In Cleveland's eyes there was nothing more despicable than thieving public servants," wrote one biographer. "We love Cleveland for his character," said General Edward S. Bragg in nominating Cleveland for president in 1884, and "we love him for the enemies he has made."

Cleveland was forty-eight when he narrowly defeated James Blaine for the presidency. Just as he had had little experience in state government before becoming New York's governor, he brought almost no experience in national affairs to the White House. His strong qualities were his honesty, his desire to do the right thing, and his common sense. One of his weaknesses, however, was his inability to delegate responsibility to others.

He was a strong advocate of the civil service system and tried to choose people who could fill their jobs capably. The tariff and the currency were important elements affecting his first administration. The farmers wanted a low tariff and cheap money. The industrialists wanted a high tariff and what they called a sound money system based on gold. Cleveland, however, felt that the tariff should be reduced and the gold standard should be kept. The fight between the supporters of silver and gold kept up a running dispute during his administration. Told that his stance might enhance the Republican campaign against him in 1888, he retorted, "What is the use of being elected or reelected unless you stand for something."

Mirroring his actions as mayor and governor, Cleveland used his veto power freely. Prior presidents had vetoed 205 bills;

Cleveland rejected 414 bills in his first term alone. Most of these bills were for Civil War pensions handed out by congressmen as special favors to their cronies, including many who had not even served in the war. While previous presidents opted to let these favors continue undisturbed, Cleveland reviewed every one of these bills, refusing those he deemed without merit.

Cleveland also demonstrated his intense dislike of paternalism in government. Vetoing a bill to assist drought-stricken Texas farmers, he wrote that he could "find no warrant for such an appropriation in the Constitution." "Federal aid in such cases," he went on to say, "encourages the expectation of paternal care on the part of the Government and weakens the sturdiness of our national character."

During this term, Cleveland's personal life changed dramatically as he married Frances Folsom, daughter of his former law partner, Oscar Folsom. Cleveland administered Folsom's estate, kept watch over the family, and fell in love with Frances. He was forty-eight years old when he proposed to the twenty-one-year-old. She accepted and they were married in the White House on June 2, 1886, making him the only president to marry while in office. The workaholic Cleveland is said to have worked up until the time of the 7:00 P.M. ceremony but took the rest of the evening off. Wrote one biographer, "Mrs. Cleveland brightened Washington society and her husband's life. With her arrival, the president became far more sociable, took more vacations, was generally less irritable, and launched bolder legislative initiatives."

In 1888, Cleveland sought reelection against Benjamin Harrison. Although he garnered more than 90,000 more popular votes than Harrison, he lost the electoral vote 233 to 168. In departing the White House, Mrs. Cleveland told one of the caretakers to make sure all the ornaments and furniture remained in place. "We are coming back just four years from today," she declared.

In the interim, Cleveland joined the New York City law firm of Bangs, Stetson, Tracy, and MacVeagh, headed by his longtime friend and adviser Francis Lynde Stetson, who counted financier J. Pierpont Morgan among his clients. There, Cleveland would serve "as counsel" and argue a complicated case before the U.S. Supreme Court.

The dispute involved Louisiana legislation to levee, drain, and reclaim land in what finally comprised New Orleans, involving some 26,026 acres and work costing several million dollars

PEAKE V. NEW ORLEANS

Cleveland argued this 1891 case before the Supreme Court, an event most notable as the first time a former president appeared before justices he had appointed during his presidency—in this case, Chief Justice Melville Fuller (pictured here) and Associate Justice Lucius Lamar, neither of whom recused himself from the case. The complicated facts of the case involved the collection of assessments from the City of New Orleans, with Cleveland's clients unsuccessfully seeking payment as holders of drainage warrants. Interestingly, both Fuller and Lamar supported Cleveland's position.

that the city took over from a defecting contractor. Plaintiff James Wallace Peake held warrants for bonds issued by the contractor and a canal company. In a lower court suit against the City of New Orleans, he prevailed and was awarded the sum of sixty-six hundred dollars, interest at 8 percent, and court costs. On appeal, however, the city was held to be an involuntary trustee and not liable as debtor to the contractor, who must look to the special assessments and to them alone for compensation. With several other counsel, Grover Cleveland argued Peake's appeal before the U.S. Supreme Court.

Justice Brewer wrote the majority opinion, affirming the lower court's opinion and rejecting Cleveland's arguments. Justice Harlan wrote the dissent, concurred in by Chief Justice Fuller and Justice Lamar. Though the latter two were nominees of former president Cleveland, no criticism was made of their participation in the case or their vote for the appellants.

In the 1892 presidential election, Cleveland beat Harrison by a large majority in the popular and electoral vote and returned to the White House, just as Mrs. Cleveland had predicted. Though very popular when he took office in 1893, his second administration soon confronted a financial panic that swept the country.

Farm mortgages were being foreclosed, railroads went bankrupt, and labor quarrels made the situation worse. The amount of gold in the treasury reached a dangerously low point. While Cleveland called a special session of Congress that repealed the 1890 Sherman Silver Purchase Act, this also engendered a party split between conservative "goldbugs" and populist "silverites."

His presidential terms also straddled some of the most serious labor strife in the country's history, including the brutal Haymarket riot and the violent Pullman strike of 1894. Cleveland used federal troops to end the nationwide boycott of trains carrying Pullman cars, which was led by Eugene V. Debs, president of the American Railway Union. Cleveland obtained a court order restoring the railroad service and enforced it with the use of the U.S. Army over the objection of Illinois Governor John P. Altgeld. Said Cleveland in the midst of the rioting, "If it takes the entire army and navy of the United States to deliver a postcard in Chicago, that card will be delivered."

Cleveland's record on racial and ethnic issues, though mixed at the time, would be subject to substantial criticism by contemporary standards. He extended concerted efforts on behalf of Native Americans, then referred to as American Indians. In his first inaugural address, he called for "improvement of their condition and enforcement of their rights," though the ultimate object was "civilization and citizenship" rather than the freedom to maintain their unique culture. Still, as one biographer wrote, "No previous president was so determined to ameliorate the appalling injustices that had been inflicted on these people by the white man."

Cleveland also believed that education would lead to "the proper solution to the race problem in the South." He pledged "equal and exact justice to all men . . . and the protection of the freedman in their rights" in his first inaugural, but he did little as president to effect these pledges. Indeed, public remarks some six years after his second presidency suggest racial prejudice and a concern more for "respectable white people in the South" than correcting injustices visited upon African Americans.

While Cleveland saw education and ultimately assimilation as the roadmap for these minorities, he was less hopeful about the "Chinese question." "Our immigration laws were designed to invite assimilation and not to provide an arena of endless antagonism," he warned during his first administration. He went on to call for legislation prohibiting reentry into the country by Chinese laborers, while during his second administration, he placed such issues low on his list of priorities.

Overall, Cleveland's years after the presidency were bright, spent with family and friends. "The older I grow," he wrote a friend, "the more near and dear such genuine and unaffected friends are to me." Though he earlier had declined a Doctor of Laws degree from Harvard (still sensitive to his lack of a formal university education), following his presidency he accepted such degrees from Villanova and Princeton. He also became a trustee of Princeton University.

In his last years, he lived at Princeton and took little part in active politics other than acting as a consultant and adviser on request. At eight-forty on Wednesday evening, June 24, 1908, the date of his departure came and the struggle ended. As he lay in his bed near the end, he said, "I have tried so hard to do right." Such words not only sum up his career but also provide a simple standard that lawyers, judges, politicians, business leaders, and others might well follow, particularly in the light of recent scandals in our nation.

RIGHTS OF AMERICAN INDIANS

"No previous president was so determined to ameliorate the appalling injustices that had been inflicted on these people by the white man." Thus wrote one biographer about Cleveland's commitment to improving the condition and enforcing the rights of American Indians. Historians are not so generous, however, in their assessment of Cleveland's record on advancing the civil rights of African Americans or Chinese Americans, matters that remained low priorities during his administrations.

★ ★ ★

Twenty-third President (1889–93)

BIRTH
August 20, 1833
North Bend, Ohio

EDUCATION
Public schools
Farmer's College
Miami (Ohio) University
Studied law in Cincinnati, Ohio, with the firm of
    Storer and Gwynne
Admission to the bar: 1853

OTHER OCCUPATIONS/PUBLIC OFFICES
Indiana Supreme Court reporter
Indiana city attorney
Civil War brigadier general
U.S. senator

DEATH
March 13, 1901
Indianapolis, Ind.

LAW CAREER IN BRIEF

While Harrison's early practice was marked by financial struggles and few clients, he attracted enough attention to be appointed city attorney. In that office, several court cases gained him publicity and clients. Subsequently, as a law firm partner, he focused mainly on debt collection and divorce cases and also served as reporter of the supreme court of Indiana. Following his service in the Civil War, a major break came in two high-profile cases: the double murder trial of Nancy Clem and the civil damages suit of Lambdin Milligan. Harrison proceeded to have a distinguished legal career both before and after his presidency, including fifteen cases before the U.S. Supreme Court and one before the International Tribunal in Paris.

Benjamin Harrison: High-Priced Counsel

Allen Sharp

In 1897, four years after Benjamin Harrison left the presidency, a one-paragraph story appeared on the front page of the *New York Times*:

> At its last meeting of the Indiana Tax Commissioners, it was voted to secure, if possible, the services of ex-President Harrison to make an argument in the Supreme Court in behalf of the State of Indiana to enforce payment of taxes assessed against the expressed companies. The Commissioners learned that he would not appear for a fee of less than $5,000. In the California Irrigation cases, he received $10,000. His largest fee was received two years ago from the Indianapolis Street Railway. It was $25,000. In the Morrison Will case, at Richmond, Ind., he received $19,000.

One of the few ex-presidents who actively practiced law after leaving the White House, Harrison had come a long way since his days as a struggling new member of the bar more than forty years earlier. Indeed, such legal fees may have befitted a man described as "probably the ablest lawyer ever to be President."

In *The Harrisons*, Ross F. Lockridge Jr. describes the remarkable political transformation in four generations of that noted family. The first Benjamin Harrison, "The Signer," was part of the aristocratic plantation slave-owning society of the James and York Rivers in Virginia. He was also a member of the Continental Congress, a signer of the Declaration of Independence, and governor of Virginia just as the American War for Independence was coming to an end. The Signer's younger son, William Henry Harrison, was governor of the Indiana Territory, a war hero of sorts, and for thirty days president of the United States. William Henry's son, John Scott Harrison, was a Whig member of the

★ ★ ★

"They were close times, I tell you. A $5.00 bill was an event."

Benjamin Harrison, describing his early struggles as a lawyer

U.S. House of Representatives from Ohio at the midpoint of the nineteenth century. Representative Harrison's son, the second Benjamin Harrison, was a Republican U.S. senator from Indiana who supported Lincoln's antislavery views and became the second in his family to serve the nation as president of the United States.

Born in Ohio in 1833, Benjamin Harrison graduated from Miami University in 1852 and proceeded to study law in the Cincinnati office of Bellamy Storer, a former Whig congressman. He "kept his nose to the grindstone," which greatly pleased Storer, whose role in formulating Harrison's legal talents was similar to that which Stephen Logan exercised on young Abraham Lincoln. After two years in Storer's office, Harrison was admitted to the Ohio bar and soon thereafter, with his new wife Caroline, he moved to Indianapolis.

The early times in Indianapolis were a real struggle, and legal fees, even small ones, were scarce. The Indianapolis bar was considered one of the best in the country at that time, and while Harrison was not immediately accepted into the established firms, he received help in getting his practice started. The U.S. court clerk helped him find office space just across from the Bates House, then the most prominent hotel in Indianapolis, and through the good offices of the U.S. marshal, he was appointed a federal court crier at two dollars and fifty cents per day. He thus had a modest job and an equally modest office. His first fee was a five-dollar gold piece for winning a false pretenses case before a justice of the peace. Of these times, Harrison later remarked, "They were close times, I tell you. A $5.00 bill was an event." His father helped support him with regular checks of twenty-five or fifty dollars.

Harrison soon captured the attention of Major Jonathan W. Gordon, prosecuting attorney of Marion County, and through him got involved in a jury trial where the defendant was accused of burglary at a place called Point Lookout. Opposing counsel in the case was Whig ex-governor David Wallace. Because Gordon was required to attend a lecture by Horace Mann at the time scheduled for closing arguments, that task fell to Harrison. The presiding trial judge heard the evening arguments in a dimly lit courtroom and though Harrison had compiled copious notes, the lack of adequate lighting caused him to throw away his written script and talk directly to the jury, utilizing his considerable memory. A guilty verdict was had and, more important, the praise of David Wallace. Thus commenced a preference for the courtroom, which would prevail in Harrison's professional life for nearly a half century.

He was soon appointed city attorney in Indianapolis, and in that capacity he assisted in the prosecution of a hotel servant charged with poisoning a guest's coffee. To prepare for the case, Harrison visited a doctor's office and spent the entire night reading books about poisons. The next day, apparently without sleep, he brilliantly conducted a slashing cross-examination based on his nocturnal research. The servant was convicted and Harrison would be renowned for his tough cross-examinations.

"Soon clients came his way and their fees were solid food to a financially famished attorney," wrote his biographer. Still, Harrison's economic situation remained extremely tight, causing great concern for his ability to support his young and growing family. Indeed, he was forced to borrow money from a federal clerk and accept further support from his father.

But Harrison's career was now on the move. He formed his first law partnership with William Wallace, a son of his former courtroom rival. In the early days of the firm, Harrison undertook tough, tedious grunt work while Wallace politicked. They had a huge collection practice, and though unglamorous, it did pay the bills. Harrison was meticulous in managing and collecting these accounts. According to his biographer, "The comparatively lax divorce laws of the state provided another lucrative source of income." Harrison's relationship with this prominent Hoosier family would deepen and last a lifetime. In Harrison's run for president in 1888, another Wallace son, Lew, would pen and publish an adoring campaign biography.

At this time, there were growing disagreements between Harrison and his father, with the young Harrison moving away from his family's ideological roots on the subjects of politics and slavery. His father was in the Congress that passed the Kansas-Nebraska Act, which Ben opposed strongly. Ben also supported

HARRISON THE YOUNG LAWYER

As city attorney in Indianapolis, Harrison helped prosecute a hotel servant charged with poisoning a guest's coffee. His quick grasp of complex medical issues and his tough cross-examination contributed to a conviction and earned him high praise.

★ ★ ★

"For Harrison, the conviction of Mrs. Clem was undoubtedly his greatest courtroom triumph."

Biographer Harry Sievers

the newly formed Republican Party and its presidential candidate, John Charles Fremont, and was the first of his family to join that party. "By June, 1856, he had shifted his political views on the slavery question sufficiently to give full approbation to the anti-slavery gospel."

In 1860, Republican candidate Harrison was elected to the office of reporter of the supreme court of Indiana. However, it provided no compensation except for a free market device permitting printing and selling of the official reports. He also continued his private practice, becoming a first-rate technical lawyer as well as a talented trial advocate and political orator. He was considered a terribly demanding taskmaster and an often humorless workaholic by office colleagues. It is said he even worked on case proofs during theatrical performances. He later bragged that he went to federal court contesting the taxability of the sales of the official reports and won.

In December 1861, with Harrison elected as reporter and Wallace elected as clerk of Marion County, their six-year law partnership terminated. Harrison would also enlist in the Union army, rising to the rank of brevet brigadier general and generally getting good grades as one of the ablest of the "political generals." When the war ended, he returned to Indiana, where he was again elected to the reporter's office.

In his closing days as reporter, his law firm was retained as special prosecutor in a sensational murder case. In 1868, a prominent businessman, Jacob Young, and his wife were murdered, their bodies found in a town near Indianapolis. Charged with the murder were three defendants, including thirty-seven-year-old Nancy Clem, who was tried separately. Her trial involved 150 witnesses, ending in a hung jury. When a new trial began in 1869, Harrison took over the prosecution, calling more than 250 witnesses and establishing that Clem's alibi was the product of bribery. After deliberating for forty-eight hours, the jury found Nancy Clem guilty of second-degree murder. "For Harrison, the conviction of Mrs. Clem was undoubtedly his greatest courtroom triumph," wrote biographer Harry Sievers. "Lawyers from all over the state had witnessed his efforts as a public prosecutor, and the Harrison name, already celebrated in Indiana, enjoyed fresh renown." Harrison also was attracting widespread attention as an orator at political meetings and especially with Union army veterans, becoming a master of the political art of "waving the bloody shirt."

He soon attracted further attention from one of the most visible post–Civil War cases, *Ex parte Milligan*. Lambdin P. Milligan, a lawyer from Huntington, Indiana, had been tried in 1864 for antiwar activities during the Civil War by a military commission in Indianapolis that consisted of twelve Union army officers. The commission found Milligan guilty and sentenced him to death. In 1866, the case made its way to the Supreme Court of the United States, which unanimously ordered Milligan to be set free, ruling that as a private citizen, he should have been tried by civil courts then operating in Indianapolis. Interestingly, one of the prevailing lawyers in this appeal was James A. Garfield.

After returning to his Indiana home, Milligan filed a state suit alleging false arrest and false imprisonment and seeking one hundred thousand dollars in damages. The defendants in the case included the Military Commission members and such prominent persons as Civil War governor Oliver P. Morton of Indiana, then a U.S. senator, and Ulysses S. Grant, former Army general-in-chief and then president of the United States. Grant sought out Harrison to lead the defense of this case, which became one of the first civil rights jury trials claiming money damages for a violation of the Constitution. Milligan retained powerful Democratic lawyer Thomas A. Hendricks, who had served in both houses of the Indiana legislature and U.S. Congress and who would later become governor of Indiana and vice president of the United States with Cleveland.

The 1871 trial lasted two weeks, resulting in massive media coverage, including verbatim front-page reporting of testimony in the leading Indianapolis newspapers. Throughout, Harrison's basic tactic was to retry the Civil War in the courtroom and to establish that in reality Milligan was a traitor. The resulting verdict was for Milligan, but for only five dollars and costs (neither of which he apparently collected).

While Harrison and Hendricks were contesting the Milligan case in a federal courtroom in Indianapolis, they were also opposing counsel in a U.S. Supreme Court case, *New Albany v. Burke*. Hendricks represented taxpayers in New Albany seeking to enjoin the city from paying interest on bonds issued to construct a railroad while Harrison represented the city. The federal

THE MILLIGAN CIVIL DAMAGES SUIT

Several years after Indiana lawyer Lambdin P. Milligan (pictured here) prevailed in the landmark Supreme Court case that bears his name—*Ex parte Milligan*—he sued the military commission that tried and sentenced him for one hundred thousand dollars in damages. Milligan stood on firm legal ground, armed with the high court ruling that the military commission had had no jurisdiction in the matter. President Ulysses S. Grant, a named defendant in the case, called upon General Benjamin Harrison to lead the defense. In the high-profile, two-week trial, Harrison's stirring arguments regarding the valor of Union soldiers and Milligan's traitorous activities bore fruit. Though Milligan won the case, he was awarded a meager five dollars in damages.

"General Harrison was by far the ablest and profoundest lawyer among our Presidents . . . recognized as one of the leaders of the American Bar."

Senator Chauncey Depew

circuit court in Indiana had issued an injunction requested by the taxpayers, and the Supreme Court reversed and ruled against the taxpayers. Thus, Harrison prevailed in his first case before the nation's highest court.

A year later, his second high court case, *Burke v. Smith*, involved the issue of whether subscribers to stock in an Indiana railroad corporation could be held liable for amounts in excess of the face amount of their subscription. The railroad had become insolvent and wanted the stock subscribers to pay more. Harrison argued for the railroad, but the subscribers, represented by Congressman Michael Kerr, won. Appearing in the case with Kerr was James A. Garfield. Thus, two future presidents were opposing counsel in the same case, probably the only such instance in our nation's history.

In 1875, Harrison was involved in another high-visibility case, this one involving alleged misconduct at the Indianapolis Deaf and Dumb Institute. A mute member of the school's senior class, Ida K. Fawkner, had been seduced and been the subject of an abortion. Harrison represented the superintendent of the Institute and one of its instructors, defendants in the case. Harrison cross-examined Ida "unmercifully" for two days, focusing on changes in her story. Both his clients were exonerated. "His legal acumen and oratorical genius had once more enhanced his political possibilities," wrote Sievers, "for few in Indiana had failed to follow the fascinating story of 'a dumb innocent that could not say him nay.'"

Soon after this trial, Harrison was involved in a case involving the so-called Whiskey Ring that operated during the Grant administration. Harrison represented Hiram Brownlee, a federal internal revenue officer who was among those accused of accepting a bribe from a distiller. While most cases resulted in convictions, Brownlee was acquitted. One of the key items in his case involved white kid gloves he allegedly wore in accepting the bribe, charges that Harrison exploded in his examination of witnesses.

The kid glove quickly became a symbol for Harrison's political enemies. In his unsuccessful 1876 campaign for governor, the Democratic press lambasted him, "Give Harrison a kid-glove client and a two thousand dollar fee and no matter how guilty the culprit may be, his intellectual grasp will readily separate crime from such respectability."

Following other high-profile cases—including his defense of railroad strike leaders and prosecution of an election fraud case—the Indiana General Assembly elected Harrison to the U.S. Senate in early 1881. While there, he was in the Supreme Court for its decision in the landmark *Civil Rights Cases* of 1883. He strongly disagreed with the decision, which severely limited governmental actions against private acts of discrimination. Notwithstanding his Virginia origins, Harrison took the view of the so-called Radical Republicans on issues of race and reconstruction. He supported the Civil Rights Act of 1875 and later, as president, he strongly supported federal legislation to protect the voting rights of southern blacks under the Fifteenth Amendment. He also backed his views with financial support. After leaving the presidency, his charitable contributions included "a sizeable annual contribution for the education of Negroes in the South."

During his term in the U.S. Senate, Harrison argued six cases before the Supreme Court. In the 1881 case of *Evansville Bank v. Britton*, he was again opposed by Thomas A. Hendricks, who appeared for the bank while Harrison argued for Britton. A closely divided Court ruled it discriminatory to tax national bank shares under a statute of Indiana without permitting the owner of them to deduct from their assessed value the amount of bona fide indebtedness. The case was a technical win for Harrison.

Two years later, Harrison prevailed in *Warren v. King*, a case involving the foreclosure of two railroad mortgages and other complicated financial transactions. The same year he prevailed in *Indiana Southern R. Co. v. Liverpool, London and Globe Ins. Co.*, a case in which former presidential candidate Samuel J. Tilden was trustee for the issuance of a million and a half bonds held by the insurance company.

Harrison also represented the Farmers Loan and Trust Company, an appellee in *Dimpfal v. Ohio and Mississippi Railroad Co.*, in which he successfully argued that the objecting minority stockholders had not exhausted all means to obtain redress of their grievances within the corporation. Near the end of his Senate term, he argued two more high court cases, *Smith v. Craft* and *Jewell v. Knight*, that were combined for argument and decision. In these cases, the Court dismissed the appeals pursued by Harrison.

"If our great corporations would more scrupulously observe their legal limitations and duties, they would have less cause to complain of the unlawful limitations of their rights or of violent interference with their operations."

Benjamin Harrison, in his inaugural address

Harrison was a strong ad-
vocate of judicial reforms
and improvements. In "the
first structural modification
of the federal judicial system in more than one
hundred years," the 1891
Congress approved creation
of intermediate courts to
relieve the Supreme Court
of its backlogged caseload
and to avoid delays that
Harrison said "amounted
practically to the denial of
justice in a large number of
cases." As senator and president, Harrison also sup-
ported increases in the
salaries of federal judges.

Politics and law constantly interacted throughout Harrison's
life, and especially during his presidency, as he carried to the
White House a series of issues and opinions that often found
expression in his legal stands. For example, Harrison was a champion of personal freedom and believed such freedom was best expressed in political terms at the ballot box. His support of the
1890 federal elections bill was consistent with positions he had
taken throughout his career to include the freedman within the
body politic. In his inaugural address he asked, "How long will
those who rejoice that slavery no longer exists cherish or tolerate
the incapacities it put upon their communities?"

Harrison was also a friend of public order who vigorously resisted mobs, violent strikes, and other challenges to that order. To
quote his inaugural address, "A community where law is the rule
of conduct and where courts, not mobs, execute its penalties is the
only attractive field for business investments and honest labor."
He was thus willing to use the army as a constabulary in such
events as the Johnson County War in Wyoming in 1890 or the
Coeur d'Alene strikes of 1892 in Idaho.

Harrison was a supporter of private
property, as were virtually all politicians
of his era. But like a growing number of
his contemporaries, and often contrary to
his party's following, he was troubled by
the corporate excesses that clearly stimulated expressions of dissent. Again to
quote his inaugural, "If our great corporations would more scrupulously observe
their legal limitations and duties, they
would have less cause to complain of the unlawful limitations
of their rights or of violent interference with their operations."
Little wonder he would later sign the 1890 Sherman Antitrust
Act and otherwise challenge monopolies that denied to others
the opportunity to achieve what those transforming generations
had achieved.

In his term as president, Harrison named four justices to the
Supreme Court: David Brewer of Kansas, Henry Billings Brown
of Michigan, George Shiras Jr. of Pennsylvania, and Howell
Jackson of Tennessee. William Henry Harrison Miller of Indiana
served as his only attorney general. William Howard Taft of

Ohio—bracketed by brief terms of service by Orlow Chapman of New York and Charles Aldrich of Illinois—was his solicitor general. Together their appointments illuminate several of the key features of his politics.

In the same manner that he sought fitness in other appointees, he looked for individuals who might bring credit upon the judicial branch. Brewer and Brown were district court justices, Shiras was an experienced Pittsburgh trial lawyer, and Jackson had a rich mixture of state court credentials. In at least one case Harrison sent a clear message to the Pennsylvania bosses, Cameron and Quay, about the limits of patronage by naming Shiras, an individual largely unconnected with their machine. Taft was later rewarded for his service with an appointment to the Sixth Circuit. Harrison was not above listening to recommendations, however. Brewer was the nephew of Justice Stephen Field, Shiras was an attorney for Andrew Carnegie, and Jackson had served in the U.S. Senate in a seat adjoining Harrison's. Miller, the extreme case, was Harrison's law partner.

A significant part of Harrison's legal career occurred after he left the presidency on March 4, 1893. He remained active in law practice until his death on March 13, 1901, reportedly averaging $150,000 a year. Although this postpresidential practice was unusual, it was not unprecedented. John Quincy Adams, as ex-president and member of the U.S. House of Representatives, argued the famous *Amistad* case before the Supreme Court in 1841 but did not otherwise engage in the practice of law. Grover Cleveland engaged in law practice with a prestigious law firm in New York between his presidencies and argued, without success, *Peake v. New Orleans*, before a Supreme Court to which he had appointed two members, including the chief justice. Of course, William Howard Taft had a distinguished tenure as chief justice of the United States following his presidency.

Early in 1895, Harrison was plaintiff's counsel in a huge and complicated will contest in Richmond, Indiana, involving the estate of banker James L. Morrison. Morrison was said to have left a personal estate worth approximately $625,000 plus real estate. The children of his deceased son challenged a will that gave most of the estate to his daughter. His opponent in the highly visible case was Republican congressman Henry Underwood Johnson. A settlement was achieved and Harrison made a huge fee (reports

CHIEF COUNSEL FOR VENEZUELA

While the press did not generally present Harrison in the most flattering manner, his legal talents were highly regarded and in great demand. In addition to frequent appearances before the U.S. Supreme Court, Harrison served as chief counsel to Venezuela in its boundary dispute with British Guiana before the International Tribunal in Paris. Though his closing argument of twenty-five hours was acclaimed "a masterful performance," the three-judge tribunal (which included Harrison Supreme Court appointee David Brewster) ruled in favor of the British. Discouraged but undaunted, Harrison believed that the decision was driven by European power politics rather than international law.

range from $19,000 to $25,000). An interesting aftermath of this trial is found in the *New York Times* of that year. Quoting a story that appeared in the *Chicago Chronicle*, it noted the following exchange in the trial when Judge Black ruled against Johnson on a key point:

JOHNSON: *"If the presence of an ex-President in this case is controlling these rulings, it is time we knew it beyond doubt."*

HARRISON: *"I assert there is no ex-President in this case. I am here to discharge the sworn duties of my profession as I see them. If the people of this country have seen cause to honor me, it is no reason why I should not appear in the capacity of counselor nor a reason why I should be driven from this court."*

Johnson later devoted a considerable portion of a signed article to putting a different spin on these proceedings, but it is not disputed that in Harrison's final argument, he vowed never again to appear in a jury case, and apparently he did not.

Harrison's most prominent representation after his presidency was as chief counsel for the government of Venezuela in a boundary dispute with British Guiana in South America. His fee was considerable—he insisted upon receiving a retainer of twenty thousand dollars and quarterly payments of ten thousand dollars until the International Tribunal in Paris rendered its decision, which added up to eighty thousand dollars for his services. After lengthy arguments, the three-judge tribunal—which included David J. Brewer, whom Harrison had appointed to the Supreme Court—ruled in favor of the British contentions, much to the consternation of Harrison and his legal entourage. Harrison may have been correct in considering the decision to have been basically driven by European power politics rather than international law. Interestingly, despite its prominence, Harrison's performance in Paris attracted far less press attention than the Dreyfus case then being tried in Rennes.

Harrison made a series of appearances before the Supreme Court of the United States between 1896 and 1898. At that time, the Court included Justices David Brewer, George Shiras, and Henry Brown, all appointed by Harrison. While press reports contained numerous references to Harrison's activities during this period, including the Morrison will case and the International Arbitration case, they did not raise questions about the propriety of an ex-president appearing before a Supreme Court to which he had appointed members. In the prior decade, Grover Cleveland appeared before a Court to which he had appointed both Chief Justice Fuller and Justice Lamar, and apparently no question arose at that time either.

Harrison's Supreme Court arguments included the cases of *Fallbrook Irrigation District v. Bradley, Triga v. Modesto Irrigation District, Forsyth v. City of Hammond, City Ry. Co. v. Citizens State Railroad Co., Magoun v. Illinois Trust & Savings Bank,* and *Sawyer v. Cochersperger.* He enjoyed mixed success in these cases, which involved constitutional questions on such matters as the Illinois inheritance tax, takings of private property for public use, and the right to determine municipal boundaries.

As the end of his life neared, Harrison appeared one last time before the Supreme Court of Indiana in *Campbell v. City of Indianapolis,* a major 1900 case dealing with the state limits on bonding authority for a municipal school corporation. A closely divided court adopted Harrison's argument for the purposes of the bonding limitation in Indiana's constitution, holding that the city and school corporation were separate and distinct, giving the latter much greater bonding authority. The legacy of this case was important to the development of public education in Indiana. At this time, Harrison also served as an active member of the Board of Trustees of Purdue University.

Indiana Supreme Court Judge Leander Monks, in his three-volume *Courts and Lawyers in Indiana,* said of Harrison: "As a lawyer, in its broad and best sense, he was considered second to no one in America." Others would echo this sentiment. In *My Memories of Eighty Years,* Chauncey M. Depew stated: "General Harrison was by far the ablest and profoundest lawyer among our Presidents. . . . After retirement, he entered at once upon the practice of his profession of the law and almost immediately became recognized as one of the leaders of the American Bar."

"I assert there is no ex-President in this case. I am here to discharge the sworn duties of my profession as I see them."

Benjamin Harrison, responding to an opposing counsel's insinuation of undue influence

★ ★ ★

William McKinley

Twenty-fifth President (1897–1901)

BIRTH
January 29, 1843
Niles, Ohio

EDUCATION
Allegheny College
Studied law with Judge Charles E. Glidden in Poland, Ohio,
    and at Albany (N.Y.) Law School
Admission to the bar: March 1867

OTHER OCCUPATIONS/PUBLIC OFFICES
Teacher and post office clerk
Civil War major
County prosecuting attorney
U.S. congressman
Ohio governor

DEATH
September 14, 1901
Buffalo, N.Y.

LAW CAREER IN BRIEF

McKinley began his law practice in Canton, Ohio, in 1867, initially in a brief partnership but then as a solo practitioner, handling routine cases and few trials. A term as county prosecuting attorney followed, during which violations of state liquor laws demanded much of his time. In the early 1870s, his practice began to prosper, fueled in part by the business his father-in-law steered his way. After his election to Congress in 1876, McKinley was involved in "every important law suit in Stark County," according to a colleague. However, his law practice ebbed with his successive elections to increasingly higher public offices.

William McKinley: A Good Lawyer

Lewis L. Gould

The day before his second inauguration as president of the United States on March 4, 1901, William McKinley said to his friend and former law intern Charles R. Miller: "Poor as I am I had rather give ten thousand dollars and go home with you on Tuesday and resume the practice of law than to be inaugurated as President of the United States tomorrow." McKinley had a way of charming people with kindly sentiments they wanted to hear, but his pleasantry had more than a little truth as well. By the time his second term opened, the president was looking forward to returning to Canton, Ohio, where he had begun his legal career more than three decades earlier. He knew that he could never again be the young attorney who had gained a foothold on the political ladder in Stark County in the late 1860s, but the memories of those formative years were warm ones for the twenty-fifth president in 1901.

McKinley did not often allude to his legal background in politics, but its impact on his approach to public affairs was significant. He learned in the law the habits of discipline, methodical thinking, and clear speaking that became his trademarks in the House of Representatives, as governor of Ohio, and in the White House. Many techniques of conciliation and the peaceful resolution of disputes were first developed in the courts and legal proceedings of Stark County. His approach to administrative duties and his skill in managing the empire that the United States acquired from Spain can be first seen during his years as a young attorney.

William McKinley Jr. was born in Niles, Ohio, on January 29, 1843, and grew up in nearby Poland. His father was the operator of several small iron mills, and William was one of nine children. The young McKinley studied at

James A. Saxton, McKinley's Client and Father-in-Law
Banker and businessman James A. Saxton "had probably more litigated cases in Stark County at that time than any other citizen," including a case in which McKinley was opposing counsel. Following the conclusion of the case, Saxton consented to McKinley's proposal of marriage to Saxton's daughter and began to direct increasing legal business to his son-in-law. He even made McKinley manager of his Stark County Bank.

"With your business capacity and experience, I would have preferred railroading or some commercial business."

Rutherford B. Hayes, upon learning of McKinley's plans to pursue a law career

local schools. He then attended Allegheny College in Pennsylvania for a time in 1859 but had to drop out because of poor health. In Poland he taught school and worked at the post office until his enlistment in the Union army during the spring of 1861. He spent four years in the military, was promoted for bravery at the battle of Antietam from commissary sergeant to the rank of second lieutenant, and eventually rose to the rank of major, a title that stayed with him in political life. Once the war ended, McKinley thought about making the army his permanent career, but family and friends argued against such a choice. He decided instead to become a lawyer and from there to pursue a political career.

McKinley began reading law in the office of Judge Charles E. Glidden of Poland in the summer of 1865. Glidden's patriotic oratory in 1861 had spurred McKinley to enlist in the army, and the young veteran plunged into "the solemnities of the marriage contract" and explored "the old customs of the Saxons and the Danes." As he worked at his studies, he so impressed Glidden that his mentor suggested that McKinley should attend law school. With financial help from his family, McKinley entered the Albany Law School in 1866, then one of the most prestigious of the more than thirty law schools in the nation. Established in 1851, the law school had grown to an enrollment of 160 by 1866. Its founders, Amasa Parker, Ira Harris, and Amos Dean, sought to enable graduates of their program "to enter at once upon the successful practice of his profession" while also "elevating the profession itself."

The cost of attendance was fifty dollars per twelve-week term, and McKinley probably spent another five dollars per week on room and board for his lodgings at 36 Jay Street in Albany. He "clubbed" with George F. Arrel, later a successful attorney in Youngstown, Ohio, who called the young McKinley "a delightful companion" and remembered his studious habits. According to Arrel, McKinley was "exceedingly industrious, and in the late afternoon of almost every day he could be found in the law library, to which the students of the class had access, studiously reading and examining" course textbooks and cases.

McKinley had to appear regularly in moot court each week. Arrel recalled that in this setting, McKinley showed his emerging ability as a speaker: "His personal presence then was, as always afterward, attractive, and his voice quite musical." Once he was paired with a student named Lewis O'Conor who years later re-called their collaboration in a letter to the White House. Formerly a Democrat, O'Conor supported McKinley in 1896 and praised the course of his administration. The president responded that he was "always glad to hear from my old associates" from the Albany Law School "and to learn that they are well and prosperous."

As he settled down to his studies at Albany, McKinley wrote to his Civil War commander in the Twenty-third Ohio Volunteer Infantry, Rutherford B. Hayes, to ask about his future, the merits of going into the law, and where a young man with a future might locate. Hayes was a little discouraging about the law as a career. "With your business capacity and experience, I would have pre-ferred railroading or some commercial business. A man in any one of our Western towns with half your wit ought to be inde-pendent at forty in business. As a lawyer a man sacrifices inde-pendence to ambition which is a bad bargain at best. However, you have decided for the present your profession so I must hush."

The two terms that McKinley spent at Albany in 1866 and 1867 involved a demanding regimen. Students attended classes five days a week, took an oral examination at the end of each week, and then had to pass a written examination at the conclu-sion of each term. In the daily lectures, McKinley listened to the school's founders and professors on topics that ranged from per-sonal property to criminal law. There were some lighter mo-ments too. At the annual reception for entering students, the daughter of Judge Amasa Parker handed McKinley a plate of ice cream. Never having eaten ice cream before, McKinley told Grace Parker: "Poor Mrs. Parker, do not tell her the custard got frozen." Miss Parker told the new student about ice cream in a kindly way that McKinley remembered when he was president. He would tell friends: "You know, I was a simple country boy."

Satisfied that he had learned enough to make a success in the legal profession, McKinley left Albany in the spring of 1867 without having graduated. He went home to Poland and passed the examination to become a lawyer in nearby Warren, Ohio. Looking for greater opportunity than his native area provided, McKinley cast about for a place to settle in his native state. His sister, Anna, taught in Canton, Ohio, and persuaded him to give the town a chance. Having done so, McKinley decided to move there permanently. He brought a letter of introduction from

"He learned in the law the habits of discipline, methodical thinking, and clear speaking that became his trademarks."

Judge Glidden to George W. Belden, a lawyer in Canton. According to later recollections, Belden was impressed with the young lawyer and gave him a case that involved a court appearance the next day. McKinley opened his argument with the words: "What we contend for in this law suit" and proceeded to win the case. Belden not only shared his fee with McKinley, but welcomed him as a partner. Their connection lasted only a year, however, because of Belden's death in 1868. McKinley became a sole practitioner.

During his early years in Canton, McKinley worked out of offices in the brick building adjacent to the county courthouse of Stark County, handling routine cases and making infrequent appearances in court. He lost little time in becoming a participant in the affairs of the local Republicans as secretary of the Stark County Republican Central Committee. In the autumn of 1869, McKinley was his party's candidate for the post of county prosecuting attorney against the Democratic nominee, William A. Lynch. The local Republican newspaper described McKinley as "a good lawyer and a fine orator," and Republican speakers stressed that McKinley's opponent had opposed the war while McKinley was fighting in uniform for the Union. McKinley won a close contest by 135 votes out of almost 10,000 cast.

During the two-year term that followed, McKinley spent most of his time prosecuting violations of the state's liquor laws at a time when temperance sentiment was strong in the local Republican Party. One particular problem had to do with liquor sales to students at nearby Mount Union College. McKinley relied on the testimony of one student who was willing to talk about this, Philander C. Knox, to help win many convictions, and he stayed in touch with Knox in later life as Knox rose in the legal profession in Pennsylvania. The fervor with which McKinley pursued his campaign against illegal liquor sales aroused some discontent among local Democrats and helped to account for his narrow defeat against Lynch when he came up for reelection in 1871. The local newspapers said that "the considerations that rate are, whiskey first, party second. The same causes would drive Lynch or any other Prosecutor who will do his duty, from the same office."

By 1871, McKinley had married Ida Saxton, daughter of a local banker, and they had begun a family. The death of their second child in infancy and the subsequent death of their first daughter a few years later helped break Ida McKinley's health. She became a lifelong invalid whose care took many hours of McKinley's time and energies.

His law practice in 1872 and into 1873 involved cases for indigents who could not afford an attorney and others in which he served as a guardian. In 1873 he won a case for his father-in-law, James A. Saxton, that produced a judgment of more than thirty-five hundred dollars. As a reward, the elder Saxton directed more of his legal business toward McKinley. By the end of 1873, McKinley was named the manager of the Stark County Bank and ran the institution when Saxton relocated to New York City to live.

As his legal career prospered, McKinley's thoughts turned to politics and a race for Congress in 1876. His friendship with Rutherford B. Hayes led him to be a significant force in Hayes's campaign for governor of Ohio in 1875 and for the presidency in 1876. As he prepared to run for Congress, McKinley became involved in a trial that illustrated his growing appeal to Democrats and Republicans alike in his district. During the late winter of 1876, a strike occurred among coal miners in the Tuscarawas Valley. The use of strikebreakers led to episodes of violence and Governor Hayes sent in troops to maintain order. As a result of the episode, several miners were arrested for disorderly conduct. Few lawyers in the Canton area wanted to take up the defense of the miners at a time when sentiments were running high against their alleged conduct. McKinley decided to become their counsel.

At the trial, McKinley's extensive preparation of the case impressed even the lawyers for the mine owners and the owners themselves. Marcus Alonzo Hanna was one of the owners who noted McKinley's skill and professionalism. Hanna had met McKinley in 1871, but the two men did not really become acquainted until this trial. Their friendship would help McKinley secure political success and put him on the road to the White House.

In the trial, McKinley effectively conveyed to the court and the jury the difficult conditions under which the coal miners

THE TUSCARAWAS VALLEY COAL MINERS STRIKE

During a coal miners' strike in 1876, the use of strikebreakers led to violence and Governor Rutherford B. Hayes sent in troops to restore order. When several miners were arrested for disorderly conduct, McKinley served as their counsel, conveying the difficult conditions in which they lived and worked. As a result, most of the defendants, while found guilty, received light sentences, and McKinley—who refused any fee for his services—gained respect from all parties for his legal knowledge and skills.

DEMOCRATIC CHALLENGER WILLIAM JENNINGS BRYAN

Though Bryan did not experience success as a practicing lawyer in 1880s Illinois or Nebraska, he proceeded to distinguish himself in the political arena despite three failed runs at the presidency. Bryan was only thirty-six years old when he delivered his famous "Cross of Gold" speech and was nominated to run against McKinley. Bryan's best known legal case was the 1925 Scopes "Monkey Trial," during which he agreed to being cross-examined by Clarence Darrow. Less well known is the fact that Bryan's spouse, Mary Baird, also was an attorney, reading law with her husband before being admitted to the Nebraska bar in 1888.

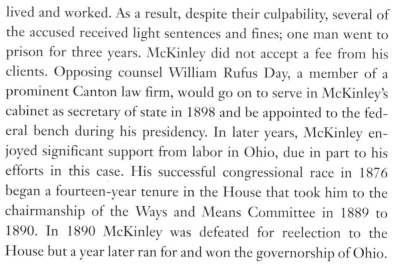

lived and worked. As a result, despite their culpability, several of the accused received light sentences and fines; one man went to prison for three years. McKinley did not accept a fee from his clients. Opposing counsel William Rufus Day, a member of a prominent Canton law firm, would go on to serve in McKinley's cabinet as secretary of state in 1898 and be appointed to the federal bench during his presidency. In later years, McKinley enjoyed significant support from labor in Ohio, due in part to his efforts in this case. His successful congressional race in 1876 began a fourteen-year tenure in the House that took him to the chairmanship of the Ways and Means Committee in 1889 to 1890. In 1890 McKinley was defeated for reelection to the House but a year later ran for and won the governorship of Ohio.

Once he became a full-time politician, McKinley's direct connection with the law ebbed, but the habits of mind that he had acquired in Canton's courtrooms stayed with him throughout his public career. One of his law interns recalled the way in which he dictated his court speeches in advance and then carefully edited them. His papers and those of his secretary, George B. Cortelyou, now at the Library of Congress, show that his working style as president retained many of the techniques he first adopted in his legal practice.

In early 1893, a business associate, whose notes he had countersigned, went bankrupt. McKinley was pressed to pay these debts and told friends that he would step down as governor and return to Canton to practice law to pay what he owed. He did not have to do so since wealthy friends, led by Mark Hanna, became McKinley's trustees and raised money from private donors to pay off the more than one hundred thousand dollars that was owed. The episode did not hurt McKinley politically; in fact, it aroused sympathy for him as another prominent American caught up in the economic turmoil caused by the Panic of 1893 and the ensuing depression. McKinley was reelected governor in the fall of 1893 and emerged as the Republican presidential nominee in 1896, as his national popularity and his endorsement of the tariff and the gold standard won him a first-ballot nomination. With Hanna as his campaign manager and chief fund-raiser, McKinley then won election to the presidency over William Jennings Bryan.

As president, McKinley relied on lawyers he had known in Canton to staff some of his key cabinet posts. In addition to his appointment of William R. Day as secretary of state in 1898, McKinley selected Philander C. Knox as his attorney general in 1901. Before Knox, McKinley had selected Joseph McKenna, whom he had known in the House, as his first attorney general. When McKenna was named to the Supreme Court in 1897, John W. Griggs of New Jersey, a friend of Vice President Garret A. Hobart, served as attorney general.

McKinley appointed other legal colleagues to key positions as well. When it became necessary to replace Secretary of War Russell A. Alger in 1899, McKinley's choice, corporation attorney Elihu Root, protested that he knew nothing about the army and military matters. McKinley's response, through a mutual political friend, was that he was not looking for someone with military experience: "He has to have a lawyer to direct the government of these Spanish islands, and you are the lawyer he wants." Similarly, McKinley turned to William Howard Taft, then a federal judge, to become president of the Philippine Commission in 1900 and help establish the islands' government and legal system under American rule. On one occasion, however, this lawyerly preference caused a constitutional stir. He asked Chief Justice Melville W. Fuller and Justice Edward D. White, both of them Democrats, to serve on the commission to negotiate peace with Spain in 1898. The justices rejected this effort to involve the judiciary in foreign policy, and McKinley turned to several senators instead.

McKinley's presidency came during a time when racial segregation was at its height in the United States. In his first inaugural address, he said that "lynching must not be tolerated in a great and civilized country like the United States; courts, not mobs, must execute the penalties of the law." Though he reiterated that position in his 1899 annual message, the Justice Department did not take any action to stop the more than 180 lynchings that occurred each year during his administration. On other civil rights issues, McKinley emphasized reconciliation of the races in the North and South, but he did little of substance to address problems of racial discrimination.

When it came to antitrust issues, McKinley consulted with John Marshall Harlan of the United States Supreme Court about

★ ★ ★

"William McKinley brought, both to the State House at Columbus and the White House at Washington, a trained and mature legal mind with which to solve the problems of the executive."

Charles R. Miller, in "William McKinley: The Lawyer"

cases that the Court had decided on the Sherman Act. In his 1899 annual message, McKinley suggested that action be taken about monopolies, and he asked Congress to address the matter in its next session. Nothing happened during the election year of 1900, when McKinley again handily defeated Bryan, but there was evidence that McKinley was moving toward a more activist policy on such issues before his assassination.

While in the White House, McKinley maintained other links to his legal background. He remained, for example, a dues-paying member of the American Bar Association. During the spring of 1901, when the Albany Law School celebrated its fiftieth anniversary, the school invited "the most distinguished graduate" to attend the festivities. While his schedule and Mrs. McKinley's illness prevented the president from attending, he sent "congratulations to the trustees of the Albany Law School upon completion of its fiftieth year of work."

Three months later, William McKinley was dead at the hands of an assassin, and his presidency passed into history. His training at the Albany Law School and his years as a practicing attorney in Canton, Ohio, had laid the basis for a political career that took him to the White House at a key point in the nation's history. As president, he used the skills acquired during his legal apprenticeship to manage the Spanish-American War, acquire the Philippine Islands, and oversee the development of the American empire. There was much accuracy in Charles Miller's observation that McKinley brought "a trained and mature legal mind with which to solve the problems of the executive." Future study of McKinley's years as a lawyer will no doubt illuminate the formative influences on one of the key architects of the modern presidency.

New Century Presidents

Law in the New Century

The lawyer-presidents of the new century presided over a country that had grown into an economic giant. The mighty struggle between labor and capital continued. As in all modern nations, interest groups—representing business, labor, agriculture, the professions, and other constituencies—struggled for control, for a share of the national product, and for the most favorable posture before the law. Controversy swirled about the issues of strikes and labor unrest, and about big, bigger, and biggest businesses.

As De Toqueville had noted some fifty years before, in the United States all political questions had a tendency to turn into legal questions. The courts, including the U.S. Supreme Court, were in the very eye of the hurricane of social change. They had taken on the job of shaping the limits of governmental power at the national and state levels. In the twentieth century, as courts ruled on child labor laws, workers' compensation laws, and other social innovations, they were seen by many as the saviors of America, and by others as almost agents of the devil.

America was a rich country and getting richer. Yet many old-line Americans felt at bay, beleaguered, their cherished values and traditions threatened. Millions of new immigrants were arriving—men and women from southern and eastern Europe—and the cities (with their vice and corruption) were growing dramatically at the expense of farms and small towns. National Prohibition, a vain attempt to stamp out the evils of the saloon, was one of the short-lived responses to this perceived crisis. More successful was the attempt to cut back on immigration—especially the immigration of the wrong sort of people.

First, Congress excluded the Chinese. Then, in the 1920s, it passed a narrow and biased immigration law, with a twisted system of national quotas that sought to stop the inflow of Greeks, Italians, Jews, and Slavs. A moral panic led to the Mann Act (against "white slavery") and stricter laws against vice, prostitution, and basically all forms of sex outside of marriage. The use of drugs was criminalized. Eugenics laws called for the protection of the country's precious gene pool by sterilizing criminals, the feeble-minded, and various undesirables. The same theories of race and bloodlines helped justify the system of apartheid in the South. It was a low point for blacks, Native Americans, and the West Coast Chinese.

Meanwhile, the law schools finally and decisively triumphed over the apprenticeship method of training. By 1910, there were seventy-nine schools that taught law in the daytime, plus forty-five that offered instruction at night. Some schools had grown to great size: the University of Michigan Law School, the largest in the country in 1901–2, had 854 students; Harvard in the same period had 632. But Harvard was in other ways the colossus of legal education. More and more law schools followed the Harvard method of instruction: casebooks and Socratic dialogue. The old lecture system was doomed, even in the night and part-time schools. As law schools expanded and proliferated, they also became, in effect, the gateway to the bar. In 1922, of the 643 men and women who took New York State's bar exam, all but nine had gone to law school.

The elite lawyers continued to worry about the fate of the profession. Were there too many lawyers? Were there too many sleazy lawyers? The American Bar Association adopted its Canons of Professional Ethics in 1908 (and Canons of Judicial Ethics in 1924). Local and state bar associations eagerly followed its lead. In the early 1920s, the ABA also set standards for legal education and began accrediting law schools. Yet the ABA was still an elite organization. Its membership was 3 percent of the bar in 1910, 9 percent in 1920. Its actions reflected the wants and needs of the upper strata of the bar. The ban on advertisement provides a good example, for Wall Street lawyers did not want or need to advertise, while storefront and local lawyers did. The ABA was also a restricted organization. Blacks were unwelcome (though three were mistakenly admitted in 1911). Women were not admitted until 1918. Women were, in general, still rare among the ranks of the lawyers; and many law schools (Harvard, for example) were exclusively for men.

The bar was highly stratified. At the top were the ABA leaders and the Wall Street lions who represented big business; at the other end of the spectrum were the ethnic lawyers, scratching for a living in the ghettos and tenement districts. The top lawyers were members of law firms; the local lawyers on the whole worked on their own. The top lawyers could aspire to high positions in Washington or seats on the board of great corporations; the local lawyers, if they were politically active, could become municipal judges, aldermen, or powers in their cities and towns. As had been the case since the colonial period, politics and the practice of law continued to go hand in hand.

And politics was, as always, a struggle for power—for command of the instruments of law, the statutes, rules, and regulations that were so important to businesses and to ordinary people. Populism made its mark on the statute books. Many states passed prounion laws. Antitrust laws aimed to curb big business or rather too-big business. Workers' compensation laws were passed in virtually all the states. Progressives made serious attempts to clean up and reform municipal government. And, in all of these issues and struggles, lawyers took leading roles as activists, movers, and shakers—on all sides of all issues. The New Deal of the 1930s, under Franklin D. Roosevelt, has been sneeringly called a "lawyer's deal." Indeed, New Deal lawyers swarmed all over Washington, drafting statutes, devising plans, and running the agencies, bureaus, and boards that carried out the New Deal program.

LAWRENCE M. FRIEDMAN

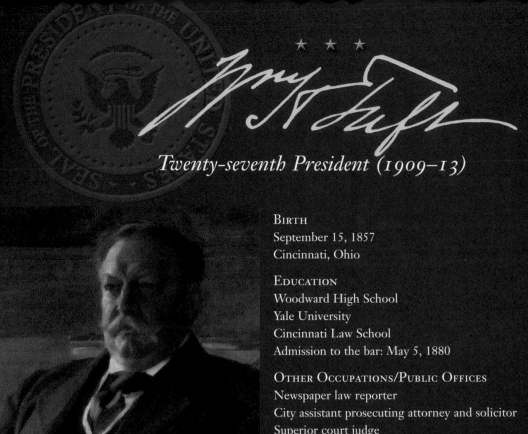

★ ★ ★

Twenty-seventh President (1909–13)

BIRTH
September 15, 1857
Cincinnati, Ohio

EDUCATION
Woodward High School
Yale University
Cincinnati Law School
Admission to the bar: May 5, 1880

OTHER OCCUPATIONS/PUBLIC OFFICES
Newspaper law reporter
City assistant prosecuting attorney and solicitor
Superior court judge
U.S. solicitor general
Federal circuit court judge
Law school dean
Governor-general of Philippines
Secretary of war with Theodore Roosevelt
Professor of law
Cochair, National War Labor Board
Chief justice of the United States

DEATH
March 8, 1930
Washington, D.C.

LAW CAREER IN BRIEF

Taft's legal résumé is by far the most extensive and diverse of the lawyer-presidents. From his work during law school covering the courts for a local newspaper in 1880, to 1930, when he completed nearly ten years as chief justice of the United States, Taft's life was immersed in the law as a government lawyer, jurist, professor, and dean. Taft even served as president of the American Bar Association a year after his presidency. During his tenure as chief justice, he championed such major administrative improvements as streamlined Supreme Court procedures, greater coordination among the federal courts, and legislation giving the high court its present home across from the Capitol building in Washington, D.C.

William Howard Taft: Mr. Chief Justice

Melvyn Dubofsky

In comparison with his twenty-four fellow lawyer-presidents, William Howard Taft pursued a career far more associated with the law than with politics. "Politics make me sick," he once wrote. The only man to serve as both president and chief justice of the United States, his preference was clear. Said Taft, "I love judges and I love courts."

Taft was a one-term president whose time in office proved a political disaster for himself and for the party he led. Taft had preceded his presidency by three years of service on the state bench in Ohio, two years as solicitor general of the United States, and eight years as a presiding judge of the Sixth U.S. Circuit Court. After losing his bid for reelection to the Oval Office in 1912, he taught for eight years at Yale Law School, followed by a decade as chief justice of the United States. In between his stints on the circuit court and at Yale, Taft served as governor-general of the Philippines and Teddy Roosevelt's secretary of war. His résumé also includes service as a superior court judge and cochair of the National War Labor Board—all in all, a long and distinguished career in public service.

However distinguished Taft's public service may have been, however, neither his contemporaries nor subsequent scholars describe him as an exceptional president, public servant, or jurist. Perhaps fellow Supreme Court Justice Oliver Wendell Holmes Jr. captured the essence of Taft's ability, when he commented on the latter's appointment as chief justice, "I never saw anything that struck me as more than first-rate second rate."

Indeed, despite notable family origins, little in Taft's adolescence and early manhood augured an exceptional future. Born in Cincinnati in 1857 to parents of New England Yankee Protestant heritage, the young Taft grew up in comfortable and secure circumstances.

★ ★ ★

"I love judges and I love courts."

William Howard Taft

"Neither law nor morals can give a man the right to labor or withhold his labor for [an unlawful] purpose."

William Howard Taft

His father Alphonso built a successful local law practice in this larger, thriving western river city, and housed his growing brood in a comfortable Victorian home located in the pastoral neighborhood of Mt. Auburn. The elder Taft, befitting his New England Protestant origins, also played a prominent role in the Republican Party. He served in President Ulysses Grant's cabinet and subsequently as the U.S. ambassador in St. Petersburg and Vienna.

Young William attended neighborhood public schools, mingled with children of similar social status, and completed his secondary school education at Cincinnati's primary college preparatory school. Already plagued by a tendency toward obesity—a condition that would subject him to periodic ridicule throughout his life—Taft was nevertheless a competent athlete and excellent dancer. A successful student, he eagerly awaited his matriculation at Yale University in 1876. During his four years in New Haven, Taft pursued his studies diligently, cemented firm friendships with like young men, and acquainted himself with many members of the extended Taft family in New England and their Yankee culture.

While at Yale he decided to follow his father's career path and practice law. Surprisingly, however, Taft rejected enrollment in an elite law school and instead chose to return home and attend Cincinnati Law School. Soon after his graduation from law school and admittance to the state bar, he spent a short time as a law reporter for local newspapers before accepting an appointment in 1881 as an assistant public prosecutor, a position he held for less than two years. Of this first political appointment to public office, Taft later observed: "Like every well-trained Ohio man, I always had my plate the right side up when offices were falling." For a short time after resigning as a prosecutor, he engaged in private law practice for the first and only time in his long career. By 1886, however, he had turned his plate right side up and ran as the Republican candidate for a judgeship on the superior court of Ohio, a race that he won. This would be his only elective office prior to achieving the highest office in the land some twenty-two years later.

Taft's four-year term as a superior court judge introduced him to a disputatious legal subject that marked his subsequent career as a federal judge on both the circuit court and the U.S. Supreme Court—the rights and responsibilities of trade union members in disputes against employers. Most unions in their charters, traditions, or rituals bound members to act together against employers deemed to be unfair to labor. Unions also sought to pressure other employers hostile to unions by refusing to supply such firms with materials or services, through what is known as a secondary boycott. In one of Taft's early cases involving a secondary boycott by the Cincinnati bricklayers' union, he ruled such actions to be malicious and illegal restraints of legitimate trade and business activities. His decision, on behalf of a unanimous court, fit neatly with late-nineteenth-century labor law, and its rationale was one that Taft would support for the remainder of his judicial career. It also reflected his considerable fear of all class-based actions that might limit the precious individual rights of all citizens.

While building his career as an attorney, jurist, and Republican Party stalwart, Taft fell in love. Not unexpectedly, the choice of his affections, Helen Herron, was the child of a family much like his own. Like Alphonso Taft, Helen's father was a successful Cincinnati attorney who raised his family in substantial comfort and security. Taft's 1886 marriage to Helen, always better known as Nellie, united Taft to a far more ambitious personality. He

probably would have been satisfied with whatever Republican judicial plums landed on his political plate; Helen's political desires for her spouse knew no limits, including the White House.

Thus in 1890, the young husband and wife left Cincinnati for the first time to move to Washington, D.C., where William would serve as solicitor general of the United States. Taft at first felt uncomfortable in his new office, owing partly to his limited knowledge of federal legal procedure and partly because, in his own words, "I do not find myself at all easy or fluent on my feet." Nevertheless he learned to master

LABOR LAW ACCORDING TO JUDGE TAFT

While a federal circuit court judge, Taft addressed a series of labor law issues that were fueled, in part, by the difficult economic times of the late 1800s. Like many fellow judges, he handed down antistrike injunctions, imprisoned union officials, and gained a reputation as an antilabor judge. This record, Taft wrote, hardly advanced his prospects for high political office: "The idea that a man who . . . is known as one of the worst judges for the maintenance of government by injunction, could ever be a successful candidate on a Presidential ticket, strikes me as intensely ludicrous."

SOLICITOR GENERAL TAFT'S BERING SEA ARGUMENT

From 1890 to 1892, Taft served as Benjamin Harrison's solicitor general. While there are varying estimates of the number of cases he handled—ranging from eighteen to thirty-six—the most notable case concerned the Bering Sea boundary dispute. In 1867, when the United States purchased Alaska, the treaty did not precisely define such boundaries and, seeking to end run the diplomatic process, British and Canadian interests sought a Supreme Court ruling that would bolster their position. Taft successfully countered this strategy, arguing that the application for certiorari should be denied "while diplomatic negotiations were going on."

federal procedure and to argue effectively before the nation's highest court, winning sixteen of the eighteen cases he argued. None of these, however, were precedent-shattering or of exceptional legal significance.

Never feeling at home in the capital's political society, and dismayed by the heat and humidity of Washington's summers, Taft used his political influence to win a seat in 1892 on the newly expanded federal circuit court serving Ohio, Kentucky, and Michigan. Taft's accession to the federal bench coincided with a crucial and controversial era in the history of the federal judiciary. Within a year of his appointment, the nation fell into the deepest of several late-nineteenth-century economic depressions. Tumbling prices for farm products, falling wages, and rising unemployment fueled rising discontent among farmers and workers. Between 1892 and 1896, third-party protest politics as exemplified by the growth of populism reached fever pitch while workers engaged in a series of turbulent and sometimes violent strikes, the most notable being the Homestead steel strike of 1892 and the Pullman strike and boycott of 1894. Because bankrupt railroads often passed into federal receivership and interstate railroads clearly fell within the national government's commerce power, federal judges often rendered judgments in cases arising out of railroad strikes. Taft proved no exception to the rule, as he handed down a number of antistrike injunctions, imprisoning several union officials and gaining a reputation as an antilabor injunction judge.

Taft's rulings in the labor cases broke no new ground, nor did they stray far from the mainstream of judicial opinion. Like most late-nineteenth-century federal judges who came from respectable and affluent family origins and who were schooled in the era's prevailing legal doctrines, Taft believed in the concept of employment-at-will and in the laborer's individual right to cease employment at any time for any reason. He also tolerated workers' collective quits or strikes aimed at their immediate employers. But he lacked tolerance for collective action that sought through the closed shop to deny employment opportunity to nonunion workers. In these instances, Taft believed, the unmitigated evil of class consciousness subverted individual rights embedded in the constitutions of the United States and the states.

In an 1893 case brought by a railroad against the engineers' union whose cars were not being interchanged with those of another line, Taft first found railroads to be quasi-public enterprises directly subject to federal law. Hewing to the mainstream of legal interpretation, Taft went on to declare that workers have a perfect right to threaten to quit work when not in violation of contract, for man has an inalienable right to his own labor. That right, however, is not absolute, and if it is used unlawfully, as for example in a sympathetic strike that is actually a boycott, then "neither law nor morals can give a man the right to labor or withhold his labor for such a purpose."

He warned Brotherhood president P. M. Arthur that the union's rules "make the whole brotherhood a criminal conspiracy against the laws of their country" as he issued a temporary injunction ordering engineers on unaffected railroad lines to handle traffic from the struck railroad. A year later in a comparable case that arose from the Pullman boycott, Taft reiterated this stance, saying in part, "The gigantic character of the conspiracy of the American Railway Union staggers the imagination. . . . Certainly the starvation of a nation cannot be a lawful purpose of a combination, and it is utterly immaterial whether the purpose is effected by means usually lawful or otherwise."

Such rulings by Taft and other federal judges, including justices of the U.S. Supreme Court, precipitated a popular outcry against judicial tyranny. The populist movement and the labor movement condemned the arrogance and elitism of the judiciary and fed a growing demand for the recall of judicial decisions and even judges. Taft's judicial rulings in labor matters did not bode well for a future in politics, as he himself later observed in a letter to his brother Charles. "The idea that a man who issued injunctions against labor unions, almost by the bushel," wrote Taft, "who has sent at least ten or a dozen violent labor agitators to jail, and who is known as one of the worst judges for the maintenance of government by injunction, could ever be a successful candidate on a Presidential ticket, strikes me as intensely ludicrous."

THE LARGE-ICAL CANDIDATE.

THE WEIGHT OF THE PRESIDENCY

Taft's rotund frame occasioned many jokes about his girth. Before, during, and following his presidency, however, he never hesitated placing that considerable weight behind the central role of the judiciary in America. He remains the only individual to have served as both president and chief justice of the United States.

"Taft considered defense of the judiciary and the rule of law among his most important issues."

Taft might have been content to spend the remainder of his life on the federal bench, remaining on the sixth circuit until he could achieve his highest ambition, appointment to the U.S. Supreme Court, preferably as chief justice. But Nellie had grander ambitions, her heart set on serving as first lady in a William Howard Taft White House. Whether it was in his own commitment to public service when asked by prominent Republicans, or in deference to Nellie's desires, Taft resigned from the federal bench in 1900 to take up service as the governor-general of the Philippine Islands.

Taft would remain in the Philippines until 1904, where he exemplified the perspective of the era's typical colonial administrators. Much in the mode of his British imperial counterparts and perhaps even eager to assume Rudyard Kipling's "white man's burden," Taft intended to bring to his "little brown brothers overseas" the blessings of Western-style education, sanitation, public health, and public administration. He clearly enjoyed the perquisites and emoluments showered on colonial rulers by deferential "natives"; yet he likely found the tropical islands environment as debilitating as Washington's heat and humidity, and the distance between his overseas outpost and the political circles likely to smooth his appointment to the Supreme Court even more dismaying.

Thus, despite his less than martial demeanor and his preference for arbitration agreements and peace movements over military preparations and war, he accepted with alacrity Roosevelt's offer to become secretary of war in 1904, a position he would hold through the remainder of Roosevelt's presidency. Roosevelt was clearly in charge of his own foreign policy and military plans, with Taft serving largely as Roosevelt's tool. In fact, because Taft served Roosevelt's ends so faithfully and appeared to share the president's political perspective, Roosevelt chose Taft as his heir to the White House, a decision both men would come to rue.

When Roosevelt anointed Taft as his successor in 1908, the nation was nearing the midpoint of a long era of Republican national political dominance, one that stretched from 1894 to 1932. Thus Taft's victory in the election of 1908, despite the Republican candidate's less than exhilarating campaign style, proved no surprise.

Soon, however, the new president's political misadventures and woeful tactics split the Republican Party. His predecessor in the White House had edged slowly to the political left during eight years in office, partly in response to shifts among the electorate and partly as a result of his own estimation about how to accommodate personal, party, and national interests. Moreover, outrage flared among masses of citizens and a bloc of GOP politicos from the Midwest against what they condemned as judicial excess. As Taft considered defense of the judiciary and the rule of law among his most important issues, he found himself in alliance with the most conservative Republicans. Whether it was issues of tariff reform, conservation, labor injunctions, corporate regulation, congressional reform, or direct primaries, Taft found himself in conflict with policies once enunciated by Roosevelt and now preferred not only by Republican insurgents but also by a new generation of Democratic officeholders and many voters.

Not that Taft was a recalcitrant or a reactionary like some Republicans with whom he was allied. Instead, Taft endorsed constitutional amendments providing for the direct election of U.S. senators and for a federal income tax; he also used the Sherman Antitrust Act to prosecute alleged corporate monopolies more vigorously than Roosevelt ever had, pursuing about seventy cases against such giants as Standard Oil and American Tobacco. Yet the principles that underlay Taft's support of constitutional amendments and antitrust prosecutions were the same ones that often brought him into conflict with Roosevelt, party insurgents, and an electorate drifting toward the left.

Many of Taft's difficulties as president flowed from his reverence for the law and the esteem in which he held judges, while many politicians, including Roosevelt, and a good part of the electorate saw the judiciary as the greatest single threat to the progressive reform agenda. For example, the Arizona and New Mexico territories adopted new constitutions preparatory to achieving statehood that included clauses providing for the recall of judicial decisions and judges. Taft opposed their admission to statehood until such clauses were purged from the constitutions. When insurgent Republicans in Congress and their Democratic allies sought to enact a federal income tax, Taft threatened a veto because he feared that such legislation would subvert Supreme

LAW STUDENT TEDDY ROOSEVELT

Roosevelt, Taft's ardent sponsor for the presidency and challenger for reelection, briefly attended Columbia Law School from 1880 to 1881. Though he initially told himself, "I like the law school very much," a classmate saw it differently: "The intricacies of the rule in Shelley's case, the study of feudal tenures as exemplified in the great work of Blackstone, were not the things upon which that avid mind must feed." Another observed that Roosevelt "was predestined for politics." Both observations proved to be correct, as Roosevelt soon left law school to pursue his political interests. This picture of Teddy (at the left) and his brother Elliot was taken just before he entered law school.

The Tafts: A Distinguished Legal and Political Legacy

The Tafts are one of those singularly accomplished, multigenerational families, like the Adamses and Jameses, who have contributed much to our nation. Alphonso Taft, William's father, was an Ohio Supreme Court justice who also served as attorney general, secretary of war, and ambassador to Hungary and Russia with President Grant. William's brother, Henry, was partner in the venerable New York City law firm of Cadwalader, Wickersham, and Taft. William had five sons by two marriages, all of whom were lawyers. His eldest son, Robert (pictured here), was a long-term U.S. senator from Ohio known as "Mr. Republican." Robert's son was also U.S. senator and his son was governor of Ohio.

Court precedent. Instead he favored a constitutional amendment. Taft was more than willing to diminish his political popularity in order to protect the courts against "irresponsible progressives." Although he believed in a strong executive, Taft took exception to Roosevelt's notion that the presidency included an "undefined residuum of power" to make policy; such a doctrine, said Taft, "might lead under emergencies to results of an arbitrary character, doing irremediable injustice to private rights."

Taft especially sanctified the U.S. Supreme Court. "What distinguishes this country from any other," he said in 1911, "is the Supreme Court . . . that has often stood between us and errors that might have been committed . . . and to turn on that court and . . . to attack it seems to me to lay the axe at the root tree of our civilization." Indeed, for Taft, judges were "high priests in the temple of justice" charged with obligations of a sacred character.

Taft not only defended the judiciary. During his presidency, he appointed six justices to the Supreme Court, including a new chief justice, the elderly E. Douglass White, whom one scholar suggested Taft chose in order to ease his own accession to the office after leaving the presidency. Among his other appointments, Charles Evans Hughes was the most distinguished and Willis Van Devanter enjoyed the longest tenure—twenty-six years, long enough to create grief for Franklin Roosevelt's New Deal as one of the more conservative and obdurate members of the Court's "four horsemen."

Taft's aggressive defense of the judiciary and his alliance with the more conservative elements in Congress and the Republican Party split the GOP. Roosevelt decided to challenge his former protégé in the election of 1912, and when Taft won the party nomination, Roosevelt broke away to become the presidential candidate of a new third party, the Progressive Party. Much of the pre- and post-Republican convention battle between Taft and Roosevelt centered on their differences over judicial practice and policy. Roosevelt criticized conservative jurists as obstacles to necessary reforms and even lauded efforts to recall judicial decisions and judges. In response Taft insisted that judges were not bound to kneel to the will of the majority and that to do so "would deprive the judiciary of that independence without which the liberty and other rights of the individual cannot be maintained against the Government and the majority." To subject judicial rulings to popular recall, he warned, "lays the ax at the foot of the tree of well-ordered freedom and subjects the guarantee of life, liberty, and property . . . to the fitful impulse of a temporary majority of an electorate." When the electorate spoke in 1912, it repudiated Taft, delivered far more popular votes to Roosevelt, and elected Democrat Woodrow Wilson to the presidency.

Taft's postpresidential years proved far more satisfying to him. His alma mater Yale offered him a professorship in the law school, which he gladly accepted and held until 1921. In 1913, the American Bar Association honored him with election to its presidency. As an elder statesman in the years just before and during World War I, Taft played a major role in the international peace and arbitration movements. After the United States entered the war in April 1917, Taft served his nation yet again, agreeing in 1918 to cochair the National War Labor Board alongside the far more radical Democratic attorney Frank P. Walsh. As cochair, Taft confounded those who saw him as a reactionary and those who admired him as a conservative defender of business interests. For the first time, this position afforded Taft direct exposure to the harsher aspects of workers' lives, including their exploitation and mistreatment by some employers. More often than not, Taft thus allied with Walsh and the labor members of the NWLB to provide a majority for decisions in favor of workers and unions.

Taft capped his postpresidential career in 1921 by obtaining the position that he had always desired most, chief justice of the U.S. Supreme Court. If he did not succeed in creating what might come to be known as a "Taft Court," he did build, to the extent possible, much harmony and fellowship among his temperamentally divided associates and much unanimity among the sharply split brethren. More important, he lobbied Congress to pass the Judiciary Act of 1922, which enabled Taft to reorganize the high court's work, reduce its caseload, concentrate mostly on cases of singular importance, and regularize the procedures and administration of the various federal districts and circuits through scheduled judicial conferences.

In all this, the chief justice played a dominant role, leading one scholar to conclude that Taft had been a weak president but

★ ★ ★

*"Many of Taft's
difficulties as presi-
dent flowed from
his reverence for the
law and the esteem
in which he held
judges, while many
politicians, including
Roosevelt, and a good
part of the electorate
saw the judiciary
as the greatest
single threat to
the progressive
reform agenda."*

a powerful jurist. His decade as chief justice also enabled Taft to show that the law could take account of changing circumstances in a manner that preserves social stability. "There will be found," he said, "a response to sober popular opinion as it changes to meet the exigency of social, political, and economic changes." In the most widely condemned and divisive Supreme Court ruling during his tenure—the 1923 case of *Adkins v. Children's Hospital* declaring a minimum wage law for women workers unconstitutional—Taft wrote the dissent. Rejecting the majority argument that legislatures lacked the constitutional authority to limit consenting adults absolute freedom to contract, Taft declared that employers and employees came to a bargain from unequal positions of power and that legislatures had a constitutional right to protect citizens against the evils of the sweating system and exploitation at work.

Justice Holmes was probably right in characterizing his "chief" as "first-rate second rate." A political failure as president, and one who split his party and thus opened the presidency to the opposition, Taft served admirably in all his other administrative and judicial positions. Yet whether as a circuit judge, colonial administrator, cabinet officer, law professor, or chief justice of the highest court in the land, Taft broke little new ground. He will probably remain best remembered as a staunch defender of an independent judiciary and as an able court administrator who brought the procedures of the federal courts, including the Supreme Court, into the twentieth century.

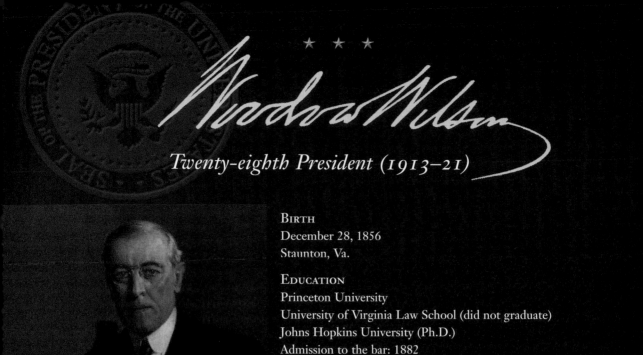

★ ★ ★

Twenty-eighth President (1913–21)

BIRTH
December 28, 1856
Staunton, Va.

EDUCATION
Princeton University
University of Virginia Law School (did not graduate)
Johns Hopkins University (Ph.D.)
Admission to the bar: 1882

OTHER OCCUPATIONS/PUBLIC OFFICES
Historian and political scientist
College professor and president
New Jersey governor

DEATH
February 3, 1924
Washington, D.C.

LAW CAREER IN BRIEF

Wilson's law career was very brief, pursued in Atlanta with Virginia Law School classmate Edward Renick in 1882. Wilson and Renick apparently spent more time following "the young lawyer's occupation of waiting" than in securing clients, cases, and fees. Having his mother as his most important client, Wilson decided in early 1883 to leave law practice and seek a graduate degree in political science at Johns Hopkins University. A long-time member of the American Bar Association, Wilson had another brief fling at law practice following his presidency, but ill health cut short the effort.

Woodrow Wilson: Reluctant Lawyer

MELVIN I. UROFSKY

Woodrow Wilson once commented that "The profession I chose was politics; the profession I entered was law. I entered the one because I thought it would lead to the other." By the time Wilson wrote these words to his fiancée, Ellen Axson, he had already abandoned the law to take up his longer and more successful career as an academic. He would finish his doctorate in government at the Johns Hopkins University and enjoy many years of success as a writer, college teacher, and president of Princeton University before embarking on the profession he had chosen so many years before—politics, serving as New Jersey governor and the twenty-eighth president of the United States.

Wilson initially realized that without a private income, he would never be able to devote his life to politics. His was not a rich family. His father, Joseph Ruggles Wilson, was a well-educated minister who was a college teacher before embarking full time on the work of God. His mother, Jessie Woodrow, was well educated for a woman in the mid-nineteenth century, but there was little money in her family either. To earn a sufficient living through the law, however, would preclude young Woodrow's going into politics. "The law is more than ever before a jealous mistress," he believed, and if a man "is to make a living at the bar he must be a lawyer and nothing else. . . . But he cannot be both a learned lawyer and a profound and public-spirited statesman, if he must plunge into practice and make the law a means of support." Perhaps Wilson was drawn to Louis D. Brandeis thirty years later because Brandeis had done what Wilson had deemed impossible—become a learned and successful lawyer as well as an effective political reformer.

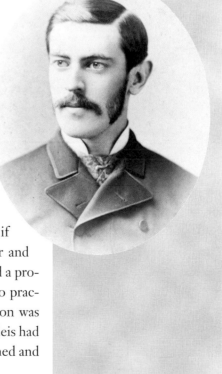

LAW PARTNER EDWARD RENICK

Renick, whom Wilson had known slightly from his time at the University of Virginia Law School, offered to share space with Wilson as they embarked upon their legal careers in Atlanta. Wilson accepted and the law firm of Renick and Wilson was formed. To a friend, Wilson described Renick as "a capital fellow," one of the "best informed and most cultivated men of my acquaintance, and a perfect enthusiast in his profession."

Wilson had doubts about the law as a profession long before he abandoned the bar and entered Hopkins; these misgivings dated back to the time he entered the University of Virginia Law School in the fall of 1879. The summer before he wrote essays on government, including "Cabinet Government in the United States" as well as unpublished pieces on "Self-Government in France" and "Congressional Government," that later led to his famous doctoral dissertation at Hopkins, also titled "Congressional Government."

Wilson's student days at Virginia as well as his relatively brief career in practice added up to what historian John Milton Cooper Jr. has termed "a miserable four years." Although he joined a fraternity and the Jefferson Society (a literary and debating group of which he soon became secretary) and "made several friends," he could not decide whether he liked the law school. The course in law, he declared, "is certainly as fine a one as could be desired," and he pronounced John Barbee Minor, then the head of the law school and one of the nation's leading legal scholars, "a perfect teacher," declaring, in fact, "I can say with perfect sincerity that I cannot conceive of a better." But toward the end of the first semester, he wrote, "Law is indeed a harsh task-master. I am struggling, hopefully but with not over-much courage, through its intricacies, and am swallowing the vast mass of its technicalities with as good a grace and as straight a face as an offended palate will allow. . . . I wish now to record the confession that I am most terribly bored by the noble study of Law."

During his time at the law school, Wilson devoted as much time as he could to nonlaw pursuits, such as the activities of the Jefferson Society and writing essays for the university magazine on politics and political leaders such as John Bright and William Gladstone. Returning for his second year, he felt "right lonely and disconsolate to-night at being left to plod out another long weary session" of law school.

Things soon turned worse. He proposed marriage to his cousin, who rejected him, and perhaps as a result, his health became problematic. He suffered from recurrent colds and stomach distress and finally decided to leave the law school in December 1880. Wilson returned to his parents' home in Wilmington, North Carolina, to recuperate, and decided that, as far as law was concerned, he could do quite as well in his father's manse as in Charlottesville. But while pursuing the goal of becoming a lawyer, he still saw his ultimate life bound up in politics. "My path is a very plain one," he wrote to a close friend. "My end is a commanding influence in the councils (and counsels) of my country—and the means to be employed are writing and speaking."

Wilson did, in fact, persevere in his legal studies, apparently in large measure to satisfy his father, who scorned Wilson's dream of a life in letters. In the middle of Wilson's first year at Virginia, Pastor Wilson had scolded his son about spending so much of his time writing and debating and had shown contempt for "a mere literary career such as you seem to dream about now and then." Settle down, he admonished, and "conquer the law, even through all its wretched twistings of technical paths of thorn." Wilson, during a long recuperation and under the watchful eyes of both parents, did settle down to his studies, although he seemed to get no more satisfaction from reading the law at home than he had studying it at Charlottesville.

After more than a year of law study and recuperation, Wilson stood ready to begin earning his living through its practice, though he had yet to decide where. As a southerner, he could find greater opportunities for entering political life in one of the states of the former Confederacy, but given the great expansion of industry in the North and the concomitant growth of law business that went with it, Wilson could expect to do far better if he settled in a northern city such as Philadelphia or Baltimore. Wherever he chose, he confided, it would have to be in a large city, "where there is at least opportunity for great things to be accomplished, whether I'm equal to their accomplishment or not. Where there's no room for ambition there's less incentive to great exertions."

By the late summer of 1881, Wilson chose the opportunity for political involvement over that of making money, although he clearly hoped to be able to earn a comfortable income as he still depended upon a monthly stipend from his father. Consulting with his parents, he chose Atlanta, a city that had by then fully recovered from its destruction in 1864 at the hands of Sherman's

★ ★ ★

"I wish now to record the confession that I am most terribly bored by the noble study of Law."

Woodrow Wilson

LOUIS BRANDEIS, THE HIGH COURT'S FIRST JEWISH JUSTICE

Controversy and debate swirled around Wilson's nomination of Louis Brandeis to the U.S. Supreme Court. A Louisville native, Brandeis maintained a Boston practice for more than twenty-five years, handling many high-profile cases and much public interest work. In 1908, he successfully argued the landmark Supreme Court case of *Muller v. Oregon* regarding the daily hours women could be made to work. His "Brandeis Brief" in the case changed the legal landscape of future briefs, as it explored the case's possible long-term social and economic repercussions along with its legal details. Still, there was strong opposition to the nomination, including that of seven former ABA presidents, among them William Howard Taft, before the Senate approved Brandeis's appointment.

army. Its strategic location had made it the rail hub of the South, with five lines serving it, and it had become a major commercial center as well, the seat of numerous manufacturing, banking, and insurance companies. Its population, then thirty-seven thousand, would double in the next ten years. The 1881 International Cotton Exposition as well as the unflagging efforts at civic promotion by Henry W. Grady, editor of the *Atlanta Constitution*, had made the city a symbol of the "New South." With the decision made, Wilson began to study the Georgia Code in preparation for admission to the state bar. He also decided to enter practice with Edward Ireland Renick, a classmate from the University of Virginia Law School.

In January 1882, Wilson received a letter from Renick, whom Wilson had known slightly in Charlottesville. Renick had graduated in 1881, and like Wilson he decided that Atlanta offered the most promise of success to a new lawyer. Renick offered to share office space with Wilson, or if Wilson preferred to have a place of his own, to at least use Renick's office until he found his own rooms. He also recommended his boardinghouse at 344 Peachtree Street.

Renick's offices were located on the second floor of a three-story building at 48 Marietta Street. He described it as "much coveted" because of its location, opposite the building housing the Georgia capitol as well as the supreme court and state library. Wilson's share of the rent would be four dollars and fifty cents a month, and they could get a servant to clean up for only fifty or seventy-five cents additional. Renick pressed Wilson to decide, since, as he put it, "I cannot very well afford to pay $9 or $10. & would wish to get some one else if you desire to make other arrangements."

Wilson decided to accept Renick's offer and, accompanied by his father, made the journey from Wilmington to Atlanta in May 1882, despite advice to delay the trip because of a smallpox epidemic. He found both the lodgings and office space acceptable, and he and Renick hit it off from the start. To a friend, Wilson described Renick as "a capital fellow," one of the "best informed and most cultivated men of my acquaintance, and a perfect enthusiast in his profession." Both men enjoyed literature more than the law, were fond of poetry, and read the *Aeneid* together.

The year they spent together as "Renick & Wilson" was much like that of many other young attorneys, with minimal business and signs more hopeful than realistic that more clients would soon come through the door. The two men proposed to divvy up the work with Renick taking on "the duties of attorney and me those of barrister, since he prefers 'office work' and I like most the duties connected with the conduct and argument of cases." As for their future success, "already some practice is coming to us and we are determined that hard work shall make it more and more."

Although not yet admitted to the bar, Wilson had already done some work for Isabelle Pratt, who had rented a boarding house from a Mrs. Kirby. Wilson attempted to get Mrs. Kirby to remove extra furniture from the building according to the terms of the rental agreement. The results of his letter, and whether he received any fee for it, are unknown. Later in August Wilson wrote that he expected to argue a tax case at the next term of the superior court in October. He hoped to give a "strong speech" in opposition to a license tax the city planned to impose. The case "will win much capital for the firm of Renick & Wilson if they can gain it—may bring them into prominence even if they don't gain it." There is no evidence that Wilson ever argued this case.

Wilson and his partner apparently spent much of their time trying to collect on "numberless desperate claims," the sort of business common to most young offices. While he had earned one or two "minute" fees, he continued to follow "the young lawyer's occupation of waiting." The two men hoped that by the end of their first year in practice together they would be able to make expenses. Things were so bad for the legal profession as a whole in Atlanta, Wilson explained, that the types of work that normally went to new lawyers "are unfairly out-bid by unscrupulous elders."

As it turned out, Wilson's most important client during his practice proved to be his mother. Janet Wilson had inherited real estate from her deceased brother, Thomas Woodrow, consisting of several tracts of land in Nebraska that, along with other assets of the estate, amounted to the rather considerable sum of thirty-eight thousand dollars. Shortly after Wilson settled in Atlanta, his mother asked him to settle the estate and signed over to him a power of attorney over the property in order to nullify an earlier proxy she had given to her brother-in-law, James Bones. As

★ ★ ★

"I perceived from the first that the charges [against Louis Brandeis] were intrinsically incredible . . . I knew from direct personal knowledge of the man what I was doing when I named him for the highest and most responsible tribunal of the nation."

Woodrow Wilson

"Wilson warned against a narrow education that looked at nothing but the law and ignored the broader historical, economic, and socio-logical context in which legal develop-ment took place."

time went on Mrs. Wilson grew to entirely distrust her brother-in-law, and she pushed her son to bring the whole sorry affair to an end. Although Bones delayed as much as he could, Wilson, pushed on by his mother, successfully secured the necessary partition of the lands between the remaining heirs and sold the tracts.

By this time Wilson had likely determined to abandon the practice of law. Josephus Daniels later wrote that in Atlanta, Wilson discovered "the depth and slime of the gulf that often separated the philosophy of law from its practice." His letters, from the time he entered law school, had never indicated that burning enthusiasm for the law that is the mark of a successful attorney. In fact, he had hardly indicated any enthusiasm at all. He revealed his desire to leave the law to his father who, while concluding that his son wanted to find an easier life, nonetheless finally approved of his decision to be a teacher. In April 1883, Wilson applied for a fellowship at the Johns Hopkins University, was accepted, and entered into a life that he not only found intellectually and emotionally satisfying, but one that would lead him to his heart's desire—politics and a chance to influence the nation's destiny.

Was Woodrow Wilson a failure at the bar? Certainly the year or so he spent in practice showed little success. One study found that the firm of Renick & Wilson never filed a single case in either the city court of Atlanta or the superior court of Fulton County. Yet such experiences would not have been very different from those of most fledgling lawyers of the time, and while Wilson and Renick never showed a profit in their year together, Wilson did spend $128 in January 1883 for law books. This purchase, however, may have been covered in part by his father, who continued to provide him with a monthly allowance of fifty dollars during his entire stay in Atlanta.

It is probably fair to say that although Wilson certainly had the ability to work hard and the intellect to have been successful at the bar, he never had the temperament to do so. Law would never be to him a vocation of love, and therefore he could never be happy in it. His interests and his passions led him elsewhere. And so he left the law, whose four years of study and practice can at best only be described as an unhappy interlude in his life. He rarely spoke about his experience, and according to his biographer, "for the rest of his life he tended to look with contempt upon lawyers as a class."

Yet Wilson never fully broke his ties with the law. In 1894, for example, he joined the American Bar Association—at that time, a very exclusive group of "establishment" lawyers and judges—delivering a paper at that group's annual meeting that surely must have jolted more conservative members of the established bar. In the talk, Wilson inveighed against the reaction of many lawyers to the domestic disturbances then convulsing the country, such as Coxey's army and the Pullman strike. While many other speakers at that meeting attacked radicalism and demanded that the government squash all protest, Wilson aligned himself on the side of the moderates and placed at least some of the blame for the current unrest on reactionary judges and lawyers who thwarted rational demands for reform. He called upon society to respond intelligently to changing events by constructive reform if it hoped to avoid revolution.

The speech also gives some insight into Wilson's disillusionment with legal education, especially the Harvard-initiated case method of study. In words that sound all too familiar today, Wilson warned against a narrow education that looked at nothing but the law and ignored the broader historical, economic, and sociological context in which legal development took place. He urged a broad liberal arts undergraduate program as the necessary prerequisite for law school, much like his own training at Princeton years earlier. Like Louis Brandeis, Wilson believed too large a gulf separated law from life. His secretary of the navy, Josephus Daniels, noted that if Wilson had any deep-seated prejudice, it was against what Wilson termed "the legalistic barriers" that obstructed justice.

Wilson, who seems to have remained an ABA member until his death, spoke one other time at its annual meeting, in 1910 in the midst of his campaign for election as New Jersey's governor. His criticism of the disjuncture between the legal profession and the great reform movements then sweeping the country sounded very similar to the message that Louis Brandeis was then delivering. Lawyers had abandoned their traditional role as leaders of the community in order to become paid handmaidens of industry,

REPUBLICAN CHALLENGER CHARLES EVANS HUGHES
Hughes was a New York City lawyer and law professor who gained prominence as chief counsel in state legislative investigations of utility and insurance companies. Following his two terms as New York governor, President Taft appointed him to the U.S. Supreme Court, where he served until being drafted in 1916 by the Republicans to challenge Wilson. Upon losing a close election, Hughes returned to law practice and also held public office, including service as President Harding's secretary of state. In 1930, President Hoover appointed Hughes chief justice of the United States, replacing Taft. Hughes remained with the Court until his retirement in 1941.

*"Like Louis Bran-
deis, Wilson believed
too large a gulf sepa-
rated law from life."*

Wilson contended, and in doing so had abandoned their obligation to the general welfare. "Let no future generation have cause to accuse us of having stood aloof, indifferent, half hostile," he concluded, "or of having impeded the realization of right. Let us make sure that liberty shall never repudiate us as its friends and guides. We are the servants of society, the bond-servants of justice."

It is difficult to determine how Wilson's legal education and brief law practice served or influenced him during his presidency—if at all. The major issues of his administration—tariff reform, overhaul of the banking system, antitrust law—were the major political issues of the day, and one needed no specific knowledge of the law to recognize their import. Wilson seems to have relied on advisers such as Brandeis, William Gibbs McAdoo, and William Jennings Bryan in fashioning these laws, and he seems not to have played any major role in the actual drafting of the measures.

His appointments to the Supreme Court seem no more instructive. One can certainly applaud his nomination of Louis Brandeis, whom he greatly admired both as a lawyer and a reformer. But his first appointment, that of Attorney General James C. McReynolds, placed on the nation's highest court for three decades one of the most reactionary members in its history. Wilson had mistaken McReynolds's hatred of trusts as a sign of progressivism; in fact McReynolds hated lots of things and was no friend of reform. He proved to be so unpleasant a member of the cabinet that Wilson took his first vacancy on the Court to kick McReynolds upstairs. His final appointment, John Clarke, was liberal and of limited effectiveness; his term was brief, as he left the Court in 1922 to work for Wilson's League of Nations.

By then Wilson had left the presidency and entered his second law practice, this time with his former secretary of state, Bainbridge Colby. The two men had apparently first spoken in January 1921 of what they would do after Wilson's term ended in March. Wilson had some fears that he had been away from the law too long and lacked the technical expertise that practice required. Colby reassured him that his job was to think and act on the larger issues involved; one could always hire technical expertise. The day before he left office, Wilson and Colby announced their intention to open a firm with offices in both New York and Washington. Colby would be in charge of the

New York office and would travel to Washington when necessary to consult with Wilson, who would head that office.

In order to practice, however, Wilson had to be admitted to the bar, a tricky situation since he had not been in practice for nearly forty years. Colby, who had strong political connections in his home state, managed to get a special bill to that effect passed unanimously by both houses of the New York legislature. In Washington, a friendly senator moved Wilson's admission, and the ex-president went to the District of Columbia Supreme Court where the entire bench, led by Chief Justice Walter I. McCoy, admitted Wilson to the D.C. bar.

The full administrative burden of running Wilson & Colby fell on Colby, who considered it an honor to be associated with the man he revered. And potential clients lined up at the door, all to be turned away. While it is common now for politicians on leaving office to resume former careers or become paid lobbyists, Wilson would not trade on his name. He refused to take any clients who sought something from the government, which, after all, was why they came to him. Whatever the prevailing ethics of the bar might be, Wilson had his own standards and would not budge.

That he might have undertaken a successful, or even a partially successful, law career after the White House was a chimera at best. Even if he had been willing to work at the law, he could not do so physically. A stroke, suffered in 1919, had left him significantly disabled, a sixty-six-year-old man with broken health. By the summer of 1922, even Wilson recognized this, and in November of that year he instructed Colby to dissolve the firm. Colby finally agreed and announced the closing of the firm at the beginning of December. The second phase of Wilson's career as a lawyer had come to an end.

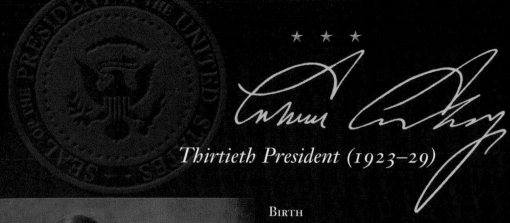

Thirtieth President (1923–29)

BIRTH
July 4, 1872
Plymouth, Vt.

EDUCATION
Public school
Black River Academy
St. Johnsbury Academy
Amherst College
Studied law with John C. Hammond and Henry P. Field
    in Northampton, Mass.
Admission to the bar: July 2, 1897

OTHER OCCUPATIONS/PUBLIC OFFICES
City councilman
City solicitor
County clerk of the courts
State legislator
Northampton mayor
Massachusetts lieutenant governor and governor
Vice president with Warren Harding

DEATH
January 5, 1933
Northampton, Mass.

LAW CAREER IN BRIEF

Coolidge began his law practice with Hammond and Field before opening his own office in Northampton in 1898, where he remained until elected governor in 1918. In 1899, he became counsel for the new Nonotuck Savings Bank, a relationship that continued throughout a practice that focused on mortgages, titles, and other real estate, estate settlement, and insolvency matters. Early on, he also served as city solicitor and clerk of courts. A self-proclaimed "country lawyer" who spent little time in court, Coolidge had a strong commitment to the rule of law, considered law "the highest of the professions," and frequently brought his legal experience and philosophy to bear in his public offices.

Calvin Coolidge: Country Lawyer

Russell Fowler

It was the Roaring Twenties, the Jazz Age, a time of unbounded energy and change. American accomplishment seemed limited only by the imagination. There were extraordinary achievements in science and technology, daring feats of exploration, creative explosions in music, art, literature, film, and fashion, and a golden era of sport. From crazy fads to flappers, from dance to art deco, so much seemed so different. For the first time, more Americans lived in urban instead of rural settings, while unprecedented numbers of women participated in education, the workplace, and public affairs. Americans enjoyed mass mobility with the automobile, mass communication with the radio, and mass marketing made possible by both. Of equal significance, mass prosperity was fueling it all. Modern American culture was born.

In a time of such excitement and excess, it may seem odd that America turned so enthusiastically to the reserved, frugal Calvin Coolidge for leadership. Yet with change came uncertainty and nervousness, conflict between the lifestyles of the past and an unfamiliar present. Most Americans also sensed a growing disrespect for religion, tradition, and other societal norms, as gangsters, corrupt politicians, and Klansmen flouted legal and governmental restraints. Calvin Coolidge was the calming counterbalance and comforting link to a simpler past and its values. But there was more to his triumph than timing and image.

The key to understanding Coolidge's remarkable career and political philosophy is recognizing his belief in the law and his ability to express and implement it. His efforts to achieve the benefits of the rule of law—security, decency, and liberty—demonstrate that he was an able and active administrator, uniquely interested in individual freedom, racial tolerance, and the challenges confronting the courts. And important challenges

★ ★ ★

"I was devoted to the law, its reasonableness appealed to my mind as the best method of securing justice between man and man."

Calvin Coolidge

*"Coolidge had a
scholarly and even
philosophical bent,
and throughout his
life, he expounded
a well-developed
philosophy of law."*

they were. Like much else in American society in the 1920s, the law was experiencing tension and change rarely witnessed since the nation's founding, and the judiciary was undergoing monumental attacks and reforms as well. During this important period, Coolidge became not only the champion of the rule of law but also of the courts.

Coolidge was born on the fourth of July in 1872 in the remote hamlet of Plymouth Notch in Vermont's Green Mountains. His mother died when he was twelve. From his loving and public-spirited father, Colonel John Coolidge, he learned the value of hard work, self-discipline, frugality, and service to others, all good New England qualities. As Coolidge said, "Our talents are given us in order that we may serve ourselves and our fellow men." His famous personality traits were apparent early, including shyness and a dry wit. Explaining his tendency to remain silent, he said, "The things I never say never get me in trouble." Beneath his frosty exterior, people also detected genuine kindness.

Young Calvin worked on his father's farm and in his general store and attended public and private schools in Vermont. He graduated cum laude from Amherst College in Northampton, Massachusetts, in 1895. Although a loner in college, he was selected to give the prestigious Grove Oration, and his essay, "The Principles Fought for in the American Revolution," won a national writing competition for college seniors.

Coolidge initially learned "the highest profession" in the locally prominent and politically connected law firm of Hammond and Field in Northampton. By day, Coolidge read law and prepared legal documents; at night, he read history, oratory, and the classics. These would be lifelong studies. His favorite writers included Shakespeare and Milton, and his hobby was translating the orations of Cicero.

Admitted to the Massachusetts bar in 1897 after less than two years of law office study, Coolidge developed a "sincere love" for the profession: "I was devoted to the law, its reasonableness appealed to my mind as the best method of securing justice between man and man. I fully expected to become the kind of country lawyer I saw about me, spending my life in the profession, with perhaps a final place on the Bench."

In keeping with his expectations, he entered politics only to further the development of his law practice. Among his earliest political posts were city solicitor and clerk of courts. Although he held more public offices than any other president, for the rest of his life he would proudly look back upon his appointment as court clerk by the Hampshire County judges as recognition of his legal ability.

Coolidge remained with the firm for seven months before opening his own office, where he practiced for twenty-one years until becoming governor of Massachusetts in 1919. By all accounts, Coolidge was a hard-working, highly ethical solo practitioner with a wide-ranging practice and an inclination to help the underdog. He was more interested in reaching fair settlements than waging courtroom battles. Most of his work involved the preparation of legal documents, wills and estates, bank title and mortgage work, and collections. Rarely in the courtroom, he faithfully stayed at his Main Street office during business hours to be available for clients. In the evenings, he increasingly took part in Republican politics, early on developing an uncanny ability of attracting Democratic votes as well. As a lawyer and politician, he skillfully used his formidable writing talents, with his crisp, clean style, to further his causes. He would be the last president not to use a speechwriter, and many have concluded that he was among the best writers to occupy the White House, perhaps equaled only by Lincoln.

Coolidge had a scholarly and even philosophical bent, and throughout his life, he expounded a well-developed philosophy of law. Eloquently expressed in speeches and writings, and grounded in the so-called classical or declarative theory, it would have a profound effect on his politics and presidency.

According to Coolidge, this traditional jurisprudence, which was the dominant view of the nineteenth century, goes to the very root of human existence individually and as a community. As he said at Amherst in 1920, "The process of civilization consists of the discovery by men of the laws of the universe, and of being in harmony with those laws. The most important of them to men are the laws of their own nature." Coolidge explained that "Men do not make laws. They do but discover them. . . . The state is most fortunate in its form of government which has the aptest instruments for the discovery of laws." He believed the American people had

COOLIDGE, THE YOUNG LAWYER

Reflecting upon his law practice, Coolidge said, "I fully expected to become the kind of country lawyer I saw about me, spending my life in the profession, with perhaps a final place on the Bench."

**GOVERNOR COOLIDGE
INSPECTS GUARDSMEN**

As Massachusetts governor, Coolidge was faced with a Boston police strike that threatened law and order. During the height of the turmoil, Coolidge sent a telegram to labor leader Samuel Gompers that catapulted Coolidge to national prominence: "There is no right to strike against the public safety by anybody, anywhere, anytime."

found such instruments in their state and federal constitutions and its systems of checks and balances, providing predictability and finality to the law, all features appealing to the conservative Coolidge.

Even with the great deference Coolidge accorded legislative branches throughout his political career, there were limits. With the progressive movement came all sorts of state legislation affecting social, economic, labor, and business activity as never before. Conservatives viewed this wave of enactments as a dangerous intrusion into individual and property rights. By the 1920s, Chief Justice William Howard Taft warned that the world would not be saved by this "overwhelming mass of ill-digested legislation." Coolidge, then vice president, agreed: "Behind very many of these enlarging activities lies the untenable theory that there is some short cut to perfection."

Coolidge had been rather progressive as mayor of Northampton, a state legislator, and governor, having earnestly supported and sponsored women's suffrage measures and bills helping workers, blacks, and the poor. Nevertheless, his growing concern about the direction of the law was apparent by the early 1920s, a direction he viewed as not just invading property rights but perilously striving to regulate morals and private personal conduct.

As vice president, Coolidge expressed his misgivings in a 1922 speech to the American Bar Association entitled "The Limitations of the Law." In it, he warned of dangers in "the attempt to raise the moral standard of society by legislation," noting that "a large part of the history of free institutions is the history of the people struggling to emancipate themselves from all this bondage." Actions in the 1920s by the Supreme Court in invalidating much social legislation—including prolabor statutes on minimum wages and working conditions—echoed Coolidge's viewpoint.

The manner in which Coolidge became president on August 3, 1923, on the sudden death of Warren Harding, presented an aura of honesty and old-fashioned values that contrasted sharply with the tawdry Harding administration and its soon-to-be-exposed corruption. By the light of a kerosene lamp, Coolidge's father, a notary public, administered the oath of office at the family homestead in Plymouth Notch at 2:47 A.M. After the ceremony, Coolidge went upstairs, knelt in prayer, and went back to bed as the thirtieth president of the United States. When he awoke, he visited his mother's grave before starting on toward Washington.

The drama and simplicity of these events captivated the nation, creating a groundswell of support for the new chief executive as he proceeded to lead the nation and confront the scandals of his predecessor's cronies. Chief Justice Taft wrote Secretary of the Treasury Andrew Mellon "that the welfare of the country is critically dependent upon the success of President Coolidge. The Republican Party has no chance without him. I don't remember a case in which a party is so dependent on a man."

Coolidge's popular appeal and political shrewdness became apparent early. In the time between becoming president and the 1924 Republican National Convention less than a year later, he purged the remnants of the discredited Harding clique, assured prosecution of wrongdoers, disassociated the GOP from the scandals, and took firm control of the party apparatus. Taft exclaimed, "He is keenly as good a politician as Lincoln." The party happily surrendered to the dominance of the "Puritan in Babylon," for he had been all that stood between it and oblivion.

Coolidge's accessibility and skillful use of the press—through regular press conferences, colorful photo opportunities, and frequent radio addresses—oddly made "Silent Cal" the first media president. Not only had the damage from Teapot Dome been contained, he swiftly managed his policies, pronouncements, and public image so as to become the personification of integrity and prosperity. In his silence, he seemed to hover above the hubbub of petty politics, and the less he said the more authoritative were his words. Adding to his good fortune was the great charisma and warmth of his beloved wife, Grace Goodhue Coolidge—the most popular first lady since Dolley Madison.

Even Democratic leaders such as Franklin Roosevelt and presidential nominee John W. Davis prefaced criticism of Coolidge with praise. In fact, the conservative Davis, a stellar lawyer but poor politician, was nominated in an attempt to out-Coolidge Coolidge. But as Roosevelt admitted, "To rise superior to Coolidge will be a hard thing." Davis proved unable to meet the challenge and became irrelevant as the president, press, and public all but ignored him. By the summer of 1924, "the Quiet

★ ★ ★

"He thought the essence of the republic was not so much democracy itself as the rule of law and the prime function of government was to uphold and enforce it."

Historian Paul Johnson

President" could survey the political landscape and see no real threats to his Republican order. The same was not true for Taft and the courts.

The aging and ailing Senator Robert La Follette of Wisconsin had accepted the Progressive presidential nomination and gathered the energy to wage a forceful campaign. In addition to attacking the administration's farm and labor policies and calling for the nationalization of railroads, "Fighting Bob" saved his most radical proposals for the judiciary, a crusade that became an obsession. Enraged over injunctions against strikers and Supreme Court rulings finding prolabor laws unconstitutional, La Follette called for electing federal judges, prohibiting inferior courts from declaring acts of Congress unconstitutional, and empowering Congress to overturn decisions of the U.S. Supreme Court.

The politically "cool [and] cunning" Coolidge wanted to ignore Davis and La Follette. He did little campaigning, due both to the inevitability of his victory and the devastating death of his youngest son, Calvin Jr., at the age of sixteen from blood poisoning. "When he went the power and the glory of the presidency went with him," wrote Coolidge. The president was never quite the same after this loss, some even believing he had suffered a heart attack. Still, Taft and Vice President Charles G. Dawes sought to draw Coolidge into the political fray and make the judiciary the chief issue of the campaign, the more so after suggestions for amending the Constitution seemed to catch the imagination of social reformers and labor activists.

The president finally determined that responding to La Follette was the proper and politically expedient thing to do. As governor, he had stood firm during the 1919 Boston police strike, and his mobilization of the state guard to restore calm evidenced his dedication to law and order. During the height of the turmoil, his telegram to Samuel Gompers catapulted Coolidge to national prominence: "There is no right to strike against the public safety by anybody, anywhere, anytime." He easily won reelection as governor, based largely on his defense of the supremacy of law.

As president, his commitment to enforce the law led him to sign a secret order directing the IRS to go after Al Capone. It was this endeavor, rather than the exploits of the FBI's "Untouchables," that ultimately proved to be the undoing of Chicago's mob boss. In foreign policy, he signed the idealistic Kellogg-

Briand Pact outlawing war as an instrument of national policy, sent five thousand troops to Nicaragua to maintain law and order, and went against many in his party and Congress by supporting American participation in the World Court.

As British historian Paul Johnson observed, "He thought the essence of the republic was not so much democracy itself as the rule of law and the prime function of government was to uphold and enforce it." Coolidge himself had said, "But in resisting all attacks upon our liberty, you will always remember that the sole guarantee of liberty is obedience to law under the forms of ordered government."

In responding to La Follette, the president offered a passionate defense of the courts. Coolidge described an independent judiciary headed by the U.S. Supreme Court as one of "the greatest contributions which America made to the science of government . . . with the sole purpose of protecting the freedom of the individual, of guarding his earnings, his home, his life." He went on to explain that the judicial power should not be "transferred in whole or in part to the Congress," which is subject to "popular demand" and "partisan advantage."

In the wake of the Red Scare of 1919 and 1920, Republican functionaries had little difficulty in making La Follette seem like the advance guard of Communism, while editorial columns and cartoons portrayed Coolidge as the champion of constitutionalism. On election day, the American people decided to follow the campaign slogan and "Keep Cool with Coolidge." The size of the landslide stunned even his most ardent supporters.

Although overlooked by most historians, Coolidge's dedication to the rule of law included a longstanding concern for the civil and economic rights of African Americans. As biographer Robert Sobel noted, "Few presidents were as outspoken on the need to protect the civil rights of black Americans as Calvin Coolidge."

There was nothing new about Coolidge's interest in human rights and his linking them with the rule of law and democracy.

As early as 1914, he urged the Massachusetts Senate to "recognize the immortal worth and dignity of man. . . . Such is the path to equality before the law. Such is the foundation of liberty under the law. Such is the sublime revelation of man's relation to man—Democracy."

During a 1924 campaign speech at Howard University, in obvious criticism of the Ku Klux Klan, he denounced "the propaganda of prejudice and hatred" and praised the contributions of black Americans in the recent war effort. As in his first message to Congress in 1923, he included language calling for tough federal antilynching laws in the GOP platform so that "the full influence of the federal government may be wielded to exterminate the hideous crime." The platform went on to state his wish that a federal commission be created to investigate the "social and economic conditions" of African Americans and promote "mutual understanding and confidence."

Coolidge personally urged black Republicans to run for public office, provided extensive party patronage to their political leaders in the South, and repeatedly called for federal funding of medical school scholarships for black students. He was "much troubled by insistent discrimination" against black Justice Department employees, calling it "a terrible thing," and pointedly instructing Attorney General John G. Sargent "to find a way to give them an even chance." Coolidge summed up his views saying, "We all live in the same world. We are bound to a common destiny through a common brotherhood."

Although these stands may have been "politically imprudent" at the time, the president never wavered in his commitment to civil rights. He would be the last Republican president to garner a majority of the black vote, and an overwhelming majority at that.

Immediately after Coolidge became president in 1923, Chief Justice Taft sought to gain influence, being so bold as to approach Coolidge on Harding's funeral train in an attempt to sway a lower court appointment. Taft found the new president "very self-contained, very simple, very direct, and very shrewd in his observations," and he was pleased to conclude that Coolidge would defend "the courts against wild radicals." Evidencing Coolidge's interest, Taft obtained his assistance in killing a bill that would limit the latitude of federal judges in their instructions to juries, but he found the thrifty president less receptive to a bill increasing judges' salaries. Taft did succeed, however, in securing White House neutrality on the issue and an agreement not to veto any pay increase. This was enough to achieve passage.

Of greater importance, Coolidge's intense pressure upon Congress on behalf of the "Judges' Bill" in 1925 proved indispensable. Along with other major procedural and jurisdictional reforms making the system more efficient and fair, this landmark act granted the U.S. Supreme Court wide discretion regarding cases it would accept for review. Freed from the burden of considering routine appeals, the high court could thereafter concentrate on important constitutional and federal law questions.

Taft's aggressive advocacy of judicial appointments, however, was not so well received. During the Harding years, the chief justice had simply conveyed his selections, which were accepted by the White House without hesitation. Unlike Harding, Coolidge could not be dictated to, indicating that "he was prepared to draw a rigid line on some subjects and ignore political considerations in matters like judicial appointments."

Coolidge was attentive to appointments at all levels, devoting particular time and effort in evaluating potential judicial nominees. As stated in his autobiography, "One of the most perplexing and at the same time most important functions of the President is the making of appointments." Reflecting the seriousness he gave the subject, he did not even discuss selections with his closest advisers but carefully considered views of bar and community leaders in the jurisdictions in question. As one historian noted, "Few Presidents have set for themselves higher standards for appointees or acted more independently of solicitors."

Although most of his appointees were Republicans and judicial conservatives, legal merit overrode political pull and ideological purity. Coolidge's circuit court appointees included such legal giants as Thomas W. Swan, John J. Parker, and Learned and Augustus Hand. As Coolidge said, "The public service would be improved if all vacancies were filled by simply appointing the best ability and character that can be found. That is what is done in private business." In contrast, Franklin Roosevelt used district court judgeships to reward local politicians. Tellingly, New Deal agency lawyers confessed that they preferred Coolidge's appointees to FDR's judges, for as one legal historian observed, "The former might be politically conservative, but more of a true

★ ★ ★

"[F]ew presidents were as outspoken on the need to protect the civil rights of black Americans as Calvin Coolidge."

Biographer Robert Sobel

lawyer, and hence more willing to accept a reasoned argument and enforce the law."

Between the 1924 election and his 1925 inaugural, Coolidge was presented with his only opportunity to name a Supreme Court justice. The doddering Joseph McKenna of California had finally been persuaded to retire. Brushing aside expectations that another westerner should be chosen, and emphasizing legal capabilities over political considerations, Coolidge nominated Harlan Fiske Stone, then U.S. attorney general and formerly dean of Columbia Law School and a Wall Street lawyer.

Chiefly known in the worlds of law and education, the robust and strong-willed Stone had been appointed attorney general in 1924 to replace Harding's appointee, the scandal-plagued Harry Daugherty. While many believed that Stone was selected because he attended Amherst with Coolidge, Stone suggested otherwise: "We were not of the same class and therefore were not intimates, although I doubt if many were intimate with him. His extreme reticence made that difficult."

To the surprise of progressive senatorial opponents, who feared Stone would be a puppet of big business given his former Wall Street connections, the new justice gravitated from the Court's conservative block. Stone's belief in self-government and judicial restraint compelled him to defer to legislative determinations even when disagreeing with their policy goals, a view that mirrored Coolidge's reasoning on prohibition. President Roosevelt would also hold Stone in high regard, later appointing him chief justice of the United States.

Interestingly, Herbert Hoover, Coolidge's successor and a man he detested (privately referring to him as "the wonder boy"), considered offering Coolidge a future seat on the Supreme Court but was dissuaded to do so by Stone. If offered, however, it would have been rejected. Coolidge was tired and wanted to be home in Northampton, as first made known in 1927 by his shocking one-sentence press release: "I do not choose to run for President in nineteen twenty-eight."

Coolidge left office amid overwhelming popularity and with the knowledge he could have had

DEMOCRATIC CHALLENGER JOHN W. DAVIS

Davis was a distinguished American lawyer who challenged Coolidge for the presidency in 1924. With a résumé that included terms as U.S. congressman, Wilson's solicitor general, ambassador to Great Britain, and president of the American Bar Association, Davis was chosen the Democratic nominee on the 103rd ballot before being soundly defeated by Coolidge in the general election. Davis then returned to the practice of law in New York City, where he further enhanced his reputation as a lawyer, constitutional scholar, and leading practitioner before the U.S. Supreme Court.

another term if he so desired. On his last day in the White House, he told Stone, "It is a pretty good idea to get out when they still want you." The former president did not live to witness the New Deal, but he witnessed the vanquishing of the party he had done so much to save and the prosperity he had represented. His usual optimism gone, he reflected, "In other periods of depression, it has always been possible to see some things which were solid and upon which you could base hope, but as I look about me I see nothing to give ground for hope—nothing of man."

As the Great Depression deepened and Republican fortunes fell, the former president's popularity never diminished as many nostalgically longed for a return to the days of "the Coolidge prosperity." There was even talk of drafting him for the 1936 Republican nomination, as if retrieving its symbol could revive an era, but as he wrote a friend, "I know my work is done." On January 5, 1933, his wife Grace found him dead of a heart attack at his Northampton home at the age of sixty. He was laid to rest beside his son in a simple grave on a quiet hillside at Plymouth Notch.

Democratic presidential nominee Al Smith concluded that Coolidge's "great task was to restore the dignity and prestige of the presidency when it had reached the lowest ebb in our history, and to afford, in a time of extravagance and waste, a shining example of the simple and homely virtues which came down to him from his New England ancestors. These are no small achievements, and history will not forget them."

The passage of time and its towering events have obscured President Coolidge's legal legacy, but his belief in the rule of law and the role of the courts, including his dedication to judicial excellence and merit selection, contain wisdom worth retaining. History (and historians) usually demands the backdrop of great events—wars and revolutions—as a prerequisite for affixing greatness, and Calvin Coolidge's presidency, a respite of peace and plenty, fell between the dramas of world war and depression. His mission, for which no one was better suited, was of restoration and respectability, and his vision of law and its administration was an important part of that mission.

Perhaps there are times when healing is as great a virtue as reform. Perhaps providing a nation with tranquility and trust in the wake of war, corruption, and change is greatness.

★ ★ ★

Franklin D Roosevelt

Thirty-second President (1933–45)

BIRTH
January 30, 1882
Hyde Park, N.Y.

EDUCATION
Groton School
Harvard University
Columbia Law School (did not graduate)
Admission to the bar: 1907

OTHER OCCUPATIONS/PUBLIC OFFICES
State senator
Assistant secretary of the navy
New York governor

DEATH
April 12, 1945
Warm Springs, Ga.

LAW CAREER IN BRIEF
Roosevelt began his law career in 1907 at the prestigious Wall Street firm of Carter, Ledyard, and Milburn, where he described himself as a "full-fledged office boy" and others considered him a "harmless bust." In 1920, following service in the state senate and Navy Department, FDR joined two friends to form the firm of Emmett, Marvin and Roosevelt, but despite his role as "rainmaker," he brought little business to the firm. In 1924, he left that partnership and entered another one with Basil O'Connor. There, he secured few clients and gave limited legal counsel, using the office more to launch his return to politics than to practice law. With his election as governor in 1928, FDR basically left law practice behind, though he made extensive use of lawyers in his presidential administrations.

Franklin Delano Roosevelt: Contrarian Counselor

JEROME J. SHESTACK

None of Franklin Delano Roosevelt's classmates at Columbia Law School would have guessed that their classmate, with barely passing grades, would become one of America's greatest presidents.

Roosevelt had entered Columbia University School of Law in the fall of 1904 at the age of twenty-two. Before Columbia, he attended Harvard, where cousin Teddy Roosevelt also studied. Franklin was only slightly better than a C student, but his extracurricular life was active; he achieved the prestigious presidency of the Harvard Crimson and became librarian of the Hasty Pudding Club. But he was rejected for Harvard's exclusive Porcellian Club. Years later he called that rejection the greatest disappointment in his life.

None of these undergraduate leadership qualities were displayed at Columbia Law School. His choice of Columbia was dictated in part by his adoration of Teddy Roosevelt, who also went there, and in part by a desire to be near Eleanor Roosevelt, whom he was then assiduously wooing. Whether this courtship diverted his attention and drained his energies, or for other reasons, Roosevelt showed no enthusiasm for law school. During his first year, he failed Contracts and Pleadings Practice but received a B in his other courses. While his second-year grades remained undistinguished—he received three Bs, two Cs, a C-plus and one D—his courtship proved successful. On St. Patrick's Day 1905, Franklin and Eleanor were married. President Theodore Roosevelt came to New York that day both to review the St. Patrick's Day parade and to give his niece away in marriage.

Roosevelt never graduated from Columbia. After the wedding, he finished the spring term at the law school and then dropped

★ ★ ★

"[I]t was abundantly clear to [FDR] and his superiors that he possessed no brilliant legal talent of any kind and, indeed, found his work often boring."

Biographer Kenneth Davis

"Unpaid bills a specialty. Briefs on the liquor question furnished free to ladies. Small dogs chloroformed without charge."

FDR, announcing his
first law job

out. The following year he passed the New York bar examination, which could then be accomplished without a law degree. Columbia's president, Nicholas Murray Butler, later told Roosevelt, "You will never be able to call yourself an intellectual until you come back to Columbia and pass your law exams." Roosevelt is reported to have replied, "That shows you how unimportant the law really is."

After leaving law school, Roosevelt dabbled in civic activities at Hyde Park in Poughkeepsie. Then, in the fall of 1907, he became a clerk in the prestigious Wall Street law firm of Carter, Ledyard and Milburn, where he received no salary for the first year, as was customary. Although the firm had important corporate clients, Roosevelt's assignments were pedestrian. In a mock advertisement of himself, he characterized his work as specializing in unpaid bills, the chloroforming of small dogs, and briefs on the liquor question for ladies. In a letter to his mother, he called himself a "full-fledged office boy."

His work at the law firm was indeed tedious, often menial, and typically boring. Most of it was in the municipal courts defending petty claims against corporate clients such as American Express. Yet, this experience cannot be regarded lightly. He learned how to get along with people of diverse backgrounds, how to use his personality to manage some rough and tumble conflicts, and how to forge agreements between opposing forces.

After about a year, Roosevelt was promoted to the firm's Admiralty Division, which he still found boring. The firm's leaders never regarded him a star, and indeed, years later a friend recalled that everyone regarded him as a "harmless bust." Nevertheless, in the light of his charm, his social and civic activities, and his family connections (which could bring in business), it was likely that he would have become a partner.

But that conventional path was not where his ambition lay. While his work at Carter, Ledyard was menial, his goals were lofty. To his fellow associates he confessed that he had no intention of making his career at law. Instead, he intended to go into politics, where he'd begin with a seat in the state assembly, and then rise to the governorship, and then "have a good show to be President." A fellow clerk, Grenville Clark, later recalled that Roosevelt "somehow managed to make it all seem proper and sincere and moreover, as he put it, entirely reasonable."

In 1910, Roosevelt was offered the opportunity to run for the New York State Senate representing the eastern shore of the Hudson. The offer was not exactly a prize since he was told his chance of winning was one in five. Roosevelt created a precedent by hiring a red Maxwell touring car to get around his district. Advisers warned that the automobile would frighten farmers' horses and lose votes, but the red Maxwell enabled him to reach every corner of his district.

To everyone's surprise Roosevelt won the election, albeit narrowly. With his wife, three children, and three servants and nurses, he moved into a three-story house in Albany. His career at the bar was put on the back burner and his career in politics moved to the fore. This may have been no great loss to the legal profession, but it marked the start of a brilliant career in the political world. As a state senator, Roosevelt was on the progressive side of most measures but took care to protect the interests of his rather conservative and puritanical constituency.

His next public office, which he obtained through a budding friendship with Woodrow Wilson, was as assistant secretary of the navy from 1913 through 1919, where he displayed splendid managerial ability and striking political skills. Roosevelt's growing reputation, his shining forensic ability, and his broad political and social connections led to his surprising selection as the vice presidential candidate in the 1920 election, with James Cox heading the ticket. It was a disastrous run for the Democrats, who were soundly beaten by Harding and Coolidge.

After the election, Roosevelt resumed his law practice at Emmet, Marvin & Roosevelt, a firm he had formed with two

FDR as a Young Lawyer

From his earliest days in law practice, FDR confessed to his fellow associates that he had no intention of making his career at law. Instead, he intended to go into politics.

LAW PARTNER BASIL O'CONNOR

On New Year's Day of 1925, the firm of Roosevelt and O'Connor opened in New York City. O'Connor was from Massachusetts, attended Dartmouth College and Harvard Law School, and had been a sole Manhattan practitioner focusing on international law. Ten years FDR's junior, O'Connor was a workaholic who complemented Roosevelt's rainmaking role. The partnership continued until FDR's move to the White House, and the friendship between the two continued throughout Roosevelt's life. O'Connor's exposure to FDR's physical handicaps also led him to pursue leadership positions with the Red Cross and March of Dimes.

friends in 1920. About that time he also accepted a position as vice president of the Fidelity and Deposit Company of Maryland, one of the nation's largest surety bonding concerns. Roosevelt was satisfied with its twenty-five-hundred-dollar yearly salary and an understanding that his participation in party politics would not be curtailed. Roosevelt also believed that his position with Fidelity and Deposit and his law partnership were compatible. As he had written to Felix Frankfurter in January 1921, "The two varieties of work seem to dovetail fairly well." In fact, they did not. He brought little business into the law firm and devoted most of his time to his political, charitable, and social activities rather than to clients.

In August 1921, he was stricken by infantile paralysis, a serious lifelong disability. Reflecting on the change wrought by his polio, Frances Perkins wrote, "Franklin Roosevelt underwent a spiritual transformation during his years of illness . . . the years of pain and suffering purged the slightly arrogant attitude he displayed. . . . The man emerged completely warmhearted with humility of spirit and deeper philosophy."

During his agonizing road to even semirecovery, he continued to classify himself as a lawyer but spent virtually no time practicing law. One obstacle to practice was the entrance to his office at 52 Wall Street, which had a flight of stone steps he could not navigate on his braced leg and crutches; rather, he had to be carried up the steps, which he found humiliating. When the building was remodeled, the flight of steps was reduced to two. Still, as Roosevelt wrote to one of his partners, "the question of even two steps is a very difficult one as I have to be actually lifted up and down them."

But that was not the most important obstacle to his law practice. More controlling was his continuing dislike of the firm's sedate practice in trusts, wills, and estates. They were "dear delightful people," Roosevelt wrote, but their "type of law business" bored him to distraction, and he received "not one red cent out of my connection with them, whereas, if I were with some real live people working along other lines I could be of material assistance on reorganizations, receiverships, etc. pulling my weight in the boat and incidentally making some money out of it."

In September 1924, he amicably ended his partnership with Emmet and Marvin. Three months later he formed a new partnership with Basil O'Connor, a lawyer almost ten years his junior. The son of an impoverished tinsmith in Taunton, Massachusetts, O'Connor worked his way through Dartmouth College; then at Harvard Law School his eyesight failed, leaving him totally blind for a while. His vision was restored by medical treatments, but even while he was blind he continued his studies, having students read to him. After passing the bar and practicing briefly in Boston, O'Connor moved to New York City to open a one-man law office with an international practice. He worked from ten- to fifteen-hour days, and took no time for hobbies or socializing. He and Roosevelt were an unlikely combination, but it turned out to be a felicitous fit.

The new firm of Roosevelt and O'Connor opened on New Year's Day of 1925. It was important to Roosevelt that their law office was in the same building and next door to the Fidelity firm. The physical proximity combined with a commonality of interests ensured that Roosevelt's two varieties of work did now actually "dovetail." Roosevelt's role was largely to give legal advice to a relatively few clients and engage in rainmaking, while O'Connor did the actual work.

Though Roosevelt was a prodigious letter writer, very few refer to his law practice, and biographers devote little space to that part of his career. However, one note from Roosevelt to O'Connor offered advice about a meeting with Owen Young, head of General Electric: "Please remind Owen Young that Roosevelt and O'Connor are entirely capable of handling all of the legal business of G.E.Co." This was indeed rather bold and exuberant rainmaking!

Continuing to struggle with his disability with uncommon courage, Roosevelt used his law office principally as a staging ground for a return to politics. This proved highly successful, as in 1928 he was elected governor of New York and in 1930 he was reelected. He was a progressive and popular governor, although

★ ★ ★

"Whatever view Roosevelt held of legal practice, he knew a brilliant lawyer when he encountered one, and early on he started to accumulate a brain trust of the best and the brightest in the legal profession."

he was considered somewhat evasive in dealing with the corrupt Tammany Hall. As young Franklin had predicted years ago to his classmates at Columbia, the governorship led to his nomination for the presidency. On March 4, 1933, Franklin Roosevelt took office as president of the United States.

Whatever view Roosevelt held of legal practice, he knew a brilliant lawyer when he encountered one, and early on he started to accumulate a brain trust of the best and brightest in the legal profession. Judge Samuel Roseman, his chief speechwriter, was one. U.S. Supreme Court Justice Louis D. Brandeis and future justice Felix Frankfurter were consulted fairly often. Thurman Arnold, A. A. Berle, Benjamin Cohen, William O. Douglas, Lloyd Garrison, Robert H. Jackson, James M. Landis, Stanley F. Reed, and Charles Wysanski were others who were part of the Roosevelt brain pool and who went on to distinguished careers. No other president has surrounded himself with so much legal brilliance.

Roosevelt's first term was devoted largely to New Deal legislation, and here arose the greatest constitutional crisis of his presidency. Many presidents had expressed dissatisfaction with the U.S. Supreme Court, but not since Thomas Jefferson had any president been as vexed by the Court as was Roosevelt. And not without cause. Roosevelt's spate of New Deal laws, designed to boost the economy and lead the nation out of the depression, were being decimated by Court edict. At the time, any one of the judges could enjoin application of a federal statute, and enjoin they did. In 1935 and 1936, some one thousand six hundred injunctions of federal laws were issued to stop New Deal programs. That was not altogether surprising. More than two-thirds of the federal judiciary had been appointed by Harding, Coolidge, and Hoover, and many manifested a conservative ideology. Roosevelt had yet to appoint anyone to the U.S. Supreme Court.

The Supreme Court, often called the "Nine Old Men," included four hard-line conservatives. Harvard's Thomas Reed Powell once summed them up as follows: Justice Butler "is playing God or Lucifer to keep the word from going the way he does not want it to." Sutherland is "a naïve doctrinaire person who really does not see the world as it is." Mr. Justice McReynolds is "a tempestuous cad" and Mr. Justice Van Devanter "an old dodo."

The three liberal members of the Court were Louis D. Brandeis, Benjamin Cardozo, and Harlan Fiske Stone. The swing votes were Chief Justice Charles Evans Hughes and Justice Owen J. Roberts. Roberts generally voted with his conservative colleagues giving them a five-to-four margin in critical cases.

On a conceptual level, Roosevelt and his advisers believed in a flexible constitutional philosophy. As the "great Chief Justice," John Marshall, had said: "We must never forget that it is a *Constitution* we are expounding . . . intended to endure for ages to come, and consequently to be adapted to the various crises of human affairs." Yet Chief Justice Charles Evans Hughes had said, "We are under a Constitution, but the Constitution is what the judges say it is." And what the high court was increasingly saying was that the New Deal legislation was unconstitutional. While the conservative justices rationalized striking down New Deal legislation as applications of strict constitutional fundamentalism, at the same time they were being highly activist, invalidating federal legislation on a wholesale basis.

"To Furnish The Supreme Court Pract ical Assistance."

THIS ACT SHALL TAKE EFFECT ON THE 30TH DAY AFT? THE DATE OF ITS ENACTMENT.

The Court overturned the National Recovery Act, the Mortgage Moratorium Legislation, the Agricultural Adjustment Act, the Municipal Bankruptcy Act, and even the New York state law prohibiting child labor, establishing a minimum wage, and regulating the hours and labor conditions of women. As it struck down one New Deal law after another, the crisis deepened and the whole structure of New Deal legislation was in peril. How was Roosevelt to deal with the Court's animus toward New Deal legislation, which Roosevelt regarded as a usurpation of legislative power? The justices were indeed old but showed no indication of retiring. The attorney general wrote to Roosevelt, "The real difficulty is not with the Constitution, but with the judges who interpret it."

At this time, Roosevelt was elected to a second term by an overwhelming vote. Rhapsodic with victory, he and Attorney General Homer Cummings devised a plan. Originally, Roosevelt contemplated a constitutional amendment to increase the number

ROOSEVELT'S "COURT-PACKING" PROPOSAL

As New Deal legislation met roadblocks in the U.S. Supreme Court, FDR devised a strategy to counteract the Court's rulings. In 1937, he submitted legislation to reorganize the federal judiciary, and though it contained provisions designed to ease the federal court workload and effect other reforms, its main purpose was clearly to get more New Deal supporters on the high court. Soon Congress, the media, the American Bar Association, and other groups actively campaigned against this attempt to pack the high court, and the bill perished in committee.

Harry S. Truman, Esquire

In 1947, the Supreme Court of Missouri received an application for a law license from Harry S. Truman, the man who succeeded FDR to the presidency in 1945. The applicant listed his residence as the "White House" and cited "all U.S. Senators from 1935 to date" and "all cabinet officers U.S.A., at present" as references. The application was returned to Truman with the request that he have it notarized, which he never did. More than twenty years earlier, Truman had spent two years at the Kansas City School of Law and served as a county court judge, a legislative rather than judicial position. Upon discovery of the original application in the 1990s, the Missouri bar admitted Truman posthumously as a member.

of justices, but realizing that the amendment process would be long and chancy, the plan took the shape of a court reform bill.

The strategy was simple. If any federal judge reached the age of seventy without resigning or retiring, the president could appoint one additional judge to that court with certain limits on the number of appointees. With respect to the Supreme Court, the maximum number was to be fifteen. The stated rationale for the bill was to ease the workload of the courts. But the disguise was transparent—its real purpose was to appoint six new members of the Supreme Court, with views more sympathetic to New Deal legislation.

Roosevelt thought his bill would pass handily. And while the initial public response was gratifying, the reluctance of Congress and the community at large to "tinker" with the Court soon gained momentum. Even many of Roosevelt's closest advisers thought his overwhelming election victory "had gone to his head," and key senators began to express opposition to what they called the "court packing" bill. Editorial comment was increasingly critical. The American Bar Association and various civic organizations fought the bill. As the days went on, the furor increased.

A severe blow was administered when Chief Justice Hughes wrote a letter in which he denied there was congestion of cases and said that an increase in justices would actually impair efficiency rather that promote it. Thus he undercut the very rationale offered for the bill. The bill's enemies circulated the letter widely and Gallup polls shifted measurably toward opposition.

The coup de grace came in late March and April when the Supreme Court announced decisions upholding key New Deal social security and labor legislation by a vote of five-to-four. In these cases, Owen J. Roberts was the swing vote that went with the liberal coalition. Professor Thomas Reed Powell quipped, "a switch in time saves nine."

Whether Roberts's switch vote actually came after the bill was introduced or before—as Roberts later asserted—the new decision undercut a pressing need for the bill's reform measures. Roosevelt's advisers thought he should declare victory and settle for less than the bill called for. Roosevelt, however, refused to do so and adamantly pressed his bill for the sake of "a generation ahead." But by now, the Senate Judiciary Committee condemned the bill as "needless, futile and utterly dangerous abandonment of constitutional principle." Ultimately, it perished in committee. This battle was one of FDR's very few misjudgments.

In time, even without his bill, Roosevelt wrought a new Supreme Court. He appointed Harlan Fiske Stone as chief justice and Justices Hugh L. Black, Stanley F. Reed, Felix Frankfurter, William O. Douglas, Frank Murphy, James F. Bynes, Robert H. Jackson, and Wiley B. Rutledge. Generally, Roosevelt's appointments brought about a new constitutional vision of civil rights and liberties that lasted through the Warren court.

The exception was Frankfurter. Roosevelt appointed his brilliant, liberal academic adviser to the Court in 1939, but Frankfurter was reborn on the Court as a didactic, uncompromising conservative. This was not the first or last time a president would misjudge the prospective views of an appointee.

Yet of all Roosevelt's Court appointees, it was Frankfurter who had the closest relationship with Roosevelt. From 1925 until FDR's death, they met often and maintained an extensive correspondence on a first name basis. Roosevelt frequently sought Frankfurter's advice on matters ranging from domestic and foreign policy to gossip, and Frankfurter eagerly gave it.

Frankfurter even gave comfort and advice on FDR's ill-fated court packing plan, though Frankfurter took pains not to go public on the issue, given FDR's stated plans to appoint him to a future seat on the high court. Following his confirmation, Frankfurter continued his correspondence with Roosevelt, some of which was patently political, notwithstanding Frankfurter's frequent admonishment against mixing judging with politics. Viewed by today's standards, this correspondence seems to have been inappropriate once Frankfurter had joined the Court.

Roosevelt's leadership during the war years is resonant with legal issues that cannot be dealt with here. Enemies criticized him for doing too much, friends for doing too little, especially with respect to refugees before and during World War II when more aggressive responses to the Nazi onslaught might have saved many thousands of lives. But no one disputed his awesome political skills, brilliant crisis management, and charismatic leadership during those perilous years.

Finally, at a time when human rights still struggle for universal acceptance, one must recall his message to Congress in January 1941. Brooding war clouds were omnipresent when Roosevelt, with uncommon vision, said: "We look forward to a world founded upon four essential human freedoms." They were freedom of speech, freedom of worship, freedom from want, and freedom from fear. These very principles underlie the Universal Declaration of Human Rights that was adopted by the United Nations in 1948 when Eleanor Roosevelt chaired the U.N. Commission on Human Rights.

How much did Roosevelt's legal background contribute to his presidency? Very likely, not much; surely not as much as with Jefferson or Jackson or Lincoln. Still, Roosevelt was a lawyer and the profession can claim him. Prominent historians rate FDR as the number one president in the twentieth century and second only to Lincoln overall. The legal profession should be gladdened that our highest-rated presidents were lawyers.

The Modern Presidency

Law in Modern America

The most recent lawyer-president, William Jefferson Clinton, was in office as the twentieth century drew to a close. He was then one of about a million lawyers in the United States. The legal profession was bigger than ever—in absolute numbers and in proportion to the population. It had grown dramatically in the last decades of the century. Demographically, there were changes as well. In 1900, the only women at the bar were lonely, isolated pioneers, strong women who defied convention to work in a man's world. A century later, women made up about a quarter of the bar, and time was on their side. They comprised almost half of the country's law students. Women were also to be found on law faculties, as bar association leaders, and on the bench. Two now sit on the Supreme Court of the United States—the first, Sandra Day O'Connor, was appointed in 1981. As of 1999, no less than twelve women were chief justices of state supreme courts. Black, Hispanic, and Asian lawyers and judges were also more common than they had been in the first two-thirds of the century. In 1967, Thurgood Marshall became the first African American on the U.S. Supreme Court; another African American justice, Clarence Thomas, replaced him when he retired.

There also were differences in law firms. Most striking was the emergence of gigantic firms. A firm of ten was considered quite large in 1900. In 1950, the biggest firms had over a hundred lawyers, and by 2000, megafirms had more than a thousand lawyers. And these megafirms developed an appetite for branching out. Many had affiliates in other American cities and in places as far away as Tokyo, Paris, or Riyadh. The old-time Wall Street lawyers would hardly recognize these new firms; they would be awed by their sheer size and amazed at their crowd of paralegals, their banks of computers and databases, and their global reach.

Historically, most American lawyers have been solo practitioners. But by the late 1990s, this was no longer the case. About 40 percent of the active lawyers worked in firms, a little more than a third were on their own; the rest worked for government, private industry, or were judges and law teachers. Many firms, of course, had but two or three lawyers. There also were somewhat larger, specialized firms—the so-called boutiques. Only about 10 percent of the bar worked for megafirms of more than one hundred lawyers, but this remained the most powerful segment of the bar in terms of wealth and influence. The massive study of the Chicago bar by John Heinz and Edward Laumann described two "hemispheres" in the legal profession. Business lawyers made up one "hemisphere"; the other "hemisphere" included lawyers who did tort, divorce, and criminal work. There was very little interaction between the two; they were, in a way, two separate subworlds of the legal cosmos.

In the United States, the population was huge, the economy gigantic, and a mass of new problems and demands invaded the legal system. More and more, a single legal system emerged as the United States, fueled by modern technology above all, had become a single economy and a single culture. Even in traditionally "local" areas like criminal and commercial law, there are now federal norms imposed by Congress or the courts (for example, the famous "Miranda warning"). The Uniform Commercial Code, drafted to iron out local differences, swept the country after the 1950s.

Our big, rich, heterogeneous country has also put extraordinary pressure on the courts. They are now asked to deal with virtually every major social and political issue. The Supreme Court of the United States has been involved in one key issue after another, including such volatile topics as segregation, abortion, and the death penalty. The high court also tore up and rewrote the electoral map with its "one-man one-vote" decisions. At the very end of the century, it even played a key role in deciding who would sit in the Oval Office.

The Supreme Court got the headlines. But state courts were also busy and significant—in the aggregate, their work perhaps as important as the work of the nine U.S. Supreme Court justices, or more so. Lower federal courts too—the last stop for many federal cases—were the pillars that supported the entire federal structure of law.

In this evolving landscape, the legal profession has been as ubiquitous and nimble as ever, as effective in defining new tasks and perfecting old ones. Lawyers have entered into many nooks and crannies of the world of business or politics or indeed of human affairs; they have performed almost any conceivable kind of work and served any conceivable sort of client. Indeed, few parties to modern controversies are now without their personal lawyer.

Many critics feel there is now too much law, too many lawyers, and too much litigation. Whether this is true was and is a matter of debate. Perhaps courts and lawyers have been a drag on the economy, perhaps the liability explosion has ruined decent businesses, perhaps judicial review has paralyzed the administrative apparatus. But on the other hand, courts have played a stellar role in dismantling segregation, promoting social justice, tearing down old structures of dominance and callousness, ensuring the right to be heard, and allocating rights, power, and legitimacy more equally.

Lawyers and courts played a part, and a crucial part, in all of this. They led, but they also responded to what was happening in society. Who played the bigger role, for example, in ending segregation and promoting racial justice: was it Chief Justice Earl Warren and the courts—or Martin Luther King, the NAACP, and its local branches? There is no definitive answer. The legal profession and the courts are reflections of the world around them. They are and continue to be a vital part of American society but in partnership with and in service to that society.

LAWRENCE M. FRIEDMAN

BIRTH
January 9, 1913
Yorba Linda, Calif.

EDUCATION
Public schools
Whittier College
Duke University Law School
Admission to the bar: November 1937

OTHER OCCUPATIONS/PUBLIC OFFICES
World War II naval officer
U.S. congressman and senator
Vice president with Dwight D. Eisenhower

DEATH
April 22, 1994
New York, N.Y.

LAW CAREER IN BRIEF

Nixon's legal career spanned several periods (1937–42, 1946–50, and 1961–68). During each, he practiced with law firms, initially in Whittier and later in Los Angeles and New York City. He also was a government attorney, serving in the Office of Emergency Management just before joining the navy. His initial practice focused on common areas of law—divorce, wills and estates, real estate, and so on—while his brief time as a Washington, D.C., lawyer provided him with a first glimpse of how government agencies operated. Perhaps Nixon's most notable period of practice began in 1963 when he joined a prominent New York City firm and later argued before the U.S. Supreme Court in the high-profile case of *Time v. Hill*. Though his side did not prevail, Nixon received high marks for his legal scholarship and oral arguments.

Richard M. Nixon: Bicoastal Practitioner

IRWIN F. GELLMAN

While the Teapot Dome scandal riveted the attention of Americans during the presidency of Warren Harding, Hannah Nixon recalled her nine-year-old son Richard sitting near the family fireplace at their Yorba Linda home with the daily newspaper spread out in front of him. Suddenly, he declared: "Mother, I would like to become a lawyer—an honest lawyer, who can't be bought by crooks." Three years later, as an eighth grader, he wrote an autobiographical essay as a school assignment: "I would like to study law," he emphasized, "and enter Politics, for an occupation so that I might be of some good to the people."

As an underclassman at Whittier College, Nixon took gradual steps toward his goal. One summer, upperclassman William Church handed Dick the Duke University Law School bulletin and suggested the university as an excellent place to study law. In the spring of his senior year, Nixon sent Duke an application along with a request for financial assistance. Duke promptly responded, awarding Nixon a $250 scholarship for first year tuition and matriculation fees and, if he maintained a superior grade-point average, renewal of his scholarship.

During the midst of the Great Depression, this assistance was essential. Nixon quickly accepted the terms of the scholarship, and by mid-September he and three other Whittier graduates drove

NIXON'S EARLY LAW PRACTICE

Nixon began practicing law in 1937 with the Whittier, California, firm of Wingert and Bewley. Within several years, he had sufficiently impressed his superiors that they made him a name partner in the firm.

Nixon Argues before the Supreme Court

In 1966, the *Time v. Hill* case provided Nixon with the dual opportunity of detailing the excesses of the press and establishing his competence as a lawyer. Though he ultimately was on the short side of a five-to-four decision, this lone appellate case of his legal career gained him respect and praise. Later, in inducting Warren Burger as chief justice, Nixon observed, "[T]here is only one ordeal which is more challenging than a Presidential press conference and that is to appear before the Supreme Court of the United States."

from southern California to Durham, North Carolina, to begin the fall semester. Due to his scant financial resources, he roomed with fourteen divinity students in a house near campus, and since everyone did not have a bed, they rotated those accommodations. For food, Nixon usually ate at a restaurant where hamburgers cost five cents. To cover these and other expenses, he worked at the university's law library and for the National Youth Administration for thirty-five cents an hour.

During his first year, his class numbered about thirty, approximately one-third of the entire student body. Almost half wore Phi Beta Kappa keys, and nineteen received some type of financial assistance. Just about everyone knew each other because class size ranged from five to fifteen. Nixon enrolled in seven courses, and his classmates recall that he took copious notes and studied prodigiously, bordering on obsessive as he would stay past midnight in the law library. He was frugal, as were many others living through the adversities of Depression life, but he seemed poorer than most. Many liked him, some becoming lifelong friends, while a few considered him stuffy and aloof. He seldom dated, never cussed, and became a passionate, effusive fan of Duke football.

Nixon grew attached to some of his professors. Lon Fuller, who taught contracts, was his most influential teacher. Another mentor, David Cavers, who had graduated first in his class at Harvard Law School, specialized in conflict of laws. Nixon, however, did not appreciate all his instructors. Douglas Maggs, who lorded over his students in torts, pounded on desks and yelled at his charges during his lectures. One of the first students to stand up to this intimidation was Nixon, even though, as one onlooker recollected, Nixon was "visibly shaking in his boots, but refusing to back down." After the completion of finals, he earned five As and two Bs, achieving an A average that guaranteed continuation of his scholarship.

Nixon took an even heavier course load in his second year, signing up for many classes with his favorite professors. Nixon also came to admire the opinions of associate Supreme Court justices Benjamin Cardozo and Harlan Stone. He was disappointed with the manner in which Louis Brandeis's Supreme Court confirmation hearings were conducted in 1916, but he was pleased that the Senate ultimately gave its consent to the appointment. Nixon also applauded Brandeis's emphasis on the public trust over the interests of big business.

As a consequence of his superior average, he was tapped for Duke's law review. He also joined the Duke Bar Association and Iredell Law Club. During his senior year, he served as bar association president. As part of his duties, he wrote a short article for the association's journal on the "Application of the Inherent Danger of Negligent Independent Contracts," which highlighted a contractor's higher duty of care in cases where its employees were injured while toiling under perilous conditions.

By his second year, about 125 students attended the school, causing class sizes to rise slightly from ten to fifteen. Nixon remained a fervent football rooter, abstained from liquor, attended dances, and occasionally saw a movie (especially enjoying love stories). He sometimes ate at the student union for thirty-five cents per meal, but often chose to drive with classmates to Mrs. Pierce's boarding house where for twenty-five cents, they enjoyed family-style all-you-can-eat meals.

Nixon participated in one notable prank in his second year. At the end of the term, when grades were not posted promptly, Nixon and two friends grew tired of the suspense. They went to the dean's office, where two of them entered through an upper transept to discover their grades. Some later asserted that this launched Nixon's criminal career, but at the time, Dean Horack found the stunt amusing. Nixon was not so pleased. He had received two As, six Bs and his only C in the trusts course. While his average dropped to a B, his financial aid was extended, but on the basis of need.

In his senior year, Nixon registered for twelve courses and continued his Spartan lifestyle. He and three other seniors rented a one-room cottage, dubbed "Whippoorwill Manor," a mile from campus. Each paid twelve dollars and fifty cents for the

"As lawyers . . . our first responsibility is to see that the legal profession provides adequate representation for all people in our society."

Richard M. Nixon

"His homework, his logic, his presentation, and his commitment also impressed his law partners, the larger New York legal community, and the reporters covering the Supreme Court."

Stephen Ambrose,
on Nixon's handling of the
Time v. Hill case

academic year, receiving what they bargained for: two old-fashioned brass double beds, a potbellied stove, and no running water or electricity. At the break of dawn in winter, Nixon tramped to campus through deep slush. As bar association president, he had an office in the law school where he kept his clothes and toiletries. He showered and shaved at the gym in the morning, went over to the student union for a quick breakfast, attended classes, and sometimes played handball or swam in the late afternoon.

In the midst of his hectic schedule, Nixon researched and wrote an article, "Changing Rules of Liability in Automobile Accident Litigation," for the Duke law review. Researched and written in six weeks, Nixon's prose was comprehensible and accomplished, unlike the stilted language in many law review articles.

Just before the article appeared, Nixon began seeking out law offices that were hiring new attorneys. One of those who interviewed Nixon was the legendary lawyer and judge, J. Edward Lumbar of the New York City firm of Donovan and Leisure. Even in the Depression, the firm had grown from fifteen to fifty lawyers, and it had a reputation for hiring bright law school graduates. Lumbar vividly recalled his impressions after talking to Nixon, where the partner "rated him considerably above average, a man worth keeping on our list for possible future reference. He stood quite high in his class at Duke. He was obviously a person who wanted to get ahead and who had worked for what he'd accomplished. He seemed alert and he expressed himself well."

Even with such a glowing evaluation, no offers came and Nixon returned to campus to finish his last semester. He continued to study energetically and organized a bar association conference called "Opportunities for Law-Trained Men." That spring he completed his course work with eight As, three Bs, and a pass. He had graduated third in his class and was selected, along with two others, for the Order of the Coif, a legal honorary society limited to the top 10 percent of his class. In June 1937, Nixon received his LL.B. degree with twenty-four other classmates. In the audience watching the ceremonies were his eighty-two-year-old "Quaker grandmother" and his parents, who had driven across the country in a 1930 Chevrolet to witness the first member of the family receive a law degree.

Nixon's next task was to pass the California bar examination. Even before graduation, he had sent in the three-dollar fee to take the test, and after returning home, he signed up for the Nix-Burly Law Review course in Los Angeles. He diligently prepped for the test through the summer, took it in the fall, and passed it that October. He was admitted to the bar a month later and quickly joined the Whittier law firm of Wingert and Bewley.

As the nation slowly emerged from Depression and marched haltingly toward world war, Nixon practiced law in Whittier and nearby La Habra. His first trial appearance came on December 7, 1937, and he continued his practice until the closing days of 1941. Rates for paying clients started at a dollar, though he sometimes worked pro bono. He kept detailed budgetary records, in total earning slightly more than $4,000. His principal client was the Milhous family, which paid him $1,339 in 1939. He took on a wide assortment of legal matters, including divorces, wills, evictions, homesteads, and estates. His employers were sufficiently impressed with their associate that they made him a partner in the new firm of Wingert, Bewley and Nixon. He also served as counsel for Citrifrost, a corporation that unsuccessfully experimented in making and marketing frozen orange juice.

To locate business prospects, Nixon joined a series of organizations, including the 20/30 Club and the Duke Alumni Association, serving as president of both. His alma mater honored him with an appointment to the Whittier College Board of Trustees. He also took acting roles in the local theatrical company where he met Pat Ryan, marrying her in the summer of 1940.

Looking for other opportunities, the newlyweds decided to leave the West Coast at the end of 1941 for Washington, D.C. Duke law professor David Cavers had recommended Nixon for a post at the Office of Price Administration (OPA), and starting in January, Nixon entered OPA's rubber rationing section's legal division. At a salary of thirty-two hundred dollars, he wrote guidelines and responded to irate constituents. For the first time, he also witnessed how

LYNDON BAINES JOHNSON, LAW STUDENT

"Am intensely interested in politics and hope to serve in one of our law-making bodies," wrote Nixon's predecessor in his 1934 application for admission to Georgetown Law School. Though accepted, LBJ's stay there was brief. He would later quip that he "only earned a B.A.—for Brief Attendance" and explain that his duties with Texas representative Mifflin Kleberg were then too demanding. Also commanding his time and attention was Lady Bird, whom he married that fall.

government agencies functioned. He worked earnestly, compiled an excellent rating, and received several promotions.

Even with such recognition, however, Nixon was dissatisfied in his assignment. Shortly before the Nixons left for the capital, the Japanese had attacked Pearl Harbor. Like many of his generation, he decided to enlist in the United States Naval Reserve. Completing basic training late in 1942, he was commissioned a lieutenant junior grade and eventually was stationed in the South Pacific as a logistical support officer. After he finished his combat duty in 1944, the navy put his legal training to use by sending him to an army industrial college in San Francisco for a month's course in contract terminations and then assigning him to the bureau of aeronautics on the East Coast to terminate naval wartime contracts.

Soon thereafter, Republican activists in his congressional district encouraged Nixon to run for the House of Representatives in 1946. He enthusiastically accepted and waged an exhausting but successful campaign. During a congressional tenure that lasted six years, he relied heavily on his legal skills by assisting in the drafting of the Taft-Hartley Act of 1947—still today a pivotal piece of labor legislation—and by shaping the Mundt-Nixon bill on the registration of members of the Communist Party of the United States of America, some provisions of which were incorporated into the McCarran Act of 1950.

Nixon's trial skills again surfaced as a member of the House Committee on Un-American Activities (HUAC), for he was the sole attorney on the committee. When Whittaker Chambers testified before HUAC on a hot, humid day in early August 1948, accusing Alger Hiss of being a communist, Nixon, sometimes acting unilaterally, guided the investigation that eventually exposed Hiss as a Russian spy and led to his conviction for perjury.

Nixon's meteoric rise propelled him to the vice presidency, where he seldom applied his legal skills to legislative matters or committee activities, though late in his second term he successfully mediated a bitter steel strike. More directly relevant to his legal background, when California Governor Earl Warren was nominated as chief justice of the U.S. Supreme Court in 1953, Nixon publicly praised the selection and supported confirmation. This came despite Warren's disapproval of Nixon's political positions and refusal to back him openly in the 1950 senatorial election against Helen Gahagan Douglas.

When the Warren court issued its unanimous opinion in *Brown v. Board of Education* a year later, Nixon concurred with the decision. He had experienced segregation while attending law school in the South and deplored it. During the remainder of his vice presidency, he cautioned against extremism from African American radicals and white supremacists. To Nixon, moderation had to prevail, and later during his presidency, he maintained that theme while he moved rapidly to desegregate schools across the nation.

Shortly after Nixon's unsuccessful 1960 presidential contest against John Kennedy, Earl Adams, an old friend and senior partner in Adams, Duque & Hazeltine, convinced Nixon to return to private practice and join his prestigious Los Angeles firm. He started in March 1961, but former president Dwight Eisenhower and others induced him to run for the California governorship against Edmund "Pat" Brown.

After suffering a bitter and humiliating political loss in that race, Nixon turned to providing a lucrative livelihood for his family. Elmer Bobst, chairman of the board for Warner-Lambert, urged him to relocate to New York City and reenter private practice as a counselor to the conglomerate. Bobst approached Bob Guthrie, a senior partner at Mudge, Stern, Baldwin and Todd, about enticing Nixon to join the firm, and by the end of May 1963, newspapers reported that the Nixons were leaving the West Coast for the East.

Nixon successfully secured admission to practice in New York and on January 1, 1964, the partnership announced its new name: Nixon, Mudge, Rose, Guthrie & Alexander. While Guthrie had raised the law firm's standing to a position just below the city's most prestigious firms, Nixon's addition moved the firm up to the premier level.

★ ★ ★

*"As president,
his most notable
legal achievements
include significantly
changing the compo-
sition and judicial
philosophy of the
Supreme Court."*

Leonard Garment, who would later become widely known for his activities as Nixon's White House counsel, was then the firm's chief litigator. One of Garment's clients was the James Hill family, which in 1952 had been held hostage in their suburban Philadelphia home for nine hours by three escaped convicts. The Hills were released unharmed and removed themselves from the spotlight to avoid unwanted publicity.

Several years later, however, *Life* magazine featured an article about a new Broadway melodrama that purported to be a dramatic reenactment of the Hill family's ordeal. On behalf of the Hills, Garment asked for an apology, but *Life* refused. A jury found for the family in the resulting lawsuit, and a New York appeals court concurred. Time, Inc., *Life*'s parent company, then appealed to the U.S. Supreme Court.

Garment asked Nixon to handle the appeal and he agreed to do so, seizing this as an opportunity to argue against the abuse of privacy by the press. He knew that a public figure suing for libel had an enormous burden of proof based upon the 1964 landmark case of *New York Times v. Sullivan.*

The high court heard the case on April 27, 1966, which was the first time that Nixon had argued before that body. John MacKenzie, a *Washington Post* reporter, described Nixon's presentation as "one of the best oral arguments of the year." Despite such praise, Nixon had misgivings. By the next morning, he sent Garment a critique of this appearance, wishing his argument had been more graphic and noting that the issue was "not the power of the state to infringe on a right but the power of the state to recognize and implement a [privacy] right."

Nixon had his chance to bolster his arguments when the court called for the case to be reargued. While Nixon presented his legal points clearly, the court sided with Time, Inc., in a five-to-four decision. Nixon's clients had lost but, according to Garment, his partner had established his "professional credentials as an appellate lawyer of distinction and this served the collateral purpose of polishing his new public persona."

Shortly after the Court decision was released, Nixon decided to run for the presidency in 1968. His victory at the polls ended his private practice, but his legal perspective had a long-lasting judicial impact. Before his inauguration, Earl Warren decided to resign, and with minimal resistance, Nixon nominated Warren

Burger, who won confirmation as the next chief justice. Nixon's choice demonstrated his philosophy of moving from the liberal, activist judges of his Democratic predecessors to more conservative, strict constructionist jurists.

In that vein, Nixon nominated Clement Haynsworth Jr., a southern jurist with similar beliefs, for the next Court vacancy. Senate Democrats controlled a lopsided majority, and with the support of other groups, Haynsworth was narrowly rejected. An infuriated president then nominated another southern jurist, G. Harold Carswell, who did not rise to Haynsworth's qualifications and also went down to an acrimonious defeat. Believing that a Democratic Senate would not confirm a conservative southern jurist, Nixon turned to Harry Blackmun from Minnesota, whose acceptance was almost guaranteed after the exhaustive, bloody battles over the earlier nominees. Lewis Powell and William Rehnquist followed in quick succession in late 1971. In the end, Nixon dramatically altered the composition of the Court with his four appointments.

While the Supreme Court moved away from judicial activism in measured steps, the Nixon presidency is best remembered for the criminal activity associated with the Watergate break-in. Initially Nixon did not perceive the damage that this burglary would do to the White House. Unable to defeat him at the polls, his opponents, who had overwhelming congressional majorities, moved Watergate from Judge John Sirica's court to the House of Representatives, where impeachment proceedings commenced. The Saturday Night Massacre, in which Nixon fired the special prosecutor as well as the attorney general and his deputy, backfired and further weakened the presidency. When Nixon defiantly proclaimed he was not a crook, others announced that he was.

Nixon also underestimated the strength of his adversaries in using obstruction of justice and abuse of power charges to remove him from office. When the Supreme Court ruled unanimously against the president's stance on executive privilege in *U.S. v. Nixon*, ordering him to release certain tapes for the criminal investigations then under way, he realized that he could not stop the momentum toward impeachment. Most of the time a stark realist, the president recognized the hopelessness of his case and resigned his office rather than face an ignominious fate.

The succession of Gerald Ford did not halt calls for a criminal indictment. President Ford, however, abruptly ended this

★ ★ ★

"The Saturday Night Massacre, in which Nixon fired the [Watergate] special prosecutor as well as the attorney general and his deputy, backfired and further weakened the presidency."

In Defense of the Rule of Law

Watergate was a trying time for all Americans, and particularly so for the legal profession, for there were many lawyers convicted of Watergate crimes as well as many others who sought to right the wrongs that had been committed. Among the latter were Judge John Sirica, Attorney General Elliot Richardson, and Leon Jaworski, Houston lawyer and former American Bar Association president (pictured here). Jaworski assumed the duties of Watergate special prosecutor upon the firing of Archibald Cox and went on to secure the unanimous U.S. Supreme Court decision that required the president to turn over certain tape recordings, leading to Nixon's resignation.

movement by pardoning his predecessor. By accepting the pardon, Ford perceived that Nixon had admitted to wrongdoing, but Nixon never conceded to any culpability and reluctantly agreed to the pardon as part of his desire to end one chapter of his life and move on to the next phase.

As part of his new life, Nixon's legal career ended with resignations from the California and U.S. Supreme Court bars. He also tried to resign from the New York bar, but as a matter of state law, he could not do so without admitting to his guilt in the Watergate scandal. Since Nixon rejected that option, a New York court disbarred him by a four-to-one vote, relying almost exclusively on the House articles of impeachment as evidence against him.

That sorrowful epilogue ended Nixon's study and practice of law, which had consumed more than four decades. He saw his profession as honorable and positive, but postwar politics turned him into a full-time politician and part-time attorney who only practiced between political campaigns. As president, his most notable legal achievements included significantly changing the composition and judicial philosophy of the Supreme Court. He also moved the nation closer to desegregation and regularly took other measures that had legal implications.

Despite these presidential actions, Watergate overshadowed all else, and yet, that burglary alone did not bring down the White House occupant. The turmoil of that time, as personified by the Vietnam War and the civil rights movement, promoted the pessimism of the era. The frenzied investigations by the press further created a climate of public mistrust. The quasi-legal procedure of a heavily prejudicial Democratic Congress added even more venom to the hostile environment.

Without doubt, Nixon shared in the blame. He gave his enemies the ammunition to destroy him, though given a similar situation, Nixon conceded he would have behaved similarly. How culpable was he? Did he deserve the House articles of impeachment and a Senate conviction? As more documents and tapes are released and studied, historians will definitively answer those questions. Until that mosaic is thoroughly pieced together, the jury will be unable to hand down a fair and equitable verdict.

$\star \star \star$

Gerald R. Ford

Thirty-eighth President (1974–77)

BIRTH
July 14, 1913
Omaha, Nebr.

EDUCATION
University of Michigan
Michigan Law School
University of North Carolina Law School
Yale Law School
Admission to the bar: July 7, 1941

OTHER OCCUPATIONS/PUBLIC OFFICES
College athletic coach
World War II naval officer
U.S. congressman
Vice president with Richard Nixon

LAW CAREER IN BRIEF

Perhaps no lawyer-president worked as hard to secure a law degree as Gerald Ford; certainly none attended classes at three law schools. Though working full-time for the Yale Athletic Department, Ford finished in the top quarter of his class before choosing Grand Rapids, Michigan, over East Coast possibilities "as a wonderful place to practice law." In June 1941, he and Michigan Law School classmate Philip Buchen opened a law office, but soon thereafter the attack on Pearl Harbor prompted Ford to enlist in the navy. Upon returning to practice in 1946, he joined Buchen in the firm of Butterfield, Keeney & Amberg, where he handled a range of general practice matters. Though he was formally associated with the firm until 1951, Ford's election to Congress in 1948 effectively marked the conclusion of his active practice.

Gerald R. Ford: All-American Counsel

David Horrocks

Until Watergate thrust him into the Oval Office in August 1974, Gerald R. Ford Jr. was best known as a star University of Michigan football player who had represented his hometown of Grand Rapids in Congress since 1949 and risen to become Republican House minority leader and Nixon's vice president. Beyond some constituents, few knew that Ford was born Leslie Lynch King Jr. in Omaha, Nebraska, in 1913, or that his mother, with babe in arms, fled a bad marriage and eventually married Grand Rapids businessman Gerald R. Ford Sr., who would prove a beloved stepfather. Fewer still knew that Ford's experiences at Yale Law School and as a practicing attorney were central to his political career. The latter is a story worth telling.

In early 1935, Gerald Ford was a college senior contemplating his future. He had studied economics at the University of Michigan, but his B.A. would be no meal ticket in the midst of the Great Depression. Despite four years of campus and summer jobs, Ford was a thousand dollars in debt, a large sum for the time. Back home, his father's paint company was gasping to survive.

At some point, Ford decided to become a lawyer, an option he may have weighed since high school. In a scrapbook preserved from Ford's youth, there is a 1930 letter from a Michigan State College recruiter to the South High football star. The official admitted, in apparent response to Ford, that Michigan State "does not offer a complete course in law or medicine."

Law school would be expensive, but Ford figured athletics might pay his way. Indeed, Ford had been a team leader as well as star player for Michigan football. His performance in the Shrine East-West game in San Francisco had impressed pro football scouts, who sought to sign him. Famed Green Bay Packers coach Curly Lambeau extended a formal offer, "We plan on signing a

★ ★ ★

"I knew I could do both—coach and go to law school at the same time. But I must say, I worked my ass off."

Gerald R. Ford

"The law demands respect for institutions, yet it relies upon individuals to bring those institutions to life."

Gerald R. Ford

center for the coming year and will pay $110.00 per game if you wish to join the 'Packers.' . . . We pay in full after each contest and all players are paid whether they play or not."

Professional football, however, was no stepping stone to law. Instead, Ford asked Michigan coach Harry Kipke to hire him as an assistant, planning simultaneously to attend law school in Ann Arbor. Kipke lacked funding, but later invited Ford to lunch with the Yale coach, Ducky Pond. By autumn 1935, Ford was Yale's assistant line coach in football and its freshman boxing coach.

Coach Ford soon sought to enter Yale Law School, but both the athletic department and the law school balked. He completed his first year coaching, spent the summer as a park ranger at Yellowstone, and diligently coached through the next academic year, 1936 to 1937.

Ford's plan, however, remained unchanged. In the summer of 1937, he took two courses at Michigan's law school and, upon returning to New Haven, pressed his case again. The athletic department was cautiously amenable, but two deans reviewed his law application and recommended against admission. Professor Myres McDougal, a young faculty member with a very distinguished future, then interviewed Ford and was impressed. During Ford's presidency, McDougal had the distinct pleasure of quoting his old interview notes: "Very mature, wise person of good judgment, good-looking, well-dressed, plenty of poise, personality excellent. Informational background not the best, but interested, mature, serious of purpose. I see no reason not to admit him." He even projected the applicant's final GPA to within three-tenths of the true result (74.5). McDougal prevailed, and Ford was admitted as a part-time student on a trial basis.

Once in the door, Ford would not be stopped. After passing his first two Yale courses in the spring, he followed Professor Harry Shulman, "a great personal favorite," to summer session at the University of North Carolina at Chapel Hill. A former Yale classmate vividly remembered how Ford "used to sit up front on the right in the large classroom." Sixty years later in retirement, Ford recalled "I knew I could do both—coach and go to law school at the same time. But I must say, I worked my ass off."

Ford earned his LL.B. by January 1941, graduating in the top quarter of his class. What had he learned at Yale Law? On the most obvious level, the undergraduate economics major had continued his business-oriented interest by taking such courses as Debtors Estates, Negotiable Instruments, and Contracts. Some of his best grades were in two courses on Income Tax; his lowest grade was in Estates I.

Harder to assess are the intangible influences of professors and fellow students, and of the intellectual discipline of law as taught and learned at Yale in the 1930s. The Yale faculty had been a fertile recruiting ground for New Deal appointees, including a young firebrand named William O. Douglas. The faculty was a forward bastion of "legal realism" which, eschewing narrow reliance on case law and formal, abstract legal theory, introduced social science and social context into its jurisprudence. Its student body, meanwhile, was very much a social and economic elite drawn predominantly from a few Ivy League schools.

One can only speculate on how this environment influenced Ford. The lessons learned may be very different from the lessons taught. Still, it does not strain the imagination to see how "legal realism," drawing from the human experience as well as formal legal theory, might have been congenial to the nonideological, people-oriented, and moderately progressive Ford. When a 1941 hometown newspaper listed Ford's "Favorite People," the list began, surprisingly, with President Franklin Roosevelt's assistant attorney general, Thurman Arnold, a former Yale professor. At the dedication of the Detroit College of Law in 1998, Ford recalled that "It was at Yale that I was first introduced to the law as a paradoxical discipline—both absolute and flexible, fixed and evolving. The law demands respect for institutions, yet it relies upon individuals to bring those institutions to life."

Upon graduation, Ford might have chosen to enter a large East Coast law firm. He had visited Manhattan frequently and received invitations to join firms in Philadelphia and New York. Moreover, his life had acquired an element of big city glamour. Ford and Phyllis Brown, a Connecticut College coed who was emerging as *Cosmopolitan*'s main cover girl, had fallen mutually and deeply in love. Through Brown's contacts, they were featured in a ski weekend pictorial essay in the March 12, 1940, issue of *Look* magazine. A very different doorway had opened to Ford, but he chose not to walk through it.

Instead, Ford and a friend in similar circumstances forged their futures back in the Midwest. Phil Buchen and Ford had become

FORD LAW PARTNER AND
WHITE HOUSE COUNSEL
PHILIP BUCHEN

Though Buchen and Ford had a law job and offer, respectively, in Manhattan, both had reasons for returning to Grand Rapids, Michigan, to forge a law partnership in 1941. Following WWII, they were partners in a prestigious local firm, and during Ford's presidency, Buchen directed the White House legal staff. Pictured here during that latter period, as counsel, Buchen advised Ford and White House staff on such matters as statutory and constitutional powers and duties, pending legislation, conflicts of interest, and judicial appointments.

close friends when both attended law school summer session at the University of Michigan. Buchen was a summer clerk at a Wall Street firm, and he had an attractive offer to remain in New York. But clerking had been a disillusioning, hazing experience for Buchen, a person described as "courtly" and a "true gentleman" in later years.

In conversation over drinks at one of their Manhattan haunts, Ford broached with Buchen the notion of opening a law partnership in Grand Rapids. The idea had strong appeal to Buchen, who was anxious to return to the Midwest and whose father had been a solo law practitioner in Milwaukee. Buchen later recalled that Grand Rapids had a federal court and "from a would-be lawyer's standpoint, it was an attractive place. The quality of the bar was generally good; the judges were generally good. In law school it was always talked about as a wonderful place to practice law."

The notion appealed to Ford on several counts. A junior position in a large firm would confine him. He liked dealing with people and their problems and didn't want to be desk-bound. He wanted to do trial work and be in court; a Grand Rapids newspaper would describe the young attorney as wanting "to be a second Clarence Darrow." In his retirement, Ford recalled, "I enjoyed all aspects of law. I enjoyed working on client problems, let me put it that way. Regardless of what the problems were. I enjoyed working on adoption problems. I didn't necessarily like divorces, but that was part of the spectrum. Wills. I enjoyed the opportunity to go over to the courthouse, to negotiate or try cases. Yes, the whole spectrum of law practice interested me."

Ford and Buchen both knew that in Grand Rapids, Ford's considerable reputation would be invaluable in building a clientele. Ford's stepfather was well known for his civic involvement and straight-arrow business practices. Ford's football exploits had made him a local celebrity, and he had returned home often. More lastingly, Ford's exceptional qualities of character had left a strong impression on those who knew him. Their comments to U.S. Navy investigators in 1942, after Ford applied for a commission, survive in the archives and attest to the young attorney's reputation.

Was Ford already planning to seek elective office? "I don't think he was that definite," said Buchen in 1979. "I think he always wanted to be involved in politics but [not necessarily] as an elected official. Those were the days when you could do an awful lot in politics without running for office yourself." This had certainly been true in Grand Rapids, where, despite nonpartisan municipal elections, city government lay under the thumb of a corrupt Republican machine led by boss Frank McKay, whose power stretched across the state.

At Yale, Ford had been smitten by Wendell Willkie's maverick antibossism campaign for the Republican presidential nomination, and he had been among the one or two thousand supporters chanting "We Want Willkie!" outside the Republican convention hall in Philadelphia. Then, he had been a volunteer at the Willkie presidential campaign headquarters in New York in 1940. When Ford returned to Grand Rapids, he immediately became active in a clean government movement called the "Home Front."

Ford and Buchen passed the state bar exam and rented a three-office suite in the downtown Michigan Trust Building, where they had easy access to the Grand Rapids Bar Association's law library. They hired a part-time receptionist, bought used books and new furniture, and decorated the office "to exude an air of prosperity from the outset." For start-up funding, Buchen received a cash loan from his father, and Ford contributed savings he had set aside while coaching. They took part-time jobs teaching business law at the University of Grand Rapids, and Ford coached football there, too. To save expenses, the twenty-seven-year-old lawyer moved back into his parents' home.

The partnership opened for business in June 1941, but there was little business to be had. Their first client requested a property title opinion, but balked at the fifteen-dollar fee. Ford and Buchen, Attorneys at Law, adjusted the bill to ten dollars and spent "at least a week" on it. Soon a feckless client would teach the new lawyers a hard lesson: "In criminal cases, you ought to get the cash up front." They found that they were targets for salesmen of life, auto, and casualty insurance but also discovered

"From a would-be lawyer's standpoint, [Grand Rapids] was an attractive place. The quality of the bar was generally good; the judges were generally good. In law school [at Michigan] it was always talked about as a wonderful place to practice law."

Law Partner Philip Buchen

"I enjoyed all aspects of the law. . . . Yes, the whole spectrum of law practice interested me."

Gerald R. Ford

that these salesmen were a good source of business referrals. The firm also offered to do tax returns.

They became active in United Way, Red Cross, Farm Bureau, Junior Chamber of Commerce, and other organizations. Community service was personally satisfying to Ford, but it was also a good way to network and to become familiar with community problems and political issues. Gradually, the Ford-Buchen firm took hold.

Ford attended Grace Episcopal Church with his parents on Sunday, December 7, 1941, and he spent that afternoon working alone in his law office. While driving home, he heard the radio report of the Japanese attack on Pearl Harbor. Presumably, Ford consulted with Buchen the next morning before taking his next step, which was to enlist in the U.S. Navy. Within barely one year, 20 percent of the Grand Rapids bar had joined Lt. Ford in military service, although Buchen, stricken by polio as a teenager, was not among them.

The firm of Ford and Buchen remained technically in existence through the war, and the two men stayed in touch as Buchen helped other firms whose men were in uniform. Eventually, Buchen joined the locally prestigious firm of Butterfield, Keeney & Amberg, securing a commitment from Julius Amberg that Ford, too, could join the firm upon his discharge. The new firm emphasized commercial and business law, with little personal injury litigation or divorce or criminal work.

In January 1946, Ford sent five dollars to the Michigan State Bar Association for his annual dues and announced his new association with Butterfield, Keeney & Amberg. An associate partner, Ford soon enrolled in a refresher program for lawyers under the GI Bill. More important, he acquired a terrific mentor in Julius Amberg. Amberg had graduated first in his class at Harvard, become one of the state's top commercial litigators, and recently served as special assistant to Secretary of War Henry Stimson. "He sort of took me under his wing," Ford recalled in 1997. "I got a real retooling in the practice of law. He was an excellent trial lawyer and a demon for research. He also stimulated my dedication to ethics. He was a real inspiration."

Amberg allowed Ford to develop an independent practice within the firm. Neil Weathers, who joined the firm about the same time, recalled Ford as "friendly, energetic, hardworking. That guy would get down here at seven in the morning or earlier.

He knew everybody in town." Ford dealt directly with a lot of clients, mostly small ones.

Amberg, a Democrat in a staunchly Republican community, became a political as well as a legal mentor to Ford. They shared an antipathy for the McKay machine, a still-powerful but waning force. Amberg was head of Citizens Action, a reform group that paralleled the Home Front, which itself had remained active during the war and even managed to make Ford's father the county chairman of the Republican Party. Almost immediately upon his discharge from the navy, Ford had renewed his involvement with the Home Front. As the postwar world unfolded, Amberg and Ford found that they also shared a strong internationalist outlook.

Amberg encouraged Ford's civic involvement. Intriguingly, within four months of joining the firm, Ford had written to the clerk of the Michigan House seeking a copy of Enrolled Act No. 2 of the 1946 Extra Session. "I understand," he wrote without elaboration, "this Act has to do with Election laws." Once Ford did run for public office, Amberg allowed his young associate to work only an hour per day while campaigning. Amberg was steadfast, moreover, when Ford's campaign provoked a serious threat of commercial reprisal against his firm.

Ford became a candidate for elected office in 1948 when he entered the Republican Party primary against incumbent congressman Bartel Jonkman, a vestige of the McKay apparatus. Jonkman was a Taftite conservative opposed to the internationalist policies strongly favored by returning veterans like Ford and by Michigan's powerful senior senator, Republican Arthur Vandenburg. After a tough campaign, Ford beat Jonkman in an open primary. The margin of victory came from Democratic crossover voters mobilized by locals of the United Auto Workers, which was led by another ardent internationalist, Walter Reuther. Ford easily won the general election and entered the U.S. Congress in January 1949.

In hindsight, the 1948 election marks Ford's final career transition from law to politics, but this was not apparent at the time. Buchen would always believe that Ford, in that first campaign, expected to serve in a prewar type of Congress with three- or four-month sessions. Ford continued his formal association with Butterfield, Keeney & Amberg at least until 1951, when he was included in the firm's new seven-way partnership. Buchen,

First Use of the Twenty-fifth Amendment

The Twenty-fifth Amendment to the Constitution, ratified in 1967, provides the details of succession in the event the president or vice president cannot perform their duties. Gerald Ford was involved in the first application of the amendment in December of 1973 when he filled the vacancy caused by the resignation of Vice President Spiro Agnew. In his acceptance speech, the new vice president quipped, "I am a Ford, not a Lincoln."

informing Ford of this development, wrote, "While none of us anticipates that you will be forced into an involuntary political retirement, it is certainly desirable to have an established practice to come back to whenever you desire." As it was, Ford handily won twelve successive re-elections from 1950 to 1972.

Ford never felt that his switch from law to politics marked a dramatic change in personal or career values. As a lawyer, he had especially liked meeting people and solving client problems. "It was easy to go from the law business with that attitude into politics," he later said, "because in reality you're solving people's problems at a different level." When Ford did make plans to retire from Congress in 1974, he had it in mind to open a small law practice in northern Michigan.

Congressman Ford quickly developed a reputation for outstanding constituent services. Over a long and eventful career, he also acquired a reputation as a social moderate, an economic conservative, a responsible Cold War warrior, and a civil and inclusive, albeit somewhat unimaginative, Republican Party partisan. He became an expert on national security appropriations, including CIA oversight, and served on the Warren Commission investigating the assassination of President Kennedy. His moderate politics, personal likability and industry, and qualities of character helped him climb leadership rungs among House Republicans. After the 1964 Goldwater campaign resulted in massive House losses, Ford became minority leader in a revolt led in part by a younger colleague from Illinois, Donald Rumsfeld. Ford despaired of becoming House Speaker when the Nixon presidential landslide of 1972 brought only meager Republican gains in the House.

Ford planned to retire at the end of that House term, but an astounding series of events sent him to the White House instead. Vice President Spiro Agnew resigned, pleading nolo contendere to charges of corruption. Under the Twenty-fifth Amendment— the first time it was utilized—President Nixon nominated Ford to become vice president, and the House and Senate confirmed him in December 1973. Nixon, already severely weakened by the unfolding Watergate scandal, chose Ford for his confirmability, their harmony on policy issues, and their cordial relationship dating back to 1949. Then, on August 9, 1974, Nixon dramatically resigned the presidency in the face of near certain impeachment and trial.

Ford occupied the Oval Office for two and a half years. The challenges of his administration included recovering an economy severely racked by simultaneous recession and inflation, forging an energy policy less dependent on Middle East oil, and stabilizing the U.S. position internationally after defeat in Vietnam. Politically, Ford contended with a strongly Democratic Congress and, within his own party, with a rising right wing that nearly gave the 1976 Republican presidential nomination to Ronald Reagan. Hanging over everything was a deep popular distrust and disparagement of government. In the 1976 general election, Ford closed a nearly twenty-point polling deficit to lose by the narrowest of margins to Jimmy Carter.

It is difficult to isolate and pull from the whole fabric of this political career the particular threads that represent Ford the lawyer. Life experiences, innate traits, personal values, and pure chance are too entwined. Seldom a reflective man, Ford's various Law Day, bar association, and alma mater speeches offer no prism. It is possible, however, to see certain connections and telling events.

Ford always accepted, as a simple proposition without elaboration, the value in government of his law training. It disciplined and sharpened his reasoning and provided technical knowledge. John Paul Stevens, Ford's only appointee to the U.S. Supreme Court, once recalled the impression left upon him by his first conversation with Ford, which had quickly segued to New York City's pending fiscal bankruptcy: "The President's precise and lucid explanation of the issues under discussion made it clear to me that he was an extremely competent lawyer."

Many Ford associates ascribed to him a decision-making style that was essentially judicial. "He told me then, and he has told me many times since," Ford aide James Cannon said, "that he prefers the combination of a good memorandum and a firm discussion, a civil and correct discussion. He treats it more as if he were a judge. He listens to one argument and the other argu-

"The President's precise and lucid explanation of the issues under discussion made it clear to me that he was an extremely competent lawyer."

Justice John Paul Stephens

ment, then he retires into his office and makes a decision on it." It is a description amply supported by the archival record.

Ford, the economics major and business law attorney, served energetically for twelve years on the House Appropriations Committee, where he acquired an acute understanding of how the government and its programs functioned. According to Buchen, one of Ford's primary gifts was that "he was very realistic about how government works and the effects of its action. . . . When [a] law passes, everybody has high expectations, but then it turns out that even the best of bureaucracies can't administer the law. He realized that."

Watergate brought to the fore the issue of respect for the law, its practitioners, and its institutions. Ford never joined the popular pummeling of lawyers as a class just because many of the Watergate malefactors had been lawyers. More to the point, he recognized the centrality of law to the whole American venture in self-government. "Our great Republic is a government of laws and not of men. Here the people rule," declaimed Ford in his remarks upon taking the oath of office. These lines, among the most famous of his presidency, derive almost verbatim from the Founding Fathers.

As president, Ford took these sentiments as a call to action, not as a mere civics book lesson. He accepted, in spirit and practice, the role of the Democrat-controlled Congress as an equal branch of government under the Constitution. His crime policy stressed timely and predictable consequences rather than severity of punishment, so that popular respect for the law and judicial process might be upheld. His key appointments in legal and judicial matters were calculated to depoliticize them.

He summoned his old partner Phil Buchen to serve as counsel to the president, and in a sense he used the scrupulous Buchen as a firewall to protect the Department of Justice and other agencies from untoward intrusions by White House staff. Ford was determined, moreover, to depoliticize the Justice Department, and he followed the recommendation of his chief of staff, Donald Rumsfeld, in appointing Edward Levi as attorney general. Levi, an eminent lawyer-scholar and then president of the University of Chicago, had no political ties to the administration and was left to do his job as he saw fit. It proved a distinguished appointment.

One of Levi's jobs would be to recommend a replacement for resigning Supreme Court Justice William O. Douglas, whom Ford had once sought to impeach in an ill-conceived episode that still lacks adequate explanation. Ford told Levi to prepare a list of worthy candidates and to ignore all political considerations. In the end, Ford selected John Paul Stevens, one of Levi's final three, after reading a selection of Stevens's opinions.

Of course, of all Ford's actions as president, none equals in fame or infamy his pardon of Richard Nixon shortly after Nixon resigned. The motives, manner, and impact of the pardon can and will be debated indefinitely and profitably. A quarter century from the event, there is at least a temporary consensus on the wisdom of granting the pardon in order to clear "Nixon and his problems" from the agenda, avoid the degrading spectacle of a trial, and get on with pressing policy issues. According to journalist Bob Woodward, Ford still carries about with him a scrap of paper with a portion of the 1915 Supreme Court decision in *Burdick v. United States*, which held that accepting a pardon was equivalent to acceptance of guilt.

One suspects, though, that in his head and heart, Ford also carries the 1974 sermon of Dr. Duncan Littlefair of Fountain Street Church in Grand Rapids. It had been welcome reading in the Oval Office after Ford had pardoned Nixon, a man whom Ford had called a friend for twenty-five years. Littlefair had often disagreed with Ford, generally taking more liberal stands. But in response to the pardon and his congregation's dismay at it, Littlefair reminded them, "Mercy and forgiveness cannot be weighed and measured and balanced and counted. It must always be free."

THE NIXON PARDON
President Ford created an uproar upon granting the former president "a full, free and absolute pardon" for offenses Nixon "committed or may have committed or taken part in between the period from January 20, 1969, through August 9, 1974." Arguing the public policy necessity of removing Richard Nixon's legal problems from the national agenda, Ford declared, "The law, whether human or divine, is no respecter of persons; but the law is a respecter of reality." Many people believed, however, that justice would have been better served in a court of law.

★ ★ ★

Bill Clinton

Forty-second President (1993–2001)

BIRTH
August 19, 1946
Hope, Ark.

EDUCATION
Georgetown University
Oxford University
Yale Law School
Admission to the bar: September 7, 1973

OTHER OCCUPATIONS/PUBLIC OFFICES
Law school professor
Arkansas attorney general
Arkansas governor

LAW CAREER IN BRIEF
Clinton's law career began in 1973 as a law professor at the University of Arkansas Law School and, following a term as Arkansas attorney general, it basically concluded in 1979 upon his first election as governor of Arkansas. Despite a brief stint as "of Counsel" in the Little Rock firm of Wright, Lindsey & Jennings following his 1981 gubernatorial setback, and though possessing significant legal talents, Clinton remained interested in public office, not in a law career.

William Jefferson Clinton: Political Lawyer

DAVID H. BENNETT

Bill Clinton, Rhodes scholar, Yale Law School graduate, former attorney general of Arkansas, was elected president of the United States in 1992. This American lawyer-president, who had served as governor of Arkansas for five terms before coming to the White House, was reelected in 1996 by a decisive margin.

Throughout his two terms, Clinton's legal training played an important role in his conduct of the office. He was famous for being not only an accomplished politician but a "policy wonk" before coming to the presidency, an individual who delighted in mastering the intricacies of public issues. But it was his training as an attorney and his background in legal education that also was critical in his handling of many complex legislative and constitutional matters.

Clinton, the third youngest person to serve as president, was the subject of intense controversy. As a candidate, he had promised to focus "like a laser beam" on the economic problems then plaguing the nation, and he went on to preside over a remarkable resurgence in the American economy. But Clinton's terms were marked by a series of alleged scandals, events that had particular resonance for this attorney-president and strengthened his relationship to the White House counsel's office.

Born in 1946 in Hope, Arkansas, Clinton's given name was William Jefferson Blythe III, after his father, William Jefferson Blythe II, who was killed in an auto accident months before his son's birth. His mother, a nurse, married Roger Clinton in 1950, and the future president changed his name to William Jefferson Clinton when he was fifteen.

His stepfather, a failed auto dealer, was an alcoholic and an abusive husband during Clinton's youth; his mother was the

★ ★ ★

"His plan after law school was to go home to Arkansas and run for public office. Whether he wrote for the Yale Law Journal, *he noted, did not matter to anyone down there."*

Biographer David Maraniss

Law Student and Law Professor

While at Yale, Clinton's tendency to skip class lectures did not necessarily translate into poor grades. Hillary described one particular instance. "Bill did a typical Bill thing in his Corporate Finance class. He never went to lectures, but then he spent a week or two cramming, and he got the highest grade in the class." When the professor asked Bill how he had managed to do so well, Bill replied, "It's just like politics. All you have to do is figure out who's [bleeping] who." After graduating from Yale, Bill and Hillary soon were together again as law professors at the University of Arkansas Law School.

powerful early influence in his life. After two years in a Roman Catholic elementary school, he attended public schools in Hot Springs, Arkansas, where he earned high grades and became a student leader. In a famous photographed incident, he visited Washington, D.C., in 1963 as a delegate to Boys Nation, an American Legion leadership training program, and was first in line to shake the hand of President John F. Kennedy at the White House.

Intensely interested in public life even at this early age, he wanted to return to Washington for college and applied only to Georgetown University. At college, he impressed classmates as a magnetic personality ambitious for leadership positions and was elected class president. He was also an avid reader with wide intellectual interests. He made a particular mark in a demanding course in the U.S. Constitution and the Law, but his interests always focused on politics. He worked one summer on a gubernatorial campaign in his home state. It was his strong undergraduate record at Georgetown as well as service as an aide to Arkansas senator J. William Fulbright that helped him win a coveted Rhodes scholarship at Oxford University.

After two years as a Rhodes scholar, he entered Yale Law School in 1970. While in high school, he had become fascinated with the law after participating in a Latin class mock trial in which he defended Cataline—Cicero's enemy. While the exercise was designed to interest students in classical texts, he told his teacher that using his rhetorical and political skills in this classroom court made him realize that someday he should study law.

In his years at Yale, grades had been all but eliminated, replaced by a pass-fail system. It freed Clinton, who held part-time jobs to supplement scholarship funds, to work on a senatorial campaign and engage in other political activities, including service as Texas state coordinator in George McGovern's failed presidential effort in 1972. In law school, Clinton demonstrated that he was an extraordinarily quick study who easily could master course materials. Friends recalled that he often did not attend class but nevertheless did very well in law school. When one professor asked him how he had excelled in corporate law after starting the exam thirty minutes late, Clinton replied, "Corporate law is a lot like politics and I understand politics. It's just a case of making sure each employer gets something out of it." A fellow student would remember Clinton's brilliance in constitutional law. Of course, it was at Yale that he met another gifted law student, Hillary Rodham of Park Ridge, Illinois, whom he would marry in October 1975.

After receiving his law degree in 1973, Bill Clinton returned to his home state to teach at the University of Arkansas School of Law. His political ambitions played a key role in the decision to return to his home state, for that is where he would seek a career in elective office. At the law school, Clinton would have preferred his first teaching assignments to be in constitutional or criminal law but was instead given courses in agency and partnership and in trade regulation. He turned discussions in the agency class to the contemporary Watergate crisis, asking students if the people involved were agents of the president. When given a course in constitutional law, he also focused on pressing political questions, spending much time on the landmark abortion case, *Roe v. Wade*.

Known for being slow in marking exams, he was an unconventional law professor in a number of ways. He rejected the Socratic method, spoke without written notes, lectured in a conversational tone, and stimulated free-flowing discussion. African American students found him particularly sympathetic. They called him "wonder boy" because, one student remembered, "he would not let race treat you different from anyone else."

While successful as a law professor, his eye was always on the political arena. He made an unsuccessful race for a seat in the House of Representatives in 1974, only a year after joining the law school faculty. But his strong showing served as a prelude to his success in the 1976 Democratic primary for state attorney

★ ★ ★

"Hillary was very sharp and Chicago and Bill was very To Kill a Mockingbird.*"*

A Yale law student, describing his classmates' moot court styles

★ ★ ★

*"The University
of Arkansas School
of Law had never
encountered a faculty
member quite
like Clinton."*

Biographer David Maraniss

general and his subsequent election to the post. As attorney general, he shaped a reputation as supporter of consumers' interests, attacking utility companies and creating a division of energy conservation and rate advocacy with a much larger litigation staff. Two years later, he was elected governor with a campaign that focused on economic development and education.

Despite Clinton's ambitious agenda, his first term was less than successful and he was defeated in his reelection effort by Frank D. White, a conservative Republican savings and loan executive. A chastened Clinton joined a law firm in Little Rock and made plans for the next race in 1982. During the campaign he persuaded voters that he had learned from the problems in his first term, and he decisively defeated White. Elected three more times, he served as governor until he won his race for the White House.

Throughout his presidency, lawyer Clinton would demonstrate the importance of his legal training. In lower court judicial appointments—particularly those in his first year in the White House—he had extensive meetings on candidates, carefully reviewing their backgrounds and legal positions. In considering Supreme Court justices, he similarly delved into the work of his nominees, choosing centrists rather than ideologues. For example, as a former professor of antitrust law, he reviewed the writings of Steven Breyer. Also, while Clinton recognized that there was some anxiety about the position taken by Ruth Bader Ginsburg on *Roe v. Wade*, he clearly understood her stance and other legal aspects of the abortion issue.

Indeed, several members of the White House Counsels Office would note that Clinton's background in constitutional law—as well as his agile mind—allowed him to immediately grasp the legal implications of numerous policy questions. The fact that he was "an attorney who happened to be a very bright fellow," one observed, made a "critical difference," for on constitutional issues his "faculty for understanding that was far greater" than that of a nonlawyer.

He spent hours with White House lawyers, for example, discussing the legal issues involved in the Securities Law Reform Act, the Brady bill, and the Oklahoma City bombing. He also sought to reverse the position of the Justice Department, which had intervened on the side of a plaintiff challenging the constitutionality of the Religious Freedom Restoration Act. One observer

JONES CASE DEPOSITION
JANUARY 17, 1998

recalls that "after discussing the case for thirty minutes or so, the president walked in and engaged in an invigorating and free-ranging debate—the kind law professors die for—about tithing, the meaning of the Religion Clauses and RFRA, and the application of the law to this case."

Later in his administration, Clinton issued school prayer guidelines for the attorney general and secretary of education, setting out in detail the principles governing what types of religious activity in school are permissible under current law. In announcing his guidelines, which were distributed to every public school district in the country, the president stated: "Our Founding Fathers understood that religious freedom basically was a coin with two sides. The Constitution protected the free exercise of religion but prohibited the establishment of religion. It's a careful balance that's uniquely American. It is the genius of the First Amendment. It does not make us a religion-free country as some people have implied. It has made us the most religious country in the world."

THE PRESIDENT'S LEGAL DEPOSITIONS

Upon President Clinton's request, Attorney General Janet Reno appointed an independent counsel, Robert Fiske, to investigate the Whitewater controversy. Fiske proceeded to depose President Clinton and Hillary in 1994, a first for both a sitting president and first lady. The president's later deposition in the Paula Jones lawsuit, especially some hair-splitting responses, generated widespread criticism.

The First Lawyer First Lady

Hillary Rodham Clinton has had a notable law career. Upon graduating from Yale, where she was a member of the *Yale Law Review* board of editors, she worked as an attorney at the Children's Defense Fund and with the special House impeachment panel investigating President Nixon. She then briefly joined her husband on the law faculty at the University of Arkansas before joining the Rose law firm in Little Rock, where from 1977 to 1992 she specialized in patent infringement and intellectual property law. During that time, she also engaged in other law-related activities, including terms on the Legal Services Corporation board and as founding chair of the ABA's Commission on Women in the Profession. While her legal practice effectively concluded in 1992, she has continued her involvement with various law-related boards and activities.

Clinton also had a high regard for lawyers. Two of his chiefs of staff were attorneys, as were several of their deputies. Many close friends and colleagues were attorneys and, of course, his closest confidante, Hillary, was a lawyer as well. It was significant that he periodically dined with members of the White House Counsels Office; he valued their judgment and they appreciated Clinton's willingness to hear their views.

Still, though he was a student of the law, Clinton primarily focused on policy matters, remaining always the adroit politician. The two merged most forcefully in the Whitewater investigation, which involved independent counsel investigations—leading to such Watergate-sounding affairs as Filegate and Travelgate—and ultimately to the Lewinsky affair and impeachment proceedings.

Throughout the independent counsel investigations, Clinton responded as a politician and as a lawyer. While he deferred to the legal judgments of White House counsel and his personal attorneys, the president's legal training made an important difference. As one close observer noted, the fact that he was a lawyer "added even more to his understanding of the illegitimacy of most of these charges . . . it added to his sense of outrage." In a final report, the last independent counsel to investigate this president concluded that there was no persuasive evidence of criminal wrongdoing in the Whitewater case by either the president or the first lady.

These "scandals" in the Clinton years had proven illusory. In part, they were the product of intense ideological conflict at this moment in American history and a new politics of personal assault. The classic American political scandals involving the White House, such as Credit Mobilier in the Grant years or Teapot Dome in Harding's administration, had involved financial corruption, the president's appointees using their positions to line their pockets. The more recent episodes of great presidential scandal—Watergate and Iran-Contra—had involved the corruption of power, the president and his aides operating outside the law to achieve their policy objectives or to stay in office. Despite allegations by his adversaries, the evidence was that none of this happened on Clinton's watch.

A sex scandal, however, was something different. It would become the focus of efforts to impeach Clinton. In 1998, Clinton admitted that he had had "inappropriate" sexual contact with a young White House intern, Monica Lewinsky. Following the first news reports about this affair, Clinton made a notorious finger-wagging denial on national television. This was a politically damaging act that haunted him during his remaining months in office.

The Republicans, however, sought to impeach him for a related incident. To an Arkansas grand jury, the president had denied allegations by a former state employee in Arkansas, Paula Jones, that he made unwanted sexual advances toward her when he was governor. When her attorneys confronted him with a surprise question about Monica Lewinsky, Clinton denied any sexual relationship with the intern. While this particular case was later dismissed, the president's denial under oath about Lewinsky became a central issue in the 1998 impeachment effort in the House of Representatives.

During the lengthy inquiry into the Lewinsky matter, Clinton's legal training—his technical understanding of where legal

★ ★ ★

"*. . . Clinton's background in constitutional law—as well as his agile mind—allowed him to immediately grasp the legal implications of numerous policy questions.*"

lines could be drawn in discussing sexual matters—hurt him on at least one occasion. Facing an independent counsel's questions about a sexual act during a televised grand jury testimony, he remarked: "It all depends upon what 'is' is." This "lawyerly" response played poorly in the court of public opinion.

While other serious charges—including obstruction of justice, suborning perjury, and tampering with witnesses—were never proved, Clinton's denial about Lewinsky in the Jones case loomed large during the angry and partisan debate leading to the House vote, along party lines, to impeach the president. During the impeachment trial that followed in the Senate, few believed that Clinton could be removed from office. There was little drama because the Senate vote, again along party lines, fell far short of conviction.

The impeachment issue—which also proved to be dangerous political baggage for his opponents—quickly faded from view. But "Clinton fatigue," that popular unhappiness with his personal behavior, lingered on in some circles. Despite his many successes in the White House, Clinton thus remains for some a controversial figure. As he is still younger than many presidents when they occupied the Oval Office, there may well be further chapters to add to the legacy of this unique lawyer-president.

Presidential Appointments

Supreme Court Justices and Chief Government Lawyers

Lawyer-Presidents and Their Supreme Court Appointments

BARBARA A. PERRY

I n his memoirs, Gerald Ford observed: "Few appointments a president makes can have as much impact on the future of the country as those to the Supreme Court." But have the lawyer-presidents, who constitute twenty-five of the nation's forty-three chief executives to date, been distinctive in their Supreme Court appointments? A look at the criteria for such appointments is a productive starting point in answering that question.

The U.S. Constitution is wholly silent on requisite qualifications or criteria for federal judges. Any reference even to the need for legal training is absent, though Alexander Hamilton in *Federalist Paper No. 78* remarked that knowledge of the laws acquired through "long and laborious study" should be a requirement for judicial service on the national courts. Recently, Henry Abraham, an astute scholar of Supreme Court appointments, identified four criteria that have most frequently guided presidential nominations to the high tribunal: (1) merit, (2) political and ideological compatibility, (3) balancing "representation" on the Court, and (4) personal and political friendship.

Merit may be deemed in the eye of the beholder, but Abraham argues that it should include strong educational background, intelligence, clarity of expression, professional ability, judicial temperament, impeccable moral character, diligence, and conscientiousness. While most presidents have made merit a threshold consideration, all have first and foremost searched for appointees from the same political and ideological stripe as themselves. In addition, many presidents have attempted to balance the Court's membership through representative factors such as geography, religion, race, and gender. Finally, our chief executives have often felt more comfortable nominating personal or political associates, an approach that at its worst can constitute

★ ★ ★

"The U.S. Constitution is wholly silent on requisite qualifications or criteria for federal judges."

★ ★ ★

"Presidents are politicians first and foremost, whether or not they have been lawyers in their pre–White House careers. Thus, their primary considera-tion for virtually all nominees to the nation's highest tribunal is ideologi-cal and political compatibility."

cronyism but at its best can assure appointment of a justice whose background the president thoroughly knows and understands.

All the lawyer-presidents have had the opportunity to name at least one justice, while five of the nonlawyer executives—William Harrison, Taylor, Andrew Johnson, Carter, and George W. Bush—have not, although the latter may still have the op-portunity to do so. Fortunately for the high court's performance and legitimacy over its two-hundred-year history, most presi-dents, lawyers or not, have placed a premium on finding merito-rious Supreme Court nominees. The summary following this article provides basic information about all the presidents and their high court appointees. But how do lawyer-presidents fare in their consideration of Abraham's criteria and in appointing quality justices as compared to nonlawyer-presidents?

The answer is decidedly mixed, though a noticeable, and per-haps predictable, difference exists in the way lawyer-presidents conceptualize merit, as they have placed more emphasis on the previous judicial and legal service of their nominees than have nonlawyer-presidents. Of the thirteen presidents for whom such experience can be identified as a criterion for their nominees, eight were attorneys. These included Jefferson, Monroe, Fill-more, Arthur, Benjamin Harrison, Taft, Coolidge, and Ford, whose own legal backgrounds ran the gamut from modest to extensive. Having served in all eras of American history, these presidents' use of the legal or judicial experience criterion indi-cates that it has been a consistent consideration for about a third of the lawyer-presidents.

One other difference in selection criteria distinguishes lawyer-presidents' nominations—geographic representation. Of the twelve presidents who utilized state or region as an obvious consideration in naming appointees, ten were lawyers—John Adams, Jefferson, Jackson, Van Buren, Polk, Buchanan, Lincoln, Arthur, Cleveland, and Franklin Roosevelt. This pattern may be traced primarily to the period in which they served, however, because all but one of these men were president before 1890, when geographic recognition was more politically relevant.

In that period, former colonies, now states, jealously vied for power, as regions produced different political agendas and sec-tional conflict over slavery would erupt in civil war and linger in the postbellum period. Thus, George Washington, a nonlawyer but a shrewd politician, nominated James Iredell from North Carolina to the Supreme Court because his state had "given no character to a federal office." All told, Washington chose justices from nine of the thirteen original states in his eleven appointments.

Lawyer-presidents had an additional geographic consideration—one based on judicial structure—that guided their Supreme Court choices. The landmark Judiciary Act of 1789 had created a three-tiered federal judiciary consisting of district courts, circuit courts, and the Supreme Court. The district courts each had a single district judge, while the circuit bench met in its various districts and was composed of the district court judge and two Supreme Court justices. Thus, the 1789 act created no separate and distinct circuit judgeships, a situation that would continue until the Circuit Court of Appeals Act of 1891 created an intermediate appellate court level in the federal judiciary. Prior to 1891, the Supreme Court justices' well-known circuit-riding duties, combined with the Court's light early caseload, had justices spending much time in their assigned circuits.

It therefore made sense for presidents to want each circuit represented on the Supreme Court by an inhabitant of that geographic area. Examples abound of this rationale in practice among lawyer-presidents. John Adams named Alfred Moore, a well-regarded member of the North Carolina bench, to replace Justice Iredell, who hailed from the same state. When ill health forced Moore from the Supreme Court, Jefferson nominated a South Carolinian, William Johnson. Jefferson also appointed Henry Brockholst Livingston of New York to replace Justice William Paterson of New Jersey. That seat remained in the possession of Empire State natives from 1803 to 1893, thanks to five appointments by lawyer-presidents and one by a non-lawyer chief executive.

When Congress later created a seventh circuit out of the new "western" states of Kentucky, Ohio, and Tennessee, Jefferson nominated Kentuckian Thomas Todd to the resulting new seat on the U.S. Supreme Court. John Quincy Adams later

CIRCUIT-RIDING CONSIDERATIONS

Prior to the passage of the 1891 Circuit Court of Appeals Act, which created a federal intermediate appellate court level to relieve the Supreme Court's backlogged caseload, high court justices were required to "ride circuit" in addition to hearing cases in the nation's capital. For this and other reasons, geography played a major role in selecting high court appointees through most of the nineteenth century. New York State, for example, kept a seat on the Court for most of that century, beginning with Jefferson appointee Henry Livingston (pictured here).

JOHN MARSHALL, "THE GREAT CHIEF JUSTICE"

Appointed by John Adams in the waning months of his presidency, Marshall always receives the highest assessment in polls of constitutional scholars and is "virtually canonized in Supreme Court lore." Yet Bushrod Washington and Alfred Moore, Adams's other high court appointees, are generally placed in the "below average" category of such rankings.

named another Kentuckian, Robert Trimble, to replace Justice Todd upon his death in 1826. Adams also placed a premium on previous judicial experience, as Trimble had served nine years on the U.S. District Court, thus becoming the first Supreme Court justice to have had federal bench credentials upon arriving at the high tribunal. Lawyer-presidents Jackson, Lincoln, and Garfield reserved the seat for the seventh circuit with three consecutive appointees from Ohio.

Upon the establishment of the ninth circuit, consisting of Alabama, Mississippi, Louisiana, and Arkansas, Van Buren nominated John McKinley of Alabama. The new justice then moved back to his native state of Kentucky so that he could live between the nation's capital and his assigned circuit. In 1839, McKinley logged ten thousand miles in his circuit riding, more than three times the average yearly distance traveled by his Supreme Court colleagues in their circuit duties. The Court briefly added another seat corresponding to a new tenth circuit that encompassed California and Oregon, to which Lincoln named Stephen Field, a Californian, in 1863. President McKinley replaced Field in 1898, after his then-record-setting tenure of thirty-four years on the Court, with California's Joseph McKenna.

Another instructive measure of comparison is through the "rankings" of Supreme Court appointees. Although such ratings or rankings are imprecise measurements, polls indicate that lawyer-presidents have appointed "great," "near great," and "average" justices in the same proportion as their total rate of appointments.

The most comprehensive poll, conducted by Albert Blaustein and Roy Mersky in 1967, covered one hundred Supreme Court appointments, including four who received multiple appointments—Edward White, Harlan Stone, Charles Evans Hughes, and Wiley Rutledge. Of those appointments, lawyer-presidents made sixty-one, which is close to the percentage of lawyer-presidents (22 or 69 percent) among the thirty-two chief executives whose appointments were rated in the poll. The poll accorded the "great" ranking to twelve appointees—John Marshall, Joseph Story, Roger

Taney, Louis Brandeis, Stone, Benjamin Cardozo, the first John M. Harlan, Oliver Wendell Holmes, Hughes, Hugo Black, Felix Frankfurter, and Earl Warren. Of those nominations, nine, or 64 percent, were by lawyer-presidents. Sixteen justices—William Johnson, Benjamin Curtis, Samuel Miller, Stephen Field, Joseph Bradley, Morrison Waite, Edward White, Taft, George Sutherland, William Douglas, Robert Jackson, Wiley Rutledge, the second John M. Harlan, William Brennan, and Abe Fortas—were rated "near great." Ten, or 63 percent, of these justices were appointed by lawyer-presidents.

Of the fifty-six justices deemed "average" in the poll, lawyer-presidents named thirty-four, or 61 percent. Only a half dozen justices— Thomas Johnson, Alfred Moore, Robert Trimble, Philip Barbour, William Woods, and Howell Jackson—fell into the "below average" category, and five (83 percent) are attributable to lawyer-presidents. Of the eight "failed" members of the Supreme Court—Willis Van Devanter, James McReynolds, Harold Burton, Fred Vinson, Pierce Butler, James Byrnes, Sherman Minton, and Charles Whittaker— lawyer-presidents were responsible for three, or 38 percent. Nonlawyer Harry Truman bears the dubious distinction of having nominated three of the eight, arguably because he relied too heavily on personal and political friendships with his appointments. Eleven presidents who were lawyers appointed no "great" or "near great" justices, though seven of those chief executives made only a single appointment.

Merely because a lawyer-president appointed a "great" justice to the high bench did not mean that he discovered the ideal set of selection criteria for such appointments. John Adams, the first lawyer-president, was a superbly trained attorney who enjoyed a brilliant career as a practicing lawyer and constitutional scholar. Therefore, he could appreciate John Marshall's superb legal mind. Yet, like all presidents, Adams wanted an ideological soul mate on the bench and he found one in his staunch Federalist appointee.

Appointed chief justice in 1801, Marshall eventually translated the party's beliefs in a strong central government and vigorous

JACKSON APPOINTEE: CHIEF JUSTICE ROGER TANEY

Despite his early career as a lawyer, prosecutor, and state court judge, Jackson was first and foremost a politician whose six high court appointments were more based on political than judicial considerations. His most acclaimed appointment, Roger Taney (pictured here), is also one of the most maligned, due to Taney's ruling in the *Dred Scott* case. Taney had earlier served as Jackson's attorney general and despite *Dred Scott*, he is widely regarded among the "great" justices.

interstate commerce authority into Supreme Court precedent, while demonstrating his impressive command of the republic's legal foundations. In his thirty-four years on the Court, Marshall established it as a co-equal branch of the federal government, primarily by exercising its power of judicial review. Long after the Federalist Party's demise, Marshall carried its banner, delivering (and probably drafting) nearly half of the 1,215 opinions issued by the Court during his tenure.

Labeled "the great chief justice," and virtually canonized in Supreme Court lore, Marshall always receives the highest assessment in polls of constitutional scholars. Yet Adams's two other nominees to the Supreme Court, Bushrod Washington, nephew of the first president, and Alfred Moore, have earned "below average" rankings. Ill health forced Moore off the bench after five years, and though Washington served almost as long as Marshall, he was overshadowed by the judicial colossus, as were most colleagues in that era.

With six appointments to the Supreme Court, including the chief justice, Andrew Jackson had the opportunity to reshape the bench and the direction of American constitutional law. He had been an indifferent student of the law, but he had considerable practical experience as an attorney, prosecutor, and justice of Tennessee's highest court. As a consummate politician, however, he was most concerned with choosing politically and geographically appropriate candidates who would hew to the tenets of Jacksonian democracy. His most acclaimed—and maligned—nominee, Chief Justice Roger Taney, managed to do just that. Until the "self-inflicted wound" of the *Dred Scott* decision, this well-trained attorney, with long experience in private practice and a stint as Jackson's attorney general, maintained the coequal status of the Supreme Court while tipping the balance between federal and state power in favor of the latter. Thus, despite *Dred Scott*, Taney rates in the "great" category.

William Howard Taft: The Only Man to Be President and Chief Justice

Though appointed chief justice some eight years following his presidency, Taft still brought more judicial experience to the White House than any other lawyer-president, having been a superior court and federal judge for more than a decade in the late 1800s. Yet other than the brilliant Charles Evans Hughes, Taft's other five Supreme Court appointments ran the gamut from "near great" to "failure."

Jackson's quintet of associate justices—John McLean, Henry Baldwin, James Wayne, Philip Barbour, and John Catron—all had previous judicial experience at the state or federal level. Yet Jackson was more concerned that they represented the right circuits and remained loyal to his Democratic Party, though their partisan fealty sometimes wavered on the bench. Justice McLean, for example, wrote one of the two dissents in *Dred Scott*, and his rationale for doing so provided the foundations of the Fourteenth Amendment. In any case, all scored "average" ratings, except for Barbour, who was tabbed "below average."

Abraham Lincoln, surely one of the savviest and most experienced lawyers ever to serve in the White House, and always ranked among the greats of the nation's presidents, had no "great" justices among the five he appointed. Two—Miller and Field—achieved "near great" status while the others—Noah Swayne, David Davis, and Salmon Chase—garnered only "average" marks.

If any president was attuned to the requirements and rhythms of the judiciary, it was William Howard Taft, having served nearly a decade on the state and federal bench before his election to the presidency. He was responsible for the brilliant Charles Evans Hughes's first appointment as an associate justice in 1910. (Nonlawyer Herbert Hoover named Hughes chief justice in 1930 to replace Taft, whom another nonlawyer, Warren Harding, had appointed chief justice in 1921.) Taft's handful of other nominees would run the gamut of rankings, from the "near great" Sutherland, to the "average" Horace Lurton, Joseph Lamar, and Mahlon Pitney, to the "failure" Van Devanter.

Woodrow Wilson was the only Ph.D. ever to occupy the White House. A scholar, philosopher, educator, and member of the bar—though he found the study and practice of law boring—he might be viewed as the number one "intellect-in-chief" to serve as president. Yet he appointed the alpha and omega of Supreme Court justices—an unquestioned "great" in the stellar Louis Brandeis and an undisputed "failure" in James McReynolds. Though the latter had been an

FDR: MEDIOCRE LEGAL CAREER; DISTINGUISHED JUDICIAL APPOINTMENTS

Other than George Washington, who made the initial appointments to the high court, no president made more such appointments than FDR. Despite his mediocre legal career, FDR's nine appointees included six rated "great" or "near great" and only one considered a failure. FDR's eye for legal talent extended to his administration, as he filled many key leadership posts with distinguished lawyers. For example, one list of America's hundred greatest lawyers includes only three twentieth-century attorneys general—Homer Cummings, Robert Jackson (pictured below), and Francis Biddle—and all were appointed by FDR.

excellent law student at the University of Virginia and a competent corporate lawyer, his nasty and bigoted persona and outdated jurisprudence made him an unmitigated disaster on the high court.

Franklin Roosevelt, another unenthusiastic student of the law, produced a mediocre performance at Columbia Law School before dropping out upon passing the bar. His periodic stints in private practice were merely brief, undistinguished interludes in his singularly successful political career, though he recruited many outstanding lawyers into government service during his years in the White House.

In addition to holding the record for times elected to the presidency—a mark that is bound to stand unless the two-term limit of the Twenty-second Amendment is repealed—FDR also maintains a unique place in Supreme Court appointment history for naming three "great" justices—Stone, who was promoted from associate to chief justice, Black, and Frankfurter—and three "near great" in Douglas, Jackson, and Rutledge. By comparison, two of his nominees, Stanley Reed and Frank Murphy, were "average." FDR's single failed justice was James Byrnes, an inveterate politician who had no desire to be on the Supreme Court and who lasted only one year there.

Although the above discussion denotes a few characteristics that have distinguished the Supreme Court appointments of lawyer-presidents, the overwhelming fact of life in judicial nominations is, not surprisingly, politics. Presidents are politicians first and foremost, whether or not they have been lawyers in their pre–White House careers. Thus, their primary consideration for virtually all nominees to the nation's highest tribunal is ideological and political compatibility. As long as controversial political issues continue to arrive at the Court's threshold, as *Bush v. Gore* reminded us, presidents (and their constituents) will care more about appointees' partisan and ideological pedigrees than any other law-related factors.

★ ★ ★

"The most comprehensive poll [on Supreme Court justices], conducted in 1967 . . . accorded the 'great' ranking to twelve appointees— John Marshall, Joseph Story, Roger Taney, Louis Brandeis, [Harlan] Stone, Benjamin Cardozo, the first John M. Harlan, Oliver Wendell Holmes, [Charles Evans] Hughes, Hugo Black, Felix Frankfurter, and Earl Warren."

SUPREME COURT APPOINTMENTS

PRESIDENT	JUSTICE	TERM
George Washington	John Jay*	1789–95
George Washington	John Rutledge†	1790–91
George Washington	William Cushing	1790–1810
George Washington	James Wilson	1789–98
George Washington	John Blair Jr.	1790–96
George Washington	James Iredell	1790–99
George Washington	Thomas Johnson	1792–93
George Washington	William Paterson	1793–1806
George Washington	Samuel Chase	1796–1811
George Washington	Oliver Ellsworth*	1796–1800
John Adams	Bushrod Washington	1799–1829
John Adams	Alfred Moore	1800–1804
John Adams	John Marshall*	1801–35
Thomas Jefferson	William Johnson	1804–34
Thomas Jefferson	Henry B. Livingston	1807–23
Thomas Jefferson	Thomas Todd	1807–26
James Madison	Gabriel Duval	1811–35
James Madison	Joseph Story	1812–45
James Monroe	Smith Thompson	1823–43
John Quincy Adams	Robert Trimble	1826–28
Andrew Jackson	John McLean	1830–61
Andrew Jackson	Henry Baldwin	1830–44
Andrew Jackson	James M. Wayne	1835–67
Andrew Jackson	Roger B. Taney*	1836–64
Andrew Jackson	Philip P. Barbour	1836–41
Andrew Jackson	John Catron‡	1837–65
Martin Van Buren	John McKinley	1838–52
Martin Van Buren	Peter V. Daniel	1842–60
John Tyler	Samuel Nelson	1845–72
James K. Polk	Levi Woodbury	1845–51
James K. Polk	Robert C. Grier	1846–70
Millard Fillmore	Benjamin R. Curtis	1851–57

Excerpted from *Justices, Presidents, and Senators* with permission of The Rowman & Littlefield Publishing Group

* Chief justice.
† Resigned without sitting.

‡ Nominated by Andrew Jackson, but not confirmed until after Martin Van Buren had assumed office.

President	Justice	Term
Franklin Pierce	John A. Campbell	1853–61
James Buchanan	Nathan Clifford	1858–81
Abraham Lincoln	Noah H. Swayne	1862–81
Abraham Lincoln	Samuel F. Miller	1862–90
Abraham Lincoln	David Davis	1862–77
Abraham Lincoln	Stephen J. Field	1863–97
Abraham Lincoln	Salmon P. Chase*	1864–73
Ulysses S. Grant	William Strong	1870–80
Ulysses S. Grant	Joseph P. Bradley	1870–92
Ulysses S. Grant	Ward Hunt	1873–82
Ulysses S. Grant	Morrison R. Waite*	1874–88
Rutherford B. Hayes	John M. I. Harlan	1877–1911
Rutherford B. Hayes	William B. Woods	1881–87
James A. Garfield	Stanley Matthews	1881–89
Chester A. Arthur	Horace Gray	1882–1902
Chester A. Arthur	Samuel Blatchford	1882–93
Grover Cleveland	Lucius Q. C. Lamar	1888–93
Grover Cleveland	Melville W. Fuller*	1888–1910
Benjamin Harrison	David J. Brewer	1890–1910
Benjamin Harrison	Henry B. Brown	1891–1906
Benjamin Harrison	George Shiras Jr.	1892–1903
Benjamin Harrison	Howell E. Jackson	1893–95
Grover Cleveland	Edward D. White	1894–1910
Grover Cleveland	Rufus W. Peckham	1896–1909
William McKinley	Joseph McKenna	1898–1925
Theodore Roosevelt	Oliver Wendell Holmes Jr.	1902–32
Theodore Roosevelt	William R. Day	1903–22
Theodore Roosevelt	William H. Moody	1906–10
William Howard Taft	Horace H. Lurton	1910–14
William Howard Taft	Charles E. Hughes	1910–16
William Howard Taft	Edward D. White*†	1910–21
William Howard Taft	Willis Van Devanter	1911–37
William Howard Taft	Joseph R. Lamar	1911–16
William Howard Taft	Mahlon Pitney	1912–22

* Chief justice.
† Promoted from associate justice.

PRESIDENT	JUSTICE	TERM
Woodrow Wilson	James C. McReynolds	1914–41
Woodrow Wilson	Louis D. Brandeis	1916–39
Woodrow Wilson	John H. Clarke	1916–22
Warren G. Harding	William Howard Taft*	1921–30
Warren G. Harding	George Sutherland	1922–38
Warren G. Harding	Pierce Butler	1923–39
Warren G. Harding	Edward T. Sanford	1923–30
Calvin Coolidge	Harlan F. Stone	1925–41
Herbert Hoover	Charles E. Hughes*	1930–41
Herbert Hoover	Owen J. Roberts	1930–45
Herbert Hoover	Benjamin N. Cardozo	1932–38
Franklin Delano Roosevelt	Hugo L. Black	1937–71
Franklin Delano Roosevelt	Stanley F. Reed	1938–57
Franklin Delano Roosevelt	Felix Frankfurter	1939–62
Franklin Delano Roosevelt	William O. Douglas	1939–75
Franklin Delano Roosevelt	Frank Murphy	1940–49
Franklin Delano Roosevelt	James F. Byrnes	1941–42
Franklin Delano Roosevelt	Harlan F. Stone*†	1941–46
Franklin Delano Roosevelt	Robert H. Jackson	1941–54
Franklin Delano Roosevelt	Wiley B. Rutledge	1943–49
Harry S. Truman	Harold H. Burton	1945–58
Harry S. Truman	Fred M. Vinson*	1946–53
Harry S. Truman	Tom C. Clark	1949–67
Harry S. Truman	Sherman Minton	1949–56
Dwight D. Eisenhower	Earl Warren*	1953–69
Dwight D. Eisenhower	John M. Harlan II	1955–71
Dwight D. Eisenhower	William J. Brennan Jr.	1956–90
Dwight D. Eisenhower	Charles E. Whittaker	1957–62
Dwight D. Eisenhower	Potter Stewart	1958–81
John F. Kennedy	Byron R. White	1962–93
John F. Kennedy	Arthur J. Goldberg	1962–65
Lyndon B. Johnson	Abe Fortas	1965–69
Lyndon B. Johnson	Thurgood Marshall	1967–91
Richard M. Nixon	Warren E. Burger*	1969–86

* Chief justice.
† Promoted from associate justice.

President	Justice	Term
Richard M. Nixon	Harry A. Blackmun	1970–94
Richard M. Nixon	Lewis F. Powell Jr.	1972–87
Richard M. Nixon	William H. Rehnquist	1972–86
Gerald R. Ford	John Paul Stevens	1975–
Ronald Reagan	Sandra Day O'Connor	1981–
Ronald Reagan	William H. Rehnquist*†	1986–
Ronald Reagan	Antonin Scalia	1986–
Ronald Reagan	Anthony M. Kennedy	1988–
George Bush	David H. Souter	1990–
George Bush	Clarence Thomas	1991–
William Jefferson Clinton	Ruth B. Ginsburg	1993–
William Jefferson Clinton	Stephen G. Breyer	1994–

* Chief justice.
† Promoted from associate justice.

Lawyer-Presidents and Their Attorneys (General)

CORNELL W. CLAYTON

L awyers have long been members of the president's cabinet, but only the attorney general serves as a "practicing" lawyer. As the nation's premier counsel—responsible for representing the federal government in court and offering legal advice to the executive branch—the attorney general's office symbolizes America's commitment to the impartial rule of law. Indeed, EQUAL JUSTICE UNDER LAW is chiseled onto the wall of the U.S. Department of Justice. Nevertheless, as one who serves at the pleasure of the president, the attorney general is also a key member of the president's political administration and, from the first appointees, they have been close personal friends and confidants of the president.

The relationship between the attorney general and the president is extraordinarily complex. It has been defined historically by a set of conflicting loyalties, pulled between the demands of law and politics. These tensions have been transformed, though not eliminated, by the emergence of other important legal offices in the executive branch, especially those of solicitor general and White House counsel. Together, these individuals today serve as the president's key legal advisers. A look at the evolution of these offices helps illuminate whether and how lawyer-presidents' relationships with these lawyers may differ from nonlawyer-presidents' interactions with them.

The attorney general's office is part of the colonial inheritance from England, where the office originated in 1472. The U.S. attorney general was formally established under the Judiciary Act of 1789, which provided for the appointment of "a meet person, learned in the law." The early office was not the powerful post it is today, as the newly formed government's legal work was meager and

AMERICA'S FIRST ATTORNEY GENERAL
Edmund Randolph, who accepted the position at George Washington's urging, complained about its ill-defined powers and difficult conditions. "I am sort of a mongrel between the State and the U.S.," said Randolph, "called an officer of some rank under the latter, and yet thrust out to get a livelihood in the former—perhaps in a petty mayor's or county court . . ."

WILLIAM WIRT: THE FIRST GREAT ATTORNEY GENERAL

Appointed by President Monroe in 1817, Wirt not only was the longest-serving attorney general (twelve years), but he redefined the office, expanding its duties, formalizing its procedures, and preserving its opinions. During his terms, he argued 174 cases before the Supreme Court, including a number of landmark cases. Though the attorney general was initially established as a "quasi-judicial" office, housed with the Supreme Court, and providing legal opinions to Congress on pending legislation, Wirt argued that the attorney general should serve as legal adviser solely to the executive branch.

the attorney general was but a part-time position. The attorney general also had no staff or office expenses, and his salary was half that of other major federal officers. Indeed, incumbents were expected to continue their private practices.

The office was not part of the president's cabinet, and early attorneys general did not even control the federal government's legal work. They lacked authority over the federal district attorneys, who were also established under the 1789 act, and over legal counsel in other federal agencies. The early history of the attorney general was thus marked by a constant struggle to consolidate control over the government's legal business. The first attorney general, Edmund Randolph, took the post out of friendship and loyalty to George Washington, but he complained bitterly about the conditions:

> *I am a sort of mongrel between the State and the U.S.; called an officer of some rank under the latter, and yet thrust out to get a livelihood in the former—perhaps in a petty mayor's or county court . . . could I have foreseen it, (these conditions) would have kept me at home to encounter pecuniary difficulties there, rather than add to them here.*

The first major changes to the office began in 1817, when lawyer-president James Monroe named William Wirt to the post. Wirt was the first great attorney general. His twelve-year tenure, longer than any other, redefined the office by expanding its duties and formalizing its procedures. Wirt was the first to reside year-round in Washington and the first to compile the office's legal opinions. Congress, for its part, increased Wirt's salary (which still lagged behind other cabinet officers') and finally provided the office with staff and expenses.

Wirt also began to redefine the office's relationship to the president. Prior to his tenure, the office operated as a quasi-judicial institution and was commonly referred to as the "attorney general for the Supreme Court." It shared office space with the Court and was considered part of the judicial branch for budgetary purposes. Moreover, in keeping with the office's quasi-judicial character, early attorneys general routinely provided Congress with legal opinions regarding pending legislation. Wirt put a stop to this practice and, in an official opinion on his office's proper role, argued that the attorney general should serve as legal adviser to the executive branch alone.

Lawyer-president Andrew Jackson had no reservations about the attorney general's political loyalty. He fired his attorney general, John Berrien, for disagreeing with Jackson's legal authority to disestablish the national bank and replaced Berrien with Roger Taney, who promptly authored a legal opinion authorizing such actions. Although Congress proceeded to censure Jackson and punish Taney by rejecting his nomination to the Supreme Court (Taney was later renominated and confirmed), an important precedent had been set.

By the time lawyer-president Franklin Pierce assumed office in 1853, the transformation of the attorney general's office was nearly complete. His attorney general, Caleb Cushing, was considered the most outstanding member of Pierce's distinguished cabinet. Cushing condemned any mixture of public office with private practice and turned the post into a full-time position. He expanded the office's duties and increased dramatically the number of opinions authored. By the end of his four years in office, Cushing's opinions filled more than three volumes of *The Official Opinions of the Attorney General*, more than all his predecessors combined. In response, Congress finally raised the office's rank and salary to match those of other cabinet posts.

Like Wirt, Cushing authored an opinion regarding the role of his office. Although the attorney general was originally established as a "quasi-judicial" office, custom and convention had thoroughly "subordinated" it to the president and fixed it as part of the executive branch. Moreover, to effectively dispatch the legal work of the executive branch, Cushing argued that Congress needed to create a law department and bring other government lawyers under the direction of the attorney general. Once again, however, Congress failed to act on the attorney general's request.

The crush of legal work following the Civil War finally goaded Congress into reforming the government's legal administration. In 1870, it established the U.S. Department of Justice and fixed the attorney general as its head. The Justice Department Act made the attorney general a member of the president's cabinet by statutory right, a major step toward consolidating control over the government's legal work. The federal district attorney offices were brought within the new department, and although agency

★ ★ ★

"In 1870, [Congress] established the U.S. Department of Justice and fixed the attorney general as its head. The Justice Department Act made the attorney general a member of the president's cabinet by statutory right, a major step toward consolidating control over the government's legal work."

A. MITCHELL PALMER

President Wilson's attorney general from 1919 to 1921, Palmer gave the Justice Department its modern structure, establishing function-based legal divisions that were each headed by an assistant attorney general. He also initiated the "Palmer Raids" that rounded up thousands of allegedly subversive aliens for deportation, though only a few hundred ultimately met that fate.

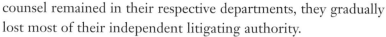

counsel remained in their respective departments, they gradually lost most of their independent litigating authority.

Though Congress was slow to centralize the government's legal work, presidents and courts had supported such change. Presidents since Washington had asked Congress to centralize government lawyering, but even creation of the Justice Department left much to be done. Lawyer-presidents Woodrow Wilson and Franklin Roosevelt were pivotal in this struggle. Each signed executive orders requiring litigation by federal agencies to be conducted by the Justice Department. The Supreme Court also helped. In *United States v. San Jacinto Tin Co.* (1887), the Court recognized the attorney general's common law authority to represent the "United States" in court even when there was an absence of specific statutory authorization to do so. Later, in *Ponzi v. Fessenden* (1922), chief justice and former president Taft clarified the constitutional basis for the attorney general's powers and the office's accountability to the president. Writing for the Court, Taft declared: "The Attorney General is . . . the hand of the President in taking care that the laws of the United States in legal proceedings and in the prosecution of offenses, be faithfully executed."

The growth of the Justice Department mirrored the general development of the federal administrative state during the twentieth century. In 1919, Wilson's attorney general, A. Mitchell Palmer, organized the department into its modern structure by establishing several function-based legal divisions, each headed by an assistant attorney general.

Today's Justice Department is a massive bureaucracy with more than forty major divisions and offices and a budget that exceeded twenty-one billion dollars in FY 2001. Most of the department's 120,000–plus employees are located in its policing and corrections divisions (which include the Federal Bureau of Investigation, the Immigration and Naturalization Service, the Drug Enforcement Administration, the Marshals Service, and the Bureau of Prisons). And most of its attorneys are located either in federal district attorney offices throughout the country or in its central legal divisions, which include Antitrust, Civil Rights, Land and Natural Resources, Criminal, Civil, and Tax divisions. In addition, the department's office of legal counsel is responsible for authoring the official opinions of the attorney general, which are binding on all federal agencies.

As the Justice Department grew and attorneys general became increasingly associated with the political administration of the president, the nature of the office changed. Early attorneys general such as Randolph, Wirt, and Cushing had been highly distinguished members of the bar, given the high level of legal acumen needed when the office was small and the attorney general functioned more as a practicing lawyer. Creation of the Justice Department, however, permitted attorneys general to surround themselves with talented lawyers, and presidents eventually began to seek incumbents more for their political and administrative skills than for their legal talents. Presidents Eisenhower, Kennedy, and Nixon, for example, appointed their campaign managers to be attorneys general (Herbert Brownell, Robert Kennedy, and John Mitchell, respectively), while presidents Truman, Reagan, and George W. Bush all named former senators to the post (J. Howard McGrath, Richard Thornburgh, and John Ashcroft).

In addition, like other cabinet appointments, the attorney general's office increasingly became a presidential vehicle for addressing the demands of influential constituencies. Lawyer-president Bill Clinton fulfilled a pledge to appoint the first woman attorney general when he named Janet Reno to the office in 1993 (two earlier female nominees, Zoe Baird and Kimba Wood, withdrew their names following revelations involving their employment of domestic workers). Similarly, John Ashcroft's appointment was arguably an effort by George W. Bush to placate the right wing of the Republican Party, just as Lyndon Johnson's appointment of Ramsey Clark in 1967 was an important signal to civil rights groups within the Democratic Party.

This should not suggest that modern attorneys general are inadequate as lawyers, only that political and administrative talents have eclipsed legal acumen as the primary qualification for the office. It is telling that the requirement to be "learned in the law" was removed as a statutory prerequisite for the office when it was reconstituted back in 1870. Even more telling, the authoritative encyclopedia *Great American Lawyers* ranks eight attorneys general from the nineteenth century among the great lawyers in history (Edmund Randolph, William Pinkney, Reverdy

★ ★ ★

"Today's Justice Department is a massive bureaucracy with more than forty major divisions and offices and a budget that exceeded twenty-one billion dollars in FY 2001."

Johnson, William Wirt, Caleb Cushing, Jeremiah Black, Edward Bates, and William Evarts), but only three from the twentieth century (Homer Cummings, Robert Jackson, and Francis Biddle) make the list, all appointed by Franklin Roosevelt.

There was an exception to this trend following the Watergate scandal in 1974. The Justice Department was deeply embarrassed by the scandal, during which four attorneys general either resigned or were removed from office. In its wake, efforts to "depoliticize" the administration of justice included congressional creation of an independent counsel's office and pledges by presidents Ford and Carter to appoint attorneys general who were less "political." Ford appointed Edward Levi, former dean at the University of Chicago Law School, and Carter appointed former federal judge Griffin Bell. Both Levi and Bell reformed the Justice Department, seeking to insulate it from improper White House influences and depoliticize conduct of the government's legal work.

These efforts came to an abrupt end in the 1980s, however, when President Reagan appointed close friends and highly partisan individuals to the position. In 1981 he appointed California friend and campaign adviser William French Smith, and in 1985 he appointed his former White House political adviser Edwin Meese. Smith and Meese were unapologetic about allying the Justice Department more closely with White House policymaking and restoring its role as a central actor in pursuing the president's political agenda. While subsequent presidents have varied in how they have viewed the Justice Department's role, they too have generally eschewed post-Watergate notions about its independence from White House politics and have expected political loyalty from their attorneys general.

As the attorney general became a more important political actor, some of its legacy as the nation's premier lawyer was transferred to the solicitor general's office. Established in 1870 to serve as a general administrative assistant to the attorney general, the solicitor general has evolved over time into an elite law office with responsibility for conducting most of the federal government's appellate litigation. The office has developed a special esprit de corps, and young lawyers who work there have usually excelled at the nation's top law schools. The office has developed an especially close relationship with the Supreme Court, where it is both the most frequent and most successful litigant. Its influence over the Court leads some to dub the office the "Tenth Justice."

In contrast to the attorneys general, recent presidents have increasingly sought solicitors general who are elite appellate lawyers and distinguished legal scholars rather than skilled politicians. For example, while John Kennedy appointed his brother Robert—a mediocre law student who had never argued a case in court—to be his attorney general, he named Harvard law professor Archibald Cox as his solicitor general. Similarly, while Richard Nixon appointed his campaign manager John Mitchell to be attorney general, he retained former Harvard Law School dean Erwin Griswold as his solicitor general. When Griswold resigned in 1973, Nixon named distinguished Yale law professor Robert Bork to the post.

In addition to the solicitor general, the White House counsel has become a key legal adviser to modern presidents. Originally established by Franklin Roosevelt in 1941, the post and title of "legal counsel" was largely honorary for decades. As late as 1970, when Richard Nixon appointed John Dean as White House counsel, it was a solo office that took on the character of its occupant. Since 1970, however, the office has become an institutionalized presence in the White House, performing a variety of duties such as advising presidents on the legal implications of legislative and presidential action, managing the administration's judicial selection process, and counseling the White House on ethics laws.

This last function is perhaps its most important. As ethics laws became increasingly complex and a new style of politics-by-scandal emerged in post-Watergate Washington, the counsel's office was transformed into an ethics watchdog. Today's counsel is expected to provide legal clarification of ethics standards to administration officials, screen prospective high-level nominees, and keep the White House out of ethics troubles.

Because the Justice Department prosecutes the same ethics laws that the counsel's office advises the administration about, the White House counsel and attorney general will sometimes become antagonists. And whereas presidents once appointed close friends and confidants to be attorneys general, they are today likely to want these individuals in the counsel's office. For instance,

ROBERT H. BORK: CASES AND CONTROVERSIES

By any measure, Robert Bork has had a distinguished legal career, having served as a Yale law professor, solicitor general, acting attorney general, and federal appeals court judge. Bork also has been at the center of major controversies, among them the Saturday Night Massacre during the Watergate saga and a contentious—and unsuccessful—fight over his nomination by President Reagan to the U.S. Supreme Court. Perhaps more than any others, Bork's experiences exemplify modern disputes about the proper separation of law and politics on the national scene.

when President Ford appointed Edward Levi—a man he knew only professionally—to head the Justice Department, he named his close friend and former law partner Philip Buchen to be his counsel. Similarly, while President Clinton named someone he barely knew, Janet Reno, to be attorney general, he named his old friend Bernard Nussbaum as his counsel. Nussbaum's ties to the Clintons went back to 1974, when Hillary served with him as staff to the House committee considering impeachment of Richard Nixon.

The counsel's dual role of enforcing ethical standards while protecting the administration from political scandal is full of pitfalls. It is precisely this delicate balancing act that sealed the fate of at least two recent White House counsel who served lawyer-presidents. John Dean was forced to resign during Watergate and Bernard Nussbaum became a casualty of the Whitewater and Monica Lewinsky scandals engulfing the Clinton administration.

When this happens, it is not unusual for presidents to look for counsel with whom they have no personal ties and who can restore confidence in the White House. Thus, when President Clinton sought to restore faith in his scandal-ridden White House, he appointed longtime Washington lawyer Lloyd Cutler as his counsel, followed by former congressman and Court of Appeals judge Abner Mikva and former U.S. attorney and D.C. corporate counsel Charles Ruff.

The relationship between the president and his key legal advisers has evolved over time as the role of law in the American political system has changed. But are there specific differences in how lawyer-presidents have managed these relationships as compared with other presidents? Has a shared professional training made any difference in how presidents relate to the attorney general and other key legal advisers?

Lawyer-presidents have appointed forty-eight of the nation's seventy-nine attorneys general. On average, these attorneys general served slightly longer in office than those appointed by non-lawyers—2.83 years on average compared to 2.48 years. Lawyer-presidents also have appointed the longest-serving attorneys general in history: William Wirt, who served twelve years under presidents Monroe and Adams; Janet Reno, who served eight years under President Clinton; and Homer S. Cummings, who served six years under President Franklin Roosevelt. It was also lawyer-presidents Tyler and Fillmore who appointed the only individual to serve as attorney general on two separate occasions, John J. Crittenden. Beyond these superficial differences, however, there are few simple patterns in how lawyer- and nonlawyer-presidents interact with their attorneys general and other key legal advisers.

Clearly, however, lawyer-presidents have appointed many of the most distinguished and capable attorneys general in history. This may reflect their greater familiarity with professional norms and their sensitivities about the most visible public position representing their profession. For example, of the greatest attorneys general during the nineteenth century—Edmund Randolph, William Wirt, Caleb Cushing, and Edward Bates—all but Randolph were appointed by a lawyer-president.

While Wirt and Cushing played crucial roles in defining the attorney general's office and making it into the powerful post that it is today, Edward Bates distinguished himself when the nation's commitment to the rule of law was put to its severest test. As attorney general for Abraham Lincoln, Bates demonstrated brilliance in finding legal rationales for Lincoln's wartime policies. In *Ex parte Merryman* (1861), for example, the Court created a dilemma for Lincoln by ordering a writ of habeas corpus on behalf of an active secessionist whom the president refused to release. Bates authored an opinion that provided the president with a way out of the legal impasse, arguing that the separation of powers permitted the president to lawfully refuse to obey a court writ during a period of crisis. Similarly, Bates authored a classic opinion to support Lincoln's authority to issue the Emancipation Proclamation in 1862, and in *The Prize Cases* (1863), he successfully defended Lincoln's naval blockade of the South before a skeptical but ultimately supportive Supreme Court.

In each of these cases, Bates's legal advocacy challenged existing legal doctrines and cut new constitutional ground. Nevertheless, Bates was mindful that the rule of law also imposed limits on government, even during civil war. He often found himself at odds with Secretary of War Edwin Stanton and other Republican radicals who were impatient with legal constraints on their actions. In one instance, Stanton attempted to bypass the civilian court system and permit direct military appropriation of civilian property. Furious with this effort to end

EDWARD BATES: LINCOLN'S BRILLIANT ATTORNEY GENERAL

During the Civil War, Lincoln's wartime policies faced significant legal challenges, and his attorney general, Edward Bates, was on the legal front lines defending them. Bates issued an opinion, for example, supporting Lincoln's authority to issue the Emancipation Proclamation and later defended Lincoln's naval blockade of the South before the Supreme Court. In all such cases, Bates steadfastly sought to respect limitations imposed by the rule of law, even though it was wartime. A native Virginian who spent his adult life in St. Louis, Bates was the first cabinet member chosen from west of the Mississippi River.

FRANCIS BIDDLE: ROOSEVELT'S ATTORNEY GENERAL DURING WWII

Biddle brought a distinguished résumé to the attorney general's office in 1941, having been counsel to Oliver Wendell Holmes, head of the National Labor Relations Board, a federal appeals court judge, and solicitor general. Like Lincoln's attorney general, Edward Bates, Biddle sought to preserve the rule of law during wartime, arguing for example with the War Department against the internment of Japanese Americans. After leaving the office in 1945, Biddle further distinguished himself as a judge at the Nuremberg War Tribunal and a prominent critic of Senator Joseph McCarthy.

run civilian administration, Bates went to Lincoln and secured an executive order requiring the president's approval for all proceedings involving government confiscation of property. Bates also refused to authorize Stanton's efforts to extend the jurisdiction of military courts over civilians. Although the practice was later authorized by his successor, Bates remained steadfast in his opposition and his view was eventually vindicated when the Supreme Court declared the practice unconstitutional in *Ex parte Milligan* (1866). In a famous explanation of his commitment to the rule of law, even during war, Bates wrote a friend: "The office I hold is not properly political, but strictly legal; and it is my duty, above all other ministers of State to uphold the Law and resist all encroachments, from whatever quarter, of mere will and power."

During the twentieth century, there were only seven lawyer-presidents, but they too appointed some of the most outstanding attorneys general. For instance, of the six attorneys general during the twentieth century who went on to serve as justices of the U.S. Supreme Court, four were attorneys general under lawyer-presidents—James McReynolds (Wilson), Harlan Fiske Stone (Coolidge), Frank Murphy (FDR), and Robert Jackson (FDR). FDR also appointed the single most talented group of attorneys general in history—Homer Cummings, Frank Murphy, Robert Jackson, and Francis Biddle. All but Murphy appear on a list of the hundred greatest lawyers in American history.

While many are familiar with Jackson's role during the Nuremburg trials and as a Supreme Court justice, the careers of Cummings and Biddle, though less well known, are no less distinguished. Cummings, who served as attorney general from 1933 to 1939, was one of Roosevelt's closest advisers and the crucial figure in the administration's battle with the Court over the president's New Deal programs. His close relationship with Roosevelt, his skilled advocacy for the administration's programs, and his criticism of the Court and its outmoded legal doctrines became the model for a more politicized attorney general's office in the twentieth century. After leaving office, Cummings and historian Carl McFarland wrote *Federal Justice* (1937), the first extensive history of the Justice Department and an important resource for scholars and historians.

Francis Biddle served in the office from 1941 to 1945. Prior to becoming attorney general, he had been a private lawyer for Oliver Wendell Holmes. He had also served as head of the National Labor Relations Board, a U.S. Circuit Court of Appeals judge, and solicitor general. World War II dominated his tenure in office. Like Bates during the Civil War, Biddle often found himself at odds with the War Department. He argued strenuously with the president against the administration's ill-conceived mass internment of Japanese Americans. Although he lost the debate within the cabinet, he made clear to the president that the Justice Department would have nothing to do with the program. After the war, Biddle served with Jackson on the Nuremberg War Tribunal. Later, he became a prominent critic of Senator Joseph McCarthy and the hearings on un-American activities, later detailing his views in one of several books he authored.

A president's background as a lawyer, however, does not mean he will share his attorney general's legal knowledge or professional commitment. Although the attorney general post is no longer the elite legal office it once was, its duties and roles still require a far stronger connection to the legal profession than the presidency. It is thus not uncommon for an attorney general to experience frustration with a president's lack of legal expertise. Francis Biddle, for example, frequently questioned FDR's legal skills. In one episode, FDR sent a memo urging Biddle to mount a legal challenge to state poll taxes, hoping this would increase the number of Democratic voters. Biddle later remembered: "The memorandum was patently F.D.R.'s own thinking, not . . . that of any other lawyer. It was naive and breathed of legal innocence that could not be dispelled by his throwing in a 'quo-warranto' and 'order to show cause.'"

Moreover, if lawyer-presidents have appointed some of the most distinguished attorneys general in history, they have also been responsible for appointing some who brought the office into disrepute. For example, Woodrow Wilson's attorney general, A. Mitchell Palmer, conducted a series of investigations and raids that one historian called "the most bizarre performance by any Attorney General" in history. In the so-called Palmer Raids, a response to a spate of letter bombs sent by left-wing extremists, he launched investigations into more than sixty thousand Americans, summarily arresting and deporting some five thousand

★ ★ ★

"Established in 1870 to serve as a general administrative assistant to the attorney general, the solicitor general has evolved over time into an elite barrister with responsibility for conducting most of the federal government's appellate litigation . . . [and having] an especially close relationship with the Supreme Court, where it is the most frequent and most successful litigant."

individuals with little regard for the due process rights of the accused. A short time later, in 1924, Warren Harding's attorney general, Harry Daugherty, was forced to resign amidst conspiracy charges relating to the Teapot Dome scandal, and in 1952, Harry Truman's attorney general, James Howard McGrath, was forced to resign amidst tax fraud and conspiracy charges.

The most damaging scandal ever to involve the attorney general and the Justice Department was Watergate. Lawyer-president Richard Nixon's first two attorneys general, John Mitchell and Richard Kleindienst, were forced from office and eventually indicted on conspiracy charges for their role in covering up illegal activities by Nixon campaign officials. Mitchell was eventually convicted and sentenced to prison.

To restore confidence in the Justice Department, Nixon appointed Elliot Richardson in 1973. But when Nixon ordered Richardson to fire Archibald Cox, the special prosecutor appointed to investigate Watergate, Richardson himself resigned in protest. Richardson's resignation set in motion the so-called Saturday Night Massacre in which the deputy attorney general and special prosecutor were also removed from office. Nixon's actions sparked a firestorm, and in the face of impeachment hearings and a unanimous Supreme Court decision requiring production of certain tape recordings, Nixon himself resigned his office in 1974.

Nixon would have done well to listen to his legal advisers. When White House counsel John Dean learned about the extent of White House involvement in Watergate, he advised Nixon to come clean and excise the "cancer" growing on the presidency. Similarly, Richardson urged Nixon to take actions to save his presidency and to comply fully with federal investigations. Nixon refused, and his effort to cover up illegal actions by others in his administration eventually led to his own downfall.

Nixon's successor lawyer-presidents similarly ignored counsel from their legal advisers, relying instead upon their own counsel. Gerald Ford's close relationship with Philip Buchen did not keep the president from making perhaps his most momentous legal decision, the pardoning of Richard Nixon, without any prior consultation with Buchen, a move that angered his counsel. And Bill Clinton, a former state attorney general and law professor himself, displayed a curious lack of attention to his relationships with key legal advisers. Despite his close personal ties to the Clintons, Bernard Nussbaum complained often about feeling isolated in the White House and lacking input into important legal policy decisions.

The relationship between presidents and their key legal advisers has been shaped far more by historical changes than by the professional backgrounds of individual presidents. As law became an important arena for public policymaking in the twentieth century, attorneys general came to be prized more for their political and administrative skill than their legal acumen. As the power and size of the administrative state grew, the need for specialization within the Justice Department led the solicitor general to become the elite appellate lawyer's office that the attorney general once had been. And as scandal-style politics and a new ethics emerged after the 1970s, the White House counsel's office became a post occupied by close presidential friends and loyalists.

Nevertheless, lawyer-presidents do interact with their key attorneys and legal advisers differently from nonlawyer-presidents. For some, it perhaps led to greater complacency and a willingness to dismiss the legal advice they received. It is hard to ignore the fact that of the four American presidents either censured or subjected to impeachment proceedings in history, three were lawyers (Jackson, Nixon, and Clinton). All would have fared better had they been more willing to follow counsel from their legal advisers. Just as lawyers who represent themselves are said to have fools for clients, the lesson here may be that lawyer-presidents who seek their own counsel and disregard their institutionalized legal advisers only court disaster.

On the other hand, other lawyer-presidents clearly have been more concerned about the rule of law and the offices most responsible for its administration. Most of the great lawyers to serve as attorneys general were selected by lawyer-presidents. Moreover, nearly all of the truly outstanding attorneys general in American history served under lawyer-presidents. Some left their mark by changing the very nature of the office they held. Others became great attorneys general by performing their duties during periods of war or national peril when the nation's legal institutions were put to their severest test. Each exemplified the profession's commitment to the rule of law, and this remains perhaps the most lasting and important legacy of the lawyer-presidents who appointed them.

THE FIRST SOLICITOR GENERAL

In 1870, President Grant appointed Benjamin Bristow, a distinguished lawyer and Union cavalry colonel, as the first U.S. solicitor general. Bristow went on to serve as Grant's secretary of the treasury, where he reorganized the scandal-ridden department and prosecuted the powerful Whiskey Ring. In 1876, he pursued the Republican presidential nomination but lost on the eighth ballot to Rutherford Hayes. Bristow later chaired the founding meeting of the American Bar Association in 1878 and served as its second president.

ATTORNEY GENERAL APPOINTMENTS

PRESIDENT	ATTORNEY GENERAL	TERM
George Washington	Edmund Randolph	1789–94
George Washington	William Bradford	1794–95
George Washington and John Adams	Charles Lee	1795–1801
Thomas Jefferson	Levi Lincoln	1801–5
Thomas Jefferson	John Breckenridge	1805–6
Thomas Jefferson and James Madison	Caesar A. Rodney	1807–11
James Madison	William Pinkney	1811–14
James Madison	Richard Rush	1814–17
James Monroe and John Quincy Adams	William Wirt	1817–29
Andrew Jackson	John M. Berrien	1829–31
Andrew Jackson	Roger B. Taney	1831–33
Andrew Jackson and Martin Van Buren	Benjamin F. Butler	1833–38
Martin Van Buren	Felix Grundy	1838–39
Martin Van Buren	Henry D. Gilpin	1840–41
William Henry Harrison and John Tyler	John J. Crittenden	1841
John Tyler	Hugh S. Legare	1841–43
John Tyler	John Nelson	1843–45
James K. Polk	John Y. Mason	1845–46
James K. Polk	Nathan Clifford	1846–48
James K. Polk	Issac Toucey	1848–49
Zachary Taylor	Reverdy Johnson	1849–50
Millard Fillmore	John J. Crittenden	1850–53
Franklin Pierce	Caleb Cushing	1853–57
James Buchanan	Jeremiah S. Black	1857–60
James Buchanan	Edwin M. Stanton	1860–61
Abraham Lincoln	Edward Bates	1861–64
Abraham Lincoln and Andrew Johnson	James Speed	1864–66
Andrew Johnson	Henry Stanberry	1866–68
Andrew Johnson	William M. Evarts	1868–69

President	Attorney General	Term
Ulysses S. Grant	Ebenezer R. Hoar	1869–70
Ulysses S. Grant	Amos T. Akerman	1870–72
Ulysses S. Grant	George H. Williams	1871–75
Ulysses S. Grant	Edwards Pierrepont	1875–76
Ulysses S. Grant	Alphonso Taft	1876–77
Rutherford B. Hayes	Charles Devens	1877–81
James A. Garfield	Wayne MacVeagh	1881
Chester A. Arthur	Benjamin H. Brewster	1881–85
Grover Cleveland	Augustus H. Garland	1885–89
Benjamin Harrison	William H. H. Miller	1889–93
Grover Cleveland	Richard Olney	1893–95
Grover Cleveland	Judson Harmon	1895–97
William McKinley	Joseph McKenna	1897–98
William McKinley	John W. Griggs	1898–1901
William McKinley	Philander C. Knox	1901–4
Theodore Roosevelt	William H. Moody	1904–6
Theodore Roosevelt	Charles J. Bonaparte	1906–9
William Howard Taft	George W. Wickersham	1909–13
Woodrow Wilson	James C. McReynolds	1913–14
Woodrow Wilson	Thomas Watt Gregory	1914–19
Woodrow Wilson	A. Mitchell Palmer	1919–21
Warren G. Harding	Harry M. Daugherty	1921–24
Calvin Coolidge	Harlan Fiske Stone	1924–25
Calvin Coolidge	John T. Sargent	1925–29
Herbert Hoover	William D. Mitchell	1929–33
Franklin Delano Roosevelt	Homer S. Cummings	1933–39
Franklin Delano Roosevelt	Frank Murphy	1939–40
Franklin Delano Roosevelt	Robert H. Jackson	1940–41
Franklin Delano Roosevelt	Francis Biddle	1941–45
Harry S. Truman	Tom C. Clark	1945–49
Harry S. Truman	J. Howard McGrath	1949–52
Harry S. Truman	James P. McGranery	1952–53
Dwight D. Eisenhower	Herbert Brownell Jr.	1953–57
Dwight D. Eisenhower	William P. Rogers	1957–61
John F. Kennedy	Robert F. Kennedy	1961–64

PRESIDENT	ATTORNEY GENERAL	TERM
Lyndon B. Johnson	Nicholas deB. Katzenbach	1965–66
Lyndon B. Johnson	Ramsey Clark	1967–69
Richard M. Nixon	John N. Mitchell	1969–72
Richard M. Nixon	Richard G. Kleindienst	1972–73
Richard M. Nixon	Elliot L. Richardson	1973
Richard M. Nixon	William B. Saxbe	1974–75
Gerald R. Ford	Edward H. Levi	1975–77
Jimmy Carter	Griffin B. Bell	1977–79
Jimmy Carter	Benjamin R. Civiletti	1979–81
Ronald Reagan	William French Smith	1981–85
Ronald Reagan	Edwin Meese III	1985–88
Ronald Reagan and George Bush	Richard Thornburgh	1988–91
George Bush	William Barr	1991–93
William Jefferson Clinton	Janet Reno	1993–2001
George W. Bush	John Ashcroft	2001–

SOLICITOR GENERAL APPOINTMENTS

PRESIDENT	SOLICITOR GENERAL	TERM
Ulysses S. Grant	Benjamin H. Bristow	1870–72
Ulysses S. Grant	Samuel F. Phillips	1872–85
Grover Cleveland	John Goode (Acting)	1885–86
Grover Cleveland	George A. Jenks	1886–89
Benjamin Harrison	Orlow W. Chapman	1889–90
Benjamin Harrison	William Howard Taft	1890–92
Benjamin Harrison	Charles H. Aldrich	1892–93
Grover Cleveland	Lawrence Maxwell Jr.	1893–95
Grover Cleveland	Holmes Conrad	1895–97
William McKinley	John K. Richards	1897–1903
Theodore Roosevelt	Henry M. Hoyt	1903–9
William Howard Taft	Lloyd Wheaton Bowers	1909–10
William Howard Taft	Frederick W. Lehmann	1910–12
William Howard Taft	William Marshall Bullit	1912–13

President	Solicitor General	Term
Woodrow Wilson	John William Davis	1913–18
Woodrow Wilson	Alexander C. King	1918–20
Woodrow Wilson	William L. Frierson	1920–21
Warren G. Harding	James M. Beck	1921–25
Calvin Coolidge	William D. Mitchell	1925–29
Herbert Hoover	Charles Evans Hughes Jr.	1929–30
Herbert Hoover	Thomas D. Thacher	1930–33
Franklin Delano Roosevelt	James Crawford Biggs	1933–35
Franklin Delano Roosevelt	Stanley Reed	1935–38
Franklin Delano Roosevelt	Robert H. Jackson	1938–40
Franklin Delano Roosevelt	Francis Biddle	1940–41
Franklin Delano Roosevelt	Charles Fahy	1941–45
Harry S. Truman	J. Howard McGrath	1945–46
Harry S. Truman	Philip B. Perlman	1947–52
Harry S. Truman	Walter J. Cummings Jr.	1952–53
Dwight D. Eisenhower	Simon E. Sobeloff	1954–56
Dwight D. Eisenhower	J. Lee Rankin	1956–61
John F. Kennedy	Archibald Cox	1961–65
Lyndon B. Johnson	Thurgood Marshall	1965–67
Lyndon B. Johnson	Erwin N. Griswold	1967–73
Richard M. Nixon	Robert H. Bork	1973–77
Jimmy Carter	Wade H. McCree	1977–81
Ronald Reagan	Rex Lee	1981–85
Ronald Reagan	Charles Fried	1985–89
George Bush	Kenneth W. Starr	1989–93
William Jefferson Clinton	Drew S. Days III	1993–96
William Jefferson Clinton	Seth P. Waxman	1997–2001
George W. Bush	Theodore B. Olson	2001–

FURTHER READINGS

AMERICAN LEGAL HISTORY

Friedman, Lawrence M. *A History of American Law.* 2nd ed. New York: Simon and Schuster, 1985.
———. *Law in America: A Short History.* New York: Modern Library, 2002.
Hall, Kermit L. *The Magic Mirror: Law in American History.* New York: Oxford University Press, 1989.
———, William M. Wiecek, and Paul Finkelman. *American Legal History: Cases and Materials.* New York: Oxford University Press, 1991.

JOHN ADAMS

Coquillette, Daniel R. "Justinian in Braintree: John Adams, Civilian Learning, and Legal Elitism, 1758–1775." In *Law in Colonial Massachusetts, 1630–1800,* 359–418. Boston: Colonial Society of Massachusetts, 1984.
Ellis, Joseph J. *Passionate Sage: The Character and Legacy of John Adams.* 2nd ed. New York: Norton, 2001.
McCullough, David. *John Adams.* New York: Simon and Schuster, 2001.
Ryerson, Richard Alan, ed. *John Adams and the Founding of the Republic.* Boston: Massachusetts Historical Society, 2001.
Wroth, L. Kinvin, and Hiller B. Zobel, eds. *Legal Papers of John Adams.* Cambridge: Belknap Press of Harvard University Press, 1965.

THOMAS JEFFERSON

Dewey, Frank L. *Thomas Jefferson, Lawyer.* Charlottesville: University Press of Virginia, 1986.
Dumbauld, Edward. *Thomas Jefferson and the Law.* Norman: University of Oklahoma Press, 1978.
Konig, David T. "Legal Fictions and the Rule(s) of Law: The Jeffersonian Critique of Common-Law Adjudication." In *The Many Legalities of Early America,* edited by Christopher L. Tomlins and Bruce H. Mann. Chapel Hill: University of North Carolina Press, 2001.
Mayer, David N. *The Constitutional Thought of Thomas Jefferson.* Charlottesville: University Press of Virginia, 1994.

JAMES MONROE

Ammon, Harry. *James Monroe: The Quest for National Identity.* New York: McGraw-Hill, 1971.
Cunningham, Nobel E. *The Presidency of James Monroe.* Lawrence: University Press of Kansas, 1996.
Preston, Daniel, ed. *The Papers of James Monroe: Correspondence and Papers, 1776–1791.* Vol. 2. Westport, Conn.: Greenwood Press, forthcoming.

JOHN QUINCY ADAMS

Bemis, Samuel F. *John Quincy Adams and the Union.* New York: Knopf, 1956.
Jones, Howard. *Mutiny on the Amistad: The Saga of a Slave Revolt and Its Impact on American Abolition, Law, and Diplomacy.* New York: Oxford University Press, 1987.
McGrath, C. Peter. *Yazoo: Law and Politics in the New Republic: The Case of Fletcher v. Peck.* Providence: Brown University Press, 1966.
Nagel, Paul C. *John Quincy Adams: A Public Life, a Private Life.* New York: Knopf, 1997.
Richards, Leonard L. *The Life and Times of Congressman John Quincy Adams.* New York: Oxford University Press, 1986.

ANDREW JACKSON

Booraem, Hendrik. *Young Hickory: The Making of Andrew Jackson.* Dallas: Taylor Trade Publications, 2001.
Cole, Donald B. *The Presidency of Andrew Jackson.* Lawrence: University Press of Kansas, 1993.
Ely, James W., Jr., and Theodore Brown Jr., eds. *Legal Papers of Andrew Jackson.* Knoxville: University of Tennessee Press, 1987.
Remini, Robert V. *Andrew Jackson and the Course of the American Empire, 1767–1821.* New York: Harper and Row, 1977.
Ward, John William. *Andrew Jackson: Symbol for an Age.* New York: Oxford University Press, 1955.

MARTIN VAN BUREN

Cole, Donald B. *Martin Van Buren and the American Political System.* Princeton, N.J.: Princeton University Press, 1984.

Fitzpatrick, John C., ed. *The Autobiography of Martin Van Buren.* Washington, D.C.: GPO, 1920.

Mushkat, Jerome, and Joseph G. Rayback. *Martin Van Buren: Law, Politics, and the Shaping of Republican Ideology.* DeKalb: Northern Illinois University Press, 1997.

Niven, John. *Martin Van Buren: The Romantic Age of American Politics.* New York: Oxford University Press, 1983.

Wilson, Major L. *The Presidency of Martin Van Buren.* Lawrence: University Press of Kansas, 1984.

JOHN TYLER

Chitwood, Oliver P. *John Tyler: Champion of the Old South.* New York and London: D. Appleton-Century, 1939.

Peterson, Norma Lois. *The Presidencies of William Henry Harrison and John Tyler.* Lawrence: University Press of Kansas, 1989.

Seager, Robert, II. *And Tyler, Too.* New York: McGraw-Hill, 1963.

Shepard, E. Lee. "Lawyers Look at Themselves: Professional Consciousness and the Virginia Bar, 1770–1850." *American Journal of Legal History 25*, no. 1 (1981).

Tyler, Lyon G. *The Letters and Times of the Tylers.* Richmond, Va.: Whittet and Shepperson, 1884–96.

JAMES K. POLK

Bergeron, Paul H. *The Presidency of James K. Polk.* Lawrence: University Press of Kansas, 1987.

Sellers, Charles G., Jr. *James K. Polk, Continentalist, 1843–1846.* Princeton, N.J.: Princeton University Press, 1966.

———. *James K. Polk, Jacksonian, 1795–1843.* Princeton, N.J.: Princeton University Press, 1957.

Weaver, Herbert, Paul H. Bergeron, and Wayne Cutler, eds. *Correspondence of James K. Polk.* 9 vols. Nashville: Vanderbilt University Press, 1969–96.

MILLARD FILLMORE

Grayson, Benson Lee. *The Unknown President: The Administration of Millard Fillmore.* Lanham, Md.: Rowman and Littlefield, 1981.

Rayback, Robert J. *Millard Fillmore: Biography of a President.* Buffalo, N.Y.: Buffalo Historical Society, 1959.

Severance, Frank H., ed. *Millard Fillmore Papers.* 2 vols. Buffalo, N.Y.: Buffalo Historical Society, 1907.

Smith, Elbert B. *The Presidencies of Zachary Taylor and Millard Fillmore.* Lawrence: University Press of Kansas, 1988.

FRANKLIN PIERCE

Cross, David. "Franklin Pierce the Lawyer." In *Proceedings of the Bar Association of the State of New Hampshire.* Vol. 1. Concord, N.H.: Rumford Press, 1900–3.

Gara, Larry. *The Presidency of Franklin Pierce.* Lawrence: University Press of Kansas, 1991.

Nichols, Roy F. *Franklin Pierce: Young Hickory of the Granite Hills.* 2nd ed. Norwalk, Conn.: Easton Press, 1988.

JAMES BUCHANAN

Fehrenbacher, Don E. *The Dred Scott Case: Its Significance in American Law and Politics.* New York: Oxford University Press, 1978.

Klein, Philip S. *President James Buchanan.* University Park: Pennsylvania State University Press, 1962.

Moore, John B., ed. *The Works of James Buchanan.* 12 vols. Philadelphia and London: J. B. Lippincott, 1908–11.

Smith, Elbert B. *The Presidency of James Buchanan.* Lawrence: University Press of Kansas, 1975.

ABRAHAM LINCOLN

Benner, Martha L., et al., eds. *The Law Practice of Abraham Lincoln: Complete Documentary Edition.* Champaign: University of Illinois Press, 2000.

Donald, David Herbert. *Lincoln.* New York: Simon and Schuster, 1995.

Frank, John P. *Lincoln as a Lawyer.* Urbana: University of Illinois Press, 1961.

Paludan, Philip Shaw. *The Presidency of Abraham Lincoln.* Lawrence: University Press of Kansas, 1994.

Stowell, Daniel W., ed. *In Tender Consideration: Women, Families, and the Law in Abraham Lincoln's Illinois.* Urbana: University of Illinois Press, 2002.

RUTHERFORD B. HAYES

Barnard, Harry. *Rutherford B. Hayes and His America.* Indianapolis: Bobbs-Merrill, 1954.

Davison, Kenneth E. *The Presidency of Rutherford B. Hayes.* Westport, Conn.: Greenwood Press, 1972.

Hoogenboom, Ari. *Rutherford B. Hayes: Warrior and President*. Lawrence: University Press of Kansas, 1995.

Williams, Charles Richard, ed. *The Diary and Letters of Rutherford Birchard Hayes, Nineteenth President of the United States*. 5 vols. Columbus: Ohio State Archeological and Historical Society, 1922–26.

JAMES A. GARFIELD

Brown, Harry J., and Frederick D. Williams, eds. *The Diary of James A. Garfield*. 4 vols. East Lansing: Michigan State University, 1967–81.

Leech, Margaret P., and Harry Brown. *The Garfield Orbit*. New York: Harper and Row, 1978.

Peskin, Allan. *Garfield*. Kent, Ohio: Kent State University Press, 1978.

CHESTER A. ARTHUR

Doenecke, Justus D. *The Presidencies of James A. Garfield and Chester A. Arthur*. Lawrence: Regents Press of Kansas, 1981.

Reeves, Thomas C. *Gentleman Boss: The Life of Chester Alan Arthur*. New York: Knopf, 1975; Newtown, Conn.: American Political Biography Press, 1991.

GROVER CLEVELAND

Nevins, Allan. *Grover Cleveland: A Study in Courage*. New York: Dodd, Mead, 1932.

Welch, Richard E., Jr. *The Presidencies of Grover Cleveland*. Lawrence: University Press of Kansas, 1988.

BENJAMIN HARRISON

Sievers, Harry. *Benjamin Harrison*. 3 vols. Chicago: H. Regnery, 1952–68.

Spetter, Allan B., and Homer E. Socolofsky. *The Presidency of Benjamin Harrison*. Lawrence: University Press of Kansas, 1987.

WILLIAM MCKINLEY

Gould, Lewis. *The Presidency of William McKinley*. Lawrence: Regents Press of Kansas, 1980.

Leech, Margaret. *In the Days of McKinley*. New York: Harper, 1959.

Morgan, H. Wayne. *William McKinley and His America*. Syracuse: Syracuse University Press, 1963; Kent, Ohio: Kent State University Press, 2003.

WILLIAM HOWARD TAFT

Anderson, Donald F. *William Howard Taft: A Conservative's Conception of the Presidency*. Ithaca, N.Y.: Cornell University Press, 1968.

Coletta, Paolo. *The Presidency of William Howard Taft*. Lawrence: University Press of Kansas, 1973.

Mason, Alpheus Thomas. *William Howard Taft: Chief Justice*. New York: Simon and Schuster, 1965.

Pringle, Henry F. *The Life and Times of William Howard Taft: A Biography*. 2 vols. New York and Toronto: Farrar and Rinehart, 1939.

WOODROW WILSON

Bragdon, Henry Wilkinson. *Woodrow Wilson: The Academic Years*. Cambridge: Harvard University Press, 1967.

Link, Arthur S. *Wilson*. 5 vols. Princeton, N.J.: Princeton University Press, 1947–66.

Smith, Gene. *When the Cheering Stopped: The Last Years of Woodrow Wilson*. New York: Morrow, 1964.

Thrash, Thomas W. "Apprenticeship at the Bar: The Atlanta Law Practice of Woodrow Wilson." *Georgia State Bar Journal* 28, no. 147 (1992).

CALVIN COOLIDGE

Coolidge, Calvin. *Autobiography of Calvin Coolidge*. New York: Cosmopolitan Book Corporation, 1929.

Ferrell, Robert H. *The Presidency of Calvin Coolidge*. Lawrence: University Press of Kansas, 1998.

Haynes, John Earl, ed. *Calvin Coolidge and the Coolidge Era: Essays on the History of the 1920s*. Washington, D.C.: Library of Congress; Hanover, N.H.: University Press of New England, 1998.

Sobel, Robert. *Coolidge: An American Enigma*. Washington, D.C.: Regnery, 1998.

FRANKLIN DELANO ROOSEVELT

Burns, James MacGregor. *Roosevelt: The Lion and the Fox*. New York: Harcourt, Brace, 1956.

———. *Roosevelt: The Soldier of Freedom*. New York: Harcourt Brace Jovanovich, 1970.

Freidel, Frank. *Franklin D. Roosevelt: A Rendezvous with Destiny*. Boston: Little, Brown, 1990.

Leuchtenburg, William E. *Franklin D. Roosevelt and the New Deal*. New York: Harper and Row, 1963.

———. *The Supreme Court Reborn: The Constitutional Revolution in the Age of Roosevelt.* New York: Oxford University Press, 1995.

RICHARD M. NIXON

Ambrose, Stephen E. *Nixon.* 3 vols. New York: Simon and Schuster, 1988–91.

Dash, Samuel. *Chief Counsel: Inside the Ervin Committee—the Untold Story of Watergate.* New York: Random House, 1976.

Garment, Leonard. *Crazy Rhythm: My Journey from Brooklyn, Jazz, and Wall Street to Nixon's White House, Watergate, and Beyond.* New York: Times Books, 1997.

Gellman, Irwin F. *The Contender, Richard Nixon: The Congress Years, 1946–1952.* New York: Free Press, 1999.

Nixon, Richard. *RN: The Memoirs of Richard Nixon.* New York: Grosset and Dunlap, 1978.

GERALD R. FORD

Cannon, James. *Time and Chance: Gerald Ford's Appointment with History.* New York: HarperCollins, 1994.

Ford, Gerald R. *A Time to Heal: The Autobiography of Gerald R. Ford.* New York: Harper and Row, 1979.

Greene, John Robert. *The Presidency of Gerald R. Ford.* Lawrence: University Press of Kansas, 1995.

Reichley, A. James. *Conservatives in an Age of Change: The Nixon and Ford Administrations.* Washington, D.C.: Brookings Institution, 1981.

Woodward, Bob. "Gerald R. Ford." In *Profiles in Courage for Our Time*, edited by Caroline Kennedy. New York: Hyperion, 2002.

WILLIAM JEFFERSON CLINTON

Drew, Elizabeth. *The Showdown between the Gingrich Congress and the Clinton White House.* New York: Simon and Schuster, 1996.

Maraniss, David. *First in His Class: A Biography of Bill Clinton.* New York: Simon and Schuster, 1995.

Toobin, Jeffrey. *A Vast Conspiracy: The Real Story of the Sex Scandal That Nearly Brought Down a President.* New York: Simon and Schuster, 2000.

Woodward, Bob. *Shadow: Five Presidents and the Legacy of Watergate.* New York: Touchstone Books, 2000.

SUPREME COURT AND JUDICIAL APPOINTMENTS

Abraham, Henry J. *Justices, Presidents, and Senators: A History of U.S. Supreme Court Appointments from Washington to Clinton.* Lanham, Md.: Rowman and Littlefield, 1999.

Goldman, Sheldon. *Picking Federal Judges: Lower Court Selection from Roosevelt to Reagan.* New Haven: Yale University Press, 1997.

Hall, Kermit L., et al. *The Oxford Companion to the Supreme Court of the United States.* New York: Oxford University Press, 1992.

ATTORNEYS GENERAL AND SOLICITORS GENERAL

Clayton, Cornell. *The Politics of Justice: The Attorney General and the Making of Legal Policy.* Armonk, N.Y.: M. E. Sharpe, 1992.

———, ed. *Government Lawyers: The Federal Legal Bureaucracy and Presidential Politics.* Lawrence: University Press of Kansas, 1995.

Salokar, Rebecca Mae. *The Solicitor General: The Politics of Law.* Philadelphia: Temple University Press, 1992.

CONTRIBUTORS

Jean H. Baker is professor of history at Goucher College and the author of nine books, including *Mary Todd Lincoln: A Biography*, *The Stevensons: A Biography of an American Family*, and a forthcoming biography of James Buchanan.

David H. Bennett is Meredith Professor of History at the Maxwell School, Syracuse University, and the author of *The Party of Fear: The American Far Right from Nativism to the Militia Movement* and other books on American history.

Cornell W. Clayton is professor of political science at Washington State University who has published extensively on American law and judicial politics, including *The Politics of Justice: The Attorney General and the Making of Legal Policy*.

Melvyn Dubofsky is Bartle Distinguished Professor of History and Sociology at Binghamton University, State University of New York, and author of numerous books and essays in U.S. history, including *The State and Labor in Modern America*.

Paul Finkelman is Chapman Distinguished Professor of Law at the University of Tulsa College of Law and author of numerous works on American legal history, race and the law, and First Amendment issues.

Russell Fowler is managing attorney of the Chattanooga Office of Legal Aid of East Tennessee and an adjunct professor of political science at the University of Tennessee at Chattanooga. He has published numerous works on legal and political history.

Lawrence M. Friedman is Marion Rice Kirkwood Professor of Law at Stanford University and the author of many books and articles on American legal history, including *The Legal System: A Social Science Perspective* and *A History of American Law*.

Irwin F. Gellman is a historian who concentrates on American foreign policy and the presidency in the twentieth century. His most recent book, *The Contender*, is the first in a multivolume biography of Richard Nixon.

Eugene C. Gerhart is of counsel to the Binghamton, New York, law firm of Coughlin & Gerhart, LLP, editor in chief emeritus of the *New York State Bar Journal*, and the author of biographies of Robert Jackson and Arthur Vanderbilt.

Lewis L. Gould is Eugene C. Baker Centennial Professor Emeritus in American History at the University of Texas at Austin and author of numerous books, including *The Modern American Presidency*.

David S. Heidler is an independent scholar and **Jeanne T. Heidler** is professor of history at the U.S. Air Force Academy. They are authors of *Old Hickory's War: Andrew Jackson and the Quest for Empire*.

James A. Henretta is Priscilla Alden Burke Professor of History at the University of Maryland and the author of numerous books and articles on American history, including *The Liberal State in America: New York, 1820–1970* (forthcoming).

Ari Hoogenboom is professor emeritus of history at Brooklyn College and the Graduate Center of the City University of New York. He is the author of three Hayes biographies and books on civil service reform and industrial development in eighteenth-century America.

David Horrocks is senior archivist with the Gerald R. Ford Library, National Archives and Records Administration (NARA). The opinions expressed in the article are solely his own and do not necessarily reflect the views of NARA or the Ford Library.

Robert W. Johannsen is James G. Randall Distinguished Professor of History, Emeritus, at the University of Illinois at Urbana-Champaign and the author of biographies of Stephen Douglas and Abraham Lincoln and an upcoming biography of Polk.

Christopher M. Johnson teaches law at the Franklin Pierce Law Center and is the chief appellate defender with the New Hampshire Public Defender Program.

Howard Jones is University Research Professor of History at the University of Alabama and the author of numerous books, including *Mutiny on the Amistad: The Saga of a Slave Revolt and Its Impact on American Abolition, Law, and Diplomacy.*

David T. Konig is professor of history and of law at Washington University in St. Louis. He is the author of books and articles on the legal history of colonial New England and Virginia and is currently working on a book on Thomas Jefferson's law practice.

John A. Lupton is assistant director and an assistant editor with the Papers of Abraham Lincoln and the author of articles on Lincoln and the antebellum legal system.

Barbara A. Perry is Carter Glass Professor of Government at Sweet Briar College and the author of many works on the Supreme Court of the United States.

Allan Peskin is history professor emeritus at Cleveland State University and the author of *Garfield* and *Winfield Scott and the Profession of Arms.*

Daniel Preston is editor of the Papers of James Monroe at Mary Washington College in Fredericksburg, Virginia.

Thomas C. Reeves is a retired Wisconsin historian and the author of several books, including *America's Bishop: The Life of Fulton J. Sheen* and *Gentleman Boss: The Life of Chester Alan Arthur.*

Allen Sharp is United States district judge for the Northern District of Indiana and the author of many historical articles, including "Presidents as Supreme Court Advocates: Before and after the White House."

E. Lee Shepard is director of the Division of Manuscripts and Archives at the Virginia Historical Society.

Jerome J. Shestack is a partner in the Philadelphia law firm of Wolf Block Schorr & Solis-Cohen and a former American Bar Association president who has written about the legal careers of several American presidents.

Elbert B. Smith is professor emeritus of history at the University of Maryland and the author of biographies of Fillmore, Taylor, and Buchanan.

Melvin I. Urofsky is professor emeritus of history at Virginia Commonwealth University and the author or editor of numerous books on American legal and constitutional history, including *A March of Liberty: A Constitutional History of the United States* and the letters of Louis Brandeis.

L. Kinvin Wroth is president and dean and professor of law at the Vermont Law School and coeditor of *Legal Papers of John Adams* and numerous other works on colonial legal history.

Illustration Credits

Except for James Monroe, Andrew Jackson, Abraham Lincoln, and Rutherford B. Hayes, the White House Historical Association provided all presidential images (many of which are details of the originals) that appear on chapter opening pages. Unless otherwise noted below, all other images are from the Library of Congress.

Architect of the Capitol (3, 12)

Massachusetts Historical Society (9)

Collection of the Supreme Court of the United States (15, 24, 191, 234, 237, 268, 299, 303, 304, 305, 307)

Washington and Lee University (16)

Virginia Historical Society, Richmond, VA (20, 77, 79)

Louisiana Travel Commission (27)

Art Commission of the City of New York (28)

James Monroe Museum and Memorial Library (30, 32, 35, 37)

New Haven Colony Historical Society (41, 45)

Morse's *American Gazetteer* (43)

The Hermitage: Home of President Andrew Jackson, Nashville, TN (52, 63)

Albany Institute of History & Art (68)

Martin Van Buren National Historical Site (75)

State Historical Society of Missouri (91, 119)

San Antonio Art League and Museum (97)

Buffalo and Erie County Historical Society (98, 187, 188)

New Hampshire Historical Society (107, 108, 115)

Chicago Historical Society (127, 149, 221)

Illinois State Historical Library (128)

The Frank and Virginia Williams Collection of Lincolniana (129, 130, 132, 141, 143, 144)

Illinois State Historical Society (138)

Rutherford B. Hayes Presidential Center (152, 154, 155, 156, 159)

Corbis (162, 176, 256, 273, 292, 295, 296, 319)

Indiana Historical Society (168, 199)

Ohio Historical Society (171)

Wayne L. Sanford and J. Thomas Willison (196)

President Benjamin Harrison Home (197)

The McKinley Museum, Canton, Ohio (207, 211)

Stock Montage, Inc. (215, 244)

William Howard Taft National Historic Site (222)

Sagamore Hill National Historic Site (225)

American Bar Association (229, 276, 306, 325)

Princeton University Library (232)

J. N. "Ding" Darling Foundation (247)

Franklin D. Roosevelt Presidential Library and Museum (255)

The Washington Post (259)

Truman Presidential Museum & Library (260)

National Archives (263, 277)

Richard Nixon Library and Birthplace (267)

LBJ Library Photo by Bachrach (271)

Gerald R. Ford Library (282, 286, 289)

Collection, The Supreme Court Historical Society; photographed by Richard Strauss, Smithsonian Institution (300)

INDEX